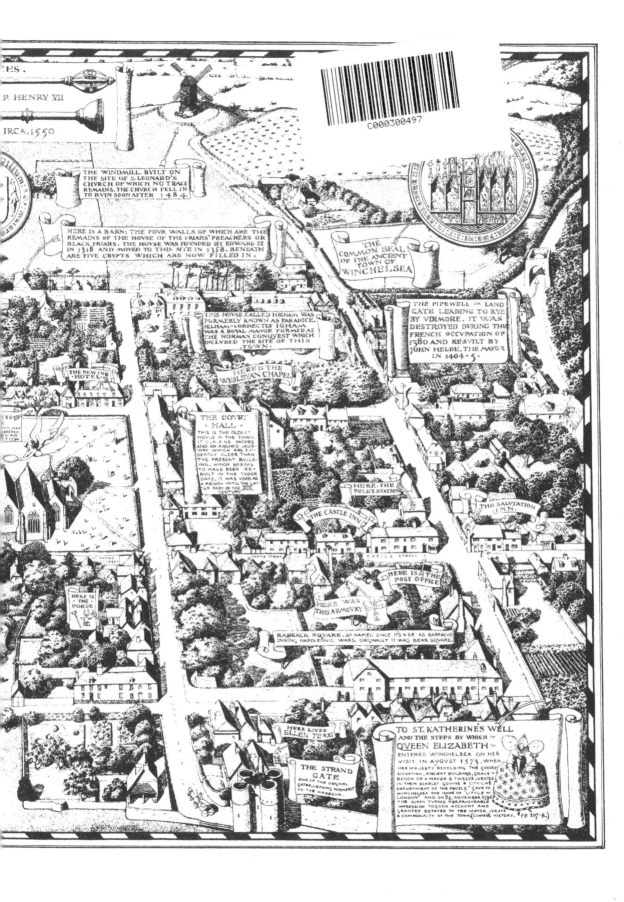

WINCHELSEA

THE TALE OF A MEDIEVAL TOWN

principally telling

the story of the Ancient Town

from the earliest times

until 1800

by

MALCOLM PRATT

with a Foreword by Lord Briggs of Lewes (Asa Briggs)

This book is for

The People of Winchelsea

*Those of them who read it may be grateful that they live in
the ancient town in the early twenty-first century
and not in medieval times.*

Published by Malcolm Pratt, 16 Downlands Avenue,
Bexhill-on-Sea, East Sussex, TN39 3PL.

© Malcolm Pratt 2005

Malcolm Pratt asserts his moral right to be identified as the
author of this work

ISBN 0 9532411 1 4

Typesetting, design and project management
David Brown, 2 West Street Farm Cottages,
Maynards Green, Heathfield, East Sussex TN21 0DG
Tel: 01435 812506
Printing
Biddles Ltd, Kings Lynn

Dustjacket photography David Brown
Front: Winchelsea Court Hall
Back: Millennium Town Sign

Endpapers
An Historical and Pictorial Map of the Ancient Town of Winchelsea
drawn by Charles Thomas (1923) © Winchelsea Corporation

CONTENTS

APPENDICES

(1) The New Inn, probably dating from the seventeenth century, has long been Winchelsea's best-known hostelry

LIST OF ILLUSTRATIONS

FOREWORD

In 1998 I had the privilege of writing a Foreword to Malcolm Pratt's *WINCHELSEA – A Port of Stranded Pride.* I am equally privileged – and happy – to repeat the experience in 2004. Malcolm Pratt's second history covers a far longer period, including years when Winchelsea enjoyed both blatant pride and enviable prosperity, making a distinctive contribution to national history as a member of the Confederation of the Cinque Ports. Its peak came in the thirteenth century and its nadir in the last decades of the eighteenth century. Yet there had been earlier decades of decay, for example, after the Black Death in the fourteenth century. In 1358 there were ninety-four properties laid waste and another ninety in ruins. Nearly half of Malcolm Pratt's book deals with the period after the accession of Henry VIII and there were some particularly devastating years in the sixteenth century. In 1548, for instance, the Corporation, the fortunes of which Malcolm Pratt follows carefully, was so short of funds that it had to sell the 'Great Chalice and the bells of the Great Cross' in order to pay off debts.

It is not only the inhabitants or former inhabitants of twenty-first century Winchelsea, more of a village than a town, who will read Malcolm Pratt's pre-eminently readable new book with interest. Most visitors respond at once to the unique charm of a unique place, witnessed through an abundance of clues to the 'heritage'. It is probably the construction of a planned medieval 'new town' that will interest them most, along with the survival of an old church with exceptionally beautiful modern windows. They may be surprised to learn of the evidence in its story both of the piracy which lay behind the wealth and of the pestilence that made it precarious. The maintenance of the church was a major local preoccupation.

The changing role of the Channel in the medieval and in the modern periods, when it was distanced from New Winchelsea, is fascinating to visitors and scholars alike. It was seldom a boundary. English and French historians intertwine: they are not separate. Wine links them as well as jurisdiction. The withdrawal of the sea and the silting of the harbour changed the basic geography, but policy was as responsible as nature for a decline in Winchelsea's fortunes that may have been inevitable. The book ends with Winchelsea serving as a garrison town during the long wars against the French Revolution and Napoleon. There is more to say of this than there is space in the book.

Winchelsea has seldom lacked historians and Malcolm Pratt, town clerk as well as historian, draws both on his predecessors and his contemporaries, the historians among the latter more professional, but not necessarily more learned, than their predecessors. The Cinque Ports are always under historical review and re-assessment. Like his predecessors and contemporaries, Malcolm Pratt confronts many unknowns and, fortunately for the reader, like them he is sometimes drawn off down tempting bye-ways. The end of this book overlaps with his first, a proof in itself of the continuity of history. Everyone in Winchelsea is aware of its powerful presence. As a former part-time resident, I revelled – and still revel – in it.

Asa Briggs, Lewes, 2004

INTRODUCTION

Before my first book, *WINCHELSEA – A Port of Stranded Pride* was published, Roger Davey, then serving as East Sussex County Archivist, was among those kind enough to read the final draft. On returning it he remarked, 'But, Malcolm, you have only written Part 2!' That volume, currently out of print but readily available through the East Sussex County Library service, concentrates on Winchelsea's story during the nineteenth and twentieth centuries. At that time, as its introduction shows, I felt that, for one as unskilled as I, without knowledge of Latin or Norman French and scarcely able to understand anything in English before the seventeenth century, the writing of Part 1 would not be within my compass.

However, prompted by Roger Davey's remark and most grateful for it, I began to compile a chronology of Winchelsea's earlier history which, as it grew, made it clear that such a task would indeed be possible, although possible, of course, only as a result of the efforts of others. I have been incredibly lucky in finding a historical research subject to occupy me in my retirement on which so much has been written in unpublished form. The work of William MacLean Homan, David and Barbara Martin and David Sylvester provides the outstanding examples. Additionally, as my bibliography shows, much has been published, particularly since 1990, which throws light upon the historical events with which Winchelsea was much involved. The publication during the twentieth century of the Court Rolls in modern English further enhanced my research. These detailed tomes, of which I earlier knew nothing, I was able to consult through the libraries of East Sussex Record Office and Sussex University.

Among the very large number of other available sources acknowledged in my notes and bibliography, it has given me particular pleasure to use the work of Margery James. Dr. James was one of my history lecturers at Goldsmiths College, University of London, many years ago. Her research into the medieval wine trade, although incomplete, was published as a tribute by her colleagues after her sadly premature death. To the best of my knowledge it remains the definitive study of the subject.

The present book, although it appears as a companion volume, stands entirely alone from the previous one. There the first nineteen pages and the openings of several chapters referred to Winchelsea's early history. Much of that material is here expanded, some is repeated, just a little is left out.

The books on Winchelsea's history by William Durrant Cooper and Frederic Inderwick were written in the nineteenth century. Although I am greatly indebted to their work, part of the enjoyment and the challenge of my project has been to bring again to life a story about which there has been no full-length book for so long. (*New Winchelsea, Sussex* by David and Barbara Martin was published after completion of my text). Additionally I believe this present volume to contain the first account in any detail of Old Winchelsea's history; a subject not attempted by any of my predecessors.

Only the very briefest mention is made in the text of Winchelsea having, in the twenty-first century, what we confidently believe to be England's only remaining unreformed medieval municipal corporation. Perhaps it is therefore worth accounting here for that strange survival. The Municipal Corporations Act of 1883 proposed the abolition of all such bodies which had survived that far. In Winchelsea's case this would have meant the loss of a head port within the Confederation of the Cinque Ports. Winchelsea's MP at the time, F. A. Inderwick KC, was able to persuade his government colleagues that such a loss would be highly undesirable and, as a result of his representations, Clause 14 was added to the act. This, in line with all the other towns affected, removed all judicial and local government powers (Winchelsea later became one of the four wards of Icklesham Parish Council) but allowed the ancient town to retain its mayor and corporation with responsibility only for maintaining its property and fulfilling the town's Cinque Ports function. And so it remains. There is, of course, a full account of these events in my earlier book.

Winchelsea's title as a head port within the Confederation of the Cinque Ports has become a matter of some controversy and good-natured banter among the present members of Winchelsea Corporation. Is it an 'ancient' town or an 'antient' town? I have always thought that the two words have separate meanings, ancient obviously meaning old and antient meaning venerable. The latter form which is unusual, attention catching, and now in general use is strongly supported by my colleagues. When, shamefully belatedly, I referred to the Oxford English Dictionary (published 1933, reprinted with corrections 1961) I discovered to my astonishment that 'antient' has no entry of its own; it only appears, without comment, in the entry for ancient as an archaic form. 'Antient' appears only very occasionally in Winchelsea's eighteenth century documents and hardly at all in the nineteenth century. This tends to confirm my view that the now universal use of antient dates only from the twentieth century. Winchelsea Corporation's legal title as defined in The Municipal Corporations Act of 1883 which allowed it to survive (First Schedule Part II) is 'The Mayor, Jurats and Commonalty of the Ancient Town of Winchelsea'. This book recounts events which took place when 'ancient' was the common usage and therefore consistently adheres to that form.

The Winchelsea which once stood in Rye Bay, probably somewhere to seaward of the present mouth of the River Rother, was never, of course, called 'Old Winchelsea' by its inhabitants or by the medieval chroniclers; it was Wynchelse or Winchellese or one of many other variations. I have used 'Old Winchelsea' because it is now universally accepted and I hope this will help clarify for the reader unfamiliar with the subject or the area that the ancient town was rebuilt as 'New Winchelsea' on its present site in the late thirteenth century.

My text was written between December 2001 and April 2004 with much later addition, correction and amendment. All references such as 'at the present time', 'now' and 'at the time of writing' should be taken in that context.

My acknowledgements show my gratitude to all who have helped with this book. Nevertheless, my inexperience makes it likely that I have misunderstood advice received and misinterpreted documents examined. Mistakes will therefore surely remain for which I am fully responsible. I shall be very pleased if those who identify those mistakes will point them out.

And so, with this book joining *WINCHELSEA – A Port of Stranded Pride*, my account of the history of the Ancient Town is finally complete. It is a study which has been time-consuming, sometimes frustrating, frequently demanding, always absorbing and finally rewarding. There can be no doubt that it is a remarkable story. It is my most earnest hope that I have managed to make it a readable remarkable story.

Malcolm Pratt
June 2005

EDITORIAL

In compiling my text I have silently standardised some medieval names to avoid confusion and modernised medieval spelling within quotations except where the original spelling enhances the effect.

I have taken the liberty of assuming that readers will be familiar with Winchelsea's geographical orientation which, for many, is unlikely. North, south, east and west are freely used in descriptions. The principal doubt is caused by the fact that, in southern England one expects the sea to be to the south. For Winchelsea it is not – it is to the east. My maps (and the position of North Street) should help.

As the chapters developed I found myself constantly using 'See page xx' to refer to earlier, or later, mention of events and incidents. This practice I later abandoned because it became an obvious intrusion on the printed page. Having numerous superscript reference numbers is sufficient intrusion alone. The index has been specifically designed for ease of reference to earlier or later mention of subjects.

It became clear early in the project that it could only be successfully brought to fruition if chronology was the key to the presentation of the material. This principle I have departed from only when returning chronologically to a topic would mean doing so fragmentarily.

The designation MP did not come into general use until the nineteenth century. I have used it from medieval times purely for convenience.

Once again I have felt more comfortable with the use of the first person when expressing an opinion or recounting my personal experience.

Many illustrations appear separated from relevant mention in the text. I have tried to ensure that captions and the index help to overcome any problems that this might cause.

It is almost impossible to make meaningful comparisons between medieval monetary values and modern ones. To place decimal values beside pre-decimal ones adds nothing by way of clarity. I have not attempted either. Pounds, shillings (twenty to the pound), pence (twelve to the shilling) and farthings (four to the penny) are referred to throughout. I can only briefly try to help younger readers by pointing out that the cost of seventy pounds for the building of a galley at Winchelsea (p. 82) was considerable, that the ten thousand pounds seized from the church by Edward I (p. 65) was enormous, and that even the wage of threepence a day paid to a sailor (p. 72) was one with which he would be by no means dissatisfied. Perhaps readers of my vintage will feel a touch of pleasant nostalgia at finding such amounts as £14 11s 5¾d appearing within these pages!

ACKNOWLEDGEMENTS

A glance through the notes on my sources and frequent mention within the text shows that I have made extensive use of the research into Winchelsea's history carried out in the mid-twentieth century by William MacLean Homan. This has proved to be an invaluable and, indeed, indispensable resource. Some documents unknown to Homan have required subsequent revision of his ideas and I have not always agreed with his conclusions but the debt remains. It gives me great pleasure that Mr. Homan's family have welcomed this use of his unpublished work.

I am indebted to all of the following for information and assistance provided in various ways: Don Alexander, Rt. Hon. the Earl of Aylesford, Robert Beecroft, John Bleach, David Bourne, Donald Cameron-Clarke, John and Margaret Charrot, Ken Chetwood, Clive Chizlett, Neil Clephane-Cameron, Pauline Colwell, Richard Comotto, Roger Davey, Bernard Doherty, Julie Ede, Ben Eggleston, Esme Evans, Major John Freeman, Graham Fulkes, David Fuller, John Gooders, Reg Hawkins, Tony Hill-Smith, the late Major Peter Hoskins, Dr. Roy Hunnisett, Denis Hyson, Tony Jasper, Dominic Leahy, Margot Leahy, The Very Rev. Canon Basil O'Ferrall, J. P. Parratt, John Parry, John Pratt, Rod Marten, Chris Milburn, the late Antony Sandeman, Michael Saville, Janet Stevenson, Michael Wardroper, Dennis Williams and Dr. Barry Yates.

My grateful thanks are due to many others:

To Winchelsea Corporation for permission to reproduce the seal of Winchelsea and to use the Charles Thomas map for the endpapers.

To Roger Davey, Michael Saville and Janet Stevenson for agreeing to read parts of my final draft and for their constructive comments.

To David and Barbara Martin who have supported the project throughout, including most helpful advice on the text, and whose expert work has so enhanced my story.

To Dr. David Sylvester whose excellent thesis was drawn to my attention by David Martin, a copy being provided through the good offices of Christopher Whittick.

To Christopher Whittick himself who, as Senior Archivist at East Sussex Record Office, has an unparalleled knowledge of Winchelsea's archives. His professional expertise in that and many other fields is amply complemented by his willingness to give so freely of his own time reading, commenting and advising.

To other staff of East Sussex Record Office whose interest, advice and support have been available to me through years of research and writing, particularly Philip Bye, Pauline Colwell and Jennifer Nash.

To the University of Sussex and the Sussex Archaeological Society for their excellent library facilities and particularly to Esme Evans, the Society's Honorary Librarian.

To Lord Briggs for once again providing a Foreword and for taking such a supportive interest in my work.

To David Brown whose skill, enthusiasm and dedication have enabled me once again to provide for my readers a volume of this kind.

To all those, listed elsewhere, who have provided or given permission for the use of illustrations.

To any who may have been accidentally omitted above and to my family who have supported the project in many ways.

ACKNOWLEDGEMENT OF ILLUSTRATION SOURCES

Winchelsea Court Hall Museum: 1 66 78. Author's collection: 3 5 12 15 18 26 28 33 34 36 39 43 44 50 53 54 58 59 61 62 67 69 71 72 75 77 79 81 83 85 86 87 88 90 95.

Melvyn Pett: 6 24. Daphne Lovegrove: 7. David and Barbara Martin: 4 21 23 30 37 51 52 60 63.

From *The Oxford History of Medieval England*: 41 from the same volume by kind permission of Chetham's Library: 8.

By permission of the Syndics of Cambridge University Library: 13.

Winchelsea Corporation: 9 11 27 31 47 68 91. By permission of the British Library: 14 32 42 45.

Tina Alexander: 16. Jill Eddison: 17 80. John and Margaret Charrot: 19. Archaeological Journal: 20. National Archives: 22. John Gooders: 25 46. Sussex Archaeological Society: 29 35 65 82.

W. D. Cooper *History of Winchelsea*: 2 38 48 49. Bridgeman Art Library: 40.

Salisbury and South Wiltshire Museum: 55. Dennis Williams: 56 57. M.C.C: 70. Reg Hawkins: 73.

Cambridge University Collection of Air Photographs, Unit for Landscape Modelling: 64.

National Portrait Gallery: 74 76 93. By kind permission of the private owner: 84.

John Collard *A Maritime History of Rye*: 89. British Museum: 92. Derek Ashby of Wade Holdings: 94.

Every effort has been made to trace copyright holders; omissions will gladly be rectified in any future edition.

PROLOGUE

Any community must take a very long period of development to become prominent in its mother country. How long it took Winchelsea we shall never know but there can be no doubt that it achieved this status, at its peak in the last decade of the thirteenth century.

At that time it had been saved from destruction by the direct intervention of its monarch. Re-sited and rebuilt in the comparative safety of the hill of Iham it was, for a time, a leading town of England and the premier port of Sussex. In its harbour at the Camber the fleet would gather at the king's command. At Winchelsea vital matters of state were argued and decided. Twenty-five thousand men were once ordered to the town for training in the use of the longbow. Its position provided travellers and merchants with a convenient and direct route to France. Perhaps best known to the modern reader, it was a leading member of the Confederation of the Cinque Ports, providing much of the country's naval requirements in both peace and war. Prominence indeed.

It has to be said that there were also less meritorious reasons for this importance. The men of Winchelsea and its fellow Cinque Ports were addicted to piracy, an activity in which they demonstrated both skill and ruthlessness. At times, with no alternative way of gaining or maintaining control of the Channel, the crown needed to appease them to ensure their vital support. Such appeasement tended to improve even further their privileged position.

Winchelsea's leading citizens added their own influence to its reputation. Two commanded the Cinque Ports fleet; others advised the monarch in matters of state and on royal commissions; perhaps most influential of all, one became Archbishop of Canterbury 'commonly regarded as a second Becket'[1] in upholding the rights of the church against the crown.

This, then, was Winchelsea's exalted state in the late thirteenth and early fourteenth centuries. Its appearance and circumstances were, as we shall see, a total contrast in the sixteenth century when it was perhaps at its poorest. Even in the late eighteenth century, at the end of the period covered by this book, Winchelsea was still struggling to overcome the effects of poverty.

Since then there have been further vast changes. Early twenty-first century residents and visitors know a community which, despite being designated an Ancient Town, has the population and facilities of a beautiful, and reasonably prosperous small village. But clues about its unique past remain – in the amazing survival of three principal medieval gateways still standing proudly astride three access roads, in the continued use of what is now the Court Hall, an important Winchelsea building for more than seven hundred years, in the visibly ruined state of the transepts of St. Thomas's Church and in the survival of the town's unreformed Municipal Corporation under the leadership of its mayor.

As we begin the story of Winchelsea long before recorded history we must search for more elusive clues.

1 . THROUGH THE MISTS OF TIME

There is no documentary evidence of Winchelsea's existence before the eleventh century. What, then, are the clues which might allow us to draw some reasonable conclusions regarding the unrecorded centuries of early development?

Archaeologically they are very few for the windswept shingle site of Old Winchelsea which existed in Rye Bay until the thirteenth century has been totally destroyed by the sea. The most recent detailed study concludes that the accumulation of shingle in the bay, driven in from the south-west, began as long ago as 4000BC. Thus commenced the promontory of Dungeness which eventually divided the coastline of the bay approximately in half. Two thousand years later men were on the great shingle barrier 'apparently using it as a stopping-off point on a trade route across the Channel to the Continent'.[1] Trade, then, was the catalyst which led to the use and eventually permanent occupation of the shingle spit on which Old Winchelsea developed. For the existence of this trade we have as a witness no less a person that Julius Caesar who recorded that there was maritime trade between Britain and France long before his conquest.[2] The nature of such trade after Caesar's landing at Deal, and his subsequent withdrawal, has been quite specifically stated as including the export of 'corn, cattle, gold, silver, iron, hides, slaves and hunting dogs' and the import of 'wine, oil, bronze furniture, finer pottery than the Britons themselves could make, jewellery, silver table-ware and glassware'.[3]

The men of Old Winchelsea would certainly have been deeply and profitably involved if they had established their community by then! But had they? It would seem that a town which eventually became so important began its early development on a purely shingle shore on which its fishing boats had to be drawn up as they still are at Hastings. When that shingle was broached to allow proper anchorage we do not know.

By the time of the second and much longer Roman occupation commencing in 43AD there would have been further opportunity for trading. The Romans were active in the area which includes the sites of both Old Winchelsea and 'New' Winchelsea on its present hill. The main cause of this activity was iron, probably first worked by the Belgae in c.250BC. There was a concentration of bloomery sites in the eastern part of Sussex, one of which, together with the remains of a Roman road, was discovered at Icklesham in 1981 by Stephen Maclean when digging in his grandmother's garden.[4] We know, too, that the Romans built a road running south from Rochester and Maidstone to cross the Weald to Hastings and the Sussex iron-working district. The road was commercial rather than military and the vast effort involved can only indicate the importance of Sussex iron to the Roman economy. Little of this activity seems to have strayed onto the Hill of Iham where Winchelsea now stands, the only evidence being the finding of a Roman coin[5] and what were believed to be fragments of Roman tiles when the site of the public conveniences was excavated.[6] The closest, more substantial, archaeological indications of Roman occupation seem to have been at Crutches Farm and at High Mills Fields, south of Wickham Rock Lane. The very name Wickham indicates a Roman site. Attempts to locate the remains of a Roman fort alleged to exist in Castle Field have been unsuccessful.[7]

If Old Winchelsea had been established in Roman times its people would have been able to gaze out upon the fleet of Roman warships stationed in the Channel to protect the merchantmen conducting the trade in iron and other goods even if they were not taking part. In those days there was no competition for control of the narrow seas for the European communities were either also under Roman control or as yet 'not awake to the wonders and riches that lay beyond the seas'.[8]

(3) The River Brede, when a formidable highway to the Weald, provided New Winchelsea with its busy inner harbour; now it wanders peacefully past the town.

It is more likely that the port of Old Winchelsea in Rye Bay began to develop in the later Saxon period on the estuaries of the Rivers Brede and Tillingham but again we are starved of evidence. The discharge of those rivers would permit the commencement of the great lagoon which eventually grew into the harbour of the Camber and succoured the prosperity of both Winchelsea and Rye. Certainly the name Winchelsea belongs to this period for at its heart is the Saxon word chesil meaning shingle; an alternative derivation also gives the Saxon ea, a stream, but the period is the same and, assuming the inlet to be originally an insubstantial one, would seem appropriate. That settlement would have been contemporary with a Saxon harbour which, the National Trust suggested in 2001 when giving reasons for declaring its land inalienable, existed at the foot of New Winchelsea's hill near the present Winchelsea Motel. A Saxon brooch has been found there and the Trust assumes that this was dropped overboard from a vessel.[9] This seems fairly scanty evidence.

Old Winchelsea's existence in the mid-Saxon period would be further supported if William MacLean Homan was right in assuming, in defiance of long and still lasting tradition, that the River Rother had altered its course to discharge into Rye Bay as early as the late eighth century.[10]

The ninth century saw Viking raiders in the Channel, an intrusion which may well have affected Old Winchelsea's trade as it did that of many communities. Homan gives one most specific example of an incident in 893 in which a fleet of 250 ships, coming from Boulogne, made its way up the Rother. The crews established themselves at Appledore.[11] If the Rother did indeed enter the sea at Old Winchelsea by then, its people were dangerously close to the action. Such raids persisted during the tenth century but without leading to permanent settlement as they did in the midlands and north of England.

Early evidence of Old Winchelsea's borough status was once thought to be provided by the discovery of a coin of approximately 964 bearing the name 'Wencles'. Only a borough would have been permitted a mint in those days. However that belief has now been discredited by no less an authority than the Victoria County History of Sussex which states: 'If the coin of Edgar bearing the mint name of "Wencles" could be assigned to this place it would prove its existence as a borough in the tenth century but in the absence of other coins and of all corroborating evidence this attribution is more than doubtful'. In a footnote the name Wencles is attached to Winchcombe in Gloucestershire.[12] It is my belief that Winchelsea was never a borough in the normally accepted sense but that its privileges stemmed solely from its membership of the Confederation of the Cinque Ports, of which much more later.

Its neighbour, Hastings, later to become the first of the Sussex ports to be adversely affected by the eastward drift of the shingle, was one of King Alfred's fortified burhs.[13] No other Cinque Port was included in this category. However, within the mints of late Anglo-Saxon England Hastings, Romney and Dover are included.[14] Hastings' decline from this eminence eventually led to its needing and seeking support from Winchelsea and Rye.

The proliferation of these mints on the south coast was at least partly responsible for renewed Viking raids in the late tenth century, raids in which plunder was the principal motive. These attacks persisted following the establishment of a base on the Isle of Wight and here we have a clue which will colour our story later – there was no effective force of English ships available to play any part in opposing such violence.

King Ethelred attempted to rectify this in 1008 by ordering every community in England of a specified size (310 hides) to build a ship.[15] This exceptional demand is recorded by the chroniclers but they make no mention of any permanent ship service due from the Confederation of the Cinque Ports at this time. Miss Murray assumes such an omission to indicate that the Confederation was not in existence at the very beginning of the eleventh century.[16]

The resulting somewhat ill-assorted collection of vessels gathered at Sandwich (still no mention of the Confederation despite being within its area) in 1009 but was totally unable to provide any reasonable defence of the country. The fleet's leaders quarrelled and fought with the loss of some of the ships, others were lost in a storm, many were 'shamefully abandoned by their naval commanders' or taken to London 'and they let the whole nation's toil thus lightly pass away'.[17] Ethelred therefore, to use the sobriquet with which he has been saddled, remained Unready and the force later to be provided by the Cinque Ports including Winchelsea remained desperately needed.

Earl Godwin tried hard to fill this gap and excelled as a freelance pirate raider along the Channel coast. He was later to be richly rewarded by King Canute but could not alone retrieve the situation when 'authority was slipping from Ethelred's grasp'.[18]

The situation continued to deteriorate and whatever community there was at Old Winchelsea at that time is most likely to have been included in the havoc caused when the Danes 'ravaged all Sussex and Kent and Hastings' in 1011.[19]

2 . IN FOREIGN HANDS

Having briefly searched for these clues about its area, we now enter the time, the reign of King Canute (1016-1035), when we have the earliest documentary evidence of Old Winchelsea's existence. Ironically it was being given away!

Canute, the form of his name which I was taught and have always used, had banished Ethelred to Normandy, assumed power, and thus confirmed the control the invading Danes had so long sought. In 1031 the king granted the Manor of Rameslie to the Norman Abbey of Fécamp. Rameslie was the main part of the most easterly coastal strip of Sussex and, vitally for us, included Old Winchelsea. This grant and its later confirmations were to have a profound effect on the history of England.

For an explanation of this apparently strange decision which gave the Normans a foothold on the English shore I am deeply indebted to the researches of William MacLean Homan. He suggests that the name Rameslie had Danish roots and possibly originated from the influence of the Viking raiders in the year 893 already mentioned. The Manor included an extensive part of the Brede Valley together with Old Winchelsea, Rye and Hastings. Its gift to Fécamp Homan explains principally by detailing extreme pressure brought by the pope.

Homan's interpretation has been challenged on the grounds of the existence of documentary evidence that the grant was originally made by King Ethelred and that his translation of it is mistaken.[1] However, I use it here because it is, to me, a reader without the skills to examine or confirm his findings through reference to the original sources, in many ways most convincing and certainly too good a story to leave out!

When Canute had established his power in England, he turned his attention on Norway. There the monarch was Olaf Haraldson, eventually, and remarkably for a man with so violent a reputation, to become St. Olaf. Olaf in his younger days had spent a good deal of time and energy plundering both England and the west coast of France, on one occasion, along with Thorkel the Tall, sacking Canterbury and murdering Archbishop Alphege. The families of Canute and Olaf were extreme rivals but Olaf's fellow Norwegians were occupying Normandy and it was while wintering with them that he was converted to Christianity. Later, in governing his native land, Olaf forced the largely pagan population to adopt Christianity, or at least its outward forms, quite probably by pointing out that the alternative was death! This mass 'conversion' gained him great standing in Rome where his efforts were much appreciated.

Such popularity did not extend to his own people who greatly resented this intrusion into their normal way of life, a fact which made Canute's eventual expulsion of Olaf from Norway a great deal easier. Olaf fled to Russia and when he returned with an army in an attempt to regain his throne, was killed by a Norwegian force in a battle near Trondheim. Canute was not directly involved in Olaf's death but the pope thought he was and he got the blame!

In those days the pope exercised vast international influence over Christendom. King Canute was summoned to Rome 'to account for his moral responsibility for King Olaf's violent end'. Unfortunately there was at least one other crime, the murder of his brother-in-law, for which recompense was demanded and, under threat of excommunication, he was ordered by Pope John XIX to make the Rameslie grant to Fécamp, favoured abbey of his sworn enemy the Duke of Normandy.[2] It must have been a bitter pill to swallow.

The town of Fécamp which lies on the Norman coast about 75 miles from Winchelsea and Rye was an ancient fishing community thought to have included a monastery since as early as

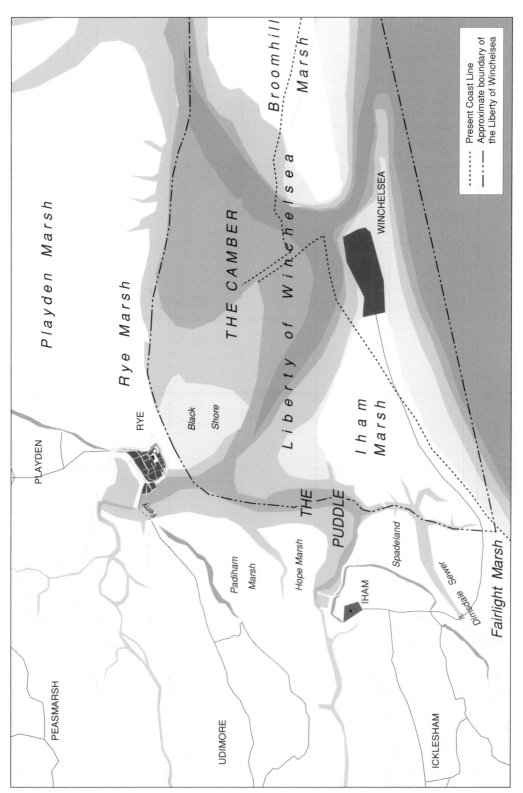

(4) Conjectural reconstruction of Winchelsea and environs, c. 1200

662. The Benedictine Abbey, whose list of abbots extends from 1000 until the French Revolution and whose architecture influenced the building of Westminster Abbey, was vastly wealthy and exerted enormous influence which was even further enhanced by its foothold on the English shore. The wording of the document states that Canute, king of the Angles, grants the manor of Rameslie in perpetuity to the abbey 'in the hope of a reward in heaven' and states that it had been King Ethelred's intention to do this but that death had intervened before he could do so. There is a list of signatories. Controversy over the document centres not only on the reservations mentioned above but also on the fact that the version which gives us the date 1031 has additions which add the Manor of Brede to the grant as well as 'two parts of the dues of the port called Wincenesel'. The date of this version certainly cannot be earlier because it names Abbot John who took office only in that year; the other signatories could also have been involved if it had originally been made beforehand.[3]

A further influence which might have provoked these later additions was that of Queen Emma, Canute's wife who had previously been married to Ethelred. It could well be that she was the influence behind the additions made in 1031 because she did not feel that the original wording was sufficient to fulfil the promise made by her first husband. Emma was the daughter of Duke Richard I of Normandy; she sought shelter in Normandy when Ethelred was in difficulties and her two sons were brought up there.[4] She therefore had every reason to seek further advancement of the Norman cause.

Whatever the truth of it all, an important Norman presence was established in England. This was subsequently frequently confirmed and lasted for more than two centuries until 1247 when King Henry III resumed control of Rye and Winchelsea by agreement and substituted other lands in less strategic places. That frequently indecisive monarch nevertheless appreciated the potential danger which had been well illustrated as early as 1033 when, thirty-three years before it eventually happened, England was threatened with invasion by the Normans. The place at which the fleet and army gathered, only to have its plans ruined by a storm? Fécamp.[5]

3 . SEEDS OF CONFEDERATION

It was Earl Godwin, already mentioned as a defender of the south coast through his piracy, who caused havoc there on his return in 1052 after fleeing the country having offended Edward the Confessor. This is important to Winchelsea's story because 'the men of Hastings and the neighbouring ports flocked to join him [Godwin]'[1] and it is apparent that by this time these ports were acting as a group. Godwin and his son Harold, the future king, also recently returned from exile (in his case in Ireland), plundered and burnt 'as in an enemy's country'.[2] Not, however, within the area of the Cinque Ports because it was the men of those ports, always ready to support anyone who provided the opportunity for gain, who were doing the plundering. The dispute eventually petered out and Godwin and Harold were received back into the king's favour.

No retribution appears to have fallen on Winchelsea or the other ports as a result of this indiscretion. Winchelsea, although not so important at this time, was to become a leading member of the Cinque Ports. Indeed, it is the continued existence of that body which has ensured the unique survival into the early part of the twenty-first century of the town's mayor and jurats despite their having no local government function.

It would appear that the earliest co-operation between the ports of the south-eastern coast of England was at the great herring fair at Yarmouth. There, before the town of Yarmouth was developed, the portsmen went during the fishing season and 'established proprietary rights of control'.[3] These particularly included judicial control over those taking part, the right to land and dry their nets on the dunes (den) and the right to sell their catch on the strand (strond). This arrangement, later frequently confirmed by charter, was, as we shall see, to cause enormous offence to the men of Yarmouth and provoke much violent dispute.

In this group of strategically placed ports of the south-east King Edward the Confessor saw the opportunity to create what in effect was a standing navy to which he could turn in times of crisis or when in need of transport. It is ironic, although typical, that they should be so disloyal to him in supporting Godwin's revolt but 'their untrustworthiness only emphasised their political importance'.[4]

The arrangement was closely defined. The ports, the original five, hence 'cinque' pronounced sink – Hastings, Romney, Hythe, Dover and Sandwich – should provide, free of all payment, fifty-seven ships for fifteen days a year, each ship manned by twenty men and a boy. That these were small ships is clear from the size of the crew; they were later to develop considerably. If this was intended to replace the need for a navy (mercenary ships had earlier been employed but had lain idle too frequently) it seems a totally inadequate provision, although, of course, the monarch could extend the service by paying for it if need be. However, Miss Murray demonstrates that it was based on likely needs for the Danish raids tended to be annual and brief and a journey to Calais in then friendly Normandy would be easily accomplished within that time.[5] Additionally the nature of these vessels would make them ideal for patrolling and scouting.[6] It is worth mentioning here a point which is often neglected, namely that the ports of the south-east were far from ideally positioned to provide transport or naval service westward. Where any urgency was required the prevailing south-westerly wind could frequently prove an obstacle.

What, then, were the privileges which attracted the portsmen to accept this obligation? These were developed, refined, restricted and lost over the years but in medieval times were quite adequate to bribe the recipients into service. The list is long and most importantly granted the

(5) The present view from The Lookout at New Winchelsea towards the site of Old Winchelsea in Rye Bay. Had the photograph been taken on a clearer day the ugly outline of the Dungeness Nuclear Power Stations would have been visible on the horizon.

right to full self-government, that is independent legal jurisdiction and exemption from national taxation (sac and soc). In exercising this right the portsmen could levy tolls and keep the profits (toll and, on bridges, pontage), exact payments for passing through their port (passage), claim duty by weight or number (lastage and tallage), charge wharf and quay tolls (rivage and cayage), keep goods unclaimed for a year and a day (waifs and strays), claim wreckage on their shores which had been floating in the sea or jettisoned from ships (flotsam and jetsam) and trade freely without restriction from any monopoly (loce-cope-free). As magistrates, to use a conveniently explanatory modern word, they could try breaches of the King's peace (mundbryce), detain and execute felons inside or outside the Ports' jurisdiction (infangthef and outfangthef), force holders of stolen goods to reveal their origin (team), punish those who shed blood (blodwit), seize those who fled from justice (fledwit) and punish minor offenders (pillory and tumbrill).[7]

One interesting addition which was used within the Cinque Ports until the sixteenth century was the custom of witherman. This was a medieval debt recovery service. If money was owed by a citizen of one Cinque Port to a citizen of another, the next man from the offending port to enter the complainant's port was arrested and sent home with a judgment demanding payment. If this was 'not successful within ten days, the unfortunate next visitor from the port which owed money had his goods confiscated for the due amount'.[8] Confiscations could accumulate until the debt was paid. Even the seizure of complete ships was not uncommon where the sum was considerable.[9] Such summary justice seems to have been effective but understandably unpopular!

This is not an exhaustive list, nor is it exclusive to members of the Cinque Ports. Such privileges were frequently granted elsewhere. Of the two which were solely granted to the Confederation, the rights at Yarmouth (den and strond) came into being at this time but the only one which still survives, that which permits representation at the coronation of the monarch (honours at court) is not first recorded until the coronation of King Richard I in 1189 although it is believed to have existed long before that time. To this last and singular privilege we shall return where it particularly affects Winchelsea.[10]

Throughout this period of privilege and controversy Old Winchelsea remained under the control of the Abbey of Fécamp. In 1054 the Abbot, John d'Alie, nicknamed Little John, travelled across the Channel to visit and inspect his Rameslie Manor and, presumably, to ensure that the original grant would be honoured by King Edward. He must have been pleased with the response for the king not only confirmed the Rameslie grant but also the grant of the Manor of Steyning.[11]

As we move towards the Conquest we pause to note, strangely in view of the events described above, that in 1063 the ships of the Cinque Ports formed part of the fleet led by Earl Harold in the campaign against the Welsh uprising of Gruffydd. With typical medieval ruthlessness they returned with two trophies for Edward the Confessor on whose behalf they had fought, 'the head of Gruffydd and the beak of [his] warship'.[12]

How much the outcome of the Norman Conquest was influenced by the Abbey of Fécamp's possession of the Manor of Rameslie, including Old Winchelsea, is a matter of conjecture rather than fact. Nevertheless it is important in our story.

4. CONQUEST

Some commentators, particularly local historians, claim that the Manor of Rameslie was vitally important and that without its being in Norman hands the conquest might well have failed.

If that is correct such importance would not necessarily include Winchelsea's ships. At this time it seems unlikely that they were influential enough, or, indeed large enough, to be included in the fleet which stood by near the Isle of Wight during William's long delay caused by contrary winds. Nor would they have been among the vessels which hurried north to support Harold against Tostig and were therefore not available in the Channel to oppose the Norman landing. It is reasonable for us to accept Professor Burrows' assertion that in 1066 Winchelsea and Rye were small fishing villages and that subsequently they rose rapidly from that condition.[1]

Even if Winchelsea's ships were impotent at this time the Manor of Rameslie was certainly in the front line. We are told, for example, that men of the Abbey of Fécamp travelled with Duke William and that, after the landing, one of them, the abbey's almoner, Remigius, was sent 'to keep the Abbey's tenants in the Manor of Rameslie in a state of quietude'.[2] This might not necessarily have been difficult for, with the Normans controlling their lives through legal jurisdiction and through tenancies, it was clear that support for William, even if passive, was in the interests of Rameslie's inhabitants. Such support may have had a more deep-seated root for the area had once been settled by men of Norway and their descendants would be more likely to take the side of 'their kinsmen the Normans, against King Harold Godwinson, who would be looked upon as the leader of their rivals the Danes'.[3]

The question we must now address is whether that support might have been active rather than passive. A paper entitled *The Cinque Ports and the Battle of Hastings* by J. Scott Pitcher, published by Adams of Rye Ltd. in 1962,[4] states quite categorically that the men of the Cinque Ports fought with Duke William at the Battle of Hastings. Mr Pitcher places them on the right flank of the Norman army under the command of Roger Bigod, Baron Montgomery. It was this group, normally shown in diagrammatic descriptions of the battle as 'Other French', which delivered the final overwhelming assault and sealed the fate of Anglo-Saxon England. If portsmen were there that would have been in accordance with their fighting character and reputation. But were they there? Neil Clephane-Cameron, Winchelsea's Sergeant-at-Mace, who is also honorary secretary of the Battle and District Historical Society and has considerable knowledge of the battle, finds such glaring errors in Mr Pitcher's account that he discounts its whole thesis. Neither can he find any reference to it in the 'Transactions' of his society which Pitcher quotes as a source.

My own researches into the sources used have been limited. It seems that Roger Bigod was present at the Battle of Hastings and 'assault[ed] the English gallantly'.[5] He and his descendants were certainly greatly in William's favour and were richly endowed with estates in Norfolk. *The Complete Peerage* assumes that this favour resulted from his service at the battle. However, I have discovered no specific mention of the Cinque Portsmen being present. In the chronicles which refer to the battle, admittedly only skimming through a vast amount of material, I found no more than 'Roger whom they call Montgomery' being instructed by Duke William to 'go on that side and attack them from that side. I rely much on you'.[6] It is therefore no more than an interesting theory based on circumstantial evidence that the men of Winchelsea, through their allegiance to Fécamp, fought with William at Hastings. If they did they might have been accompanied by others from Rameslie but, as we shall soon see, the portsmen further east had little sympathy for William.

Further circumstantial evidence of the influence of Abbey and the Manor lies in suggestions that William's right flank was protected by its existence there and that, as he moved east after his victory, the villages and communities of the Manor were left untouched while others were ravaged.

One particularly violent reaction of the Conqueror was visited upon New Romney. Here he devastated the community in revenge for the killing of a number of his knights who are variously reported as having been on a reconnaissance mission, constituted an advance party, or landed when blown off course. They were given short shrift by the men of New Romney who 'were punished harshly for their attack'.[7] News of the extreme violence meted out travelled ahead of the conquering army and cowed many into submission. Despite considerations of whether or not William had a better claim to the throne of England than Harold's, at a distance of well over nine hundred years it must be our inclination to sympathise with the defenders rather than the invaders in this conflict. Certainly that feeling remains in New Romney to this day for, when mention is made at Cinque Ports gatherings of Romney's defiance, a cheer invariably ensues from its delegates!

We must not stray too far from Winchelsea's story. Following news of Romney's treatment Dover succumbed and the Conqueror went on to his coronation. By Easter 1067 William felt sufficiently secure to travel to Normandy to celebrate his enormous success. The French chronicler William of Poitiers describes how locals in the Norman towns through which he passed came out to greet him, to see the hero and to applaud. Significantly for us the celebration was sealed with a service of thanksgiving in the church of St. Trinité at Fécamp 'to which came a crowd of clergy, people and knights ... to offer congratulations, and William made show of various trophies brought back with him'.[8]

King William's confidence in his security was, temporarily at least, misplaced. There was an uprising in Wales led by Eadric the Wild. The Conqueror hurried to repress this revolt and another at Dover whose inhabitants temporarily supported Eustace of Boulogne, the king's former ally, in an invasion which was firmly repulsed. The port which William chose for this speedy return from Normandy to action? Old Winchelsea.

Like his predecessor, William fully appreciated the significance of the ports of the south-east coast in providing the kind of service already described. It may well have been during his reign that the seeds of confederation grew into something more formal. Certainly by 1069 there was no question of defection such as Dover's support for Eustace. In that year a Danish attack was 'driven off from Dover and Sandwich'[9] by Portsmen united in defending William's kingdom 'and henceforth the south was loyal'.[10]

(6) These medieval painted boards, on display in Winchelsea Court Hall Museum, were once believed to have come from the ancient church of St. Leonard, Iham, whose foundation long pre-dated New Winchelsea. They have recently been identified as depicting not St. Leonard but St. Peter (above) and, partially, St. Paul and may be a rare survival from an earlier Court Hall.

5. DOMESDAY AND BEYOND

Unravelling Winchelsea's entry in Domesday Book is a daunting task. Perhaps it would be safer to say that it is an impossible task because Winchelsea is not mentioned! Nevertheless the Manor of Rameslie does feature and is shown, as we have seen, as having been granted by the king (William I) to the Abbey of Fécamp which had held it from Edward the Confessor. It is within that entry, then, that any information about Old Winchelsea is contained.

The modern version which I am using[1] translates 'Rameslie' as 'Rye' which is obviously incorrect but otherwise sets out clearly the Manor's details as they were recorded by the king's officers surveying the country. Within it there were five churches. It has been suggested, on the very reasonable grounds that the Abbot of Fécamp later controlled their advowsons, that these were the churches of Brede, Winchelsea, and Rye, together with All Saints and St. Clement's in Hastings.[2] Alternatively, William MacLean Homan, who discounted the inclusion of any part of Hastings within Rameslie, listed St. Leonard's of Iham (where New Winchelsea's windmill stood until 1987), Icklesham, Brede, Udimore and 'either St. Mary's of Rye or St. Giles's of Winchelsea'.[3] I do not know on what grounds he assumed that the church of St. Giles in Old Winchelsea was older than that of St. Thomas. We must treat both these lists with further caution for the former gives Winchelsea one church only and the latter includes Udimore which was never part of Rameslie.

Rameslie also contained a 'new Borough' which had 64 burgesses. Here again theories are hedged by uncertainty although Rye seems likely. Hastings is separately mentioned as having '4 burgesses and 14 smallholders' and anyway had been a borough in the ninth century and had a mint in the tenth – concrete evidence of its borough status.[4] However, that status must have applied to the Hastings west of the castle; the Domesday 64 burgesses may have been in the then newer Hastings which we now call the Old Town. Old Winchelsea is generally accepted as an unlikely candidate for 'new Borough' in view of its named inclusion in the confirmation of Canute's grant and its likely greater antiquity than Rye because it was closer to the sea. Added to this, it was thought never to have achieved borough status, although modern research has suggested otherwise.[5] L. A. Vidler certainly claims the 'new Borough' status for Rye and he goes so far as to suggest that this 'newness' was caused by its having to be moved inland to a safer site long before this happened to Winchelsea.[6] An interesting possibility.

Having hovered round the outskirts of Old Winchelsea's record in Domesday, we must examine what must be its most important, if oblique, reference. The Manor of Rameslie contained one hundred saltpans. Given its site on the shingle bank, an extremely suitable place for salt production, in Rye Bay, many of these must surely have been associated with Winchelsea. What is even more important is that, even if the figure of 100 is assumed to be an estimate, it represents more than one third of all the saltpans recorded in Sussex.

The manufacture of salt was a vital medieval industry which flourished in Old Winchelsea for many years. Even as late as 1266-1272 there were considerable sales of salt from Winchelsea to 'French, Dutch and other merchants' despite the havoc which must have been wreaked to the saltpans by the storms of 1250 and 1252. By 1350 Winchelsea, however, was importing salt.[7] The only way of obtaining this vital salt in the south of England was from the sea. Sea water was admitted into broad, shallow pans or ponds with clay bottoms. After three or four days, given the right weather, the water would be reduced to a strong brine by the heat of the sun. It was then boiled in shallow iron vessels and allowed to cool at which time the salt crystallised out and the

(7) The workings at Pett Level which are believed to have been the remains of ancient saltpans and may have been associated with Old Winchelsea.

remaining liquor could be drawn off.[8] Conditions for this work would have been ideal where the sea water either naturally percolated through the shingle bank or was artificially admitted. When natural these breaches would have been intermittent and the drift of the shingle from the west, caused by wind and tide, would repair them. As the eastward drift became stronger and the shingle bank thinner, the percolation of sea water to the marshes behind would have become more common. Recent research suggests that 'the weakest point would have been towards the south-west end of the barrier, but some distance out from the shelter of the Fairlight hills'.[9]

In 1965 Captain Herbert Lovegrove CBE RN, Winchelsea's leading historian of the time, four times its mayor and twice Speaker of the Confederation of the Cinque Ports, made a fascinating discovery which he attributed to the effect of the construction of the new sea wall from Pett Level to Winchelsea Beach in 1950. The former sea-defences in front of the new wall were gradually being eroded by wave action thus 'uncovering the underlying bed of forest clay whose surface lies some 3 to 7 feet above low water. In doing so it has exposed a series of artificial workings cut in the clay'. In his article describing this discovery[10] Captain Lovegrove considers the possible causes of these diggings, discounting any association with sea-defences, fishing activity or holiday visitors and points out that, even by December 1965, they were becoming obscured. He concludes that as the site was near the channel known as the Great Fleet[11] 'where tidal water, having access within the shingle bars and being thus protected from the sea waves, could be tapped with safety through its retaining dykes. It seems possible therefore that they are the remains of medieval saltpans'.[12]

Although I am sure that they have long disappeared, I cannot but hazard the suggestion that these diggings may have been the only archaeological evidence ever to have been discovered resulting from the existence of Old Winchelsea.

Before we leave the Domesday Book it is relevant to examine what it tells us about the members of the Confederation of the Cinque Ports. The most complete entry is for Dover which records its ship service duties (20 ships for 15 days each with a crew of 21) in return for which the king had 'remitted to them the sac and soc'. Service and resulting privilege are also mentioned, though only in general terms, for Romney and Hythe.[13] Certainly there is no collective mention of the Cinque Ports at this time, although one would hardly expect it as Domesday was a survey of communities and manors, not of associations.

There was, however, a book deriving its name from Domesday and known as 'The Domesday Book of the Ports' which listed the Cinque Ports, their duties and privileges. Had this volume survived much which is uncertain would have been revealed. However, not only did it disappear during the reign of Charles II, but up until that time it was constantly amended rather then added to[14] so the ports' composition in the eleventh century and whether Winchelsea was then a member would not have been revealed.

As we try to follow Winchelsea's story beyond Domesday and into the twelfth century there is not a lot to go on! We can imagine it developing steadily encouraged by an increasing involvement with the Cinque Ports which may have caused grief within the town for the Ports' fleet was lost in great storm when providing ship service on an expedition to Scotland in 1091.[15] We know that the Abbey of Fécamp kept an eye on its condition for Abbot William de Ros visited Rameslie in 1103, paying particular attention to Rye and the construction of a stone church at St. Mary's.[16] The town of Yarmouth was developing and becoming more incensed at Cinque Ports intrusion on its annual herring fair. This feeling no doubt provoked a Cinque Ports attack on a Yarmouth church which had been built near the huts which were occupied during the fair. The portsmen expelled the chaplain, intending to take the premises over for their own use and later they repulsed the sheriff who was sent to sort things out.[17] If the men of Winchelsea were involved, this kind of behaviour would have been in character.

We can assume more about the growing importance of the port of Winchelsea from an agreement which was made in 1130 between the Abbot of Fécamp and King Henry I. They agreed to share the tolls due in certain respects from ships at Winchelsea and would hardly have bothered about such an arrangement had those tolls not been of increasing significance. The abbot retained all other income from the port.[18] Such evidence is reinforced by the inclusion of Old Winchelsea in the Pipe Rolls of the following year. These records list the ports and the taxes levied on their merchants.[19]

While Winchelsea's growing importance at this time is clear, we are left without direct evidence as to its borough status. It is my belief, as already stated, that Winchelsea was never a royal borough in the normally accepted sense but obtained its great privileges and status only as a result of its membership of the Confederation of the Cinque Ports. There has been much research into the boroughs of Sussex in recent years. One resulting article[20] accords Old Winchelsea borough status in '(?) c.1150'. The co-author of this piece, John Bleach, has allowed me to say that the question mark is the most important part of the reference! Despite further research which he kindly carried out as a result of my inquiry he can find no definite evidence.

By this same year, 1150, the Cinque Ports Court of Shepway had come into existence. This well illustrates the Confederation's privileges in which Winchelsea was included, for it was the equivalent of the Shire Court, presided over by the Lord Warden who had similar powers to the Sheriffs of the counties of Kent and Sussex from which his area was taken. The ports provided the judges and the time allowed for the court to be summoned provides us with an interesting pointer to the infrastructure of the times. Forty days' notice was required. This was because the portsmen might well be at sea and the only method of recall was to send a boat after them.[21] Also, if you wished to travel from Winchelsea, for example, to the site of the Shepway near Lymne, afforestation and the appalling nature of such roads as existed made it unthinkable to do so by any method other than by sea.

This court was powerful. Death sentences which it ordered would be carried out the next day. As we move forward into the second half of the twelfth century we find further evidence of such power influencing the growing importance of both Winchelsea and the Confederation.

6. CHARTERS AND HONOURS

Strangely this growing importance was despite some disadvantages. The accession of King Henry II in 1154 brought Winchelsea within the enormous Angevin Empire stretching from the Pyrenees to the Cumbrian moors. Ports in Brittany and the Bay of Biscay became friendly and accessible and this tended to move the focal point of trade westwards to Southampton, whereupon a rivalry, sometimes a violent rivalry, between Southampton and the Cinque Ports came into being. It is clear, too, that this change of influence reduced the importance of Winchelsea and the Cinque Ports in royal transportation. Of twenty-eight royal crossings of the Channel in Henry's reign only five were carried out by Ports ships, four between Dover and Wissant and one from Dieppe to Winchelsea.[1]

Nevertheless all the Cinque Ports privileges were renewed by charter at the beginning of the reign as was customary. Charters, however, were granted to individual ports and not to the Confederation. Winchelsea and Rye 'were given freedom from pleading "otherwise than as the barons of Hastings and the Cinque Ports plead"'[2] which confirms their involvement as members of Hastings rather than as Head Ports which they later became. The king was seeking to secure the loyalty of the ports through their privileges and his doubts about that loyalty, as we shall see, were in coming years to be well justified.

Winchelsea and Rye were in trouble as early as the year 1164-5 when they were fined 100 marks each, a considerable sum. Unfortunately we do not know the reason for this fine but 'it has been suggested that it had some connection with the quarrel between the King and Thomas a' Becket'.[3]

To that quarrel we must briefly turn. Becket had been appointed Archbishop of Canterbury in 1161, seen by the king as the perfect man to 'put the church in its place' and control it 'within the customs and laws of the realm'.[4] Henry wanted to ensure that the bishops could not take action against royal officials without consulting him and he wanted the clergy to be subject to the king's courts, not only to those of the church. Becket did not fulfil these hopes. Following the king's frustrated and ill-judged 'Who will rid me of this turbulent priest?' the four knights who took him literally divided their party and hurried to Canterbury, two crossing via Dover and two via Winchelsea. The assassination led to the dedication of Old Winchelsea's principal church to St. Thomas the Martyr, a dedication which survives today in New Winchelsea. It was altered at the Reformation to St. Thomas the Apostle but restored in the 1930s.

The Cinque Ports were providing their traditional ship service in 1174 when patrolling the coast of Flanders and in the 1180s served for pay when, in wartime, their traditional fifteen days were necessarily exceeded. The growing relative importance of Winchelsea within this service is illustrated by its assessed value with Hastings of 100 marks when Chichester and Bosham were only valued at 20 marks each.[5] Modern researchers have suggested that this growing importance also stemmed from a major breach in the shingle barrier which enhanced the value of Old Winchelsea's harbour while the town remained protected, for the time being at least, from the erosion which eventually destroyed it.[6]

Henry II landed at Winchelsea from Dieppe in 1188 but there were to be no further opportunities for reputation enhancing royal visits for Winchelsea during his reign for the king died the following year and it is the coronation of his successor, Richard I, which next demands our attention. It is the first recorded occurrence of the Confederation's Honours at Court.

Churchill records, with typical flair and style, that 'Richard was crowned with peculiar

(8) The coronation, not of Richard I but of his brother King John, as depicted in a contemporary manuscript.

state, by a ceremonial which, elaborating the most ancient forms and traditions of the Island monarchy, is still in all essentials observed today'.[7] The chronicler Roger de Hoveden, describing the ceremony tells us that 'a canopy of silk, supported by four long lances, was held over [the king and queen] by four barons'.[8] It is in a subsequent letter written by a Canterbury monk that the barons are identified: 'The archbishop presented to [the tomb of] the Blessed Thomas … a certain pall [canopy] which belonged by ancient custom to the barons of Dover and the Cinque Ports'.[9] As we have seen, it was singularly appropriate for the people of Winchelsea that the canopy should be placed in homage on the tomb of Thomas a' Becket. In later centuries the canopies, normally one for the king and another for the queen, were divided between the eastern and western ports and allocated in turn. Even this apparently even-handed arrangement led to disputes and if Winchelsea was ever allocated such a remarkable and valuable object the mayor and jurats no doubt sold it! The title of Barons of the Cinque Ports, originally applying to all free men of the ports and later more exclusively to the most prominent citizens, usually jurats, arose from their medieval claim to be the equals of earls and barons as a result of their ship service.[10] The title survives only for those attending a coronation and since at the time of writing we are celebrating the Golden Jubilee of Her Majesty Queen Elizabeth II, the fifty years which have passed since her coronation mean that there are currently no surviving Barons.

Another privilege accorded to the Barons of the Cinque Ports for several centuries was to dine at the king's right hand after the coronation. Eventually this was withdrawn when they fought for the privilege with others who had taken their places! We must not dwell too long on all this for it is really the history of the Cinque Ports rather than specifically of Winchelsea but it is a remarkable survival and, should Honours at Court be granted at the next coronation, Winchelsea's mayor will be entitled to attend.[11]

Richard I, following tradition, also issued charters at the beginning of his reign, among them one to the men of Rye and Winchelsea. This confirms the privileges already mentioned and relates them to 'both sides of the sea, wherever they may come throughout our whole land'. Their right, already mentioned, to be subject only to the jurisdiction of their fellow portsmen is confirmed for they are 'To be quit of Shires and Hundreds, and if anyone desires to implead them they are not to answer or plead otherwise than as the Barons of Hastings and the Cinque Ports plead'. The charter goes on to define Rye and Winchelsea's ship service responsibility as, in return for these liberties, 'towards our full service two ships to complete the number of the twenty Hastings ships'.[12]

This ship service duty was soon to be put to the test for Richard I left the country not long after his coronation and needed a large number of ships to take him and his considerable army on the Third Crusade. Of approximately one hundred vessels required thirty-three came from the Cinque Ports. Of these thirteen were due from Hastings, two of them provided by Rye and Winchelsea.[13] Shoreham and Southampton sent three each; nine were given by the king and individuals; the origin of the remainder is not known.[14] Some sources[15] suggest that Rye and Winchelsea had been accepted as Head Ports by this time but such a division of ship service makes it much more likely that they remained 'members' of Hastings, helping that port which was the first Cinque Port to suffer from the debilitating eastward drift of the shingle which had destroyed its original harbour.

There are no records to show which ships went how far in support of the Third Crusade but, assuming that the two ships came one from Rye and one from Winchelsea, it is clear that some men of Old Winchelsea were, at least initially, involved in that enterprise. We do know, however, that the Cinque Ports had to meet one-third of their costs and that the majority of the ships had crews of between twenty and thirty.[16] The size, construction and manning of these vessels, one of which is depicted on Winchelsea's seal, we shall soon consider.

7. THE ALARDS, THE COGS, AND THE LOSS OF NORMANDY

But first to some of the men who sailed those ships.

Winchelsea was, in the late twelfth and early thirteenth centuries, rapidly expanding. In fact it was a remarkable growth because records of harbour dues paid by merchants in 1204 at the ports of the south and south-east coasts show Old Winchelsea third after London and Southampton, with a total of £62 compared with Rye's £10, and twice the trade of any of the other Cinque Ports.[1] Cooper claims that, at this time, Old Winchelsea was more important than New Winchelsea ever became. That seems doubtful but it is certainly reported as being 'A town of great trade and accompt, having in it when it flourished 700 householders'; a very large population for a medieval English port. Other chroniclers tell us that Old Winchelsea was 'well frequented', 'a pretty town and much resorted to' (which makes it sound like a medieval holiday resort which it certainly was not) and that it 'once had in it fifty inns and taverns' (much more likely!).[2]

Recent research suggests that the River Rother altered its course much earlier than the usually accepted time of the 1287 storm to join the estuaries of the Brede and Tillingham at Old Winchelsea late in the twelfth century and thus provide important additional opportunity for such development.[3] Certainly Hastings was complaining in 1199 that 'Winchelsea and Rye, becoming rich, refuse their former service'.[4]

One of the leading influences in the increasing expansion and importance of Old Winchelsea came from the Alard family. Theirs was a long tradition, the name being derived from the Saxon Aethelwald. They were closely involved in Winchelsea's vital wine trade and not averse to including in their maritime operations a good measure of privateering and piracy. One of their number, James, son of Alard, was among those buying up land in the marshes near Old Winchelsea; land of potential value for draining and development.[5]

These activities led them, at this time, to resent the Abbot of Fécamp's overlordship which restricted their potential influence. The abbot was no absentee landlord. In 1200 he exercised his rights and reinforced his power by paying for the building of a prison in Old Winchelsea[6] and in the same year, sensibly it would seem to us, arranged for the market to be moved out of the cemetery.[7] He was paid tithes for many areas of his Manor of Rameslie, provoking the Rector of Brede and James, son of Alard, into unjustifiably claiming that some of these tithes had been granted to them by charter. The monks of the abbey counter-claimed that the charter was forged. When the matter eventually came to court and the claim was shown to be fraudulent, the rector appeared in person but James Alard prudently stayed away![8]

In later years the Alards' influence came principally through maritime service to the monarch, a privilege which they frequently exploited and sometimes abused. In 1225, for example, William, son of Alard, Paulin 'de Winchelse' and Thomas, son of Godfrey, all members of leading Winchelsea families were 'granted protection for three years' (presumably against accusations of piratical activity) in return for their active part in an expedition to Gascony with the king's brother. After this expedition William Alard was paid for the wages of 'himself, 30 sailors and 30 serjeants-at-arms, and also for anchors and ropes which he had lost in Gascony'. Fourteen years later the same three appear documented as taking charge of 'repairs to certain galleys at Winchelsea' and William Alard's influence extended to being 'excused the onerous honour of knighthood'.[9] The less prestigious activities of the family can be briefly represented by a complaint from men of Barfleur that ships with a cargo, principally of wine, 'had been seized off the coast of Brittany by William Beaufiz, Stephen, Henry and John Alard. On this occasion Stephen Alard had been entrusted with the command of a squadron of thirteen ships. In the same year, 1235, Reynard Bernard, a merchant of Peregoz, complained bitterly that the same Stephen Alard had 'robbed him and carried off his brother Stephen to Guernsey'. The king in this case gave rather less than enthusiastic orders that Stephen Alard should be arrested and the stolen goods recovered 'if [you] can lay hands on him'.[10] These activities lasted into the early fourteenth century when 'Alard, son of John Alard, with others of the Cinque Ports' was excused a charge of outlawry on condition that he served in the fleet accompanying a military expedition to

(9) The seal of Winchelsea – the obverse or ship side

Scotland.[11] Of the Alards who gained national reputation as commanders of the king's fleet and advisers at court we shall learn later.

What, then, of the ships in which the Alards and others carried out their activities, both legal and illegal? The ships of the Cinque Ports were principally cogs. There are such vast variations in the evidence about these vessels that it has been suggested that the word cog was used as a generalisation in medieval times, just as we would use 'ship'.[12] However, the definition that they were 'large sailing merchantmen, broad and deep in the hold, with a single mast and a great square sail'[13] seems most feasible. The classic example engraved on the seal of Winchelsea certainly does not, however, give the impression of such size, and while it is almost certainly a representational distortion, it is likely that the early cogs, built on the shingle beaches of the confederation ports as a communal rather than a specialist activity, were appreciably smaller than their successors became. The Winchelsea seal cog is likely to be an early version constructed in the thirteenth century for it shows the curved rear sternpost which would not satisfactorily accommodate a rudder. The later modification which added the rear rudder and removed the steerboard on the 'starboard'[14] side greatly improved the seaworthiness of the cogs. They were originally principally for the vital fishing and transport industries, their construction being greatly assisted by the plentiful availability of timber from the forests of the Weald. Later, however, their size increased and, by the addition of permanent 'castles' their use changed to include most successful battle action when needed. By the time of the Battle of Winchelsea in 1350, as we shall see, the Cog *Thomas* of Winchelsea which served as the king's flagship is reputed to have carried 360 men, 124 of them sailors. We have already noted that the crew of a cog when the conditions for Cinque Ports ship service were devised was only twenty men and a boy but even then the cogs were used in wartime for the Winchelsea seal shows not only the superstructure, but also the trumpeters who acted as signallers during sea battles.[15]

The adaptation for battle came from the addition of fore- and after-castles. These 'castles', originally temporarily installed when needed and later part of the ships' permanent structure, were designed to add height to the deck and thus facilitate boarding an enemy vessel in the days when a battle at sea was little more than a hand-to-hand land battle. This is the origin of the term 'bridge'

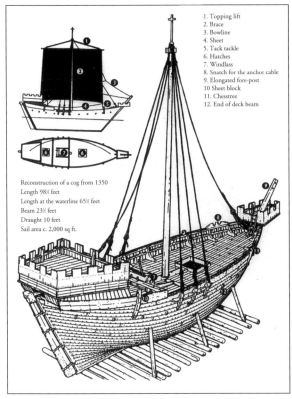

1. Topping lift
2. Brace
3. Bowline
4. Sheet
5. Tack tackle
6. Hatches
7. Windlass
8. Snatch for the anchor cable
9. Elongated fore-post
10 Sheet block
11. Chesstree
12. End of deck beam

Reconstruction of a cog from 1350
Length 98½ feet
Length at the waterline 65½ feet
Beam 23½ feet
Draught 10 feet
Sail area c. 2,000 sq ft.

(10) A cog of c.1350.
This image gives a better idea of the nature of these vessels
than the representational Winchelsea seal

for the highest part of a ship provided a bridge from which to attack.[16] The castles also, at least when temporary, tended to make the vessel considerably less stable. The mast-head look-out point served when necessary as a 'fighting-top' for from it archers had a great advantage in firing arrows or throwing other offensive materials down upon the enemy.

Whatever sophistication may eventually have been used, the medieval limitations in navigational skills ensured that the cogs, when they fought, were almost exclusively involved in fighting in inshore waters. Intercepting an enemy at sea was uncommon and a matter of chance.

While I have concentrated here largely on the cog's potential for battle and for the piratical use to which they would have been put by the Alards, it remains true that 'The vast majority of ships on war service for the English crown were unmodified merchantmen with their usual crews, taken up to transport troops or supplies overseas'.[17]

With the disastrous rule of King John the cogs of the Cinque Ports under men like the Alards who commanded them came into their own. The seamanship of the crews and the manoeuvrability of the vessels made them a great influence when fighting the French. King John, whose kingdom originally extended on both sides of the Channel, showed a considerable lack of resolution in defending Normandy against attack from the south. He also showed a tactless propensity for making matters worse by, for example, issuing a royal proclamation from Hastings that all ships passing up and down the Channel must lower their sails as a mark of respect whenever they met a vessel in his service. Initially this caused little controversy but when Normandy was lost it was an extreme provocation.[18]

In all this the king's Norman barons perceived an excuse to change their allegiance and his English barons greatly resented his mismanagement in many respects. The seeds of Magna Carta were sown.

The Channel which had 'for years been virtually an Anglo-Norman lake'[19] now became a battleground on which England must be defended. The Cinque Ports vessels played a vital part.

For the men of Old Winchelsea the change was particularly startling for their port found itself, through the overlordship of the Abbey of Fécamp, under the heel of a foreign power.

8. LOUIS AND EUSTACE

After the loss of Normandy which affected them so severely, King John attempted to secure the loyalty of Winchelsea and the Cinque Ports by confirming all their charters and rights in 1205. He appreciated that the ports' claim that 'they always have been [and] yet are esteemed to be the gates that are open or shut to the peril or safety of the nation'[1] was largely justified. Nevertheless the king was by that time beginning to develop a maritime presence independent of the Cinque Ports' ship service and in the same year as his confirmatory charters were issued he had two of his own galleys either stationed or laid up at Winchelsea.[2] The potential for conflict with France made even these combined resources inadequate. In 1207 the monarch issued instructions to 'Wimund de Winchelsea' among others to arrest all the ships that they could find[3] and in 1208, more controversially, he ordered that the Cinque Ports were to select some of their most competent men to serve in his own ships which were based as far away as Portsmouth. These men would bring with them 'their detailed knowledge of the narrow seas with their tide rips, their currents and their danger areas'.[4] I do not know whether the two incidents are connected but it was in this same year that the Cinque Ports, at that time even more at variance with King John's government than with the French enemy, threatened to leave the country[5] and thus ensure the vulnerability of their stretch of coast. They may well have over-reached themselves on that occasion for they had to pay 1000 marks to recover the king's goodwill.[6]

Eventually, when King John's misrule inevitably provoked the English barons into rebellion I believe that Winchelsea and the Cinque Ports, despite the claims of some sources, continued their enmity with the French as John would have wished, not through loyalty or patriotism but because of their intense annoyance at the interference being caused to their vessels in the Channel by French privateers.

Be that as it may, Winchelsea was certainly at the centre of events. At Easter in 1213, alarmed by the threat of a French invasion in support of the rebellious barons, King John hurried from Portsmouth to Winchelsea 'where he stayed three days and received the ambassadors of the French king'. While he was in the town he demonstrated his loyalty to the pope, who was supporting him, by his religious observance and by providing alms to feed the poor.[7] There must have been a period of very dry weather at the time for the king is recorded as travelling by road to support and encourage the army he had mustered in the southern ports from Arundel to Lewes on 24 April, and on the following days to Battle, then Dover, and back to Winchelsea.[8] Road travel was far from easy in those days and this seems a considerable achievement.

While in Winchelsea the king would have been able to observe its use as a royal dockyard for in that same year, 1213, the then very large sum of £1260 was paid for the building there of '10 galleys and 10 boats' and for repair work on the king's great ship *Deulabeneie* and numerous other vessels.[9]

All this activity may well have been a contributory factor in ensuring success in the sea battle off Damme in which the fleet under William de Longspee mounted a highly effective attack on the French invasion fleet during which they 'seized or burnt three hundred French ships'.[10] L. A. Vidler, Rye's popular historian, claims that this was the first recorded English victory at sea since the Norman Conquest.[11] The men of Rye and Winchelsea undoubtedly contributed to that victory. The immediate threat of invasion was thus removed but when de Longspee attempted to take up the battle ashore he was soundly beaten.

King John's anxiety to ensure the loyalty of the Cinque Ports led him, in 1215, the year of

Magna Carta, to send Anfred de Den and Godfrey de Craucumb to take custody of Hastings Castle and the towns of Rye and Winchelsea with strict orders to defend them with all the forces they could muster. The barons of these towns were instructed to give all the help they could.[12] One of the actions which de Den took was to release into the king's service three ships of Yarmouth which had been seized and detained at Winchelsea in furtherance of the Cinque Ports' long dispute with that port.[13]

And so we come to 1216 when the barons, whose main aim in dictating the terms of Magna Carta had been to get rid of King John, an aim in which they had signally failed, rose in open rebellion and offered the throne of England to the French Dauphin, Louis, if he would mount an invasion in their support. It is at this time that the fleet of the Cinque Ports is alleged to have joined the rebels.[14] Clearly King John

(11) The Strand Gate, a view towards Rye, probably eighteenth century.

did not accept that that was what they had done. Rather to the contrary, he sought to protect them in two ways. The first was to give instructions to the barons of Winchelsea that, if Prince Louis invaded and sought to capture their town, they should offer 200 marks 'to exempt the town from fire and damage'.[15] It may well be that it was through similar orders that the Cinque Ports, or at least all of them except Dover, fell into the hands of the enemy, rather than by offering active support. The king's second direct intervention was to promise to Hastings, Winchelsea, Rye, Pevensey and Shoreham that he would grant additional privileges if they would remain loyal.[16]

Prince Louis did invade – initially with great success for he took London and the Cinque Ports with only the castles of Windsor and Dover holding out against him. The king then took further supportive action by appointing William, Earl Warenne, 'to keep and defend [the Cinque Ports] on his behalf. This is the earliest appointment we have of an officer to supervise the ports generally'.[17] Later, of course, this position would become that of Lord Warden.

Prince Louis' initial success was undermined by the death of King John on 9 October 1216 which brought to the throne the young Henry III and into power the majestic William the Marshal who, unlike his previous royal master, inspired trust, loyalty and obedience. Prince Louis' mounting problems were made worse by the fierce and determined defence of Dover Castle by Hubert de Burgh who thus held the gateway to the kingdom. If Dover had been lost such a prestigious victory might well have attracted to Prince Louis sufficient support to alter substantially the history of England.

We must not here stray too far from Winchelsea's own story but there is little danger of that for the strange events which ensued were again centred in the ancient town. After defeat at the Battle of Lincoln, Louis made his way to Winchelsea with some difficulty but was unable to embark because 'he found the road to the sea closed'.[18] Presumably this was a metaphorical road, closed by the Cinque Ports fleet standing off-shore. Much bloodshed seems to have ensued and the fleet sent from France to rescue Louis was trapped at Dover by bad weather with the exception of one vessel commanded by a strange character and notorious pirate known as Eustace the Monk. Eustace he may have been, monk he certainly was not, although the nickname originated from his upbringing in a monastery. Eustace was a much hated turncoat who had previously employed his prowess as a privateer in support of King John but was now, equally actively, on the French side. His ship, unlike those of his fellows, made its way with great difficulty along the shore to Winchelsea where he is said to have been well-known.[19] After capturing English ships in the harbour he successfully sustained a short siege by building a large platform on one of them from which he might successfully keep up the pressure on the defenders by firing heavy missiles from a trebuchet mounted there. The size of this structure created wonder in the eyes of the Winchelsea men who are recorded by one chronicler as observing that it 'overpassed the sides of the ship in every direction'.[20] However, it did not take

(12) The Norman church of All Saints with St. Nicolas, Icklesham.
Much of the land for the establishment of New Winchelsea was taken from the ecclesiastical parish of Icklesham.

them long to mount a sortie during which they succeeded in boarding the adapted ship and towing or sailing it offshore where, no doubt with energy and enthusiasm, they chopped up the platform 'in full view of its builders'. Despite the poor view which the English held of him, Prince Louis here displayed considerable leadership for when this insult was blamed on poor watch-keeping; the men responsible had refused to keep watch at night because they were too hungry, Louis offered to keep watch himself. The trebuchet was a medieval engine of war from which large, heavy objects could be slung great distances. The English action did not prevent the French from getting trebuchets ashore and mounting attacks on Winchelsea, and on Rye across the bay.

Rye was at the time in English hands but the following day the remainder of the French fleet reached Winchelsea, took off Louis and his hungry followers, and entered Rye where the garrison, heavily outnumbered, judiciously withdrew.[21] Louis and Eustace then left others to continue the invasion and departed for France.

In August 1217 the French fleet, under the command of the same Eustace the Monk, and helped across the Channel by favourable winds, returned. Hubert de Burgh, successful defender of Dover Castle, was eventually placed in command of the English fleet with orders to repel this new invasion. Initially there were some problems in persuading the men of the Cinque Ports to join. Cinque portsmen were not at this time practised in set-piece battles at sea. They were used to piratical and random attacks encouraged by the thought of personal gain. It was therefore necessary for William the Marshal to offer bribes and inducements to persuade them to meet the French. This type of profit no doubt was more to their liking and was sufficient to encourage them to 'act in complete unison as an attacking fleet'[22] for the first time. They learnt their lesson well.

The Battle of Dover which ensued was a vital factor in the defence of England and an amazingly innovative event in the development of warfare at sea. As we shall see when we reach the story of the Battle of Winchelsea nearly a century and a half later, medieval sea battles were fought like land battles mounted when fleets drove into each other on collision course thus enabling the combatants to board each other's vessels. Hubert de Burgh, however, used much greater subtlety for instead of heading straight for the enemy, the English fleet passed well astern of them. Eustace completely misinterpreted this and thought they were heading for Calais which he had left largely undefended. However, when the English fleet had gained the advantage of being astern and to windward of the French, they altered course and attacked. 'Thus the English were able to defeat and capture most of the enemy fleet'.[23] One tactic used in these captures was distinctly unorthodox and, except that they approached from downwind, as potentially dangerous for the attackers as for the attacked. Bags of quicklime were hurled at the enemy vessels. These were light bags designed to burst on impact and blind the enemy sailors.[24]

Eustace's own ship, still weighed down by one of his trebuchets, was straggling astern of his fellows and was among the first to be captured. Poor Eustace did not show great bravery when hauled from a hiding place in the hold of his vessel. He pleaded for his life, offered large sums for his safety and promised once again to become loyal to the English crown. But it was too late. 'There was one Stephen of Winchelsea who reminded him of the miseries he had inflicted on him on land and sea and gave him the choice of having his head cut off either on the trebuchet or on the side of the ship'.[25] By medieval standards that was a merciful offer. Sentence was carried out and 'the severed head of the arch-enemy Eustace was hoisted on a pole and paraded through the Cinque Ports'.[26] Stephen of Winchelsea's involvement must have ensured that his home town was included in this gruesome display. I like to think that Stephen was an early Alard – his actions and behaviour were entirely in character.

9. EARLY FRIARS AND EARLY STORMS

Within seven years of the Battle of Dover the Greyfriars, who were to exert such an influence over life in Winchelsea until the Reformation and the remains of whose chapel still stands there, landed at Dover and soon made their way along the coast. It seems they must have been extremely well received for when Winchelsea was moved to its new site almost seventy years later it was specifically laid down that the Franciscans should be the only friars with premises in the town. The Dominicans or Blackfriars came only later when influence at court favoured them strongly.

The early religious houses had little contact, except as landlords, with the communities around them. They tended to be 'comfortable retreat[s] from the cares of the world'.[1] St. Francis of Assisi in approximately 1206 'after an early life of dissipation … determined to retire from the world and seek a new life in absolute poverty'.[2] He was among those to resolve that the Christian life should include some beneficial influence on the common people and, quite apart from poverty, should feature good works as well as preaching God's word. His Franciscans, with the full support of the pope, were among those whose activities increased the number of religious houses in England from approximately 700 at the time of the death of King John in 1216 to almost 900 a century later.[3] The nature of the members of the orders also changed. The earlier practice of recruiting very largely from the children of aristocrats who were sent to the monasteries to be educated gave way to voluntary enrolment only from those over sixteen. 'Conscripts [were] replaced by volunteers.'[4]

This, then, was the type of community which established itself in Winchelsea, probably in the late 1220s. The evidence for this date is circumstantial. What we know for certain is that the Franciscans, initially a mere nine in number, made their way to Canterbury via Dover in 1224.[5] The startling fact which attracts our attention is that they set out from Fécamp in Normandy whose abbey was then in possession of the Manor of Rameslie including Old Winchelsea. This connection must surely have led them to the town fairly soon. It is also unlikely that, because of their natural caution, they would have set about the great effort involved in establishing a monastery in the town if they had known of the great threat which hung over it from storms and encroachment of the sea. This threat was clearly apparent by the mid-1230s. The only certainty is that the Greyfriars were well established in Old Winchelsea by 1253 when they benefited from the will of St. Richard of Chichester who died in that year.[6]

While the Greyfriars were establishing themselves and before the storm threat became obvious life in Winchelsea proceeded in its often violent way. It was not long after their invaluable service at the Battle of Dover that the men of the Cinque Ports were 'summoned to account for their unofficial activities of piracy, robbery on the high seas and pillage'.[7] We have to presume Winchelsea implicated in the charges for 'only Hythe and Rye were apparently blameless'.[8] The power and influence of the confederation members was such that their extremely mild punishment was an exhortation to cease these activities. They did not comply for 'in the thirteenth century the men of the Cinque Ports were the most famous pirates of the day, possessing a reputation for atrocity that the Barbary corsairs might have envied'.[9]

Sometimes, indeed, these atrocities were carried out on the direct instructions of the monarch. In 1242 King Henry III, smarting from his lack of success on an expedition to France, ordered the men of the Cinque Ports to attack the French coast and shipping. Under these instructions they set to with a will, wrought havoc in the French coastal towns and 'slew and plundered like pirates' earning the nickname 'the king's pirates'.[10] It will be well for us to bear such incidents in mind when considering later the French raids on Winchelsea. Violence was sometimes internal as well. In 1221 the Constable of Dover Castle had to intervene in a riot in Winchelsea which took place between sailors of St. Sebastian and of Rye. The wine which was the subject of this dispute was being held in Winchelsea.[11]

An earlier and equally unsuccessful expedition provides us with a good example of the pitfalls involved in the ship service required of the Cinque Ports. In 1229 all the 'Great Ships' from Southampton, Shoreham and other south coast ports were ordered to Portsmouth.[12] This led to an important dispute because Hubert de Burgh, indomitable and partisan strategist and victor of the Battle of Dover, was at the time responsible for gathering together such fleets. Realising the futility of the king's proposed expedition, de Burgh, at his own peril, delayed the arrangements and when the king arrived there were not enough ships available to carry his army overseas. There was a furious row during which the king 'drew his sword and rushed

(13) Medieval friars

upon [de Burgh], reproaching him with having betrayed his trust and being bribed by France'.[13] When the expedition eventually set sail in 1230 (at the king's expense for the Cinque Ports' fifteen days of duty had already been vastly exceeded) de Burgh's worst fears were justified but the incident led to his eventual downfall. Of the Cinque Ports' ship service requirement, Hastings had been ordered to send twenty-one vessels, but of these fifteen were supplied by Winchelsea (10) and Rye (5).[14] The Ancient Towns were still clearly members of Hastings and not yet head ports.

We must not presume that the men of Winchelsea were solely preoccupied with piracy and ship service. There were many ways at this time that their influence spread more widely. In 1236 we have the first direct evidence of the town's involvement in Honours at Court. Orders were issued to Winchelsea to take one of the king's galleys to Witsaund where they were to meet the bishops of Hereford and Ely, escorts to Eleanor of Provence who was on her way to England for her wedding to King Henry III. After bringing her to Dover the barons of Winchelsea joined their fellow portsmen at the king and queen's coronation where, according to Matthew Paris's account: 'The barons of the Cinque Ports carried over the king wherever he went the silken cloth four-square, purple, supported by four silver spears with four little silver-gilt bells, four barons being assigned to each spear … likewise the same [barons] bore a silken cloth over the queen coming after the king which said cloths they claim as their right, and they obtained them at court ... and, moreover, the barons of the Cinque Ports claimed as theirs the right of sitting at the king's table, the same day, on the right hand of our lord the king. And they did so sit'.[15] This report also notes that the barons were allocated to these duties in a random way 'lest port should seem to be preferred to port'. On this occasion the barons' right to carry the canopies and dine at the king's right hand was challenged by the 'wardens of the March of Wales … but the claim was considered somewhat trifling'.[16] Disputes about precedence, about the ownership of the canopies which Paris calls silken cloths, and about the right to dine at the king's right hand were to echo down the centuries!

Winchelsea's influence was recognised in other ways. In 1235 the king called a conference at Dover to discuss progress, or lack of it, in the current war with France. He badly needed advice from experienced mariners and Winchelsea was instructed to send eighteen of its best men, the largest Cinque Ports delegation involved.[17] This influence was further enhanced by the importance of Winchelsea as a centre for shipbuilding. In 1235 Old Winchelsea and Rye 'possessed a striking display of naval strength'.[18] Winchelsea had nine ships and Rye four. Later there were royal dockyards and storehouses in both towns. The king had a covered slipway for two of his galleys built at Winchelsea in 1237.[19] The men of Winchelsea were entrusted with the care and maintenance of these vessels. Their skills were not only used in their own port. In 1231 the bailiffs were commanded to send William Wade, carpenter, to Portsmouth 'to repair the king's great ship there'.[20] The carpenters of Portsmouth must have been mortified. Spying, too, seems to have come within their orbit for in 1242 the barons of Winchelsea were required to send a fishing boat, no doubt of innocent appearance, 'to foreign parts [the French coast] to examine there and inquire into rumours in those parts' and report back to the king.[21] In the following year a lasting truce with France was eventually concluded; a truce which held for fifty years until Winchelsea was well established upon the hill of Iham. In terms of official warfare this brought some relief to the town.

But there was no similar relief from the elements.

The earliest evidence I have found of the cataclysmic thirteenth century storms which were to have such a profound effect upon Old Winchelsea came in 1215 when a French fleet, on its way to support King John in his civil war with the barons, was destroyed by a 'great tempest off Calais'. Thousands of French knights and their retainers were drowned.[22] This may have seemed, to the English, like divine intervention but it turned out to be a portent of things to come.

In 1233 'thunder and lightning were incessant for fifteen days, accompanied by hurricanes of wind and rain' and three years later the Thames, 'excited by a storm', broke into the Palace of Westminster and inundated Westminster Hall.[23] This violence of the weather profoundly affected Old Winchelsea whose site on its shingle bank was becoming increasingly vulnerable through influences such as the inning of marshes to the east and the erosion of Fairlight Head to the west. Jill Eddison records that great floods occurred on Romney Marsh during the appalling weather of 1236 which F. A. Inderwick relates only to London. She notes that there was exceptionally heavy rain in the first three months of the year which flooded 'roads, bridges and causeways'. Later in the same year further exceptional flooding 'caused much damage and loss of life'. Three officials were sent by the Archbishop of Canterbury, who owned large areas of Romney Marsh, 'to see to the preservation of the marsh against inundation by the sea'.[24] Winchelsea must have been severely affected for at this time it petitioned for help.[25] Eight years later, increasing storminess was affecting Old Winchelsea's shingle and increasing alarm affecting its inhabitants.[26] This alarm was noted outside the town for in 1249 Winchelsea was given a large grant by the crown 'on condition that they are diligent in repairing and preserving the town against the sea'.[27]

What work was actually started in fulfilment of this condition we do not know but within twelve months an onslaught began which would have rendered any progress useless. On 1 October 1250 the chronicler Matthew Paris recorded that 'the moon being in its first quarter, there appeared a new moon, swollen and red in appearance, as a sign of coming tempests. The disturbed sea transgressed its usual bounds, the tide flowed twice without any ebb and emitted a frightful roaring sound. At Winchelsea besides the salt-houses and abodes of fishermen, the embankment and mills which were destroyed, more than three hundred houses and several churches were thrown down by the tempestuous rise of the sea'.[28] The salt-houses, so important to Winchelsea's economy as we have seen, and the fishermen's houses might well have been particularly vulnerable. St. Thomas's Church survived. Another chronicler, John Stow, gives a similar account in which he describes Paris's 'frightful roaring sound' as 'heard a great way into England'. He adds that 'the sea seemed to be on fire, the waves fighting with one another [so] that the mariners were not able to save their ships' and concludes by reporting that 'the arsenal for the king's galleys and the lighthouse at the peninsula point were carried away by the flood'.[29] Such events must have had a devastating effect but there was to be no relief for reconstruction. The men of Winchelsea had no alternative but to continue what had become a running battle with the elements.

We have no specific reference to Winchelsea as the storms continued in 1251 but 'at the time of the equinox the sea overflowed its usual bounds, causing no small injury in the provinces of England lying near the coast, and the shore was inundated six feet higher than had ever been seen before'.[30] Winchelsea must surely have been affected if this generalisation is to be believed. Anyway, whether as a result of this new threat, or of the 1250 storm, the king set up an inquiry 'to examine how Winchelsea could be saved and defended from the sea'.[31] The inquiry was to extend to all lands between Old Winchelsea and Hythe.[32]

There was to be no let up in the battering Winchelsea was receiving. Yet again in 1252 the elements struck. Once more we rely on Matthew Paris for the information that on 13 January in that year 'the east wind blew till it stirred up the south wind to blow also so that at Winchelsea which was a port to the great use of the English and especially to the people of London, the waves

(14) This eighteenth century view of the south front of St. Thomas's Church contains the earliest known depiction of the present Court Hall

of the sea, as if indignant and enraged at being driven back the day before, covered the places adjoining the shores, took possession of mills and houses and washed away a great many of the inhabitants'.[33] This is the first mention we have of loss of life during the storms but throughout this period fear of this possibility must have heightened the anxiety of the townspeople.

The agony was to be ongoing. Thomas of Walsingham records that, not only in 1252 but also in 1254, Winchelsea's sea wall was breached and the effect on the community and the local economy was worsened by the deposit of layers of salt on cultivated areas.[34]

William MacLean Homan adds an interesting sidelight on Matthew Paris who provides us with the majority of our information about this frightening time. Homan suggests that Paris, 'monk of St. Albans and famous chronicler of the thirteenth century' is likely to have been a Winchelsea man himself and cites in evidence his remark quoted above about Winchelsea's importance and his comment on the damage caused by the 1252 storm as what 'he knew and was acquainted with'. It is Homan's theory that we know so much of the storms' impact on Winchelsea only because Paris's personal interest gave them, and other events related to the town, more prominence in his writing than they would otherwise have received. Aided by his detailed study of surviving documents, Homan is able to add that the name Paris appears among the property holders of the Manor of Iham in 1285, but, no doubt to his disappointment, the name does not feature in the rent roll of New Winchelsea seven years later. He goes on to add, 'One does not know, but it is not altogether unlikely that Matthew Paris may be reckoned Winchelsea's most illustrious son'.[35]

It seems to me that that distinction, as we shall see, might better be accorded to Archbishop Robert Winchelsey or, indeed, to Gervase Alard, but Homan's suggestion is certainly convincing in that so much has come down to us about Winchelsea from Paris's writing.

Some medieval commentators would, less charitably, have attributed the awful storms as visitations of God in retribution for the piracy and violence to which the men of Winchelsea were addicted. They were soon to have much opportunity to wreak havoc on 'friend' and foe alike for the steadying influence of the Abbey of Fécamp's overlordship of Old Winchelsea had, before the worst of the storms, been withdrawn.

10. RESUMPTION AND REBELLION

In fact it was in 1247, three years before Matthew Paris's 'frightful roaring sound' of the sea rent the Sussex air, that King Henry III decided to resume control of the ancient towns of Rye and Winchelsea. He must have been on good terms with the then Abbot of Fécamp, William de Vaspail,[1] for no objection to the arrangement was raised by the abbey, probably because the monks did rather well out of the deal. They received in return valuable lands in Gloucestershire and Lincolnshire, together with confirmation of their title to the Sussex manors of Steyning and Brede.[2]

The king was provoked into ending the grant of Edward the Confessor which had operated for more than two centuries in order to protect, as he saw it, the security of the realm. The charter of resumption refers particularly to the potential danger that, with the French the greatest potential enemy, two such vital ports as Rye and Winchelsea would be unavailable to the crown in time of war should they remain in French hands. He was also anxious to 'conceal from foreigners the intelligence of affairs at home, and stop them of such convenient ports of passage'.[3] This seems to suggest an alertness and foresight with which Henry III is not always credited. However the men of Rye and Winchelsea were not to repay this compliment to their importance with the loyalty it deserved.

Geoffrey Williams, historian of the heraldry of the Cinque Ports, suggests that the return of Rye and Winchelsea to the English crown would be highly likely to require the manufacture and adoption of a new seal for the Ancient Town of Winchelsea. Although the seal which is so proudly preserved by Winchelsea Corporation to this day is more likely to be a version made about fifty years later, the design probably originated in 1247.[4]

The independence which the men of Old Winchelsea assumed was their right after the departure of their overseers, the monks, led them into activities which were certainly not envisaged by the king when he freed them from that control. There were many acts of piracy but the principal problems arose from the extreme rivalry between the Cinque Ports and Yarmouth, a rivalry caused mainly by jealousies over control of the annual Yarmouth Herring Fair. The most dramatic incident involved preparations for a visit by Henry's queen, Eleanor of Provence, and Prince Edward (later Edward I) to Bordeaux to discuss arrangements for the prince's marriage. Whoever made the transport arrangements must have been woefully ignorant of the situation for Winchelsea was to provide a ship for the queen and Yarmouth one for Prince Edward. Winchelsea was 'content to supply a good

(15) The surviving gable at the west end of the chapel of St. John's, probably the oldest and most important of Winchelsea's three hospitals

seaworthy vessel but the Norfolk port provided a far handsomer ship, and no doubt taunted their rivals upon its superiority'.[5] Thus provoked, the men of Winchelsea attacked and destroyed the Yarmouth vessel whereupon the royal party understandably 'refused to trust either escort'[6] and hurriedly departed to sail from Portsmouth.

In the face of this kind of violence the king and his officers vainly tried to uphold the Cinque Ports' traditional rights, even on one occasion threatening the men of Yarmouth with the loss of their lands if they failed to allow 'the barons of Hastings, Rye and Winchelsea all the liberties and customs they have been wont to use'.[7] I am not aware why this particular stricture applied only to the western ports but we can be pretty certain that Winchelsea led the way when it came to this kind of disorder for in 1253 twenty-four men of Winchelsea were ordered to appear before the king's council at Oxford 'to receive and do justice in the contention between the men of the Cinque Ports and the men of Yarmouth'.[8] The other ports only had to send six men each!

Winchelsea's leading position within the Confederation, and her sailors' propensity for piracy, ensured her strong participation in events affecting King Henry's dispute with the barons in the Barons' War. Naval domination of the Channel was vital in this conflict for it ensured the safe passage of foreign supporters of the monarch's cause. It was one thing for the king to nominate a Constable and Warden of Dover to control the Ports and quite another to enforce that

(16) The New Gate, eighteenth century

control. Initially Henry tried flattery by entertaining the portsmen at his Christmas feast at Canterbury in 1262. Simon de Montfort was later infinitely more effective by offering unlimited opportunity for piracy and plunder.[9] Winchelsea's support for Earl Simon, the strongest within the Confederation, may well have been bolstered by encouragement from the Franciscans,[10] at that time the only friars in the town.

Attention focused on Winchelsea when King Henry stopped there on the journey which culminated in his defeat at the Battle of Lewes. The king's purpose was still, by now in some desperation, to ensure the support of the Ports. He was defied, although some whom he had taken hostage offered to recruit ships for him and were released on that eventually unfulfilled promise.[11] The people of Winchelsea would have deeply regretted the king's choice of stopping place for he had his whole army with him and they stayed four days. The soldiers were tired and 'fell eagerly upon Winchelsea's large stocks of wine and soon were exceedingly drunk'.[12] Rape and destruction ensued.

Such events hardened the Ports' resolve to defy Henry and they 'formed the core of a fleet which gathered at Sandwich to prevent foreign assistance reaching [him]'[13] after his defeat. Three hundred of the barons' archers were sent to garrison Winchelsea while its ships were with the fleet at Sandwich and the town played host to the Countess de Montfort when things began to go badly for the rebels and she was making her way to safety at Dover where a hundred Winchelsea sailors fought with de Montfort's soldiers in defence of the castle.[14]

Winchelsea was to pay for this solidity with de Montfort and the barons. Before payment was exacted, however, the Cinque Ports were rewarded with full licence for their piracy during which, among other horrors, 'they flung overboard the crews of every ship they met, whether it was foreign or English'.[15] For this they received reward rather than punishment for their ship losses were met by a tax levied on the clergy and their representatives were specifically named in the summons to de Montfort's parliament in 1265.[16] The reason that they were rewarded is made clear in an account of an expedition to Calais where they 'pillaged all those they could find ... and the ... Earl of Leicester [Simon de Montfort] and his sons received as was said one-third of the whole pillage'.[17]

Simon de Montfort's defeat and death at the Battle of Evesham changed all that.

Well, perhaps not quite all, for until the decisive intervention of Prince Edward, one of de Montfort's sons, also Simon, who took refuge at Winchelsea after his father's defeat, actively encouraged the portsmen to continue terrorising shipping in the Channel during which they 'scour[ed] the seas so effectually that no merchant vessel could pass and, an entire stop being put to trade, the prices of imported articles rose enormously'.[18] It was during the malicious influence of Simon junior that the Cinque Portsmen sacked and burnt Portsmouth, a town which had been warned to expect attack but presumably not from its own countrymen![19]

The situation became intolerable and Prince Edward set out to exact revenge. Ford Madox Ford, amusing but not always reliable as a historian, records how, when this became apparent, Hastings and Rye sent grovelling apologies to the king while 'Winchelsea rebelled boldly and took its punishment'.[20] Ford's assertion about Hastings is supported by the town's letter which, after much which might well be described as 'grovelling', 'humbly implore[s] the clemency of your royal majesty'.[21]

The prince commenced his campaign by taking Dover Castle, travelled north to mop up other pockets of resistance and finally turned his attention on Winchelsea which would not grovel and was only forced into submission by a combined land and sea assault.[22] The men of

Winchelsea, aware of what was in store, are reputed to have planned to abandon their town and to have sailed away with their wives and children. This may well have been the occasion when Portsmouth was largely destroyed. Later, however, they decided to return and face the music.[23]

In the assault to which they were subjected the forces were led by Prince Edward himself and by Roger Leyburn, a former steward of the royal household with a subsequently somewhat chequered career who was at this time again a strong supporter of the prince. As a 'Kentish noble'[24] he benefited from local knowledge. Leyburn and the prince gathered together a fleet from the east coast ports, particularly Yarmouth (it would not have been hard to persuade them to serve!) and 577 Welsh archers, most of them for two days, but a substantial number for only one. Campaign costs included a payment of 3d per day to the archers, the same pay as was received by Cinque Ports seamen when their fifteen days free service had transpired.[25] These combined land and sea forces 'probably represented the strongest force which the government could muster without summoning a parliament to the south-east and exacting military service'.[26] A salutary reflection of Winchelsea's strength.

The leading citizens were slain but the majority were spared with a leniency unfashionable in those days. Perhaps it was an unwise leniency for the following year (1267) the royalist triumph of obtaining the submission of London 'was momentarily endangered' by yet another revolt in Winchelsea. This was repressed with smaller forces while Roger Leyburn was still hurrying there to see what was going on. The prisoners were taken to Rochester.[27] We can assume their fate.

However, the wisdom which Edward displayed as king manifested itself earlier when, after the mayhem of these campaigns, he assumed the position of Lord Warden of the Cinque Ports and became their protector instead of their enemy. This reconciliation came as a great relief to shipping in the Channel, both English and foreign, for disputes and piracy were greatly reduced.[28]

Such a reconciliation better disposed the prince towards the men of Winchelsea and he never forgot the quality demonstrated in their determined and persistent resistance. Similarly he never failed to recognise the town's importance to the country as a provider of shipping, a centre of trade and a creator of wealth. If he had withheld this recognition, Winchelsea would eventually have been lost for ever like Dunwich.

11. THE ROAD TO FINAL DESTRUCTION

Prince Edward's attacks on Winchelsea ceased with its eventual submission and his reconciliation with the Cinque Ports, but attacks by the elements continued.

The barons of Old Winchelsea, in this context, as we have seen, a name used in medieval times to refer to the leading citizens, were, in 1262, made a grant for seven years for urgent work on sea walls 'because of imminent peril from the sea which was constantly threatening the town'. Things were no better when the grant ran out and it was renewed for another five years.[1] The situation was worst to the south of the town[2] which is consistent with the generally assumed reason for this growing problem, namely that Fairlight cliffs were eroding, thus exposing Winchelsea to a far more direct threat. Fairlight Head then stretched far further out to sea than it does now but the problem exists to this day.

Measures were prudently taken to try to raise funds. One of the ways in which this was done is described in the ancient customs of Brighton where 'shares' in the catch of the fishing boats were apportioned between the crew, the costs, the vicar, the master and the churchwardens. The churchwardens' share was specifically to be used for 'building of fortes and walls towardes the sea for the defence of the saide towne ... and maintenance of the parish churche'.[3]

Among Winchelsea's sites which suffered at this time was the market place which had to be moved elsewhere.[4] By 1271 the quay alongside St. Thomas's Church lay in ruins and the church itself, much in need of the churchwardens' share, had been partly destroyed.[5] Two years later, as harbour dues and other sources of income rapidly declined, never to recover to their previous levels,[6] further murage grants were made for sea defences and in 1276 an additional 5000 square feet of land was granted to the townsmen to rebuild the quay and defend it.[7] We have just one glimpse of the personal hardship being suffered by townsmen and fishermen as a result. On 3 July 1276 King Edward I, as Prince Edward had by then become, decreed from New Romney that Matthew de Horne of Winchelsea should be granted 'a place 100ft by 50ft, lying between his house in Winchelsea and the king's port there, so that the said Matthew may make a quay upon the said place for the defence of his house against inundation of the sea, and build upon it'.[8] This was practical help resulting from personal involvement for the king had visited Winchelsea the previous day to examine the situation for himself. That visit was to have even more important repercussions later.

As the elements eroded it mercilessly, the town somehow managed to remain a principal importing centre for wine from France, mostly from friendly Gascony which was under the jurisdiction of Edward I as duke. Matthew Paris, with the very personal and specific knowledge which we have already noted, tells us that the Winchelsea of those days provided a large proportion of the fish which was consumed in London.[9] Transport to London was not as we would expect. The appalling condition of inland routes and the often impenetrable forests of the Weald meant that, even from as far west as Winchelsea it was much quicker to take goods to London by sea than it was by land from communities a great deal closer to the city.[10] Winchelsea was well equipped in terms of ships to take advantage of this and was helped further by a shorter route than would be available now because Thanet was still an island.

It was a matter of prudence and good sense that Winchelsea's extensive fishing and trading activities should be supported by proper assistance to shipping in using the harbour, particularly entering it at night. For this purpose a hermitage at the eastern entrance kept a light burning[11] and this service was officially recognised by permission to levy a toll of twopence on every ship carrying merchandise 'for maintaining the light which they had at their port for the safety of sailors entering at night'.[12] The history of Trinity House notes that 'elevated fire' was used in the ancient world to guide ships into port, the best known examples being the Colossus of Rhodes and the great Pharos of Alexandria. The Romans, too, used this technique; one of their lighthouses survives at Dover. In medieval times, however, the light operated at Winchelsea by 1261 is the earliest recorded in England; one is known in the Channel Islands almost fifty years later and at St. Catherine's Point on the Isle of Wight in 1323. 'These were usually maintained by monks and hermits as acts of charity'.[13] A building providing this lighthouse service, or the remains of it, survived until 1536 when it lay 'on a shingle bank called Old Camber Head, half a mile out to sea'.[14] Disaster then struck for it was destroyed by 'the men of the admiral of Sluys'[15] who 'burnt the hermitage of the Camber in despite (sic) and hewed an image of St. Anthony with their swords, bidding it call upon St. George for help'.[16]

In 1273 the barons and bailiff of Old Winchelsea were ordered to expel all the Jews who were living there. At that time the Jews were being severely taxed and their activities strictly controlled by the new administration of King Edward I. For sufficiently long to become a matter of custom there had been places where the Jews were permitted to live but Winchelsea was not one of them. Clearly the town had taken them in and they were apparently welcomed in assisting with, and becoming involved in, its trade. However, orders of this kind issued by the king in those days were certainly not disobeyed and the Jews were duly evicted although with nothing like the violence and depredation involved in the general expulsion from England in 1290 for the instruction included the phrase, 'without any damage to their bodies and goods'.[17]

Although Old Winchelsea continued to be pounded by the elements and thus steadily

(17) The old Ship Inn at Winchelsea Beach surrenders to the sea. That it would have been just as difficult to protect Old Winchelsea is suggested by Jill Eddison in 'Romney Marsh: Survival on a Frontier'.

(18) The 'Blackfriars' Barn in Rectory Lane was once used as a barn but was never associated, except in its present name, with the Blackfriars. It is an important building which dates from the foundation of New Winchelsea, possibly a high-status house but more likely a public building.

undermined, the men of the town still had to carry out their ship service obligations as members of the Confederation of the Cinque Ports. In the 1270s this principally involved the king's Welsh wars. It is recorded that in 1277 a fleet of ships 'arrived in the estuary of the Dee under the command of the Warden of the Cinque Ports' and that this fleet took a leading part 'in the reduction of Anglesey and the subsequent reduction of Wales'.[18] Although I cannot recall having seen the exact figures for the number of ships from each port which served in this campaign, evidence for the period gives Winchelsea such prominence that its vessels must have played a leading part.

Edward I greatly valued such Cinque Ports service and so, in the same year, sought to placate them in their ongoing dispute with Yarmouth over the annual herring fair. The men of Yarmouth were told that they must keep the strand and den (dunes) clear of obstructions so that there was room for the Cinque Ports to exercise their right to land and dry their nets. They must allow the portsmen to collect their traditional rents and to administer justice and control the prison, jointly with the provost of Yarmouth, during the fair. They must be allowed to collect dues to maintain fires on the beach, presumably navigational fires like Winchelsea's hermitage light, although Yarmouth could collect the dues and carry out this duty if the Cinque Ports failed. It must have been a further insult to Yarmouth that the barons were to receive the not inconsiderable sum of six pounds on their departure.[19] While it reinforced the king's support of the Cinque Ports, this declaration obviously did nothing to end the controversy or reduce the number of disputes.

In the following year, 1278, Edward I confirmed his support still further by issuing his Great Charter which applied generally to the Cinque Ports rather than to individual towns. This document states the number of ships which must be provided by the ports, in some cases assisted by their limbs, as follows: Hastings 6, Rye 5, Winchelsea 10, Romney 5, Hythe 5, Dover 21 and Sandwich 5.[20] Some authorities add the Hastings, Rye and Winchelsea contingents together to make Hastings equal to Dover with 21. There are many theories about exactly when Rye and Winchelsea became head ports in their own right as the two Ancient Towns. I count this charter as signifying that new improved status.

The Patent Rolls of 1280 and 1283 record respectively that, by then, Old Winchelsea was 'for the most part submerged' and, 'already in great part submerged by the inundations of the sea and in danger of total immersion'. W. M. Homan, in reporting this, adds, 'One must, however, ... make allowance for the exaggeration so dear to the medieval clerk'.[21] That may be true but I think we cannot fail to get the message!

If Winchelsea was to survive, positive action could wait no longer. In 1280 'the king's steward was sent to obtain land with a view to moving the settlement to a new site safely up on the hill of Iham'.[22] As we shall see, he was the first of many who became involved in the project.

We will first, however, by-pass their efforts and reach the climax of Old Winchelsea's fate. The threats and alarms fed the despair of the inhabitants of the ancient port until 1287 when the axe finally fell. There were, in fact three major storms in rapid succession in 1287-1288[23] and these storms 'must have generated surges that raised the sea to an unprecedented level'.[24] I shall, however, place the blame firmly on the one which I have always thought occurred on 4 February 1287 but some sources place it exactly one year later.[25] This, like the later problem of dating the 1360 French raid, is probably the result of a calendar confusion. On that occasion the sea 'rose or swelled so high in the marsh of Romenal [Romney] that it brake all the walls and drowned all the grounds so that from the great wall of Appledore as far as Winchelsey, toward the south and the west, all the land lay under the water lost'. It was probably this same storm which is recorded as having 'made pitiful waste of people, cattel and of houses in every place'.[26] It is also noted by Thomas of Walsingham that 'lightning passed through the chamber where the king and Queen Eleanor were conversing, killing two of the attendants'.[27] Provision was already in hand for those people of Winchelsea who survived this final onslaught. For residents of the settlement of Broomhill on the opposite eastern side of the Camber, there was no such provision and from that moment the community to all intents and purposes vanished leaving only its ruined church.[28] This storm was of such ferocity that the shingle ridge it threw up on Dungeness can still be identified more than seven hundred years later.[29] There was nothing inhabitable or recognisable left. The site must have become exposed at low tide for some years but no direct archaeological evidence of Old Winchelsea's existence has ever been found and no extant map purporting to identify the site was made until more than three hundred years later.[30]

Apart from my suggestion about the saltpans, mentioned earlier, we have just one more indirect clue about archaeological remains from Old Winchelsea. It was in 1743, that the Rev. Jeremiah Milles, a Cornish clergyman, toured Sussex. He was informed by fishermen local to Winchelsea that 'they had often anchored their boats on the ruins of the old city and had brought up rubbish and mortar when they weighed their anchors'.[31] I suspect that they were either eager to please or that they found ballast discarded, for once, at sea instead of in the harbour.

12. THE HILL OF IHAM

We have already noticed King Edward I's visit to Old Winchelsea in 1276 following which he assisted Matthew de Horne in his fight to defend his home against the elements. Having assessed the situation for himself and appreciated its hopelessness the king sent John Kirkby to carry out further inquiries and thus, according to Cooper, 'a site was fixed on which a new town should be built'.[1] Kirkby had served King Henry III and on his son's accession remained in office under the crown. He enjoyed the king's confidence and favour and in 1284 assumed the post of Treasurer of England, later being installed as Bishop of Ely. This latter position was, in medieval times, a perk in return for royal service rather than an important ecclesiastical appointment. Others no doubt carried out the bishop's diocesan responsibilities while Kirkby 'hurried back to his duties at the exchequer immediately after his consecration'.[2] Kirkby remained a distinguished figure in both Winchelsea and the country. He was prominent throughout the regency of the king's cousin, Edmund of Cornwall, while Edward was in Gascony between 1286 and 1289, putting down a Welsh rebellion led by Rhys ap Maredudd. I have found no evidence that Winchelsea, through its Cinque Ports service, was required to help him. As the rebellion took place in 1287 it might well not have been in a fit state to do so. Perhaps Kirkby is best known to historians for his great influence on the royal finances, particularly through an inquiry about royal dues which became known as 'Kirkby's Quest'.

The king continued to take a personal interest both in Kirkby's investigation and subsequent ones, often visiting the home of his friend William of Etchingham at Udimore when doing so. It was already clear that the site best physically suited for the task and most conveniently available was on the hill of Iham. 'Not only was it at a safe height and at a safe distance from the sea, being separated from it by about a mile of cultivated marshland, but it was about six miles up a tidal river.'[3] The chosen land could readily be defended, having cliffs on three sides. Its position on the then much wider and more important River Brede might be a potential disadvantage for its trade – it later became an extreme disadvantage – but it was further defence against an enemy attack by sea. New Winchelsea was never a sea port. It is a popular misconception that the waves lashed the cliffs of the hill of Iham. The sea may have affected Winchelsea in many ways, finally fatally, but not by eroding its cliffs as it did, for example, at Rye. In 1280 the king gave instructions for acquisition to proceed.[4]

What, then, of the hill of Iham where Winchelsea still stands. Cooper tells us that the site, covering one hundred and fifty acres, was principally of sandstone and was 'fit only for and used as a rabbit warren'.[5] The hill lay within the Manor of Iham largely owned by William de Grandison and his wife Isabella from whom it was purchased on the king's instructions. Other required land was owned by John Bone, John Langhurst and Battle Abbey and much of the total lay within the ecclesiastical parish of Icklesham. William Durrant Cooper records that, when his *History of Winchelsea* was published in 1850, £10 per annum was still being paid to the Vicar of Icklesham in compensation.[6] The Town of Iham, associated with Hastings in the Confederation of the Cinque Ports, lay on the western slopes with its Church of St. Leonard and was not taken into the new town.

With the land secured, planning could begin and here the design of Edward I's French bastides became highly influential. The king, as Prince Edward, had built a number of these towns in Gascony, intending them to be independent and well defended units which could conduct their wine trade without outside interference. Entirely new towns needed entirely new names and one of them, Libourne, was named for Roger Leyburn, Winchelsea's subduer.[7] 'Thirty years later it [was] largely with a view to encouraging and protecting the wine trade with Gascony that [the king]

(19) Monségur (Gironde), a bastide town like Winchelsea.
The survival of Monségur's regular street pattern is clearly shown

interested himself in the building of New Winchelsea.'[8] The bastides, as communities built as a unit rather than developing over time, were laid out on a regular grid pattern and New Winchelsea followed this example. Because of its topography the bastide which compares best with New Winchelsea is Monségur in the Gironde. Monségur is much smaller but its configuration is remarkably similar. Powicke plays down the importance of defences to the bastides but uses as his example 'the liberties of Monségur' which describe them as 'settlements of houses laid out in plots of fixed length and breadth, arranged in streets, and surrounded by ditch and earthen walls, rapidly constructed. The settlers had facilities for cutting wood, a market, assigned weights and measures and currency, a governing body of elected jurats and a scribe.'[9] There are remarkable similarities here, not only in the layout but in the fact that New Winchelsea was probably similarly defended initially and certainly had similar facilities and responsibilities. In the early twenty-first century Winchelsea claims to be the only community in England where the office of jurat survives and I have, as town clerk, the privilege of being successor to the scribe! There is another delightfully appropriate coincidence. The name Monségur means, 'hill where you are safe'.[10]

W. M. Homan, remarking that there are many surviving bastides, states that, 'Winchelsea is, however, probably the only thirteenth century town in England where a layout of this nature can be traced and reconstructed in detail', adding with his usual forthrightness that 'it is to be hoped that the Town ... will not be destroyed by modern building schemes controlled by persons with more influence than knowledge'.[11] I know that he did not, and would not, approve in some particulars of what has happened to Winchelsea in more than sixty years since that was written[12] but basically his hopes have been fulfilled; the original street pattern remains.

Before we reach Homan's importance in interpreting the layout of New Winchelsea to which he refers in that quotation, we must go back to the late thirteenth century and consider the next stage of the planning process initiated by Edward I. In 1283 he established a commission to carry the project forward. Here again, as with John Kirkby if not quite to the same extent, the importance of the establishment of New Winchelsea is emphasised by the highly influential nature of the men appointed. They were Stephen de Pencestre, Henry le Waleys and Gregory de Rokesle.

Stephen de Pencestre was the first Warden of the Cinque Ports to hold office on a regular and permanent basis. The office had been in existence since 1206 when the Earl de Warenne was made keeper (or warden) but the position, in the gift of the crown, was formalised only in 1268 on the installation of de Pencestre who 'functioned as both the barons' representative [in dealings with the king] and the king's authority in the Ports'.[13] An exceptionally tricky double responsibility in those days! He had taken over as Bailiff of Winchelsea and Rye after their uprising during the Barons' War with the task of keeping them under control and his presumably good job in this respect was rewarded with the more senior position in which he exercised considerable influence. His name is an earlier version of Penshurst, his family seat.[14] He

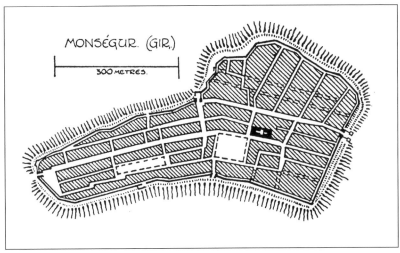

(20) A plan of Monségur showing how similar in shape its site is to that of New Winchelsea.

had a sadly controversial career as a judge in London which makes clear his influence outside the Ports but falls quite outside the remit of this book. There is still a Pencester Road in Dover, his headquarters as Lord Warden.

The careers of Henry le Waleys and Gregory de Rokesle ran strangely parallel and at one time in conflict. Le Waleys, a wealthy London merchant, was mayor of the city at the time of his appointment as a Winchelsea commissioner and had earlier been mayor of Bordeaux which sounds odd to us but in those days the latter was an office in the gift of Edward I who ruled Gascony as duke. De Rokesle had served as joint warden of the exchanges at London and Canterbury for a revision of the coinage vital to Edward I's financial plans. Both 'had grown rich and bought up many manors in town and country whose rents provided capital for wider business'.[15] Le Waleys was a reformer in London. Among other measures he started the practice of 'dragging bakers convicted of fraud through the streets of the city', set up a new prison and instituted new methods of trial.[16] All this annoyed many of the more conservative aldermen and they elected de Rokesle in his place with a mandate to nullify these reforms. The king then appointed a special judicial inquiry under Winchelsea's sponsor, de Kirkby, and de Rokesle was ordered to the Tower to answer for his actions. He resigned in protest and de Kirkby then took the city under the direct control of the monarch. Its mayoralty was not, in fact, restored until 1298.

Fortunately by then Winchelsea had, less controversially, been permitted its own mayor and was governed by him and his jurats. It might be this sequence of events which led Celia Fiennes to report in 1697 that 'if the Lord Mayor of London meets the Mayor of Winchelsea, the Mayor of Winchelsea must have precedence',[17] a tradition not elsewhere noted or observed!

Winchelsea's desire to use its clout to acquire a mayoralty and thus become largely self-governing was laid down in an undated petition to the king which must have been submitted at some time during, or more probably before, the commissioners' work and the actual construction began. W. MacLean Homan dealt with this petition and the king's replies in detail[18] and, although I have paraphrased and summarised, I rely here, gratefully, on his account.

Winchelsea's citizens wanted it confirmed that, in the new Winchelsea on the hill of Iham, their courts and other privileges should be the same as before; this the king agreed. They asked that their land should be allocated on the same terms as before; this would be at the commissioners' discretion. They wanted their liberty to extend half a league (approximately one and a half miles) all round the town; this the king said would be impossible – it would mean taking too much land from the Abbot of Fécamp and others. They sought permission to hold their traditional fairs, one of 15 days and the other seven, and their market on three days a week as in Old Winchelsea; 'Let it be so'. They required that there should be no religious houses in New Winchelsea save that of the Grey Friars, long established in Old Winchelsea; the king replied that he did not wish there to be any religious houses in Winchelsea 'except by the will of the Barons of Winchelsea'. They requested royal assistance in making roads and enlarging the harbour; the king made no response (a cautious avoidance of commitment to public expenditure!). They asked that all who came to the fair and the market should be excused payments for seven years to give the opportunity for the town to be improved; agreed. They requested convenient sites for the building of St Thomas's and St. Giles's churches; at this point the king's response became somewhat tetchier – 'Let them take from the sites so assigned'. Finally came the most controversial request, already mentioned, that Winchelsea should be governed by a mayor and jurats. Initially the response was disappointing, 'Let them have bailiffs as they have been accustomed'. By at least 1292, the king had changed his mind. We do not know what brought about this change but it must have had to do with Winchelsea's very considerable, economic and political influence.

This document concludes with either the appointment or confirmation of the appointment of Stephen de Pencestre, Henry le Waleys and Gregory de Rokesle 'to assess the town' and allots de Pencestre and de Rokesle the particular task of surveying the land of John Tregoz, much of which had been acquired from William de Grandison.

Two points from these representations need brief development here:

Possibly interpreting as hostile the request that there should be no friars except them, the Grey Friars jumped the gun! In 1285, well before plans were completed or the layout decided, they acquired quite independently part of the estate of John Bone and began building. This was later, as we shall see, to cause the regular nature of Winchelsea's plan to be distorted to allow for their existing property.

The ancient office of jurat, I believe, survives in England only at Winchelsea. Jurats also continue to be appointed in Jersey where they retain a judicial function lost by the Winchelsea jurats who were ex-officio magistrates until 1886. This office has existed since long before the time of King John to whom the people of Jersey made representations similar to those of the people of Winchelsea to Edward I. They 'claimed the right to be governed by the laws of Normandy and to have twelve jurats, natives of the island, with exclusive jurisdiction over all causes, civil and criminal, arising within the island'.[19] Both claims were successful. In Winchelsea the jurats administered justice with the Mayor and in Jersey with the Bailiff. Other English jurats have either become magistrates or councillors, as in the Cinque Ports, or had their positions abolished as in Romney Marsh.

With the commissioners' work complete the land on the Hill of Iham was formally handed over by John de Kirkby, still closely involved, acting on behalf of the king during Edward's absence in Gascony. The ceremony took place on 25 July 1288 'in the presence of the Sheriff of Sussex and other nobles, as well as knights, and many others of the said county'.[20] Winchelsea's new site was at last fully available.

13. NEW WINCHELSEA

With work in progress and the land officially handed over, the men and women of Winchelsea could now at least climb the hills, formidable then and still formidable now, from the strand and the ferry and take a proprietary interest in the development. There must certainly have been frenetic activity during the second half of the 1280s and until 1292 when the land allocated to individuals was confirmed through the rent roll.

It is therefore to that rent roll, two copies of which are preserved in the National Archives, that we must turn for the amazing amount of detail available about how and to whom the New Winchelsea land was allocated. The plots were laid out in thirty-nine numbered blocks as, we are told, was Old Winchelsea. These blocks are officially called quarters, are usually referred to as squares, and the majority are distorted rectangles! St. Thomas's Church had its importance emphasised by being allocated a complete un-numbered quarter, a privilege only equalled by the Greyfriars, who were already in situ, and the market, vital focal point of any medieval community. St. Giles's Church occupied part of Quarter 21. Other slight distortions were probably caused by features such as, for instance, Hogtrough or Deadman's Lane which, together with the Greyfriars clearly affects the alignment.

This regular pattern, in England probably best preserved at Winchelsea both in the surviving town and beneath the fields, was the fashion of the time. We have seen that the French bastides were laid out in that way as were many English towns. Salisbury and Ludlow are examples of earlier similar foundations. Contemporarily, King Edward I would dearly have liked to develop Poole, another vital port, to this pattern, but the project failed for lack of support from potential inhabitants.[1] Later Brighton, or Brighthelmstone as it then was, followed Winchelsea's example.[2] Perhaps, even later, New York did too, for Winchelsea's east-west roads were First Street (now North Street), Second Street (Mill Road/Mill Lane), Third Street (High Street), Fourth Street (Back Lane/Rookery Lane) and others now lost.

Reasons given for the regular layout are many and various. Anthony Freeman, a distinguished resident of the twentieth century, assumed that the wide and regular streets were fire-breaks made necessary by the construction close together of so many wooden buildings.[3] David Sylvester claims that this device was used 'to facilitate defence and street access and to eliminate wasted, untaxable bits of land'.[4] In a development of Sylvester's defence theory I remember reading somewhere that the straight streets would enable troops to move faster but I am not quite sure why they could not run round corners! The idea about obtaining maximum taxation income is convincing but I think the pattern was merely decided according to the fashion of the day for all 'new towns' with the considerable width of the streets facilitating the passing of heavy-laden carts carrying hogsheads of wine or loads of stone.

For our extensive knowledge of how the plots within the quarters were allocated we have to thank William MacLean Homan. His painstaking and perceptive interpretation which brought to life the rent roll, originally only a list of names, measurements and rents, has been acknowledged and used by all subsequent writers on Winchelsea's history. The existence of documents not available to Homan which would have affected his conclusions had he seen them, and a few minor and uncharacteristic errors, have been pointed out in what is now the definitive interpretation of the layout[5] but Homan was the pioneer to whom we must remain grateful.

The key to Homan's interpretation is his assertion that in the Middle Ages the east was taken

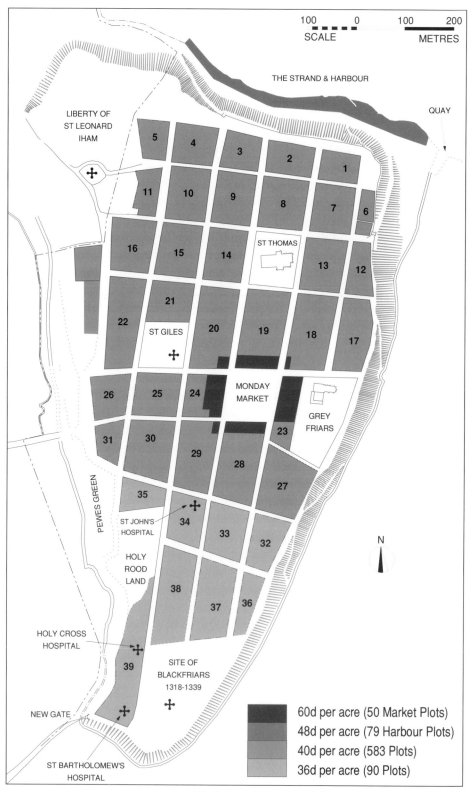

(21) The layout of New Winchelsea

to be the top of any map or plan rather than the north as it is today. This same importance of the east as the point of the rising sun was the reason churches and graves faced that way. It is not known whether any plan was drawn to accompany the 1292 rent roll, if it was it does not survive, but Homan deduced that the quarters would be numbered from the east and the existing town layout placed Quarter 1 in the north-east corner.[6] I have never quite fathomed how he further deduced that the rent roll list of plot owners in each quarter started in the south-east corner and went clockwise from there but that was his theory. Historical and archaeological investigations since have, with very minor exceptions, proved him right. Thus we now refer to 'Homan's rule'.[7] The measurements in the rent roll were, of course, another important factor in determining the exact position of each plot. The linear measurement was a virga, of sixteen feet six inches. Virga is Latin for the more recently used 'rod' as in 'rods, poles and perches' for those old enough to remember them. Areas were in acres as we should understand the term.

By these methods were allocated a total of 802 plots, 723 on the hill and seventy-nine beside the River Brede at its foot. The influential residents were allocated more than one plot, often including one by the harbour, but almost ninety percent of the people had a single plot either at the harbour or on the hill.[8] Presumably where there was multiple plot ownership the additional land was used as garden or smallholding; alternatively it may have been rented to someone whose name does not appear in the roll. There are 690 citizens listed and from this figure various attempts have been made to estimate Winchelsea's population in 1292. It has to be borne in mind that households were much larger in those days than they are now. Homan's estimate is that the population was between four thousand and six thousand.[9] That assumes an average of about seven persons per household. Others go as low as three thousand and as high as seven thousand. Whoever is right we cannot escape the fact that for a medieval port New Winchelsea had a very large population, reflecting its importance.

It is remarkable evidence of medieval thoroughness and skill that the allocation of these plots was done in such intricate detail, including increased values for sites surrounding the market, and lesser ones for those to the south, outside the principal area. A further example of this precision is that the total rental due to the king of fourteen pounds eleven shillings and fivepence three-farthings was exactly the same as that which had been due from the land on the hill of Iham taken over for New Winchelsea's construction.[10]

Quite apart from allowing us to know where these original New Winchelsea residents lived, the rent roll gives us their names which have been rendered in translation by W. D. Cooper.[11] I am sure that this normally staid gentleman must have enjoyed this task and possibly used some imagination and a sense of humour in carrying it out for he includes such delightful examples as Sander de brokeye long, Walter Spytewymbel, Stephen Blaunchpain, John Squathard, Wymarch Piggesteil, William Halfhering and Geoffrey Ponderous. He also, of course, includes the all-powerful Alards, eleven of them if we assume John Alard and John, son of Reginald Alard, to be different people. The Alards' dominance is reflected in their ownership of up to a maximum of four plots each. Among other leading families who will feature in this book were the Paulins, the Godfreys and the Selys. The list also demonstrates that, unlike the problems attending Edward I's attempted development of Poole, mentioned above, Winchelsea attracted through its predominance and potential, either before or during the move, a considerable number of those whose original residence was elsewhere. They include William of Romney, John of Dover, Andrew of Folkestone, Hamo the tailor of Rye, John of Sandwich, William Mot of Hastings, Stephen of Canterbury, Stephen of Biddenden and Peter of Portsmouth. It is worth noting that the first five were Cinque Portsmen. It is also worth noting that the list includes forty-eight women, widows and heirs, owning property in their own right. Frederic Inderwick laments the passing of the formidable Anglo-Saxon women and comments that these names are predominantly Norman, such as Alice, Juliana and Matilda. He draws particular attention to no fewer than twelve who bore the 'now unremembered' name of Petronilla.[12] Winchelsea residents who read this may know that the name was not entirely unremembered in the twentieth and early twenty-first century for it remains in use at Petronilla's Plat and it was the name of the late 'Peter' Barclay. She always insisted that it must be 'spelt the Winchelsea way'.

Inderwick also provides us with an analysis of the occupations of the residents. Among those identified by occupation within the roll, associated with the military and the defence of the town there were a professional wall builder, an armour maker, several gatekeepers, a pikeman, a trumpeter and a crossbowman. Serving the civilian population were ten bakers, six butchers, five cooks, four cobblers, one cordwainer, several coopers, two carpenters, two water-carriers, two barber surgeons, two cutlers, several reapers, numerous masons, two shipwrights, several ships' caulkers, two house builders and several carters. Also identified by occupation are six goldsmiths and jewellers, two gilders, a farm bailiff, some fishermen, two or three horse-dealers, a tiler, a stone-cutter, two tailors, five smiths, two grocers, two horse-breakers, four tanners whose tanyard was then south of the present Sandrock Hill, pewterers, inn-keepers, two bird-catchers, a comb maker, a tin man, and a bell maker. The list even explains one of the names which caused me amusement, that of Walter Spitewymbel. It appears that Walter was a 'botcher or needle and thread man'.[13]

Also allocated land in the southern part of the town, alongside some of those included in this delightful miscellany of medieval occupations were the hospitals of St. John, St. Bartholomew and Holy Cross. St. John's Hospital's relative importance is emphasised by the placing of its site nearest the centre of the town. It has been suggested by Capt. Herbert Lovegrove in his study of education in Winchelsea that this foundation included a training place for squires[14] but I have found no other source for this information. The gable end of one of the St. John's buildings, probably the western end of its chapel, remains and is a well-known Winchelsea feature. St. John's had moved with the town from Old Winchelsea and is likely to have been the oldest of Winchelsea's hospitals for 'rents had been assigned to it from time immemorial from the issues of Great Yarmouth'.[15] It is a mistake to think of medieval hospitals in the modern sense, almshouses is a better comparison. St. John's and St. Bartholomew's were certainly under civic rather than monastic control. Nevertheless this did not preclude regular religious observance for 'at many of the hospitals the master or prior, chaplains, brethren and/or sisters followed a rule and wore a religious habit, and that often applied to the leprous and other inmates as well'.[16] Clive Chizlett, in his study of the 'life-threatening environment' which Romney Marsh provided for its residents for centuries, concludes that medieval hospitals like those at Winchelsea were 'normally clean, [and] well-aired, with patients' beds set well apart. The day-to-day routine was rule-governed, disciplined, and, of course, hallowed'.[17] If he is right, applicants for admission must earnestly have hoped for mayoral approval.

We have most information about the mayor's responsibilities at St. John's which he had to visit once a year and where he was authorised to remove 'any objectionable inmate'. In consultation with the jurats he most importantly controlled admissions. They 'might admit any poor man or woman who had been "in good love and fame all their time"'.[18] Such inmates were cared for without any charge. The corporation was also responsible for appointing the master and mistress of both St. John's and St. Bartholomew's which they did as late as 1559, at which time they were probably combined on the St. John's site.

Holy Cross and St. Bartholomew's had originally been in the extreme south, in quarter 39 near the New Gate. Holy Cross, later described as a 'hospital or free chapel' and possibly referred to in 1287 as 'the church of the lepers' came, like St. John's, from Old Winchelsea having been in existence since at least 1252 but St. Bartholomew's which provided for 'brethren and sisters' was probably a foundation contemporary with the construction of the new town. Holy Cross appears not to have survived as long as the other two for in 1570 the corporation denied all knowledge of its existence since its mention in old records a hundred years earlier.[19]

It would seem that the king was anxious about the establishment of a working economy in New Winchelsea for he granted a seven-year exemption on the rents listed in the rent roll to encourage further immigration but David Sylvester has discovered that in fact these were collected so the circumstances of the grant remain obscure.[20] The most likely explanation has been suggested to me by David Martin, namely that the seven-year exemption began in 1285 when the Winchelsea men were beginning to develop their holdings and ended in 1292, thus making necessary the compiling of the rent roll. I find this totally convincing.

Perhaps there should be brief mention in this account of the layout of Winchelsea and its rent roll of what I presume to be the family which lived longest in the town, the Coggers. Their name indicates the occupation of ship's caulker, a vital occupation for the medieval Winchelsea community. Richard, Alice and Mabel Cogger are listed in the roll. An old gentleman of their name, reputedly a direct descendant, died in Winchelsea in the late nineteenth century.[21]

During the arduous years spent building their town anew, the men of Winchelsea gained vast experience which was to be utilised by King Edward. The merciless assault the king's forces made on Berwick in an early campaign against the Scots resulted in 'sack and slaughter which shocked even those barbaric times. Thousands were slain'.[22] The king needed Berwick rebuilt and he summoned a gathering of experts to a parliament at Bury St. Edmunds to advise him how best this should be done. Among them was Thomas Alard of Winchelsea.[23]

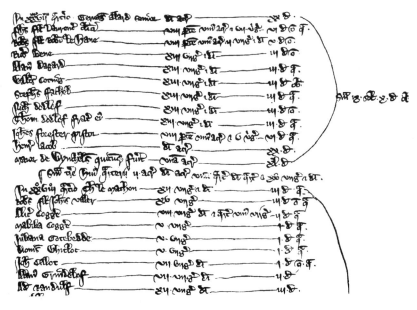

(22) Part of the Winchelsea Rent Roll of 1292

14. THE CELLARS

To New Winchelsea on the hill of Iham, built under the supervision of men like Thomas Alard, came, with Old Winchelsea's residents and hospitals, its principal trade, the wine trade. As early as 50BC, long before we know whether or not Winchelsea existed, the principal trade in wine with the continent had shifted to the ports of the south-east from further west.[1] In 1180 the custumal of Battle Abbey required its villeins to bring salt, herrings and wine to the abbey from Winchelsea.[2] In 1204 Manasses of Winchelsea, the town's bailiff, was a vintner,[3] like many of his leading citizens including the Alards. In 1213 Daniel Pincerne (the butler) of Winchelsea is recorded as having sold 50 tuns of wine to the king's agent.[4] As the thirteenth century progressed records show a steadily increasing trade between the Cinque Ports, particularly Winchelsea, and Gascony. The trade was further encouraged in 1278 when Edward I excused the Confederation from the royal prise on wine in recognition of its ship service.[5] Dr. M. K. James remarks that, in 1285, cellars indispensable to the wine trade were being hired by Gascons and used as bases, even as homes.[6] She does not refer specifically to Old Winchelsea where, it seems likely, there were no unflooded cellars at that date! We do know, however, that King Edward I hired New Winchelsea cellars in 1297 to store his wine.[7]

Perhaps the most important of Winchelsea's archaeological features lies in its remaining medieval vaulted cellars which are contemporary with the construction of the new town. Despite its present village-like appearance and size it stands, in this respect, for sheer numbers, alongside Southampton, Norwich and Chester although even in the last mentioned many of the cellars are neither vaulted nor underground. The historian of Winchelsea cannot resist noting that, while the town has thirty-two accessible medieval vaulted undercrofts, 'a smaller number' survive at Rye![8]

Cellars, then, were an integral part of the Winchelsea economy and their construction was a top priority in the intense building activity which we have noted as taking place during the years before 1292. Indeed, it must have been the first major building activity for the cellars were of a 'cut and cover' type which had to be built before the private houses and public buildings above them. Most of those which remain have their access by stairs leading directly from the street; many are on corner sites where the most important merchants lived; some have openings to admit daylight; others are entirely without natural light. The majority are barrel vaulted, that is they were constructed with parallel stone arches while those of the wealthiest citizens are of quadripartite construction, where pairs of arches meet in the centre and cross. Of these the best remaining examples are at Salutation Cottages and at what is now known as Blackfriars Barn in Rectory Lane. The former has all three bays built by this method and the latter two out of three.[9]

There has been some controversy over the intended uses of these cellars. W. M. Homan, to whom we turn again for intricate detail about the town's history, had no doubt that they were solely for the bulk storage of imported wine. P. A. Faulkner in 'Medieval Undercrofts and Town Houses' has argued that the existence of such cellars in inland towns and the fact that some cellars are far more elaborate than would be necessary for a bulk storage facility, means they were more likely to have been showrooms and shops.[10] David and Barbara Martin consider that the truth is likely to lie between the two, some with no artificial light falling into the former category and some elaborately lit examples into the latter.[11] I can only add a brief anecdote from personal experience. One very hot afternoon I joined a group taking a guided tour of six of the Winchelsea cellars under the leadership of Jurat Dominic Leahy. As we emerged from the cool, even temperature of the cellars to the considerable heat of the day, their excellence as wine stores was instantly and effectively demonstrated. In later years, of course, uses became far more varied. For example, the Homan drawings which I have used in writing this section are prefaced with a list of the names of the medieval occupants and an assessment of each accessible cellar's value as a potential Second World War air-raid shelter![12] Dominic Leahy has carried out a study of the temperature and humidity of his cellar at Five Chimneys with a view to demonstrating its qualities as a wine store. Between September 2002 and April 2003 the outside temperature varied between 25.4°C and −2.3°C, inside the cellar the variation was between 16.5°C and 11.4°C. The recommended ideal temperature for storing wine is between ten and fifteen degrees centigrade. Humidity readings carried out over the same period demonstrated the cellar's similar steadiness.[13] Point proved.

It is also to Dominic Leahy that I am indebted for allowing me to see and to use the results of his study of how the cellars were built and his conclusions which suggest how this was done. Since, as already mentioned, they were of cut and cover construction and had to be ready before the houses above could be started, the first requirement was to dig a big hole! In this the side walls were built up to a height of about three feet. From them were 'sprung' the arches, made of blocks of Caen stone or local sandstone, cut five-sided in uniform pattern and supported by a wooden construction of poles 'perhaps standing in pots of sand to assist striking slowly'. It could have taken up to twelve months to build each cellar and bring it into use primarily because of the setting-time of the lime-mortar used. When the arches were sound and thoroughly dry the supports were removed and wooden planking laid longitudinally onto the arches with local Kentish ragstone mortared end-on above it to form the roof. Eventually the planks would be

(23) The barrel-vaulted cellar at Firebrand, High Street.

struck out or left to decay at which time the cellar was complete and building above could commence.[14] It is clear that when this process was finished the arches served very little purpose for they have been removed from several of the cellars without apparent detrimental effect, although the one of these that I know best, at New Cottage, Mill Road, has only garden above it, no longer a building.

Quite apart from the vaulted cellars considered here, there is a row beneath Nos. 1-10 Barrack Square, properties built in 1763 for the growing cambric manufacturing industry in the town, and later used as barracks in Napoleonic times, hence the name. The Department of the Environment's listing of these properties states, 'This range of houses is built on a series of high vaulted cellars partly above ground which date from about 1300'. If this were true it would be inconceivable that they were ignored in W. M. Homan's cellar study and Homan's conclusion has more recently been confirmed by David and Barbara Martin who comment: 'Extensive brick barrel-vaulted cellars beneath 1-10 Barrack Square ... show no indications of incorporating work pre-dating 1763, although it is possible that the present work incorporates some earlier remains of vaulted cellars.'[15] A further clue is that none of Winchelsea's genuine medieval vaulted cellars is 'partly above ground'.

An interesting further insight into the construction of the Winchelsea cellars was provided by the detailed excavation and examination of one at the corner of Mill Road and Higham Green, currently the property of Jurat John Gooders. The work was carried out by Hastings Area Archaeological Research Group and the report is dated May 1999. It notes that this cellar was constructed not in a purpose-dug pit but in an irregularly shaped one. As the land acquired by King Edward I from Sir John Tregoz for the site of New Winchelsea is recorded as including seven acres of quarry it is suggested either that existing pits in the quarry were used for the cellars or that the Tilgate stone, a geological feature of the Hill of Iham, was quarried from the cellar areas and used in buildings in the town.[16] Seven acres would be the approximate area of three of Winchelsea's quarters. Cellars are a feature of the northern part of the town where this one is situated and it is the area in which the Tilgate stone is closest to the surface.

There is no doubt that the availability of local material, combined with the wealth and eminence of some of the citizens for whom homes were being constructed, helps to explain the number of secular and private buildings in the town which were of stone.

15. THE OTHER SURVIVORS

Just a few of those buildings, in part at least, are among the ones which survive today, along with the cellars, from the late thirteenth century creation of the town. The vast majority, the wooden ones, are, of course, all gone. What then does remain from the initial period of New Winchelsea's construction?

Since the Greyfriars jumped the gun, acquired their land in 1285 from John Bone, and laid out their plot in such a way that its pre-existence distorted the regular plan of the town, the ruins of their chapel can be assumed to be the earliest of the other survivors. These ruins are remarkable because they are the only remaining example of 'an apsidal [that is semi-circular, although in this case three-sided] termination to a church of the Mendicant Orders in this country'.[1] The Mendicant Orders were those which relied for their income on alms from the communities in which they lived. Pevsner confirms the quality of this building: 'Considering the dearth of Franciscan remains in England, this is one of the most impressive there are.'[2] The Greyfriars' buildings consisted of the large chapel of which the ruins are those of the quire, and all the dormitory, refectory and other provisions which one would expect. These are all lost although the foundations of the cloisters are visible as scorch marks in dry weather.[3] The principal cause of the loss was the rebuilding of the western range as a gentry residence for the then owner, Richard Stileman, in 1819.[4] Half the quire was almost similarly lost when Stileman's gardener proposed that it should be knocked down and a greenhouse built against the other half![5] Fortunately this plan was not adopted.

The Greyfriars, by moving on to the Hill of Iham so early, had the choice of their site which they obviously thought to be a good one because, unlike the Blackfriars who came later and moved three times, they stayed there until the Reformation. Choosing such a good place for their friary was apparently uncharacteristic of the Greyfriars for, according to E. B. Poland, 'Their first house in London was near the Shambles in Newgate on a spot appropriately called Stinking Lane. In Cambridge they occupied the decayed town gaol; in Norwich the water-side close to the town walls'.[6] I suspect that this resulted from the availability of land and the proximity of a supportive population. Both were assured in Winchelsea for we have already seen that the Mayor and Corporation petitioned that this Order should be the only one in the town.

The rector and officials concerned with the Church of St. Thomas had no need to make any similar choice of site, this was done for them. A complete un-numbered central quarter was allocated for the construction of St. Thomas's and for its graveyard. This was fully in accordance with its predominant position in the community. We must assume that the building, or at least its preliminary stages, began very early and not more than three years after the Greyfriars. There has always been doubt about whether in fact it was ever completed. If it was, it was of cathedral size and almost reached the western churchyard wall. There would be nothing incongruous in Winchelsea having a church as large and impressive as a cathedral. The ancient town's influence and importance make this quite likely and, in this story, we are reaching the time when that influence and importance were at their height.

What remains for us to see in the early twenty-first century is the chancel with its central and side aisles, the sanctuary with a crypt beneath, and the ruined transepts. The west wall of the chancel has been filled in and a sixteenth century porch inserted. The most recent study of Winchelsea assumes that, as New Winchelsea enjoyed such great success during its first fifty years, St. Thomas's was completed and that 'Given the amount of [later] demolition undertaken within the town for stone and other building materials, the most likely explanation is that after the collapse of the population the church was simply sized down and the unwanted part sold for materials'.[7] Supporting this assertion David Martin points out that, with the chancel side-aisles taken over as chantries (see below) St. Thomas's would, without the nave, simply not have been big enough to accommodate its large congregation.[8]

It will be convenient here, since we are considering survivals from New Winchelsea's early days, to take into account recent research which has closely examined, or rather re-examined, St. Thomas's most famous attribute, the tombs in the north and south aisles.[9] Despite earlier supposition that those in the north aisle might have been brought from the former St. Thomas's in Old Winchelsea, all are now firmly dated as contemporary with the new church, and were constructed during the early years of the fourteenth century, those in the south aisle slightly pre-dating those in the north.

Two chantries where prayers were to be said for the souls of the founders and their close relations were endowed at St. Thomas's during this period, one by Stephen Alard in 1312 and one between 1319 and 1323 by Robert Alard. Stephen's

(24) This tomb is believed by long tradition to be that of Gervase Alard

was recorded as being in 'the Chapel of the Blessed Mary' and was for the benefit of the souls of 'himself, his parents, his father's other wife, Alice, and all his ancestors and heirs'. Robert's was 'in the Chapel of St. Nicholas' where four priests were to hold daily services 'to say masses for the souls of his late brother Henry, his late wife Isabel and himself'.[10] Scholarly re-examination published in 2000 concludes that the three tombs in the north aisle are those of Robert Alard, his brother and his wife and that Stephen Alard's chantry was in the south aisle with his tomb to the east and that of one William Maufe to the west. This conclusion means that the original dedication of the side chapels must have been reversed since medieval times, the Lady Chapel now being in the north aisle and the Chapel of St. Nicholas in the south.[11] The dedications, together with the chantries, having been abolished at the reformation, the blame for their reversal during the twentieth century generally falls on W. D. Cooper who placed them this way round without giving supporting evidence.[12]

The conclusion that the north aisle tombs are those of Robert Alard, his wife and brother I find completely convincing. Those on the south side cause me more of a problem. Many readers will know that the eastern one has long been believed to be that of Gervase Alard Junior, Winchelsea's first known mayor and one time Admiral of the fleet of the Cinque Ports and the southern coast. Of him we shall hear more later. I could accept that 'his' tomb is in fact that of the chantry founder, Stephen Alard, at least it is still an Alard, and I already take care to refer to 'the tomb which is, by tradition, that of Gervase Alard'. However, William Maufe puzzles me much more. Maufe's family had long been associated with Sussex and the barons of Winchelsea were, in 1278, ordered to pay to him and his wife £10 a year out of their Winchelsea rents.[13] He is identified from the arms on the

(25) This head, generally believed to be of Edward I, looks down on Gervase Alard's tomb.

tomb but why would he be here in such a prominent position? I cannot answer that question but I want it to be Stephen Alard.

One last point arises from this report regarding the identification of the carved heads which appear on either side of the south aisle tombs. I asked Claude Blair whether he and his team would include them in the report but he said that they were not identifiable but were representations of kings and queens. That disappointed me because I have always believed that those on the eastern tomb are of King Edward I and his second queen, Margaret, and on the western one those of King Edward II and Queen Isabella during whose reign Stephen Alard also served as admiral of the Cinque Ports fleet. Learned publications have used these images as portraits of them and their presence is said to be a tribute recognising service to the nation. The reputed image of King Edward II certainly bears a remarkable resemblance to the effigy on his tomb in Gloucester Cathedral.[14] That the other is Edward I was undoubtedly Frederic Inderwick's opinion. Referring to the opening of that monarch's tomb in 1774, he stated that the features were 'distinctly traced and [bore] a close resemblance to the effigy of the King still to be seen over the tomb of Gervase Alard in Winchelsea church'.[15] It is also difficult to believe that the highly skilled and dedicated masons of the day would carve the effigies, their dress and armour in such immaculate detail, on the tombs and then put any old king or queen on the canopies.

I shall therefore adhere firmly to the tradition that those entombed in the south aisle are Gervase and Stephen Alard who were honoured by having representations of the kings and queens they served so well placed upon their tombs.

The faces of the kings and queens are not the only ones upon the canopies of these famous south-aisle tombs. Gazing down from the apex of both is a green man. The medieval significance of this figure is not known. It is often assumed to be a pagan image but surely that would rule out its inclusion in such a fiercely Christian place as St. Thomas's and in so many other medieval churches, abbeys and cathedrals. I like to think that the green man must have been, as he was later recognised, either a source of spiritual regeneration through his depiction of nature or a symbol to ward off evil. Or, indeed, both.

In considering the buildings which have survived in Winchelsea from those turbulent early days we turn now to the present Court Hall. It was not in 1292 the town's principal civic building, that lay elsewhere, but 'the shell of the present building undoubtedly dates from the late thirteenth or very early fourteenth century and incorporates beneath its western end (and perhaps the remainder) an un-vaulted undercroft – an unusual feature for Winchelsea where most of the known undercrofts are vaulted'.[16] It is therefore a prominent survivor. Its walls, and those of the garden, were part of the original structure, much larger than we see today and almost certainly extending to the north as well. The present magnificent roof dates from the fifteenth century. The first floor, now the museum, originally had two rooms and was known as the Freeman's Hall or Freeman's House. The Court Hall stood where the garden now is and was used as such by 1538. In 1666 the Court Hall was demolished and the two rooms of the upper floor of the adjoining building became known as The Court Hall and The Freeman's Hall.[17] To the subject of these changes we shall return.

In 1292, or whenever it was completed, it is confirmed by the rent roll that the building was a private residence. The question arises as to which leading Winchelsea resident would have been influential and wealthy enough to have such a magnificent stone house when the vast majority of Winchelsea's homes were of wood. Homan originally deduced that the land on which the Court Hall now stands was allocated in 1292 to Reginald Alard. His later research led him to alter his conclusion. Winchelsea Corporation's copy of *The Founding of Winchelsea* contains an amendment in Homan's hand which changes Reginald Alard's name to that of Gervase Alard junior.[18] This alteration has recently been confirmed by David and Barbara Martin's research.[19]

So, although I have to swallow my disappointment that Gervase Alard's tomb is only his by tradition, I can at least rejoice in the fact that the annual mayoring ceremony, more than seven hundred years after he was Winchelsea's first recorded mayor, takes place each Easter Monday in his former home.

Gervase Alard junior was by no means the only wealthy citizen who could afford a stone-built home. Three of the others survive, although they are not recognisable externally as such today. Two are present-day homes, Firebrand and The Armoury, the third, the Blackfriars Barn in Rectory Lane, now a ruin, may have been either an opulent home or a public building.

This last, despite the name by which it is now known, never had anything to do with the Blackfriars. It was, however, converted into a barn by 1763 and remained in that use until the early twentieth century. The building, originally contemporary with the construction of New Winchelsea, or at least dating from the early fourteenth century, has been extensively investigated by archaeologists, together with an adjoining house to the north. Evidence is strong enough to conclude that the 'barn' was originally a large house, 'or, given its exceptionally large open hall and dearth of private accommodation, a guildhall or similar'.[20] The inclusion of a large garderobe (lavatory) and a cesspit bigger than would be required for domestic use tend to support the theory that this was some sort of public building, quite possibly the town's Court Hall, long before the present building had that use. Today the most remarkable surviving feature at Blackfriars Barn is the cellar. This has three rooms, two quadripartite and the central one barrel vaulted and is by far the largest in Winchelsea. The eastern room contains a fireplace – the only known example of a heated cellar in the town.[21]

There is no doubt about the original and present domestic use of The Armoury in Castle Street although other uses have intervened. The name derives from Winchelsea's days as a garrison town during the Napoleonic Wars. Earlier it was a pub, 'The Bear', and more recently a bakery.[22] The present façade in no way reflects the building's original appearance but much survives within. The principal range is dated c.1300 and included an open hall, probably of two bays. An original southern range has long been lost but the building was extended in that direction in late medieval times. Here there is a six-bay barrel vaulted cellar.[23]

No clue as to its origins can be found, either, from the present appearance of Firebrand on the corner of High Street and St. Thomas's Street. It, too, is dated c.1300 and, 'is a crosswinged hall house with services to the east (away from the corner). The service doorways and rear entrance door to the hall still survive. Beneath the services is the barrel vaulted cellar with parapetted entrance steps leading down from the street'.[24] The name derives from the building's long use as a forge. Among the timber work, most of which dates from the fifteenth century, are some 'barge boards' which once formed part of Firebrand's south-facing gable and were later incorporated into the present rafters.[25] The owner, Richard Comotto, kindly invited me to have a look at them. The original purpose of these carefully carved boards was to prevent rain driving in under the projecting section of the roof and the boards' pronounced moulding would clearly encourage the water to run clear. The use of these boards within a much-modified building must be an unusual survival. Richard Comotto believes that Firebrand's roof-space previously had another most unusual feature. He has been told by a descendant of the Marten family, long-time owners, that the attic once had a hollowed-out tree trunk running through it to carry away rainwater.

Another well known survivor is the gable end of the chapel of St. John's Hospital, already mentioned. I am told that such gables (there is another at Midley, near Lydd) may have been deliberately left standing as a way of avoiding particular tithe payments.[26]

While we are considering those buildings which survive, in part at least, from the time of the construction of New Winchelsea we must not, of course, forget the three town gates. As the name New Gate was being used in 1330 and the Pipewell Gate was probably rebuilt, in 1399 or 1404, it is the Strand Gate which I presume to have been the earliest. This magnificent bastion, now sadly obscured by trees from the point of view made famous in paintings by Turner and Millais, stood commanding the town's principal entrance from the waterfront. Through it would flow the merchandise on which Winchelsea prospered and the men who manned the ships which carried that merchandise. If the Strand Gate was built between the years we are at present considering, 1285-1292, it may well have been principally to exhibit to the world Winchelsea's prominence and wealth for it was originally a much more formidable structure than we see today. However, it would not have been long before it was needed for its main purpose, defence against an enemy. By 1294 England was at war with France and by 1295 the situation was such that King Edward I 'authorised a special customs duty on goods entering the port and town of Winchelsea to assist the town in building its walls'.[27] This duty was to be levied for five years, presumably considered sufficient for the work to be completed. If so, that was not how it worked out.

The war which made all this necessary was, partly at least, provoked by the men of Winchelsea and the Cinque Ports.

(26) Firebrand, High Street, despite its present external appearance, contains many features dating from the foundation of New Winchelsea

16. ESCAPE, ENMITY AND EXPEDITION

Having examined the building of New Winchelsea between 1285 and 1292 and the surviving features, we must now turn to other events affecting the town during that period and a little beyond.

It is somewhat frustrating that Winchelsea's first known mayor was Gervase Alard junior in 1295 but we know nothing of his predecessors. Rye's first mayor, Henry de Rakele, was appointed in 1289, a date claimed to represent the incorporation of the town, and of Winchelsea, as a municipal borough.[1] The fortunes of the two towns in such respects ran remarkably parallel and such a date for Winchelsea's first mayoralty, early in the period under consideration, seems highly likely. However, the subject of Winchelsea's establishment as a municipal borough developing through the privileges granted as a Cinque Port has already been examined and cannot be assumed to coincide with its first mayoralty. Hastings, for example, was one of King Alfred's burhs in the 880s[2] but was not granted a mayor until 1588.[3] In a letter to Jurat John Knox, a leading Winchelsea resident at the time, Leopold Amon Vidler, historian of Rye wrote, 'In spite of what Homan says [that Winchelsea's mayoralty probably dates from 1293] I think the first date should be 1289, the same as Rye'. Vidler goes on to claim that the absence of an individual charter granting Rye (and presumably Winchelsea) this status can be explained by the presence of the king 'otherwise we should probably have one and would know exactly when the honour was conferred'.[4] Whether attendance of the monarch would remove the need for a written charter seems highly unlikely.

If that was the correct date, Winchelsea's first mayor or his successor might well, as supervising authority for the port, have been forced by statute to take some local part in the general expulsion of the Jews from England the following year. With characteristic and understandable asperity, Simon Schama writes, 'In 1290 England acquired the distinction of becoming the first country in Christian Europe – or anywhere else for that matter – to expel its Jews as if they were a contagious disease.'[5] This is not the appropriate place to discuss the background to Edward I's order, except, sadly, to say that it was a popular measure at the time. There is no direct documentary evidence that Winchelsea, previously shown to have welcomed the Jews, was involved. However, large numbers of those expelled are recorded as having left through the Cinque Ports. They were granted immunity from punishment at their port of embarkation but many horror stories exist about what happened to them after their ships set sail. W. M. Homan concludes that the character and nature of Winchelsea's seamen implicates them but no more.[6]

Another year later came the survey known as Pope Nicholas' Taxation. This assessed the value of the buildings and land owned by all the churches in England. It 'became the basis for clerical grants to the crown [and] is the most precious survey of ecclesiastical property in the Middle Ages'.[7] The intention was that such a tax, authorised by the pope, departed from the church's usual exemption from national taxation and should be used for crusades. Edward I interpreted this loosely! As we shall shortly see, such taxation was to embroil Archbishop Robert Winchelsey in a dispute with the crown which was fatal to his career. When assessed, all three of Winchelsea's churches were listed as being within the Deanery of Hastings and the Archdeaconry of Lewes.[8] Their relative values were: St. Thomas's £10 13s 4d, St. Giles's £6 13s 4d and St. Leonard's £4 13s 4d.[9] It is not clear how St. Thomas's was so precisely valued for, while its land would have been allocated, its building cannot have been complete. No doubt plans were far advanced.

If the monasteries as well as the churches were included in this survey, the Franciscans of Winchelsea would have had other matters to worry about had they felt unfairly treated. In the early 1290s things seem to have been difficult for them. E. B. Poland attributes this to the preoccupation of Winchelsea's inhabitants with the construction of their new town which reduced their interest in matters religious and, even more importantly in almsgiving. Combined with this he asserts that food supplies were unreliable and that 'the roughness and cruelty of the sailors of this period was notorious'.[10] Into this disturbed atmosphere for a monastery came one Friar William of Pershore, a Benedictine, who was used to a far calmer existence within his order but sought a more active life. It proved considerably too active for his liking.

W. M. Homan discounts Poland's theories about how rough life was for Winchelsea's Franciscans and thinks that William would have wanted to get away from the Benedictines because of their regime which he describes as 'a strict rule and, if strictly observed, an uncomfortable one involving much wakefulness, long prayers, little food, few clothes and very few baths'.[11]

Whatever his reason for requesting the move, Friar William had been formally accepted into the Order of Greyfriars and was therefore bound to them. He soon began to yearn for the comparative quiet of his former life. This yearning became so strong that, without seeking official approval, he escaped and fled to the Benedictine Abbey of Westminster where, against all the rules of the religious orders, he was taken in. To add insult to injury he had stolen a number of books from the Greyfriars' library and taken them with him.

The abbot and friars of the Winchelsea Franciscans were outraged. They discovered where William was and demanded his return. They wanted the books back too! Although not denying the facts, the Abbot of Westminster declined to give William up. An appeal was then made to the Archbishop of Canterbury who implemented a papal authorisation of excommunication against Brother William and anyone harbouring him. The Abbot of Westminster appealed and the appeal was heard in Rome on 4 April 1291. The outcome, for the abbot, was disastrous. He was ordered to apologise in public, recognising the Franciscans' right to demand William's return; to assist in capturing William; to pay a fine of '100 marks or the expenses'; to express his regret to the Archbishop of Canterbury and to return the books. 'Silence was to be maintained regarding the dispute now terminated'.[12] How this last condition was possible when the matter had been publicly announced is not clear.

Perhaps the Abbot of Westminster had failed to take into account that both the Archbishop of Canterbury and the pope were Franciscans!

This story has, for us, an unsatisfactory ending because we do not know what happened to William or the books. If he was returned to Winchelsea he must have had a singularly unpleasant time. All we do know by way of conclusion is that payment of the fine, divided between Lichfield (which had been burnt) and Winchelsea (which had been drowned) was not completed until 1295.[13] Cooper supports the view that the fine was intended to help support the Winchelsea Greyfriars who were among the 'poor houses of these friars'.[14]

Whatever our doubts about the conclusion of William of Pershore's story, there can be no doubt about Poland's assertion that the roughness and cruelty of the sailors of this period were notorious. This was being amply demonstrated while William's story was unfolding or at least during the time taken to pay the fine.

Thomas of Walsingham records that in 1292 the crew of a Cinque Ports ship and the crew of a Norman ship came to blows while taking on water near Bayonne. The death of a Norman

(27) This artist's view (eighteenth century) of the Greyfriars Chapel ruins in their then agricultural setting also shows the monastic building lost when the present house was built.

sailor in this fracas so incensed his comrades that they 'seized an English ship in the Channel and hanged some of the crew from the yardarm. They added insult to injury by hanging a number of dogs alongside them'.[15] This same form of affront is reported by Burrows who implies that the French king had given orders for such actions as a deliberate provocation. Burrows writes: 'They [the Normans] paraded their ships before the English ports with the bodies of Englishmen they had slain hanging alternately with the carcasses of dogs from their yardarms'.[16] Such calculated insults were understandably intolerable to the English seamen and were guaranteed to lead to trouble.

Feelings ran high but not high enough to prevent mutual arrangements being made by an intermediary for the matter to be fought to a conclusion like a duel between fleets. The English fleet, augmented by Irish, Dutch and Gascon vessels, gathered at Portsmouth 'disguised as a trade convoy,'[17] allegedly to deflect suspicion about the involvement of the Cinque Portsmen who formed its nucleus. The English fleet sailed to an agreed rendezvous marked by a standard hoisted on board an empty ship anchored off St. Mahe.[18] The French fleet, also augmented, in their case by Flemish and Genoese, totalled two hundred warships and is stated, by the English chroniclers at least, to have vastly outnumbered the enemy. Probably numbers were about even. Both sides flew the red streamer or bausan signifying death without quarter.[19] As the French sailed out from the mouth of the Charante with the English lying at anchor and in wait, a great gale blew up. The English fleet scattered, but in order and under strict discipline. Aided by this discipline and their expert seamanship in such conditions they fell upon the foe whose ships were running before the storm and annihilated them. Few French vessels reached port again.

The men of the Cinque Ports used the flying of the bausan as an excuse for the ruthlessness of the attack and claimed that it removed from them any need to account for their actions or pay restitution.[20] No direct evidence associates Winchelsea with this massacre but the town's prominence within the Confederation at the time and the fact that prizes were taken to Winchelsea after the battle[21] leave no room for doubt.

All this and subsequent incidents off Gascony finally snapped the patience of the Parlement of Paris. The French declared Edward's duchy of Aquitaine forfeit and in 1294 war ensued.

Winchelsea was, as always at this time, deeply involved. Orders were given that the fleet must be strengthened and that Winchelsea should provide two large galleys, each of 120 oars. 'The competence of the town for such work in the matter of shipwrights and the supply of materials is shown by the fact that it and Bristol were the only two out of ten places including London where more than one galley was to be constructed'.[22] We know no more about this work in Winchelsea but a fascinating account survives about how the Southampton galley was built.

This states that work was immediately put in hand on receipt of the royal command. Four master-builders were summoned, together with thirty skilled workmen, recruited from Shoreham and the neighbouring ports. An empty sea-shore fenced plot was hired, neighbouring properties were requisitioned as workshops or offices and two boys were engaged to keep watch night and day. Timber, iron, sails, masts and spars were acquired and finally, with the fighting castles fitted, the vessel was 'hauled to the sea down a ditch it had taken twenty men six days to dig'. The total time taken was seventeen weeks, an amazing achievement particularly as the winter of 1294/95 is recorded as have been extremely wet. The galley was provisioned, armed, and, crewed by a master, three constables and one hundred and twenty sailors, taken on its four-day voyage to join the fleet at Winchelsea.[23]

We can only hope that, when the Southampton galley arrived, the shipbuilders of Winchelsea had done as well and that their two vessels were similarly ready.

Certainly, as they approached, the Southampton men would have witnessed frantic activity. The king was using Sir William de Etchingham's manor house at Udimore as a base while supervising the military preparations and even went so far as to prorogue parliament in the autumn of 1295 because of the need to stay near Winchelsea to control what was happening.[24] A sitting of parliament in those days, of course, required the presence of the monarch.

Evidence exists of the scale and urgency of this activity. Edward was desperately seeking to recruit a new army. During 1295 he ordered twenty-five thousand men from the counties between Norfolk and Dorset to come to Winchelsea to train in the use of the longbow 'knowing perfectly well that only a tiny proportion of them would have much aptitude for the weapon'. In the same year he pardoned poachers and criminals more likely to be able to use weapons competently on condition that they accepted military service.[25]

The king was also urgently gathering an adequate navy. In this respect he ordered Thomas Alard of Winchelsea, together with William de Thorntoft, to take and make ready all the ships they could find in Sussex, Southampton, Dorset, Somerset, Devon, Cornwall and Gloucester. Instructions were given to the sheriffs requiring them to permit this requisitioning.[26]

All was designed to lead to the departure of a great expedition to Gascony with the purpose of re-establishing Edward's government there. The expedition was to be led by his brother, Edmund of Lancaster. Ships and men gathered at Plymouth as well as Winchelsea, but a delay until January 1296 was caused by the illness of the designated commander. On 1 January in that year Edward asked for special prayers to be said 'in every diocese of England and Wales ... for

Lancaster's expedition'. This was enthusiastically supported by Robert Winchelsey, Archbishop of Canterbury, not, as will become clear, an automatic supporter of the king. Despite these prayers, when in Gascony Edmund was able to achieve little more than his predecessors had done. 'Within a very few weeks of the army's arrival its funds were exhausted and its commander was dying. Edward had preserved a foothold in Aquitaine but little else had been achieved.'[27]

The importance of Edmund's expedition to this story is that we know the names of the Winchelsea ships included and many of their commanders. Of the Cinque Ports ships doing their ship service duty on this occasion, Winchelsea supplied thirteen, Sandwich twelve, Dover seven, Rye seven, Romney five, Hythe three and Hastings three. Homan, quoting from documents at the National Archives, gives the Winchelsea list as follows:

Name	Master	Constable	No. of Mariners
The Cog *St. Edward*	John Pate	John Alard	48
The Cog *St. Mary*	Adam Stonhard	Edmund Andrew	48
The *Plente*	Wm. Kingessone	Robert atte Carte	43
The Cog *La Lunge*	Reginald Payn	Cok Badding	48
The *Nicholas*	John Muleward	*name not given*	43
The Shallop *St. Giles*	Henry Baker	Henry Baker, son of Benedict	48
The *Nom Dieu*	Bendedict Alard	Henry Alard	40
The *Bocher*	Benedict Seman	Richard Spayn	48
The *Fantun*	Gervas Tonman	Roger Tonman	48
The Shallop *St. Thomas*	Elyas Lambyn	William of Ihamme	35
The *Margaret*	Robert Germayn	Matthew Batell	33
The *Langeton*	Hendman Aubyn	Robert Paulin	38
The Ship *Bishop of Durham*	John de Meghefeld	William Heved	43

Thirteen ships with officers and five hundred and sixty three seamen – a formidable contribution.[28] As is made clear by the way the list is set out, the constable ranked immediately below the master in the hierarchy of each vessel. It is assumed by some that Gervase Alard gained some of his wide experience by sailing with this expedition. However, as he was serving as mayor at the time, this seems most unlikely.

Not only do we know the names of the Winchelsea ships and their officers but, thanks to recent research by David and Barbara Martin based, of course, on Homan, we know where many of the officers lived and so can identify the modern properties on those sites. For example, Henry Baker, son of Benedict, Constable of the *St. Giles*, lived at Plot 6, Quarter 9 where 'Firin' and 'Westway' now stand. Robert atte Carte, Constable of the *Plente*, lived in Quarter 6 ('The Retreat'), Elyas Lambin lived in Quarter 7 (6 Barrack Square), John de Meghefeld, (Quarter 14 - Wesley's Chapel) also had a Harbour Plot (Tanyard Lane). There are no buildings where Adam Stonhard's home stood in Quarter 16 – it was beyond the cricket sight-screen at the opposite end of the ground from Rectory Lane. No fewer than four expedition officers lived in Quarter 20. The homes of Henry Baker, master of the *St. Giles*, and Henry Alard, constable of the *Nom Dieu*, stood on the Rectory Lane side of Wall Field. John Alard and Robert Paulin had large plots where Mariteau House now stands. William of Iham lived on the far side of the field behind the New Hall (Quarter 21). Cok Badding lived near the north-west corner of the allotments (Quarter 22). Robert Germayn, master of the *Margaret*, lived, like Henry Baker and Henry Alard, in Wall Field but further to the south in Quarter 24.[29]

The survival of such precise information after more than seven-hundred years somehow seems to bring much closer these men of the Winchelsea of long ago. On this occasion they were serving their monarch rather than seeking gain through violence. Let us therefore hope that they returned safely and were properly paid for the long time the expedition must have taken beyond their statutory fifteen days.

(28) The house now known as The Armoury takes its name from the time of the Napoleonic Wars but, despite its much-altered external appearance, dates from the foundation of New Winchelsea. The adjoining Town Well post-dates the period covered by this book. It was built in 1850 and was the main source of water for Winchelsea's ordinary people for more than fifty years.

17. THE CRISIS

Because of Winchelsea's involvement, we have been skirting the edges of national history. Now we must plunge right in. No excuse is needed. The great crisis of 1297 almost brought England to a state of civil war. One of its major causes was a dispute between Winchelsea's founder and Winchelsea's most distinguished son. More than that – a substantial part of the climax took place within Winchelsea's walls.

Robert Winchelsey was Archbishop of Canterbury from 1293 until 1313. 'He derived his name from Old Winchelsea where he was probably born'.[1] He was originally Robert of Winchelsea and many in those days took their names from their places of birth and upbringing. This evidence is certainly quite enough for me to include him here as an important part of my story. The variation in spelling makes no difference. The present use of Robert Winchelsey, the Earls of Winchilsea and the Ancient Town of Winchelsea merely demonstrate that in medieval times the spelling of proper names was constantly variable. Standardisations are a comparatively modern phenomenon. Robert's origins seem to be taken beyond doubt by the bequest of 100 marks for the fabric of St. Giles's, Winchelsea in his will.[2] The fact that both the Dictionary of National Biography and Winchelsey's twentieth century biographer[3] place Old Winchelsea in Kent is only a minor irritant!

Homan states that Winchelsey was 'said to have been "born of mean parents"'.[4] I assume him therefore to be a self-made man who, with resources unrevealed save for his reputed excellence in grammar, went to school in Canterbury, studied arts in Paris and later theology at Oxford. He was appointed Rector of Wood Eaton in Oxfordshire and became a canon of Lincoln Cathedral. With Wood Eaton so close to Oxford he continued his studies and his close association with the university, eventually obtaining various further degrees and becoming its chancellor. 'Winchelsey gained praise as chancellor of the university for his support of the rights of students and as a prudent man with a sense of justice.'[5] These characteristics were to stand him in good stead, in the eyes of the church if not in the eyes of the king.

He became Archdeacon of Essex and a prebendary of St. Paul's, earning an outstanding reputation for his theology, teaching and pastoral care. This reputation led to his appointment as archbishop by a committee of distinguished clergy and with the approval of the king. Other characteristics must have recommended him. He gave freely to the poor, supported students in difficulty, 'was cheerful in temperament, corpulent in body, a hard worker and a good man of business'.[6] If Winchelsey was, indeed 'corpulent in body' it was because he had a large frame and not through over-eating. It is said that, when served a joint of meat he would, to the intense annoyance of his servants, give the best cuts to the poor and eat only the scraggy bits himself. He was also reputedly a very plain dresser, having only two suits of clothes, both of coarse cloth.

The list displayed in Canterbury Cathedral shows him to have been the fiftieth archbishop since St. Augustine which is somewhat ironic as he spent a good deal of energy during his period of office in dispute with St. Augustine's Abbey, adjoining his cathedral! His selection was unusual in his times in that he was a secular cleric, not a monk or a friar.

The appointment had to be confirmed by the pope. Robert travelled to Rome but there was a papal vacancy and he was long delayed there. While he was away the problems which provoked his dispute with Edward I escalated rapidly.

Edward was desperately in need of money to finance his Scottish campaigns. Since the time of William the Conqueror the judicial and financial affairs of church and state had been largely separate. Edward, frustrated by this lack of funds, ordered money to be physically seized from churches. As an excuse he issued an order to 'search out counterfeit and clipped coins'.[7] The money which he seized, more than ten thousand pounds, could only have been rightly his had it been collected for a crusade. It had not. The amounts taken were faithfully recorded but only about two thousand pounds was ever repaid. The resentment created among the clergy was greatly increased by 'the way in which entry was forced to churches and chests then smashed when keys could not be found'.[8] Hardly a tactful approach.

(29) These medieval floor tiles which were found near Rye in the early 1930s are thought to represent (left) King Edward I and either Thomas a' Becket or, more likely, Archbishop Robert Winchelsey for the tiles date from his time

Edward, as we shall see, had been seeking and obtaining taxation of the laity pretty mercilessly and the church had to be his next target. In Winchelsey's absence the response of its leaders was initially weak. The king took advantage of this by calling an ecclesiastical council which he addressed in person. He stressed the urgent need for funds in the national interest, emphasising that the laity were not only financing the campaigns but risking their lives by fighting in them. He tried to excuse and even apologise for his earlier actions, but the demand for money remained. Under this pressure the clergy offered double what might have been expected in times of emergency but far less than Edward wanted. He was furious. We have seen how Winchelsea's churches were assessed during Pope Nicholas' Taxation in 1291. The total of this survey for the whole country was £200,000. Edward wanted half and actually collected about £70,000.[9]

In 1295, with Winchelsey back in the country, a parliament, including the clergy, was held at which further demands were made. The clergy offered a tenth, that is one tenth of the value of their movable goods. Winchelsey demonstrated his wisdom and fairness by speaking of the national interest, of the king's need to defend his kingdom, and of his right to seek money from the church in times of such need. However, he totally rejected Edward's assumption that he could demand such a tax; it could only be paid with the full consent of the church, and only when the country was under threat, not on a regular basis. The clergy readily confirmed this: 'Consent to direct taxation by the king was not obligatory. The grant depended on the clergy's concerted opinion. That this opinion was united in a firm policy is a mark of their confidence in the archbishop'.[10] The tenth was offered and rejected. No persuasion by Edward could change their minds. Winchelsey's leadership had unified the church and antagonised the king.

This dispute would continue to fester while another was developing. The high-handedness which led Edward to order churches to be entered by force also led him to antagonise his barons by the introduction of the maltote, or 'bad tax', on wool. He first suggested to a selected gathering of barons that all wool should be seized to prevent its export to France. He would, of course, then have reaped the profits. The resulting protests led him to impose an alternative tax of approximately 30 marks on every sack of wool. This had not been approved by parliament in the normal way and resentment rapidly grew.

The barons felt that the provisions of Magna Carta were being ignored. They were offended by other writs and requirements of the king and his clear determination to ignore the written assurances obtained from King John. They claimed that Edward had not only introduced an unlawful tax on wool but had made seizures of corn, leather and cattle to which he was not entitled and had enforced the forest laws with unjustifiable harshness.[11] He was also alleged frequently to have defaulted on tallies, that is to have refused to pay debts of which clear evidence existed.[12] They wanted these unlawful activities reduced rather than expanded and gained much from the perceived justice of their cause.

And so we move towards Winchelsea.

It was Edward's avowed intention to lead an expedition to Flanders in 1297. The French had gained ground there which he wanted to regain and he also had in mind the establishment of a French truce in order that he might concentrate on dealing with the Scots. It further annoyed the barons that the writs issued required them to go to Flanders where their military service had never been required before.

Winchelsea was chosen as the port of embarkation. Orders went out for the gathering of ships, men and supplies. This was a massive undertaking. The sheriffs of counties all over England were ordered to despatch ships capable of carrying forty tuns; if the order was fully obeyed hundreds of vessels must have appeared. In fact three hundred and five ships eventually sailed for Flanders, of which the Cinque Ports provided seventy-three, forty-six of them serving free for their statutory fifteen days.[13] Some fifty-thousand men and large numbers of horses poured into the neighbourhood, among them between five- and seven-thousand Welshmen. The Welsh had to undertake something of a forced march, two hundred miles in a week, if they were to arrive within the permitted time. Supplies, too, came from all over the country. They included such items as 53 quarters of wheat, 32½ carcasses of oxen, 280½ pigs, 124 cheeses, 154½ tuns of wine and 34½ tuns of cider (or ale). The logistical problems must have been vast. Storage was required in Winchelsea and records show that Edward requisitioned cellar space for this purpose. 'Some of the cellars referred to are probably among those still in existence.'[14] Sylvester describes how storage of these supplies helped the local economy. 'Payments for hoisting and bringing the goods to shore, for moving them to their storage facilities within the town, and for guarding them, put over £40 into the hands of local labourers and property owners.'[15] A large sum in those days.

It was while he was in Winchelsea supervising this vast undertaking that Edward met with a mishap which is one of Winchelsea's most widely remembered historical events, 'the king's leap'. We owe our knowledge of the incident to the chronicler Thomas of Walsingham. He describes how the king approached the cliff to observe what was going on at the harbour-front below. The cliff was in fact so steep that the defences at the top were probably provided by only an earth bank. As the king approached, his horse, frightened 'with the noise of [a] mill and the quick revolving sails' held back. Edward violently urged the beast forward whereupon it set off at speed, leapt the bank and disappeared from the view of the appalled onlookers with Edward still in the saddle. They thought their monarch must have perished. 'But Divine Providence so disposing, the horse fell upon his feet, even from such a height, into a road, which from recent rains was softened with mud, into which the horse was able to slip for twelve feet; and yet did not fall.'[16] To general relief and rejoicing the king reappeared, unharmed. Professor Prestwich, illustrating what he believed to be Edward's volatile temper says: 'This almost certainly explains why he sold a horse to Robert de Bures for 50 marks, buying one in exchange valued at 100 marks, surely a transaction decided in a fit of temper'.[17] If that is correct, Edward was uncharitable; most of the witnesses would have felt that the horse deserved congratulation rather than condemnation. In concluding this account I have to say that the name 'King's Leap', as at present applied to a property in Winchelsea, is possibly misleading. Although the fall may well have been onto what we now call Spring Steps, topography suggests that it could equally well have been onto Ferry Hill with the return through Pipewell Gate.

As the departure for Flanders approached Edward's disputes with both the church and the barons were escalating. As this affected Winchelsey and the church the reasons are complex. We need to note here only the outcome, namely that those churchmen unwilling to pay the taxes required were to be fined in a way which effectively instituted 'a forced tax on the income of the clergy'. This amounted to accusing the recalcitrant clergy of treason and sentencing them to outlawry.[18] Even a meeting with the king at which Winchelsey acted with tact and circumspection failed to defuse the situation. Edward inflexibly confirmed his position, even going so far as to legislate to prohibit the archbishop from excommunicating those who were putting his (the king's) orders into force.[19]

Things were going no better in the monarch's dealings with the barons. Their leaders the Earls Bigod and Bohun were growing in strength and confidence. They set out their grievances, described above, in a document of complaint and it is likely that this was presented to Edward when he was in Winchelsea. The messenger is not to be envied! The barons reinforced their determination by, on the morning of the king's proposed departure, entering the exchequer and forcibly forbidding the collection of unannounced taxes.[20] Civil war was imminent. The people of England, or those who knew what was going on, must, indeed, have been apprehensive.

(30) Remains of Winchelsea's eastern wall, adjoining Rookery Field

Frederic Inderwick, here as elsewhere, is prone to exaggeration and imagination in his account of Winchelsea's history, but, apart from his precise placing of the meeting in 'the great square of Winchelsea', he gives a perceptive and succinct account of what happened when the barons arrived in the town determined to win the argument or take up arms in defence of their rights.

> 'A word of impatience on the part of the king, a moment of flinching on the part of the barons, and the whole country might have been plunged into civil war. But the king knew the temper of his subjects – he had learnt early in his life what King Charles learnt only on the scaffold, not to drive the English people to extremes, and he recognised that the barons in their demands were within the limits of reason and of right. Like a great statesman and powerful ruler he knew by intuition when to make concessions and by frankly accepting the position he secured at once the peace of the country and the confidence of the people.'[21]

Unfortunately we shall see that his concessions, however worthy they may have seemed, were considered by him to be made under duress and were not to be relied upon.

There was not time for formal signature of any agreement but, on the strength of Edward's assurances, the fleet sailed for Flanders with Edward himself travelling in the Cog *Edward*, probably owned by John Alard of Winchelsea.[22] As a sign of loyalty, before the departure, Edward was handed the great seal and returned it for safe-keeping during his absence.[23] The barons withdrew their earlier objections to the expedition and joined him in support.

Before we turn to the disgraceful behaviour of the men of the Cinque Ports when the king's soldiers and their supplies had been landed in Flanders at the mouth of the River Swyn and the consequences of that behaviour, it will be convenient to conclude briefly the story of the great crisis and the career of the unfortunate Archbishop Winchelsey.

For Edward the need to confirm his uncharacteristic submission to the barons' demands was made more urgent within three weeks of his departure by William Wallace's victory at the Battle of Stirling. A truce with France was imperative. He must concentrate on the Scottish campaign and he must, for the time being at least ensure the support of the barons and the church. This was achieved by issuing at Ghent a confirmation of Magna Carta, an assurance that recent forms of taxation would not be perpetuated, a promise that future taxation would be implemented 'only with the common consent of the whole kingdom and for the common benefit of the same kingdom',[24] and that the maltote tax on wool would be abolished.

Capitulation indeed. The crisis was over. Edward's subsequent wish to renege on almost all of this, and his request to the pope to absolve him from his promises must be mentioned but falls outside the scope of this book.

As for Archbishop Winchelsey, although the future was not bright, so far he had been outstandingly successful. His insistence on the independence of the church removed the direct involvement of the exchequer in collecting taxes from the clergy. Winchelsey himself controlled such payments and permitted them only when he believed that a state of national emergency existed.[25] Anyone who could achieve that in defiance of Edward I must indeed have been a strong and determined character.

It is clear that the king, temporarily at least, recognised this strength, accepted and respected it. In 1299 Winchelsey carried out, without challenge, his duty as archbishop of marrying King Edward to his second queen, Margaret of France, in his cathedral at Canterbury.

Prestwich comments that he was 'Briefly on relatively good terms with the king'.[26]

It did not last. The following spring Winchelsey was ordered by Pope Boniface personally to deliver a critical papal bull to the king who was campaigning in Scotland.[27] A hazardous journey and an unenviable task. By 1301 tensions between Edward and the pope had greatly eased and Robert Winchelsey's position consequently weakened. As a result of court actions he had taken, he was accused of 'contravening his oath of fealty to the king'.[28] Accusations were made about the misappropriation of church money collected as national taxation. None of this was justified. Worse followed. In 1305 Bertrand de Got, Archbishop of Bordeaux and a former royal clerk in the service of Edward, was elected Pope Clement V. The following year he suspended Archbishop Robert from office. Exile resulted. The pope would not even agree to grant Winchelsey an interview but neither would he agree to a replacement being appointed.

Recall came when Edward II succeeded his father in 1307 for the new king sought reconciliation with the man who was still his Archbishop of Canterbury. The pope eventually agreed and Robert returned to conduct the new monarch's coronation. He was, however, a man too principled to curry favour. During the early years of Edward II's reign Winchelsey's position as one of the leading Ordainers who sought to restrict the powers of the king and his fierce opposition to the position of Gaveston at court estranged him from a second monarch.

Robert Winchelsey died on 11 May 1313 at his Manor at Otford in Kent after becoming ill at the beginning of the year. His body was taken to Canterbury to be met by a vast gathering of distinguished clergy. At his funeral the Bishop of Llandaff preached on the text, 'Know ye not that there is a great prince called Abner fallen this day in Israel?'[29] His tomb in the cathedral survived until the time of the Reformation but was then destroyed. No doubt Henry VIII felt as strongly as Edward I had done about those who sought to limit the powers of the crown.

It is not easy to assess whether or not such a famous son of Winchelsea and temporary hero of this story was indeed 'a great prince'. He himself would probably have been appalled by Maud McKisack's statement that he was 'commonly regarded as a second Becket'.[30] He was, however, 'a forceful and courageous archbishop, and also a man who, though belonging to no religious order, had lived a simple and devout life. He had shown a single-minded concern for the welfare of the English Church'.[31] The Oxford History of England pays tribute to Winchelsey's 'highly meritorious career' but regrets his inability to maintain co-operation with the king. This is attributed partly to his being 'the victim of a rigid conscience but probably more of the strains and stresses at court after the outbreak of war with France'.[32] No Archbishop of Canterbury in his time could avoid becoming involved in the politics of both church and state. Pope Clement, full of resentment, spoke of the archbishop's 'vicious policies and perverse acts'.[33] It is hardly surprising therefore that campaigns for Robert Winchelsey's canonisation failed.

18. THE ADMIRALS

As the great crisis of 1297 developed and well before the king's promises to Archbishop Winchelsey and the barons, the need for some overall control of the English fleet was becoming increasingly apparent.

In 1295, for example, a French galley squadron attacked the Channel Islands, sailed as far as Dover which was partly burnt and mounted an unsuccessful attack on Winchelsea and Hythe. There seems to have been little organised resistance. The Cinque Ports ships were elsewhere. Quite astonishingly, the failure of this assault on Winchelsea is attributed to the intervention of a fleet from Yarmouth.[1] In view of the long-running feud between the Cinque Ports and Yarmouth which was soon to explode into increased violence, I am sure that this intervention on behalf of Winchelsea must have been accidental. Perhaps the Yarmouth ships scared the enemy away by appearing on the horizon in force when passing by.

It was in the same year that King Edward I appointed England's first admiral. He was William Leyburn whose kinsman Roger has already featured in these pages. Leyburn's command was wide-ranging. He was responsible for the seamen 'not only of the English ports, but of all places "where ships ply within the kingdom and our authority including Bayonne, Ireland and Wales."'[2] However, he was not an admiral in the modern sense; he was an administrator. Leyburn's brief was to supervise the recruitment of soldiers and sailors who would serve in the navy; to ensure that enough shipbuilding took place and to purchase an adequate supply of stores for his ships whenever needed. The admiral did not go to sea! Understandably Leyburn proved impotent in controlling his navy once it had left home shores.

It was the Cinque Ports versus Yarmouth feud which most noticeably demonstrated this impotence. In the months before the departure from Winchelsea of the king's great fleet and army for Flanders several incidents had occurred. Ships from both Hastings and Winchelsea had been destroyed in Yarmouth harbour; a Winchelsea captain and his crew, properly authorised to lie in wait off Orford Ness for Calais pirates were 'ambushed and murdered by Yarmouth mariners'; and, most provocatively, when Yarmouth ships arrived at Winchelsea in obedience to the 1297 muster, some of their sailors went into the town and killed five citizens.[3]

In view of these calculated insults it is clear that the men of Winchelsea would have been deeply involved in the carnage to come. However, it is worth pointing out at this stage that we could assume that they were there, even without this preliminary evidence. It has been calculated that between 1282 and 1347 Winchelsea contributed no fewer than thirty-four per cent of the Cinque Ports ships required for ship service by the king. The town's total was 102, compared with Sandwich 58, Dover 43, Rye 31, Hastings 26, Hythe 21 and Romney 20. Winchelsea's dominance at that period is further illustrated by the national figures commencing a little later in 1301 which show, significantly, only Great Yarmouth (133) exceeding Winchelsea (82).[4] I therefore feel quite justified when telling this story in assuming that where evidence has survived of the activities of the Cinque Ports fleet in the thirteenth and fourteenth centuries, Winchelsea's ships were heavily involved.

We return now to the vast array of vessels and men which left Winchelsea with the king still smarting after the confrontation there, on Edward I's Flanders expedition in 1297. The fleet landed safely at Swyn. Soldiers, horses and supplies were successfully landed. Those on shore, including the monarch, then watched horrified as the men of the Cinque Ports and of Yarmouth fell upon each other in bloody battle. On this occasion the Cinque Ports won. 'A terrible carnage of the Yarmouth crews took place, the Portsmen burning some twenty of their ships and slaughtering many of their

(31) An early nineteenth century view of the west front of St. Thomas's Church

crews, the king himself standing powerless to intervene.'[5] Several investigations have assumed somewhat varied totals of the Yarmouth ships destroyed and men killed. The most convincing seems to me to be that of David Sylvester who extracts from 'a royal inquisition into the melee' the fact that 'at least 165 men were killed, 17 ships were burned and another 12 were looted, while total damage cost £5000'.[6] These people were on the same side! 'The king's entire military campaign was placed in jeopardy – his Wardrobe ship carrying his treasury was nearly destroyed and he was only able to restore order by taking hostages from both sides.'[7] Again it seemed the conflict had been pre-arranged. 'According to one account the king heard of the intention and forbade it, but to no effect.'[8]

Something more effective clearly needed to be done. The immediate result was the removal of privileges from both sides for a period of two years, but without the combined strength of these combatants the defence of the south and east coasts was seriously weakened. The king's Scottish campaigns suffered similarly. In less than a year he was forced to reinstate the privileges for he needed support. In an attempt to end the dispute Edward therefore ordered four representatives of each of the Cinque Ports and twenty-four men of Yarmouth to London. 'The eventual "peace settlement" required every shipmaster and two leading mariners to take an oath before leaving port that they would keep the peace and arrest anyone who breaks it.'[9] Such an arrangement would not last long.

What was needed was a respected and experienced Portsman who could bring order to the Cinque Ports fleet. The king chose Gervase Alard of Winchelsea as his second admiral but with a reduced command – he was to lead the whole fleet of the south coast from the Cinque Ports to Cornwall, a wider mandate having become unnecessary. Understandably his instructions included a requirement that if ever the men of Yarmouth were involved, they were to be kept well away from those of the Cinque Ports!

Although there were Gervase Alards in several generations of the medieval family, we know that this was the same person who served as Winchelsea's first recorded mayor and lived in what is now the Court Hall. He was a highly experienced seaman who could command the respect of his fellows and is most unlikely to have been a land-bound admiral like his predecessor. 'He had served with Edmund Crouchback, Earl of Lancaster, the brother of King Edward I in Gascony, Flanders, Scotland and Normandy ... and was described as "beated and chopped with tann'd antiquity."'[10] Several members of Gervase Alard's family served with and after him. They served not only the king but also their own self-interest. 'It is characteristic of the traditional callings of the men of Winchelsea that at much the same time as the Alards held these royal appointments they were widely engaged in the lucrative practices of piracy and ship-wrecking.'[11]

Edward I's expedition to Flanders which began with the Cinque Ports versus Yarmouth fracas was unsuccessful militarily but successful in providing the opportunity for a truce with France. He returned to England via Sandwich and having, temporarily at least, disposed of one enemy, set about the defeat of the Scots.

This is where the skills of Gervase Alard were required. The sailors of the fleets which supported Edward's armies were largely recruited locally, as were many of the soldiers. Alard knew the men of Winchelsea and those of the other Confederation members and they knew him. Frequently he took family members. The Alards, together with the Paulins, dominated both land and ship ownership in Winchelsea; 40% of Winchelsea's identifiable ships were theirs.[12] Other men of the town and the neighbourhood would be encouraged to volunteer by their wish to keep in with this powerful group. When Gervase Alard sailed with his first expedition to Skinburness in 1300, carrying and gathering supplies for Edward's army in Scotland, Justin Alard and Pate Alard were among his captains. Captains had an overall responsibility – masters were in charge of individual ships. Five ships from the town were included, the Cogs *St. Edward, St. Mary, St. Thomas and St. Giles,* and the Snake *St. Thomas.* All were commanded by Winchelsea residents. This expedition lasted from 10 July until 26 September. After the statutory fifteen days had passed, Alard was paid two shillings a day, his captains one shilling, the masters and constables of the ships sixpence and members of the crew threepence. The fleet even took a chaplain who was included on the payroll at the same rate as a master.[13]

This was Robert of Sandwich, the first named chaplain to be discovered by Gordon Taylor for his history of the chaplaincy service in the navy. Taylor records that, for his fee which totalled one guinea, the chaplain should minister to all seamen regardless of rank,[14] a principle which has applied in the navy ever since.

Seeking out and delivering supplies took Alard's fleet to Skinburness, to Ireland and to Kirkcudbright during this period. This means of transport was infinitely superior to overland travel which, at the time, was extremely difficult because the roads were appalling. The fleet was not intended to be involved in combat but frequently had to defend itself against enemy attack. For this Gervase Alard and his men were well prepared and no doubt sought plunder when the opportunity arose. Professor Burrows states that 'the Cinque Ports fleet [under Alard in 1300] is said to have captured 28 ships and routed 16,000 men, but this is by no means certain'.[15] If the fleet really was as combative as that, it would have been well in character. We can be certain, through surviving documentary evidence, that Alard again served as admiral in 1303 and 1306. In 1303 his duties included transporting a considerable Irish army to Scotland to fight for Edward; they sailed in 'a very substantial fleet of 173 ships'.[16] He would also have had to arrange the transport of a 'machine' which had been repaired and was to be taken to Scotland by the Cinque Ports fleet. This was a trebuchet, a device for projecting stones at the enemy, like that used earlier by Eustace the Monk. 'Several types of these were in use in the fourteenth century'. Homan also suggests that the trebuchet was taken from Winchelsea and had formed part of the town's defences. There would have been some excuse for reducing Winchelsea's readiness at that time because of the peace treaty with France.[17]

Of the 1306 campaign we have less detail but in February of that year the king ordered that stores should be collected for a summer campaign[18] and Alard must have been involved. Cooper reports that Alard was again at Skinburness with the southern fleet during this year.[19] Gervase Alard's leadership had become an important factor in what Edward saw as a vital part of his policy and his credibility.

Throughout these campaigns Edward I was almost always desperately short of money. For this he blamed Archbishop Winchelsey and on one occasion Alard's leadership was tested when this problem affected Winchelsey's home town for 'the men of Winchelsea stated that they would make no preparations for a campaign because they had received no payments to meet the debts the king owed them. Instead the clerks of the Wardrobe had broken the tallies which provided evidence of these sums'.[20] There is nothing to suggest that this protest lasted long. Maybe Alard intervened.

After his valuable service to the nation Gervase Alard returned to his home town and was again elected mayor in 1308. He had been appointed king's bailiff for life in 1306 but was replaced by Henry Paulin the following year.[21] If the life appointment was a reward for loyalty he must have relinquished it voluntarily in order to resume as mayor. We do not know the date of his death. Whenever it took place he is reputed to 'have died full of years and honour, leaving a reputation of which the Cinque Ports were proud'.[22] The king expected him to 'establish good order and military discipline in the king's name'.[23] As far as Edward was concerned Alard had achieved this in good measure.

The king, however, did not live long after Alard's last term as admiral and it was Edward II who, appreciating and making use of the mettle of the men of Winchelsea, later appointed Robert Bataille in this capacity in 1322 and subsequently Stephen Alard in 1324.

(32) *The ruins (eighteenth century) of the refectory of Robertsbridge Abbey, an important local foundation whose iron foundry aroused the wrath of the men of Winchelsea and the Cinque Ports.*

19. MISDEMEANOURS MULTIPLY

Robert Bataille and Stephen Alard were to be more than adequate successors to Gervase Alard in their skills both as admirals and pirates. This is, to us, a strange mixture of activity but as Winchelsea's peace-time merchant vessels served also as wartime combatants it is perhaps unsurprising that their commanders and crews took a liberal view of the nature of the 'line that separated licit maritime activity from outright piracy'.[1]

The piracy, of course, was perpetrated indiscriminately upon the ships of enemy countries and of rival home ports. In 1303 inquiries showed a constant continuation of the fierce feud between the Cinque Ports and Great Yarmouth. Winchelsea was deeply involved. In one instance, at Plymouth, Jack Paulin and Benedict Seman, members of leading Winchelsea families, led their men in capturing a Yarmouth ship and killing the captain and the crew. Another Winchelsea ship, captained by Henry Hathelard, seized a Yarmouth vessel and stole eighty tons of wine.[2] I include here only instances where Winchelsea seamen are specifically mentioned as being involved. The situation was serious and there was widespread further killing.

Things became so bad that the following year the Archbishop of Canterbury, Robert Winchelsey, sent a letter urgently requesting the men of both sides to observe a truce ordered by the king.[3] Winchelsey's support of the king at this time is perhaps a little surprising but no doubt he felt the influence created by his humble origins as a Cinque Portsman might help in stemming the violence. Sadly this seems unlikely for the request had little effect.

The quarrelsome and overbearing behaviour of Winchelsea seamen helped such incidents increase rather than decrease. In 1305 they were involved in a serious quarrel with an Irishman at Ross. The leading residents of Ross, fully aware of the appalling reputation of the Winchelsea men, urged their citizen to 'go and seek the goodwill of the Portsmen lest ill come to the town by them'.[4] He refused and these fears proved fully justified. Four Ross ships, two of them quite unconnected with the man involved in the quarrel, were attacked in Brittany by Winchelsea sailors. £400 was taken and the terrified Ross crews paid a further £20 to save their lives and their ships.[5]

It was, of course, the important nature of their special service to the crown which allowed the men of the Cinque Ports to get away with such acts. This was well demonstrated in the same year by the men of Sandwich who had been directly commissioned by the king to patrol the Channel 'for the security of merchants and others crossing'.[6] Under this cover £300 was stolen from London merchants who most certainly did not benefit from any security as a result of the commission.

In 1310 the continuation of this kind of outrage was officially investigated in relation to particular offences against Flemish ships. The inquiry 'did little to stem such activity'.[7] The monarch was still too much beholden to the Portsmen for support to take effective action. Rivalry with the men of Flanders was by no means all one-sided. Ten years later a Winchelsea ship the *Johanette* belonging to 'our beloved merchant Stephen Alard, baron of Winchelsea' was seized off Beachy Head by Flemish ships. In arbitrary retaliation King Edward II ordered that goods to the value of £120, stored in England but belonging to Flemish merchants, should be seized.[8] The goods, of course, did not necessarily belong to the guilty parties. The king was unable to use such ploys in disciplining his own men.

Profits from piracy became so valuable that it may well have been one of the reasons that the men of Winchelsea began to try to wriggle out of the very service which allowed them the

*(33) Ferry Farm House stands close to the present Ferry Bridge, the site of the ferry to Udimore,
once Winchelsea's only overland route to Rye.*

privilege! For example, as a regular and proper requirement of their ship service, the Cinque Ports fleet was told to be at Skinburness by 24 June 1314. They were given almost three months' notice. 'Most of the Cinque Ports disobeyed the order, showing how dissatisfied they were with the war which had lasted for twenty years and had brought them neither profit nor glory'. Lack of profit would have been a major motivation. On this occasion Winchelsea's excuse is recorded. Two of its ships (why this was less than its quota is not explained) had set out but had been prevented from reaching the required destination by bad weather.[9] If the king believed this he was gullible indeed.

The Winchelsea men were much more likely to have been too busily involved in wrecking, another of their illegal activities. In that same year two incidents occurred in which they were implicated with accomplices from Rye and Romney. One occurred off Dungeness where the *Blessed Mary of Fonte Arabia*, carrying an extremely valuable cargo to Gascony, was wrecked and plundered.[10] The other occurred in Gascony itself when an English ship, the *Mary of Bayonne*, was wrecked on the coast with a cargo worth £2000, a vast sum in those days. The Winchelsea, Rye and Romney men carried off their spoils with a will![11] A certain Robert de Kendale had the misfortune to be Lord Warden of the Cinque Ports at the time with responsibility for judicially inquiring into such events. When he ordered that an investigation should be held at Winchelsea, 'the men of that town and of Rye and Romney, by force and violence prevented the investigation from taking place'.[12] I wish we had more details of how they achieved this! The only clue comes from the Victoria County History which states that 'a riotous assembly made up from the three ports prevented him from carrying it [his inquiry] into effect'.[13] Reporting the same obstruction,

Miss Murray, in a comment laden with implication for Winchelsea and the others involved, writes: 'but the Warden's authority in maritime matters was generally recognised by the more law-abiding members of the community'.[14]

Astonishingly, in the same year, Edward II 'granted a licence to the barons of Winchelsea to fit out two ships to protect the coast,'[15] following which they are alleged, well in character, within a very short time to have carried out numerous further acts of piracy.[16]

In 1315 we have confirmation that Winchelsea had assumed the status and responsibilities of a head port within the Confederation which seems odd in view of all that its citizens had been up to. As already indicated, I assume that such status was conveyed by King Edward I's general charter to the Ports in 1278 but it is not directly stated. On this occasion the evidence arises from Winchelsea and Rye being pardoned for their failure to provide the correct number of ships for ship service. Winchelsea's pardon was sent direct to the officers of the town; Rye's was directed via its head port, Hastings. Rye, according to L. A. Vidler, was not to achieve head port status for another twenty years.[17]

It was not only general pardons, but personal ones which were issued at this time in connection with various piratical and other misdemeanours. In 1320 John Lambot of Winchelsea who had apparently given excellent service to the king in his Scottish campaigns was forgiven, in view of that service, 'for all manner of trespasses and felonies committed by him in the realm'.[18] He needed pardoning again very soon for by the end of the same year he was implicated in an attack off the coast of Essex on vessels from Brabant. In this incident 'the men and servants of the merchants had been driven out of the ships and the goods carried off to various places'.[19] Almost certainly including Winchelsea!

Whether John Lambot was involved in perhaps the worst of these multiplying misdemeanours in the following year we do not know. The men of Winchelsea definitely were. They were on official duty at the time having been authorised to patrol the Channel armed 'to control the seas'.[20] What they actually did was to terrorise the whole of the south coast, particularly Southampton whose growing importance was no doubt a particular irritant to them. Thirty Winchelsea ships sailed within sight of the Hampshire port. The Winchelsea seamen's reputation was quite enough to alert Southampton's burgesses to the danger. They hurried to placate this formidable fleet by offering two fully equipped Southampton ships to join them and assist in their Channel patrols. This very fair offer was totally ignored. On 30 September 1321 the men of Winchelsea landed at Southampton and burned fifteen of the town's ships which were drawn up on the Strand. Not satisfied with this they returned the following day to destroy a further two ships. The marauders eventually sailed off 'leaving damage estimated six years later at over £8000'.[21] The amount of this loss was probably exaggerated in the interests of any claim Southampton might make in its long-running disputes with the Cinque Ports. For us the attack illustrates the widespread enmity which existed between the men of Winchelsea and not only the king's enemies but also his subjects.

It is extremely doubtful whether King Edward II would have been in the least disturbed by such an incident for he knew perfectly well what the men of the Cinque Ports were up to. His favourites, the Despensers, father and son, were banished from the country for their unlawful activities. 'All the chroniclers agree that, whereas the elder Despenser had accepted his sentence and gone abroad, the younger had embarked upon a career of piracy in the Channel, robbing merchant ships and basing his activities on the Cinque Ports, with the king's full connivance.'[22]

We have already noted that in 1322 Robert Bataille of Winchelsea was made Admiral of the

Cinque Ports fleet by King Edward II. Incidentally, *The Victoria County History of Sussex* accuses the same Robert Bataille of leading the despicable attack on Southampton.[23] Bataille's importance to the king was that, like his predecessor, Gervase Alard, he was to lead the Cinque Ports fleet in supplying the army in Scotland. In an attempt to ensure his loyalty Bataille, too, was granted a pardon for 'all offences committed on land or sea'.[24] In this pardon was included his accomplice and successor as admiral, Stephen Alard. Further assurances were needed before Bataille would carry out his duty to the crown. He was told that all the goods which he and his fellow merchants gathered together and transported for the support of the army in Scotland would be purchased rather than 'arrested' i.e. requisitioned. The very existence of this reassurance indicates that this was not always the case. 'But this evidence still suggests that trading on behalf of the crown in wartime could be profitable.'[25]

The piracy continued. In the same year Bataille and his ships attacked Sherborne merchants off Portsmouth and 'carried off about £80 worth of cargo'.[26] In 1323 Reginald Alard joined Robert Bataille and his successor as admiral, Stephen Alard 'in similar escapades'.[27] In 1327 the ship *Rykenbergh*, on its way from Norway to Southampton, 'was plundered by certain men from Sandwich and Winchelsea'.[28] Later in the same year we have the names of the culprits. They were Alexander le Keu, Benedict Sely and John Badding, all of Winchelsea, who took an amazing assortment of items from a ship trading between Waterford in Ireland and Bruges. The list included, '42 sacks of wool, 12 dickers hides (a dicker is 10), 3 pipes salmon, 2 pipes cheese, a bale of cloth, silver plate, mazer cups, a tiercelet (a male hawk) and jewels and goods to a total value of £600. The crew of the ship were forced to give a letter of acquittance and were sent to Flanders. We do not know what happened regarding the claims for compensation'.[29]

All this became even more discreditable in 1336. The new king, Edward III, was struggling to establish the kind of control over the Portsmen which had been forfeited by his father and never fully achieved by his grandfather or his great-grandfather. While one of Edward's own ships, *Nicholas,* lay at anchor at Winchelsea 'it was boarded by men of the town who stripped her of all her tackling and gear. If they had the audacity to do that to a king's ship lying in harbour, what fate awaited strangers at sea!'[30] Of that fate many examples have been cited in these pages.

We are now approaching the outbreak of the Hundred Years War in 1337. Before examining the sinister influence of that conflict on the history of Winchelsea we will consider the legal and more appropriate activities of the men of the ancient town, conducted in parallel with, and sometimes in unison with, their piracy.

20. FROM WINE TO WAR

Prominent among those legal activities was the wine trade with Gascony. The survival of the cellars in New Winchelsea which the town's trade required has already been considered. In the early fourteenth century the trade itself was remarkably prolific and important both to Winchelsea and the country. In 1303-4 twelve Winchelsea ships carried 1575 tuns of wine from Bordeaux. The names of the ships and the masters have come down to us through the Bordeaux accounts[1] so we cannot necessarily assume that all of this considerable quantity entered the country through these ships' home port. It is, however, likely that a great deal of it did. Even more detailed statistics for the period 17 September 1306 to 19 May 1307 indicate that of 605 shipments of wine exported from Bordeaux during that time, 305 were in English ships of which twenty-one shipments were in thirteen Winchelsea ships. Again the quantity carried was considerable, 2923½ tuns.[2] This has been computed as 737,000 gallons of wine contained in 14,400 hogsheads,[3] or, even more readily understandable, four million bottles. A considerable amount!

For clarification it should be made clear that the ton, used widely before decimalisation and still for calculating the size and capacity of ships is synonymous with the tun because it derives from the amount of space required in a medieval ship for a tun cask of Gascon wine. In fact the Winchelsea wine was seldom carried in tun casks, they were too big; as shown above it was carried in hogsheads. Hogsheads were barrels carrying a quarter of a tun. They were much more manageable in the days before cranes and W. M. Homan makes the interesting point that 'The entrances to the medieval cellars in Winchelsea appear almost invariably to have been about four feet two inches wide which would suit the handling of a hogshead'.[4]

Of the other Cinque Ports which might have been expected to trade similarly, Sandwich is shown by the 1306/7 accounts quoted above to have equalled Winchelsea with twenty-one shipments; Rye had five. The others do not feature.[5] David Sylvester further illustrates Sandwich's trading equality with Winchelsea, in quantity if not in value where Sandwich seems to have been pre-eminent. He shows that during 1307/8 '163 ships called at Sandwich while 161 anchored at Winchelsea.[6]

However, if we consider only Winchelsea's own county of Sussex, the town had no rival. The trade of the county was concentrated there. Its advantages were its excellent harbour facilities, its proximity to the mouths of the Rother and the Brede, both then important inland trading highways to the Weald, and its convenient position providing a good direct route from Sussex to the Continent.[7] It was the Weald which provided Winchelsea with its principal export. Wood made up the vast majority of shipments out with salt, salt herrings, wheat and horses lagging way behind.[8]

This trading prominence was not achieved without considerable problems. The wine harvest in Gascony was seriously affected during the summers of 1310 and 1311, producing a comparative slump. After three better years 'it was again suffering from another decline, no doubt as a result of the advent of pestilence in Gascony and elsewhere'.[9] Even when the wine was plentiful, transporting it between Gascony and England was a hazardous business. In times of 'peace' there were plenty of pirates, from France, Spain and elsewhere who were quite capable of matching the spirited attacks of the men of the Cinque Ports upon alien trading vessels. In times of war such assaults were accepted as legitimate. As early as 1301 King Edward I had issued instructions to the Warden of the Cinque Ports that ships sailing to or from Gascony or any French port should keep together in convoys for mutual safety and that if they landed to trade en route they 'must do so prudently so that they may return safely to their vessels'.[10] Such requirements sometimes involved demands that the ships of the

(34) Strand Gate and Strand Hill, probably early eighteenth century

Cinque Ports should act as escorts as part of their ship service.

1315 was a year of famine in England but there seems to have been no lack of supplies of wine or other commodities in Winchelsea. When King Edward II and Queen Isabella visited the town on 16 June having spent the previous day at Hastings, they were able to purchase considerable stocks, presumably because of shortages elsewhere. Certainly they were too great for immediate consumption. Unsurprisingly the principal purchase was of wine. They bought six tuns of wine, three from Reginald Alard for £8 and three from Robert Alard for £8 10s 0d. Robert Alard was to become Winchelsea's bailiff, a royal appointment, in the same year. His activities in that role will soon be featured. Whether he achieved the extra price for his wine because he was in royal favour or because of its extra quality is a matter of speculation. Other purchases in Winchelsea on behalf of the royal household included large quantities of bread, wax and kitchen supplies. The queen attended mass while staying in the town.[11]

The direct effects of royal influence on Winchelsea were felt three years later when the Blackfriars were permitted a site there. King Edward II, like his mother but unlike his father, was a supporter of the Blackfriars. Readers may recall that Edward I had given an undertaking not to allow any of the monastic orders except the Franciscans or Greyfriars to have premises within the town. W. M. Homan assumes that this concession was sought by the men of Winchelsea with the Blackfriars and their sinister reputation particularly in mind.[12] Edward II, his own inclinations enhanced by pressure from the pope, granted a site near the New Gate near the edge of the town. This area had been reserved by the monarch at the founding of New Winchelsea and was allocated in order that the Blackfriars 'may build a church and houses for the brothers of the order'.[13] Unfortunately for the brethren their initial enthusiasm on being permitted access to the prosperous Winchelsea community was tempered by the discovery that they were too far outside the town and 'few persons came to worship in the church and alms bestowed were small'.[14] It is not easy to understand how their next move, to land close to the northern end of the Hill of Iham but in the Brede Valley, was expected to solve this problem. It did not. Three years after moving there the Blackfriars sought the pope's permission for another move 'because their convent was in danger of being swept away by the sea'.[15]

While the Blackfriars were occupying their original site they stand accused of violent conflict with the townsfolk who 'did not at first take very kindly to these newcomers ... and among other places where the religious and townsmen quarrelled and came to blows, Winchelsea is mentioned'.[16] Homan strengthens this allegation, reporting that in various places including Winchelsea the monks and the people, 'rose up and in a merciless manner killed each other'.[17] However, we must be cautious about accepting this story for E. B. Poland, referring to the original source, states that no mention was made of the friars or even of the religious, but that 'the commonalties of Winchelsea and Faversham rose up and in a merciless manner killed each other'.[18] We shall meet the Blackfriars again later, at last gaining a foothold within Winchelsea's walls.

If Poland is correct in his interpretation of this matter I have no idea why the men of Winchelsea should have been involved in such strife. There is, though, evidence that the town suffered deprivation and damage at this time. In February 1326 Simon de Croyseur was appointed by the king to succeed Robert Alard as bailiff of Winchelsea, Rye and the Manor of Iham. Submitting his accounts up to 1 June 1327 he stated that 'a large number of houses in both Winchelsea and Rye had been so utterly destroyed that one could not even tell where the houses had stood'.[19] These houses would, of course, have been of wood. Robert Alard, too, used this deprivation to excuse himself from payment of some of the dues owed to the king during his time as bailiff. The inclusion of Rye, unless its inhabitants had also started attacking each other and burning each other's houses, suggests that this was the result of the first of the French raids which were to affect the two ancient towns so seriously.

Nevertheless, even with many of its houses apparently destroyed, Winchelsea continued to prosper in its wine trade. In 1328 it was ranked ninth among the wine importing towns of England with no Sussex port above it and only Sandwich of the Cinque Ports. It functioned as a centre for incoming wine shipments, as a base for the prosperous wine traders of the time whose activities included re-exporting the wine, and as a stopover place for ships heading for other ports. For example, in the very early days of the Hundred Years War, Bernard de Compre, master of the *Prymerole* arrived in London with a shipment of wine and had it confiscated on the grounds that it came from a town loyal to the French king. He was able to regain custody of his wine by explaining that, when he left, his Gascon port of departure was 'still loyal to Edward III and that his journey took some time because he stopped at Winchelsea'![20]

Winchelsea's prosperity in the wine trade must have been much enhanced by the Cinque Ports privilege which allowed it not to charge a gauge fee, thus making it a cheaper port of entry than many others. A gauge fee was a tax of one penny on each tun of wine imported into England when the wine was measured and checked by the royal gauger or his deputies. The buyer and the seller each paid half but not in Winchelsea.[21]

Sadly this prosperity was not to last. In 1333 Edward III launched an attack on Scotland and, although not officially at war with England, the French supported their traditional allies, the Scots, and the situation in the Channel and on the high seas rapidly deteriorated. By 1336 things were so bad that the Seneschal of Gascony was ordered not to allow the wine fleet to sail until ships arrived from Bayonne to make an even larger convoy and provide an escort.[22] These restrictions were disliked by the individual masters concerned who felt they limited their opportunities for enterprise and for gain. Many continued to sail alone. Eventually the king issued instructions that ships which attempted to trade overseas unprotected were to be seized, together with their cargoes. All this, added to the more and more frequent requisitioning of trading ships for royal service, resulted in an acute shortage of wine in England and, no doubt, in Winchelsea. Action had to be taken. This was achieved by arranging for the wine fleet to sail armed and for it to include ships released from royal service for the duration of the journey to Gascony and back.[23]

In the same year, 1336, Winchelsea proved well able to pull its full weight when ship service was required. Whether the service was to protect the trading fleet or for other duties we do not know but, of the thirty Cinque Ports ships, no fewer than nine, almost a third in number and more than a third in tonnage, were from Winchelsea. These vessels carried an average of seventy-one men, some of whom were archers to defend against attack. Of her immediate neighbours, Rye had the two largest ships in the fleet, each with ninety-four mariners and men-at arms; Hastings sent no ships at all.[24]

The strength of the Winchelsea contingent is quite surprising because this ship service coincided with the first surviving evidence that Winchelsea was having trouble with its harbour, that is the quayside harbour on the River Brede close to the town rather than the anchorage at the Camber which was still quite adequate for the gathering of the English fleet. This inner harbour was fully tidal and relied on the scour of the ebbing waters to keep the River Brede between Winchelsea and the sea navigable. The reclaiming, or inning, of land in the Brede Valley reduced this scour and permitted more and more silting. There were also problems at the entrance to the river. A Patent Roll of 3 May 1336 states, 'In the entrance to the harbour sea-sand and gravel have accumulated and are found in such quantities that ships carrying no more than twenty tuns of wine hardly can get in or lay-to at the town on account of the filling in and deposit'. A tax was authorised of fourpence for every ship arriving at Winchelsea with goods for sale and twopence for every pound's worth of goods within those ships.[25] This tax, by paying for dredging work and permitting the construction of a breakwater,[26] must have considerably eased the situation because it was more than sixty years before the silting of Winchelsea's harbour became increasingly, and eventually terminally, serious.

(35) The Greyfriars Chapel ruins from the south and other then surviving features, eighteenth century

One year later in 1337 the Hundred Years War between England and France broke out in earnest. The causes of this conflict – Edward III's claim to the French throne and his refusal to do homage as a vassal for his lands in Gascony; King Philip of France's support of Scotland and his counter-claim to sovereignty over Gascony – need not, beyond those few words, delay us here. This story must concentrate on the war's effects which were the most important influence on Winchelsea's history and the catalyst for the town's decline over more than the next century.

Initially the French fleet in the Channel was in the ascendant. Winchelsea was among the towns set to work to construct the fleet of galleys which Edward required to counter this threat. Massive problems of construction were caused by the need for a great mast able to support the single sail, the yardarm and the topcastle in such a vessel. The 1337 Winchelsea galley probably had a mast several feet in diameter and standing approximately a hundred feet above the deck.[27] Winchelsea's shipwrights must have been grateful for the forests of the Weald nearby. The total cost of the galley, at seventy pounds,[28] was substantial, although it sounds ridiculously small to the modern ear.

This galley, with the others the king had ordered, was completed far too late to attempt to save south coast ports from the enemy ascendancy during the first year of the war and beyond. In early skirmishes Hastings, Rye, Folkestone, Winchelsea and Dover were reportedly victims 'and a little later a squadron of French ships destroyed every single ship in Romney and Hythe'.[29] Cooper gives an account of the attack on Rye and Winchelsea, the French having diverted their attentions to those towns when they saw the county militia waiting for them in strength at Sandwich, their original target. Considerable damage was done before the attack was aborted when 'a squadron of English came up with them, whereupon the Frenchmen hoisted sail and fled before them'.[30] The supposed French ascendancy did not work in this case for the enemy ships were pursued to Boulogne where, with typical medieval thoroughness, the town was fired and twelve captains of the guilty fleet hanged.[31]

This type of violence, sustained over time, had an appalling effect on the wine trade. Prices increased as a result of the cost of extra ships for protection. They were also adversely affected when things became so bad that wines were frequently carried overland in England instead of being transported along the more dangerous sea routes.[32] This was considerably more expensive and the known condition of medieval roads, particularly in winter, emphasises how bad the situation must have been. Fighting on land in Gascony made matters even worse. Between 1337 and 1340, campaigns in the region of the Dordogne Valley and surrounding areas 'led to the virtual disappearance of the wines of this district'.[33]

Desperate measures were needed to counter the enemy threat. It was the unenviable task of the Lord Warden of the Cinque Ports to attempt to sort things out. In 1338, by which time more ships were available, the then Lord Warden, the Earl of Huntingdon, who will soon, if briefly, become important in this story, was ordered to take offensive action in an attempt to seize the initiative.[34] He was also instructed not to pester the Abbot of Battle to supply soldiers and horsemen for the defence of the coast of Kent because the abbot was responsible for providing men for this duty in the Winchelsea area.[35] Senior clergy often doubled as military officers in medieval England and the Abbot of Battle retained this responsibility, with varying degrees of success, throughout most of the fourteenth century.

In such enterprises the abbot should have been able to expect support from the bailiffs of Winchelsea and the surrounding area but, sadly, the evidence shows that they are more likely to have been expending their energies lining their own pockets.

21. BAILIFFS MALICIOUS ...

We have seen how, albeit reluctantly, King Edward I permitted Winchelsea a mayor by 1295 and almost certainly a few years earlier. This did not devolve all power in local matters to the people themselves for the king retained his bailiff who represented him within the town and collected rents and dues owing to the crown. In the years before 1527 we know more about the bailiffs than we do about the mayors for only from that date do the records of Winchelsea Corporation survive. Because the bailiffs were the king's officers, their appointment, their instructions and their offences became the subject of entries in the Court Rolls of the monarch and it is from these that so much information can still be obtained.

Winchelsea's bailiff between 1317 and 1324 was Robert Paulin, a member of a leading local family. One of his duties was to seize the lands of those whose property, in accordance with the law of the time, should have reverted to the crown on their death without legitimate heirs. In the case of the de Rakele family, among others, he was alleged to have co-operated in their avoidance of these requirements and taken the profits himself. This led to his temporary suspension from office but he must have managed to clear himself of the charge for he was reinstated only two months later.[1]

Such disputes between the bailiff and the king are unlikely to have troubled the people of Winchelsea unduly but many of his other activities outraged them. It was the practice of Paulin and his officers, for example, not to approach the masters of vessels arriving at Winchelsea with goods liable to customs dues. When these ships were about to sail their officers and crews would be imprisoned and their vessels seized on the grounds that they had illegally avoided payments. Release was achieved only by submitting to demands for excessive fines which were demanded by Paulin through blackmail. One unfortunate Dartmouth master was fined ten marks, (£6 13s 4d) for an unpaid duty of twopence. W. M. Homan quotes several other examples of appalling injustice which resulted. One southern European master and crew who declared that 'neither they nor their people would ever come [again] to Winchelsea'[2] were undoubtedly not alone.

All non-residents who brought goods to sell in Winchelsea were required by law to obtain permission from the bailiff or his officers 'before offering goods for sale to the public or commencing to bargain'.[3] Another of Paulin's fraudulent practices was to instruct his representatives to approach such people to negotiate prices and buy goods but only then to produce their concealed staffs of office and arrest the 'offenders'. Another of his ruses for profiting through his office was to persuade 'immoral women and others' to bring false charges. Those charged were arrested, thrown into prison and released only when Paulin 'had robbed them to his satisfaction'. The charges were then dropped.[4]

Excessive fines for trespass or debt in the bailiff's court caused further resentment within Winchelsea and things became so bad that the townsmen submitted their complaints in detail to the king. 'The king's bailiff and his underlings, they said, caused the town to get such a bad name that no merchants or mariners who had once been there ever returned.'[5] The petition is undated so we can only speculate on whether it resulted in Paulin's removal but David Sylvester comments, 'This is a forceful example of how communal pressure could be brought to bear on an individual who compromised community interests, even a member of the powerful Paulin clan'.[6]

Robert Paulin was also Bailiff of Rye but there is no record of similar extortions there. Indeed, L. A. Vidler speaks quite favourably of him, pointing out that 'His account of the quitrents due to the king is the earliest extant. It gives us a most valuable account of the buildings and inhabitants of the town'.[7] Apparently this record also shows that Paulin lived in a large house near St Mary's Church in Rye for which he paid two shillings and threepence a year. Clearly he was not as ready to swindle

(36) Surviving features are clear reminders of the Lower Court Hall's earlier use as the town prison. The outer door is no longer there but its securing bar rests on the window-sill.

his neighbours in Rye as he was the residents of Winchelsea and its visiting traders.

In 1321, during Robert Paulin's period of office as bailiff, King Edward II ordered that Winchelsea's defences should be improved by the repair of the walls and the digging of a ditch.[8] To finance this operation, and additionally to raise enough money to pave the town, permission was given to charge, for a period of seven years, additional taxation on goods being imported at Winchelsea. It is difficult to believe that Paulin did not find ways of benefiting from this taxation; certainly he was included among those responsible for the document is addressed thus: 'The King to the Barons, Bailiffs and Freemen of the town of Winchelsea, greetings,'[9] but its importance to us here, is that specific mention is made in the grant of all the items which could be taxed and the amount to be charged. While it is tempting to over-simplify Winchelsea's trading activity as being principally wine in and timber out, this list, reproduced in full by Homan, shows how much the ordinary residents of the town relied on imported goods and includes an enormous variety of items deemed important enough for inclusion.

The early entries are reasonably conventional and include: 'For every measure of corn for sale one halfpenny, for every horse, mare, ox or cow for sale one halfpenny, for every cart carrying salt meat for sale one penny, for six sheep, goats or pigs for sale one penny and for every whole piece of cloth for sale one penny'. Later entries become more substantial: 'For every ship coming to the town laden with iron for sale one penny, for every ship coming to the town laden with salt for sale two pence, for every hundredweight of tin and copper for sale two pence, for every jar of oil for sale four pence, for every jar of honey for sale four pence,' and, the highest valued, 'for every hundredweight of grain for sale ten pence'. These are only a very few of the items included. Perhaps the valuation of oil, honey and grain as the most expensive seems to us surprising. The list is extensive, including even monkeys and falcons at one halfpenny each and the final proviso covers all omissions: 'For any merchandise which has come to the town for sale not mentioned, and does not exceed twenty shillings in value one halfpenny'.[10]

When the ditching paid for by this taxation was carried out great offence was caused to the Abbot of Fécamp. The ditch crossed some of the abbot's land retained when Rye and Winchelsea were resumed to the English crown, cutting it off from the remainder and he demanded to be recompensed 'by exchange or otherwise'.[11] He was faced by a typical government delaying tactic, being told that the matter 'would be considered by the Council'.[12] The outcome of the Council's deliberations is not known but the disputed land remained within the Liberty of Winchelsea.

Robert Paulin was preceded and succeeded as bailiff by Robert Alard. It is difficult not to interpret this as suggesting considerable rivalry between these, the two most influential Winchelsea families of the time. The extent of the Alards' influence is illustrated by events which led to an execution in Winchelsea in 1322, while Robert Paulin was bailiff and only one year after the walling and ditching had been authorised. In that year Stephen Alard was a sufficiently influential figure in royal circles to be granted lands in Kent which had formerly been the property of Bartholomew Badlesmere. Badlesmere had been given, as a royal favour, custody of Leeds Castle in Kent. While he was absent from the castle, Queen Isabella, expecting obedience and subservience, arrived intending to break her journey there. Badlesmere's wife (who would very soon be his widow as a result of all this!), 'with her husband's approval for reasons which are not quite clear, refused the queen admission'.[13] The queen was not amused! Royal forces stormed the castle and Thomas Culpeper, presumably Badlesemere's appointment as governor for he had earlier been his close associate, was taken with eleven of his knights. Culpeper appears to have been a Winchelsea man for he was sentenced and executed in the town.[14] If readers recognise the name Thomas Culpeper it is probably because those bearing it were an ill-fated lot. A more famous Thomas Culpeper was also executed by royal command; in his case by King Henry VIII for his liaison with Queen Katherine Howard.

The importance of the men of Winchelsea and the Cinque Ports in national politics, whether it be through their trade, their vital ship service, their vicious reputation at sea, the influence at court of such families as the Alards or, indeed, their malicious bailiffs, becomes clear in the same year as the Winchelsea execution of Thomas Culpeper through their first summons to parliament since the time of Simon de Montfort.

When the people of Winchelsea petitioned in 1832 to be allowed to retain their right to elect two members to parliament, they claimed that right had been granted by Edward I. In writing about this in my earlier book I said that in fact it was granted by Edward III.[15] This remains technically correct because I was referring to the granting of membership as of right. However, it is now clear to me that Winchelsea's parliamentary attendance, by regular invitation, had begun more than forty years earlier. *The History of Parliament – The Commons* demonstrates that the Lord Warden was, from 1322, issued with writs seeking the attendance of the Portsmen and that although no returns were actually made until 1366 'there is ample evidence from local records to show that barons of the Ports did attend parliament' between these dates.[16] Sadly, this information came from the records of other ports for those of Winchelsea for the fourteenth century have not survived.

No doubt the Alards were included in that representation for their influence grew until the end of Edward II's reign at which time Robert and Gervase Alard were acting jointly as bailiff. Their appointment was by Queen Isabella, then in power with Roger Mortimer.[17] Robert and Gervase Alard may have been Paulin's rivals but they followed his practices sufficiently successfully for the young Edward III to instruct the Lord Warden of the Cinque Ports, in 1331, to order their appearance 'before the treasurer and barons of the exchequer' and to appoint a substitute bailiff. The men of Winchelsea had again been incensed by the behaviour of their bailiffs and had accused them of 'behaving ill, committing extortions and hardships and owing divers arrears'.[18] Homan goes on to suggest that while there may have been genuine complaints, the young king would readily have grasped the opportunity to remove from office members of a family formerly closely associated with his mother.

Under the new king, Robert Alard's fortunes declined rapidly and in 1334 he was accused of murder. The accusation was made by Isabel Sely whose husband had been the victim. It was not only against Alard but also five others, all leading citizens. They included 'Vincent Herbert (alias Finch),'[19] ancestor of the Earls of Winchilsea. Homan gives a fascinating account of what would happen in such a case if the accused elected to stand trial: 'According to the custumal of Winchelsea the accused person gave the bailiff [at that time Stephen of Padiham] the names of thirty-six persons from [whom] to select a jury and, if one of these did not obey the summons to appear, the accused was considered guilty; if all thirty-six appeared in court, twelve of them were chosen and if these twelve swore that the accused was innocent he was acquitted. If one of the twelve refused to swear to his innocence [the accused] was hanged on the gallows in the saltmarsh north of the town'. If this system did produce an acquittal there was trouble for the accuser! With typical asperity and tongue-in-cheek cynicism, Homan comments, 'Quite a simple procedure and probably no worse than those of more recent times'.[20]

However, in this case there was a sensation in Winchelsea. The accused were not prepared to submit themselves to such a trial by reputation. They fled and their guilt was automatically assumed. Stephen de Padiham was instructed to confiscate all their property while it was considered whether it should belong to the king according to the customs of the Cinque Ports.[21] We know nothing of the fate of the others, but the self-seeking former bailiff, Robert Alard, is believed either to have died or to have been arrested and executed soon afterwards.[22]

Even with the Alards disgraced and their predecessor Robert Paulin long removed, the bailiffs of Winchelsea continued to come under fire. Ten years after the murder of Andrew Sely the men of Iham submitted a strong complaint that 'free access for their boats to the water leading from Iham had been interfered with by the Bailiff of Winchelsea who had prevented its use by driving stakes into the river bed and stretching chains across the water'.[23] The bailiff was ordered to remove the obstruction or he would have to recompense those aggrieved.

This action was untypical of John Glynde, bailiff since 1341, who, rather than being, like his predecessors, a persecutor, was himself persecuted.

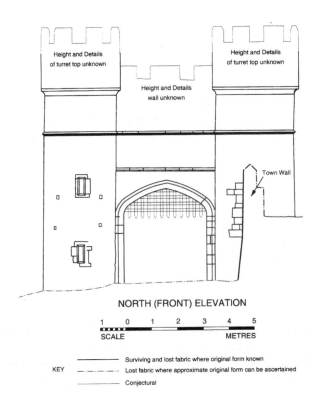

NORTH (FRONT) ELEVATION

```
1   0   1   2   3   4   5
SCALE                  METRES
```

KEY
——— Surviving and lost fabric where original form known
—·—·—·— Lost fabric where approximate original form can be ascertained
——— Conjectural

(37)
The Strand Gate as it stood when it guarded New Winchelsea's principal entrance (partly conjectural)

22. ... AND A BAILIFF MALIGNED

It is a strange anomaly that, in 1345, one of the duties of the bailiff who was persecuted rather than persecutor, was to conduct an inquiry into 'tenements laid waste by submersion by the sea'.[1] Obviously the steady withdrawal of the sea and the silting of the River Brede, major factors in the longer term decline of Winchelsea, had been temporarily reversed.

This bailiff, John Glynde, was appointed, jointly with John Marchant, on 1 March 1341. They replaced Stephen de Padiham in circumstances which considerably offended him. Glynde and Marchant also served as bailiffs of Rye and the Manor of Iham until October of that year when Marchant retired and Glynde continued to serve alone.[2] The circumstance which led eventually to Glynde's downfall was that since 1337 he had been Rector of Winchelsea. Perhaps, after the doubtful activities of his predecessors described above, the king was seeking the service of someone of far greater reliability and integrity. All the evidence suggests that, had Glynde been allowed to act without interference, Edward would have achieved that aim. Nevertheless it was an extremely unusual appointment. In Edward I's reign Archbishop Pecham, Archbishop Winchelsey's predecessor, had even gone so far as to issue instructions that the clergy were not to accept such positions.

The bailiff's duties, apart from collecting rents due to the monarch and carrying out his orders, also included, as Winchelsea was a leading Cinque Port, dealing with money due to the Lord Warden, another royal appointment. The Lord Warden of the time, the Earl of Huntingdon, was outraged that the rector should be undertaking these responsibilities. His main suspicion was that if the church obtained a foothold in the administration of royal dues the money would find its way into church coffers. While this was unjust in Glynde's case, it is understandable because the church was pretty acquisitive at the time.

Unfortunately for Glynde, Huntingdon was a vindictive man and his well-established position in affairs of state permitted full rein to this aspect of his character. The Lord Warden's family had been prominent at court for almost two hundred years, since the time of Henry I. He was well established in his office, having served since 1330, and, in the year of Glynde's appointment, had taken over the duties of Admiral of the Cinque Ports fleet previously held by leading Winchelsea citizens.[3] When ambassadors were needed, long before the establishment of permanent embassies abroad, Huntingdon was often called upon, for example in 1337 when he was one of the leading members of 'an elaborately equipped embassy', that is one which involved considerable show and display, in search of allies in Flanders.[4] His elevation to an earldom in that year would have emphasised his personal importance in such negotiations.[5]

Several Earls of Huntingdon have appeared in the pages of English history, although they were new creations, not descended from this Lord Warden whose line died with him. In the case of titles this is, of course, not unusual; Dukes of York and Lancaster pop up all over the place. The repetition of Christian names and surnames is, however, less common. Jack Straw was a leader of the 1381 Peasants' Revolt before he became Home and later Foreign Secretary. Thomas Cook was a renowned medieval warrior before he started selling holidays in the nineteenth century. The name of the Earl of Huntingdon, although not exactly coinciding, would similarly have struck a chord in the ear of late twentieth and early twenty-first century readers – it was William Clinton.

William Clinton's real place of favour in the eyes of King Edward III lay in his involvement in the downfall of the king's mother's lover, Roger Mortimer, who, as the gruesome end of the king's deposed father approached, had been, with Queen Isabella, ruling England. Churchill describes how in 1330 parliament was meeting at Nottingham Castle in the presence of Mortimer and Isabella who were closely guarded. Carefully laid plans ensured that, with the Commons and the Lords present, the young king also was near at hand to be proclaimed in his rights as ruler should the opportunity arise. Unfortunately for them 'Mortimer and Isabella did not know the secrets of the castle. An underground passage led into its heart. Through this, on an October night, a small band of resolute men entered, surprising Mortimer in his chamber which, as usual, was next to the queen's, and dragging them both along the subterranean way, delivered them to the king's officers'.[6] Mortimer was hanged and Isabella imprisoned.

(38) The seal of John Glynde

Among this 'small band of resolute men' was William Clinton, instantly rewarded with the post of Lord Warden of the Cinque Ports and Constable of Dover Castle and with the king's complete trust. That trust led King Edward to believe the earl's malicious assertion that 'John Glynde, the king's bailiff of Winchelsea, was attempting to escape abroad with a large sum of money he had collected in Winchelsea and Rye for the king, including eighty pounds due to the Earl of Huntingdon who was entitled to receive [this sum] per annum from these towns'.[7] Huntingdon was abetted in this claim by Stephen de Padiham, still smarting from the rector's appointment in his place. The king ordered Glynde's arrest. Initially imprisoned at Dover Castle he was later transferred to the Fleet prison in London. To say that conditions there were bad would be a gross understatement, they were appalling. In desperation Glynde petitioned the king for his case to be reviewed and an inquiry was ordered. Three times during the eighteen months that he languished in the Fleet, Glynde was brought to court. Each time a part of his alleged debt was shown by the production of various receipts and account books to have been incorrectly calculated. The books either justified the expenditure or provided evidence that he had properly used or transferred the money. On one of these occasions Huntingdon's own receipt for the £80 alleged to be missing was traced by Glynde's representatives and produced. Despite the gradual reduction of the totally false charge, John Glynde was each time returned to prison until at last it was shown that he had spent the final outstanding £21 protecting marshland near Winchelsea.

Finally and belatedly pardoned by the monarch, the rector was released but by then he was a broken man. He returned to his duties as rector, but not as bailiff – unjustly the treacherous Stephen de Padiham was restored to the post. An attempt at some recompense was made by the town in 1345 when Glynde was one of Winchelsea's representatives at the Yarmouth herring fair, an appointment which included some perks. Similar recompense was possibly attempted by the king with the grant of a house in Winchelsea.

Unfortunately this tale does not have a happy ending. The documents of the case describe him as having lain in prison 'to the great danger of his life'. Whether prison deprivations were the cause of his death at a comparatively young age we shall never know. He died at his home which stood in what is now the garden of Glebe, adjoining the present rectory in 1348 or 1349.[8]

These years are gruesomely significant. There is no doubt that researchers requiring information about the Black Death would automatically have assumed that Glynde's death and his replacement as rector in 1349 by John of Scarle were caused by the terrible visitation of plague which struck England at that time. Those researches revealed that almost half the clergy died.[9]

The evidence about the effect of the Black Death upon Winchelsea is almost exclusively circumstantial but it was clearly such a massive feature in the decline of the town which is one of the themes of this book that we must examine it and the demise of John Glynde provides a good opportunity.

There will be brief mention below of the Battle of Crécy in 1346 as we continue to examine Winchelsea's part in the Hundred Years War. The English celebrations and the prestige which followed victory in that battle were cut short by one of the worst natural disasters ever to strike England. The Black Death, carried in ships' cargoes by rats and their parasites, reached the country through Melcombe Regis in Dorset in July 1348. This was pneumonic plague, a more serious version than bubonic. 'The evidence, which is patchy, suggests that in rural areas of southern England between forty and fifty per cent of the population died. The mortality in the towns can only be guessed, for there is hardly any evidence apart from the hyperbole of the chroniclers. It must have been higher.'[10] Simon Schama supports this view by recording, 'The areas around the southern ports were most immediately stricken by the plague'.[11] Winchelsea as a town and port was therefore dangerously vulnerable. Schama, in typically dramatic style, also reports that King Edward asked the Archbishop of Canterbury to organise penitential prayers but the Archbishop himself fell victim to the plague before he could do so.[12]

Attempts were made in Italian and Sicilian ports to stem the spread of disease by forcing vessels manned by sick or dying crews 'to lie offshore for forty days (una quaranta) until the sickness had run its course, a system which gives us the word quarantine'.[13] If the port of Winchelsea attempted to follow this practice the relentless inland spread would have rendered such a precaution largely ineffective.

(39) Glebe, St. Thomas's Street, stands close to the site of John Glynde's home and contains the remains of a fifteenth century crosswing and other early features. It was almost certainly built by Maline Farnecombe in 1477 and its main range rebuilt in 1583 by the mayor, William Morley.

We know that closed communities such as monasteries and hospitals, of which Winchelsea had five at that time, were severely stricken. A Franciscan brother in Ireland set down in graphic detail the horrors of the effect on his community and concluded his account by writing that he was 'waiting among the dead for death to come'.[14] Such direct evidence as exists about this vulnerability suggests considerable variations. 'Christ Church, Canterbury escaped with the loss of only four monks; but St. Albans lost its abbot, prior, sub-prior and forty-six monks within the space of a few days in 1349. Westminster lost its abbot and twenty-six monks and in a number of other houses the losses were such as to produce a state of serious emergency.'[15] At least one of Winchelsea's religious communities suffered. It was probably more. If either the Greyfriars or the Blackfriars were affected, they might well have been among those which never again reached their full complement of monks, a development arising from a reduction in enthusiasm for monasticism as 'a centrally important part of religious life'[16] as well as from the deliberate failure to recruit replacements so that remaining funds would go further.

Another piece of circumstantial evidence which catches the eye is noted by Nigel Saul when he writes, 'The landscape everywhere gave proof of physical decay – houses had collapsed, fields were grassed over or were being invaded by bushes; manor houses were abandoned; some parishes could no longer maintain their churches'.[17] This was not written about Winchelsea but it might well have been and the most striking similarity exists in the circumstances of St. Thomas's Church whose foreshortening is highly likely to have resulted, partly at least, from the great reduction in the size of its congregation.

Now, then, to the direct evidence. We know that, had he been writing about Winchelsea, Nigel Saul would have been correct in recording the collapse and decay of its properties. A Schedule of Decayed Rents which is held in the National Archives shows that in 1358 there were ninety-four properties 'waste and uninhabited' and another ninety in ruins. This was almost one third of the town and must have been at least partly as a result of de-population.[18] The worst of the French raids were yet to come.

Depopulation was certainly affecting lands surrounding Winchelsea, particularly Romney Marsh. Schemes to reclaim more and more marshland from the sea had been actively pursued during the early part of the fourteenth century but were put on hold after the Black Death because of reduced demand.[19] On the marsh the number of labourers who might have carried out reclamation work was also greatly reduced. Those who survived realised the value of their labour and pressed for higher wages with the result that 'In the hundred years between 1310 and 1410 the average wage went up from three shillings to eighteen shillings a year'.[20]

Incidentally, these figures, if correct, emphasise the near impossibility of comparing medieval financial values with modern ones, a task that I have deliberately avoided throughout this book.

We have some direct indication of King Edward's concern about the reduction in Winchelsea's population for, fearing that the situation would worsen, he gave instructions to the mayor and bailiffs that nobody was to be allowed to leave the port except 'a merchant, notary or king's messenger'.[21] That instruction seems restrictive. A more understanding example came in an edict dated 6 August 1355 'in which the king "out of compassion for the state of the Hospital of St. Bartholomew, Winchelsea, which since the pestilence is depressed in many ways in its facilities, pardoned the master and brethren of the hospital for ten years from this date the six shillings of rent due to him yearly"'.[22]

Sadly John Glynde had long lost his duties as bailiff and his life. Otherwise he would, as a result of this relief, have been six shillings short in his annual returns!

23. THE WAR DEVELOPS

While John Glynde languished in the Fleet and the Black Death raged, much which affected Winchelsea happened during the early years of the Hundred Years War.

Initially the French and their allies had control of the Channel and attempts to reverse this trend started pretty chaotically. Glynde's persecutor, William Clinton, Earl of Huntingdon, the Lord Warden, received instructions to assemble the ships of the Cinque Ports and the Thames at Winchelsea. All those men who had received 'charters of pardon', that is had been forgiven crimes on condition that they served the king in time of war, were also instructed to report to Winchelsea to serve in the navy.[1] This did not bode well. It cannot have been only the pressed men who were less than enthusiastic for, in 1339, the required total southern fleet of 111 ships, ordered to gather at Winchelsea and Portsmouth, 'fully manned and victualled for three months' service' did not materialise. To their credit, the only ships reporting were from the Cinque Ports.[2] They may well have been concentrated in the defence of Winchelsea for on this occasion the town did not suffer although, when a strong Franco-Genoese fleet attacked, Rye was burnt[3] and Hastings 'was completely destroyed'.[4]

Clearly the Cinque Ports fleet had done something useful for, early in 1340, when they were again assembling for action, they were promised that half their costs would be met by parliament 'not as a precedent but from "special grace"'.[5]

This reward and compliment was immediately repaid with effective action. The men of the Cinque Ports and Winchelsea captured a Boulogne ship and set about the interrogation of four merchants whom they had taken for their ransom value. Anxious to co-operate in return for their safety – the ship's seamen had probably all been killed already – the merchants revealed that eighteen galleys, beached at Boulogne, were guarded only by six watchmen. What an opportunity! The Cinque Portsmen, aided by a heavy mist, achieved complete surprise and entered the harbour before being spotted. They sealed off the lower town, thus enabling them to destroy the galleys and their equipment unhindered. The fate of the watchmen is not recorded; if they had any sense they fled. It took some time for the French to muster a force adequate to drive the invaders off. By the time this was achieved, after heavy fighting and much bloodshed, twenty-four merchant ships had suffered the same fate as the galleys.[6]

Viewed from the English point of view, even better was to follow. The French fleet, in support of their king's invasion of Flanders, gathered in the River Swyn off Sluys and took up defensive positions, chained together in groups ready to repel any English attack. 'This was a traditional galley or longship tactic, serving to make the naval battlefield as much like a battlefield ashore as possible, but, of course, it removed any possibility of manoeuvre and resigned the initiative to the enemy.'[7] The English fleet led, nominally at least, by King Edward himself in his flagship the Cog *Thomas* of Winchelsea, took little time in seizing that initiative. Approaching with the wind, sun and tide to their advantage, the English sailed to the south of the Flemish islands and thus succeeded in attacking from the rear. A fierce and terrible fight ensued, principally upon the decks of the restrained enemy vessels. A chronicler records, with somewhat regrettable relish, how 'an iron shower of quarrels from crossbows and arrows from longbows brought death to thousands of people; all those who wished or dared to do so fought hand to hand with spears, battle-axes and swords; stones hurled from the turrets of masts dashed onto the brains of many'.[8] The size of the enemy Spanish ships reduced the impact of the onslaught for them but the French succumbed and suffered a major naval disaster. Courtiers were too frightened to give King Philip the ghastly news. Eventually they delegated the job to the king's fool who is reputed to have done so in a riddle:

> *Q. Why are the English knights more cowardly than the French?*
> *A. Because they did not jump in their armour into the sea like our brave Frenchmen.*[9]

King Edward, writing to his son, the Black Prince, then only ten, informed him, probably exaggerating, that only five thousand of the forty thousand French soldiers and sailors escaped and that, 'We have heard from some who were taken alive that the bodies are scattered all over the coast of Flanders'.[10] Such was the nature of medieval warfare.

King Edward III was to win only two major naval battles during the Hundred Years War. This, the Battle of Sluys, was the first; as we shall soon see, the Battle of Winchelsea was the second, and in both his flagship was the Cog *Thomas* of Winchelsea.

Sluys was, nevertheless, a somewhat hollow victory. The strains of the war were to weaken the resolve of the Cinque Ports and other towns of the south coast on which he relied so much and, within a year, Winchelsea, like others, was being ordered to provide the names of two of its ships for use as part of a fleet to protect the coast from renewed raids.[11]

Such demands were far from being the only way in which the maritime communities of the south and east were affected by the war. They were also frequently required to guard the coasts. Large numbers of men were constantly being called away from the land to keep watch and provide a first line of defence. When this happened at important times in the farming year such as harvest there could be very serious problems for the local economy and the welfare of the inhabitants. Jonathan Sumption tells how, at this time, the economy of Great Yarmouth, traditional enemy of the Cinque Ports and the biggest ship provider in England, virtually collapsed.[12] Taxation to support the war effort was another drain on the country's resources. A war tax was levied in 1340. The king was in urgent need of money. However, in this regard Winchelsea had no complaint; it does not appear among the Sussex towns required to pay because of its Cinque Ports privilege of exemption, enjoyed also by Hastings and Rye.[13] Other port towns in the county enjoyed no such privilege and there would have been much sympathy with 'the rowdies of Chichester who attacked the bishop's servants in the streets and tore up the letters which they carried calling for prayers for the king's wars'.[14]

It was another twenty years before attitudes to such taxation changed through intense fear for the safety of the country. Such a change would take place only after Winchelsea had been grievously harmed.

Winchelsea may not have been financially deprived by war taxation but demands for ships were constant and the livelihood of the town's fishing and sea trade industries certainly suffered. The spirit of the men of the town ensured that other ways were found in which they could serve their own interests by not toeing the line. In 1342 a disputed succession led to civil war in Brittany. A large English fleet, led by the king and including twenty-four ships from Winchelsea went to take advantage of this instability. On this occasion only transport duties were required. After the king and his army had been landed many of the vessels did not want to waste time hanging about for the return journey so they deserted, 'leaving the king and his troops "in very great peril"'. Edward was understandably furious and issued instructions to the bailiffs of their home towns (eight of the deserters were from Winchelsea) that the offenders should be arrested, their property seized and that masters and mariners should be committed to Newgate.[15] We do not know how successful the bailiffs were. The likelihood is that they were not successful at all!

This type of insubordination was partly countered in the same year by the granting of official royal permission to the Cinque Ports and others to attack French ships whenever the opportunity arose and to keep one third of any profits. The men of Winchelsea no doubt took full advantage for 'these privateers were very active ... but indiscriminate in their choice of victims and not over-scrupulous in accounting for their takings'.[16]

Enormous problems arose from this kind of official piracy and in 1345 things became so bad that Miss Murray comments, 'pirates of Winchelsea prevented the fleet from assembling at all'.[17] The Close Roll to which she is referring requires the mayor and bailiffs of Winchelsea to recall all ships of their town to port as the king has been told that 'certain pirates maintain themselves at sea in a ship and fluvi (large flat vessels of shallow draft with two masts and two rudders) of that town and commit wrongs upon the king's subjects and other aliens ... wherefore the ships he has ordered to go to Sandwich in his service do not dare to do so'![18]

Action to control such defiance was urgently needed and it was taken in the form of the reinforcement of the powers of the Admiral which, as we have seen, had been limited. A distinguished and respected person was needed for the Portsmen could not otherwise be brought into line. The Earl of Arundel was appointed. The Admiral was told that he must govern and rule the men of the Cinque Ports while at the same time upholding them 'in all their laws and customs'. In return the Portsmen must obey his orders, must not set sail without instructions, must keep as close to the flagship as possible, and must not enter port or leave the fleet without permission.[19]

Discipline of a kind was certainly achieved during preparations for the Crécy campaign the following year. Winchelsea, with other important ports such as Dover, Sandwich and London, was felt, because of the constant comings and goings at its harbour, to be an easy target for enemy spies. These towns were therefore ordered to prevent anyone, whatever their rank, from leaving the country for fear that the English plans would be revealed.[20] Secrecy was all important. Remarkably the plan worked so well that, 'Even the English army itself believed it was going to Gascony.'[21] In fact it was going to Normandy to be put ashore by a large fleet including ships of Winchelsea and the Cinque Ports. The beach on which King Edward III and his army were landed became, 598 years later, Utah Beach on D-Day.[22]

After landing the army the fleet wrought havoc in the fishing communities of Normandy suspected of providing and supporting French control of the Channel and similar attacks in England. 'They burned more than a hundred ships, including sixty-one which the French had fortified for war service.'[23] At this point discipline broke down. The ships were so crammed with booty that temptation overtook their masters and many deserted, hurrying to cash in on their good fortune at English ports. The army was therefore left, again, in France without adequate naval support for

(40) The Battle of Sluys

supplies or as a means of withdrawal. A hundred ships had to be
requisitioned to replace the deserters. They sailed from
Winchelsea in convoy with both men and supplies.[24] It is
tempting to assume that the Winchelsea sailors, having made
large profits from their looted goods, then rejoined this fleet!

Success at Crécy was followed in 1347 by the siege of
Calais. Once again Winchelsea was deeply involved,
supplying twenty-one ships and 596 men. This was one of
the largest contingents from the forty-nine south of England
ports which contributed.[25] Assuming that all the Winchelsea
men were on Winchelsea ships, the trend towards the use of
much larger vessels than were envisaged in the original ship
service arrangements is emphasised here. In fact the
Winchelsea ships may have needed to supplement their crews
from other ports for Miss Murray explains that at least sixty-

(41) A gold noble issued by Edward III to celebrate his victory at Sluys. The ship is very similar to that on the seal of Winchelsea

five were needed to man a ship of the size normal in 1347. In terms of ship numbers, demands on
the Cinque Ports were thus reduced by half[26] and the Cinque Ports representation was just
fourteen percent of the total.[27] Hastings only managed even this reduced responsibility by buying
a ship from Winchelsea.[28]

Adequate supplies for the besieging troops were essential for the success of the campaign.
Attempts were made to facilitate this by persuading ships' masters and their supplying merchants
that, 'whoever would take victuals, bows, arrows or bow strings to Calais for the supply of the
army, should be protected from loss or molestation and should be free to sell their commodities
for such price as might be agreed upon between the buyer and the seller'.[29] In other words, cargoes
would not be seized or requisitioned. The promise about loss or molestation was at least partly
kept for we know that Peter Foulk of Winchelsea was given a ship called the *Michel* of Fowey as a
replacement for his own which the king had ordered to be sunk at Calais.[30] What the people of
Fowey thought we do not know!

After Calais fell the English garrison continued, of course, to need regular supplies.
Sandwich's more advantageous position geographically meant that it became the principal port of
departure for this regular trade. Nevertheless the king's ships also continued to be based at Calais
and Winchelsea in an attempt to maintain the upper hand which they had temporarily gained in
the Channel. Benedict Sely of Winchelsea, master of the ship *Laurence*, was probably both
patrolling and transporting when he entered his home port with profit in mind. Instead of
proceeding to Sandwich with his cargo of flour destined for Calais, he sold it at Winchelsea. This
misappropriation was discovered by the authorities and taken extremely seriously. The *Laurence*
was to be seized and Sely imprisoned in the Tower of London. Had Sely's cargo reached Calais he
would not have been able to take advantage of being allowed to sell it for a price agreed with the
purchaser – it already belonged to the king![31]

The English freedom to supply the Calais garrison, that is when the supplies were not sold
elsewhere by men like Sely, was a constant irritant to the French. The sixty-one war-prepared
vessels destroyed by the English in Normandy had been a devastating loss. King Philip urgently
sought money to replace them. He must be able to continue harrying the English coast.[32]
However, he was only partly successful and a truce was being negotiated when the Black Death
struck both sides and put warfare largely out of their minds for the next two years.

24. THE BATTLE OF WINCHELSEA

We have already examined the largely circumstantial evidence of the impact of the Black Death on Winchelsea. Whatever may have been the extent of its impact, all danger of infection must have passed by the summer of 1350 for the town was then acceptable as a base for King Edward III and a large gathering of important personages as they prepared for the Battle of Winchelsea, also known as the Battle of L'Espagnol sur Mer.

In my account of this event I depart from the line taken by the man who has informed and, indeed, inspired much of this book, William MacLean Homan. Homan took an extremely poor view of the Plantagenets. He writes scathingly of their gratuitous violence. Where he deals with the Black Prince's exploits in France there may be much to support him but the Plantagenets ruled in days when the only language which earned the respect of the people and thus permitted stable government was the language of strength. The fates of Edward II and Richard II are examples. Such strength had to be reinforced by decisive action and, if possible, by victory in battle. The way in which these requirements were met, by, for example, hanging, drawing and quartering those being summarily executed and displaying parts of their bodies in various places as a warning is, to us, appalling. But I think it is dangerous to apply mid-twentieth century standards of behaviour (Homan was writing in 1941/42) to medieval times which were consistently violent and where that violence was accepted as normal. The twentieth century can hardly be exempted from barbarity anyway.

Homan describes the Battle of Winchelsea as, 'a sordid and disgraceful ... act of piracy on the part of King Edward',[1] on the grounds that this was a trading fleet from a country with which England was not at war, returning home peacefully. However, there is much evidence that the Castilian ships involved, and others, had been causing havoc among English vessels and seriously hazarding trade. This began in 1349 when 'a famous freebooter called Don Carlos de la Cerda ... seized some English wine ships off Bordeaux and murdered their crews'.[2] The importance to the whole of England of such interference with the wine trade is emphasised when considering the single example of wine consumption at Battle Abbey. The abbey relied upon Winchelsea for the import of its wine. It was 'above all a wine drinking community ... the monks were permitted a ration of one pint of wine per day and received one gallon each on special feasts'.[3] No wonder such vast quantities of wine were considered essential for the country's economy.

Initially the government reacted by granting a subsidy of one shilling on every ton of wine to help finance the convoy system used for its transportation.[4] This was not enough. In 1350 the Castilian fleet sailed through the Channel to Flanders 'taking some English prizes on the way'.[5] de la Cerda added insult to injury by carrying within his ships a major consignment of wool for sale to the Flemish. This trade had been an English monopoly for as long as anyone could remember and Edward III, outraged, was bent on revenge. His call to arms in such circumstances was highly popular and many distinguished soldiers rallied to it.

Assuming that the Spanish would, in accordance with their normal practice, return home 'before the equinoctial gales' the king planned an interception. 'The Earls of Huntingdon and Arundel were to organise the gathering of a great fleet at Sandwich, together with a large number of mariners, bowmen and spearmen.' Winchelsea men became involved at an early stage when William Passelawe and Robert Shipman, constables of the king's flagship, the Cog *Thomas* of Winchelsea, were empowered to 'impress one hundred of the best seamen of Kent and Sussex to man the vessel'.[6] All this was supposed to happen by mid-June but at the end of the month the

British Library Harl.4379f.60v

(42) Ships of the French/Genoese fleet, similar to those of the Castilians defeated at the Battle of Winchelsea

number of ships present in Sandwich harbour fully supplied and manned was disappointing. Clearly the sailors were not as keen as the soldiers! Many had delayed their response in order to defend their own ports against imminent attack.[7]

The king seems to have been undeterred by this shortcoming and eventually mustered thirty-five vessels; not really enough for his purpose. This fleet included four from Winchelsea, all cogs, his flagship the *Thomas*, with the *Blithe*, the *Sainte Marie* and the *Johan*.[8] The preparations he had made to ensure his own comfort at sea become clear from a list of the contents of his supply train on the journey from London. Among the items transported for his use aboard the *Thomas* were four folding seats, three bed blankets, four nightcaps, four pillowcases of fine linen, eight 'footcloths', two mattresses 'of linen of divers colours', and a featherbed.[9] The king was dressed in black velvet and wore a small beaver hat 'which became him much'. His minstrels, who would play 'a German dance, Sir John Chandos', as the enemy approached, boarded with him.[10] He seems to have been better prepared for a cruise than a battle.

But a battle it was to be. A fruitless attempt to seek out the enemy in the North Sea (they were in harbour at Sluys) was followed by Edward's acceptance of his commanders' advice that they should head for Winchelsea where further supplies would be available and the fleet could be supplemented by ships from further west which were still responding to the call. On the evening of 26 August the king's fleet dropped anchor in the Camber.[11] John Cammidge's detailed account of these events records that Queen Philippa was staying nearby at Udimore and that the king and the young Black Prince went there to greet her. On their return 'the king and the Black Prince were entertained in the Court Hall by Stephen Alard, descendant of a long line of tall Sussex seamen and leader of the Cinque Ports Squadron'.[12] Cammidge quotes no source for information of this kind but what he says is certainly possible. However, if royalty were, indeed, entertained by Alard, it is likely to have been, not at whatever was then the official Court Hall, but at the present one which was, in the fourteenth century, a private residence belonging to his family.

After receiving news that the Spanish were sailing down Channel the king ordered his fleet to sail. The fateful day was 29 August 1350. From the chronicler Froissart's seemingly highly imaginative account of the battle, quoted in detail by Cooper,[13] and other evidence it is generally accepted that the battle was fought at sea off Dungeness after the Spanish ships had been successfully intercepted. The Castilian vessels were considerably larger than the English but this did not deter the king from ordering his fleet to approach in line and board them. The enemy made no attempt to avoid battle which their larger size and greater speed would have made possible. Their commander, de la Cerda, had boasted that he would defeat the English fleet, 'obtain dominion over the English sea and then invade England and exterminate its people'.[14] Unfortunately for him the extermination was to be suffered by large numbers of his own men.

The cog *Thomas* of Winchelsea led the way and was first to grapple the enemy. She is reputed to have been one of the largest cogs ever built[15] and to have carried on this occasion a complement of no fewer than 360 men, mariners, soldiers and the king's entourage.[16] The ships of the fleets crashed together and mayhem ensued. The bowmen of both sides rained arrows upon the enemy and rocks were thrown from the taller Spanish ships with devastating effect. Nevertheless, with the fleets locked together, the larger numbers of English soldiers managed to board their opponents' vessels and where they gained the upper hand they mercilessly slaughtered the Spaniards, or, without taking the trouble to do so, threw them into the sea to drown. Both King Edward and the Black Prince had narrow escapes when their craft foundered under the onslaught but superior military strength allowed their attackers to be overwhelmed, and safety gained upon captured enemy ships.

Some of the Castilians escaped but those which had not been sunk were sailed in triumph back to Winchelsea whence the king hurried to Udimore to celebrate with the queen and his courtiers. 'The next day there was a solemn thanksgiving service in St. Thomas's Church and later in the Court Hall the king thanked and dismissed his faithful subjects.'[17] Before doing so he no doubt delighted the community by dispensing goodwill and 'granting pardons and patronage to several of the town's residents'.[18] Whether or not they deserved the patronage, they probably merited the pardons!

The Battle of Winchelsea was hailed as a great victory. Certainly the defeated Castilians were a hostile enemy and not innocent merchants as W. M. Homan chose to believe. It is, however, worth examining whether this, the only battle to bear Winchelsea's name, had any real importance in the context of medieval warfare and the Hundred Years War and whether it actually achieved anything.

There are three reasons why it merits note in this context. In terms of English naval history it us believed to have been the first occasion when guns were used in battle at sea, although the chroniclers do not mention this. Guns are similarly believed to have been used first on land in the Battle of Crécy four years earlier. In those days of early development they would have been much more dangerous for the firer than for anyone they were aimed at and extremely difficult to use effectively against a close vessel standing higher or lower than the weapon. In fact they would have been used not against personnel but to disable ships by bringing down masts, spars and rigging.[19] The battle was certainly remarkable in that it involved, when methods of navigation were primitive in the extreme, a successful deliberate interception at sea, probably achieved more by luck than judgement.[20] It is almost certainly the last occasion when opposing fleets engaged in action by approaching each other in line on collision course and used the men on board to fight what was to all intents and purposes a hand-to-hand land battle.[21]

Whatever may have been its place in the history of naval warfare, reports of what happened afterwards vary. About fourteen of the enemy ships were far enough from the principal encounter to escape when they saw how things were going. N.A.M. Rodger implies that this was quite sufficient, with reinforcements, to continue to harry shipping in the Channel but that it was a Castilian civil war which kept them at home for twenty years rather than defeat at Winchelsea.[22] Jonathan Sumption on the other hand thinks that their departure for that reason was long delayed, that they readily obtained their reinforcements from the French Channel ports and 'hovered off the east coast before withdrawing northward to spend another winter at Sluys'. The mere presence of the Castilians in northern waters for another year caused immeasurable damage to England's commerce.'[23] Expensive convoy systems, like those supporting the wine trade to Gascony, had to be introduced across the North Sea.

Only a little more than seven months after the battle, in April 1351, Andrew Offord, a leading member of King Edward III's household was despatched to meet the ambassadors of the Count of Flanders on official court business. He arrived at Dover demanding transport to Calais. Enemy dominance of the Channel seas was such that no one would take him. Determined to use his rank and royal instructions to overcome this reluctance Offord hurried to order the mayor and bailiff of Dover and the lieutenant governor of Dover Castle to provide a ship for him. Like the townsmen they refused. They went so far as to tell him that 'they would not do it even if the king were here himself'. Somewhat ignominiously, but with admirably grit, Andrew Offord eventually reached Calais in a rowing boat![24]

If the king's intention in fighting the Battle of Winchelsea had been to clear the Channel seas for English control, he had most certainly not succeeded.

25. A DECADE AT HOME ...

We now turn from the war to look at life in Winchelsea during the decade (1350-1360) which separated what the inhabitants would have looked upon as a glorious victory from what was undoubtedly a disastrous defeat.

During that decade several events foreshadow Winchelsea's eventual decline, but, taking in what happened shortly before the Battle of Winchelsea, the shipbuilding industry seems to have continued to flourish at this time. In 1346-1347, the last year of his life, Stephen de Padiham, the bailiff who had so cruelly regained that office by giving false evidence against John Glynde, was responsible for fitting out a new galley for King Edward III at Winchelsea.[1] Just after this Richard Large of Winchelsea was authorised to spend the vast sum of £377 2s 5d on refitting the king's flagship, the cog *Thomas,* and on constructing two smaller boats, the *John* and the *Jonette* with material recycled from a larger ship. The work took about six months, employing shipwrights of varying degrees of skill, labourers, sawyers, 'castlewrights' and watchmen. When the task was completed numerous labourers were paid threepence a day each to dig a channel through which the ships could be launched.[2] The channel digging took three days. The land where the building and repairs took place was 'the float', near the present Bridge Inn, and David Sylvester comments that, with its 'excellent supply of Wealden timber and iron, the port town was an important centre of shipbuilding and was designated for the storage and repair of royal galleys'.[3] Despite this furious activity and the constant involvement of the seamen of Winchelsea and Rye in the ship trades, in fishing, in sea transport and in warfare, things were not to go well in the long run. Major centres of marine activity were, before another fifty years were out, to be found further west. This provokes James Williamson into the perceptive comment that, had Geoffrey Chaucer lived a hundred years earlier (he died in 1400) he might well have made his typical English shipmaster a man of Rye or Winchelsea. In the circumstances of his time he described him as a west countryman of Dartmouth.[4]

It was Stephen de Padiham's successor as king's bailiff, John Longe, who was instructed in 1349 to inquire into the ruined nature of the 'parsonage house' of St. Thomas's and to ensure that the rector had somewhere reasonable to live. It appears that the house in which John Glynde died had been 'seized into the king's hands' on the death of a previous owner without heirs. It lay on the eastern side of the churchyard and was probably fairly basic for it was found to be worth 'five shillings per annum and not more'. This property, most likely adjoining the present site of Glebe, was granted to John Glynde's successor as rector 'for the inhabitation of himself and his successors, rectors of the said church'.[5]

At this time Winchelsea was also attempting to deal with problems more serious than a dilapidated rectory. Additional taxation on trade to finance the king's wars placed a burden on the economy which was further exacerbated by food shortages. Following the Black Death the embankments protecting cultivated marshland round the town from the sea had been neglected. These embankments, the medieval equivalent of the modern sea wall, were being breached to such an extent that the land to the east of the town, from below the Strand Gate to the sea, then known as Spadeland 'was inundated by salt water at every high tide'[6] and its use for agriculture became impossible. The king issued instructions that the walls and ditches must be repaired.[7]

The town's condition and trading influence was further reduced in 1353 when Chichester was chosen as the Sussex Staple port for the export of wool. This legislation required that all Sussex's wool had to be taken to Chichester and taxes paid before its export was permitted. Before

*(43) The Bridge Inn stands close to the present bridge over the River Brede
and the site of Winchelsea's medieval quay*

this date the mayors of both Winchelsea and Chichester had been allowed to control the wool trade in this way. Taxation on wool was extremely high at this time. 'In 1341 the duty was fifty shillings a sack, an enormous sum in those days.'[8] So much for the king's grandfather's promise to abolish the maltote or bad tax on wool!

Two deaths occurred in 1354; one likely to have been greeted with regret in Winchelsea and the other to have passed unnoticed.

Reginald Alard died on 15 April and his graveslab in St. Thomas's Church lies in front of the reputed tomb of Gervase Alard in the south aisle. In line with the establishment of the church's Alard chantries, the slab 'offers fifty days' indulgence to anyone praying for Reginald Alard's soul'.[9] Cooper states that the slab has been moved and that when this was done 'the bones and a glass bottle' were found beneath it.[10] This may have been the same Reginald Alard who had been a leading citizen of New Winchelsea and had sold wine to King Edward II. As he would have reached a great age by this date, at a time when few people did, it is more likely to have been a family member of the same name. Alard was a considerable landholder in the Manor of Frenchcourt in Fairlight parish and could possibly, therefore, have been an early owner of Wickham which was part of that manor.

The unregretted death would have been that of the Earl of Huntingdon, persecutor of John Glynde. Perhaps there is some satisfaction in noting that he had no heir and 'his honours became extinct'. Earls of Huntingdon appear, however, in later pages of the history of England. The next creation was made at the coronation of Richard II when Sir Guichard d'Angle, the king's former governor, was granted the title. He had a career almost as chequered as that of his predecessor; left for dead on the field of Poitiers when fighting for the French, he later fought for the English and became established at the English Court. d'Angle, however, was the medieval equivalent of a life peer; his title was not hereditary.[11] Later creations led to the earldom remaining in existence to this day. The field of Poitiers, on which d'Angle was left for dead, will soon become relevant to this story.

We have already noted that Winchelsea was a major exporter of timber from the Weald and during the fourteenth century it led the Sussex ports in this respect.[12] Large amounts of this timber were exported either as charcoal or firewood. Certain hazards arose from the manufacture of charcoal, the burning being carried out in such an enthusiastic manner that it became a hazard to shipping and orders were issued that the manufacture of charcoal should be confined to an area above Sloghdam, where the ships would not be endangered.[13] Such methods would also have reduced the quality of the charcoal.

Sloghdam, beyond which the timber must be burnt for this purpose is important to Winchelsea's story because it heralds one of the major reasons for the town's decline. It was, in fact, a sluice, built in about 1330. The potential for silting of the channel by the exclusion of the tidal flow was thus created and over the next quarter of a century the problem grew to such an extent that it came to the king's attention. A Close Roll of 24 April 1357 'orders the removal of the obstruction made at Sloghdam to the flow of the sea water descending into the harbour of Winchelsea so that it may be cleared of filth and refuse'.[14] The 'filth and refuse' must have included considerable quantities of silt.

Attempts were made to regulate the export of brushwood in its pre-charcoal state. All vessels carrying any such cargo from Winchelsea must report to Sloghdam to have the brushwood checked if the ship-owners were Winchelsea men exercising their privilege to export free, and subjected to customs duty if they were not. Apparently the free export privilege had been much abused. Mariners had been sailing to such other ports as Smallhythe, 'and there plac[ing] wool, wool fells, and hides in the bottom of their ships and brushwood above, to defraud the king of his custom, and cross[ing] secretly thence both by day and by night'.[15] A very early example of Winchelsea men indulging in smuggling.

However much of an impediment the silting of the Brede was, it was insufficient to deter a growing trade in pilgrim transportation. This became an increasingly important part of the Winchelsea seamen's potential income in the fifteenth century and we shall return to the subject, but during the decade under consideration the seeds were sown. As will be shown, pilgrims needed great determination and no little pluck to undertake pilgrimages, principally to the shrine of St. James of Compostela in Spain. Such journeys were all the more hazardous while the Hundred Years War continued. The masters of Winchelsea ships were, nevertheless, pleased to supplement their incomes by providing the opportunity to travel. We know that, in 1356, a licence for this purpose was granted by the crown to Simon Salerne of Winchelsea. We know, too, that the increased taxation on trade to finance the war already mentioned applied to pilgrims as well. The going rate was twopence for each pilgrim returning from abroad to Winchelsea. The masters made sure that their passengers footed the bill![16]

While some Winchelsea trades suffered and others grew, the Cinque Ports' constantly simmering enmity with Great Yarmouth continued, and eventually required royal legislation to attempt to control it. Winchelsea plaice and Rye whiting had achieved a fame which allowed them to be classed with the valuable Yarmouth herrings. That fame had been greatest in the thirteenth century when Winchelsea is recorded as providing plaice by the thousand to royal tables at Winchester and Westminster.[17] Even though this prominence was on the decline, the fact that the two ancient towns should be part of the Cinque Ports contingent demanding, as of right, facilities and judicial control at the annual Yarmouth herring fair was bound to cause resentment in Yarmouth and never failed to do so. Murders, skirmishes and numerous more orderly legal disputes ensued.

King Edward III, in 1357, increasingly frustrated by this disorder within his kingdom, intervened. He confirmed, no doubt to Yarmouth's annoyance, that the Cinque Ports had the right by the tradition of centuries 'to send bailiffs to Yarmouth to administer justice and collect certain profits for the duration of the 40 day herring fair'.[18] At that time seven bailiffs were sent, one each from the head ports including Winchelsea. There were other provisions in the legislation. Among them it was decreed that no man must carry armour; every master must ensure that his crew were on board their ship between 'the going down of the sun unto the sun rising', subject only to weather conditions; ships attending the fair must load and unload at Yarmouth and nowhere else 'on pain of losing the ship'; no brewer might sell a gallon of the best ale above twopence, or second best above a penny; and there must be no challenge to the right of the Cinque Ports to 'den and strond', that is the right to land and dry their nets on the dunes (den) and the right to sell their catch on the strand (strond).[19]

Despite its obvious attempt to be even-handed, this did not, in the short term, really solve anything. However, in the longer term, it proved a very thin end of a very large wedge. Within six years the number of bailiffs attending had been reduced by the Confederation from seven to four. Hastings continued to send one, with Rye and Winchelsea, New Romney and Dover, Sandwich and Hythe, co-operating to send the other three.[20] The significance of the premier position of Hastings in this connection is not clear. It arose probably because of Hastings' traditional position at the head of the 'west to east' list of the head ports. It is fairly safe to say that, in maritime terms, it was the least influential at that time. One important point arose from this change affecting the men of Winchelsea who, in turn with men of Rye, were chosen. In the past bailiffs like John Glynde had had a responsibility for supervising only the ships and men from their own port. Now the chosen four undertook a general control of the Cinque Ports contingent.[21]

Returning to Winchelsea from disputes further afield, we find the Blackfriars finally achieving a settled location within the walls of the town. This was in Quarter 4 near the Pipewell Gate and they proceeded to build themselves a substantial establishment including a sizeable church measuring approximately 140 by 60 feet.[22] Following their desperate complaint in 1342 that their property at the foot of the hill was in danger of inundation by the sea, the pope had ordered the Bishop of Chichester to find them a site within the walls. The bishop had no power to do this without royal agreement and King Edward III was currently 'on bad terms with [both] the pope and the church'.[23] However, by 1358 when the land in Quarter 4 was granted, Edward was anxious to secure the pope's support in his attempt to have himself acknowledged as King of France. W. M. Homan suggests that this was a major factor in allowing the Blackfriars full access to Winchelsea, its services and its potential almsgiving, facilities from which the inhabitants had so long tried to exclude them. It seems that they were not unsuccessful in making themselves at home for by the time of the dissolution much Winchelsea property was under their control.

Quarter 4 today provides us with no remains above ground and no clear evidence from earthworks to indicate the exact extent of the Blackfriars' buildings. However, archaeological investigation and the evidence of aerial photography suggest that the slope of the site led to the principal buildings being to the north of the church, that the friars had a cemetery to the south and east, and that there was a substantial entrance gate near the Pipewell Gate. The remains of this

(44) Many Winchelsea cellar entrances were very public, no disadvantage when the cellar was used legally, but a great discouragement to smuggling use. This one is at The Stone House, Barrack Square

gate feature in a Turner painting. It was eventually destroyed during road-widening.[24]

What, then, of the walls inside which the Blackfriars sought to establish their community? We are not even sure that there were any! Certainly the entrance gates had been constructed but the steep nature of the hill on the north, east and south made stone walls unnecessary but on the more vulnerable west side the arrangement is uncertain despite foundations which suggest that part at least may have been of stone.[25] Thomas of Walsingham, writing before the end of the century but recently discovered to have been quoting third-hand from a mid-fourteenth century, possibly eye-witness, account 'stated that the town was not enclosed by a stone wall but by earthen entrenchments carried to the height of a man, surmounted by a projecting wooden roof, with intervals, and through these bulwarks was the lookout towards the ships'.[26] General assumptions about town defences of the period make it clear that 'ditches and earth banks, sometime surmounted by a timber palisade, [were] the only protection enjoyed by some towns until the late Middle Ages'.[27]

If that was how Winchelsea was defended, and if those defences had been neglected as had the Spadeland embankments, much is explained of how disaster and destruction came so easily to the town in 1360.

26. ... AND DEVASTATION FROM ABROAD

One of the causes of that disaster and destruction occurred four years previously, in 1356, on the field of Poitiers to which we must make a brief excursion. Despite being heavily outnumbered in that cruel encounter, the English army led by the Black Prince was victorious. The French were under the command of their king, King John II, who showed outstanding bravery during the battle. Sadly for the French he was eventually surrounded by a crowd of English knights who, initially with some trepidation, demanded and obtained his surrender. The king requested escort to the Black Prince's tent, during which decorum collapsed and great arguments broke out among those who claimed to have made the capture and therefore to be entitled to a share of the ransom. Eventually King John was extricated from the quarrelling mob by the Earl of Warwick and taken before the Prince of Wales.[1]

For France this was a desperate blow. Little could be worse in the chivalric ideals of the Hundred Years War than your king being held prisoner by the enemy with the inevitable consequence that vast sums of money would be required to secure his release.

Negotiations were lengthy but eventually King John was taken to London where, with his son and other captured French knights, he was 'given a tumultuous welcome by the city population'.[2] No doubt this reaction was motivated more by triumph than warmth of greeting.

Much remained to be decided about how to ensure maximum benefit from such a fortuitous situation. While the debate continued the French king was taken to Somerton in Somerset where he was held in the luxury proper to his rank but well away from any possible attempt by his countrymen to obtain his release. Unfortunately the English parliament sadly misjudged the relative strengths of the opposing Channel fleets at this time, assuming that 'the French no longer represented a threat to the coasts of England or the livelihood of its inhabitants'.[3] How wrong they were.

No doubt encouraged by this complacency and with truce negotiations stalled, King Edward III sailed to France to renew the campaign, taking with him a large army and a substantial proportion of the fleet.

More through bad luck than design, Winchelsea suffered the dire consequences of these miscalculations on 15 March 1360.

A pause is necessary here to clarify the authenticity of this date. W. D. Cooper follows a number of sources and is followed by others in claiming that the French attacked twice, on 15 March 1359 and exactly one year later.[4] W. M. Homan, on the other hand, makes it clear that this arises from a dating confusion within the surviving documents and that only one raid took place, on the latter date. He explains 'that the year in fourteenth century England ended on 24 March and not on 31 December, so what we now call 15 March 1360 would at the time be spoken of as 15 March 1359'.[5] The Close Roll transcripts that I have been able to examine confirm Homan's view.

One raid was quite enough!

News of the threatened invasion, with the purpose of freeing the French king, brought something like panic. Orders were given that King John was to be moved from Somerton to Berkhampstead; all men who could carry arms were to hurry to defend the coast; all ships in south coast ports were to be drawn up 'far from the sea' to prevent their capture.[6]

The French fleet, under Admiral Jean de Neuville, was cruising unmolested in the Channel, largely because such English ships as were available had been ordered to the mouth of the Thames as a result of inaccurate intelligence. In the matter of intelligence the French were even less successful. They were heading for Sandwich 'apparently believing that Somerton was close by'.[7] Held back for almost a week by the weather, they eventually managed to land a considerable force in Rye Bay. There were between fifteen hundred and two thousand men, 'mostly bowmen and footsoldiers' but including less well trained volunteers. 'They formed up on the beach in three battalions and marched along the shore until they came to Winchelsea.'[8]

British Library Cotton Nero EII pt2.f.166

(45) The capture of King John II of France at Poitiers

Winchelsea was just as ill-prepared as England was. Large numbers of the able-bodied men among a population greatly reduced by the Black Death were either serving with Edward III in France, as members of the Cinque Ports contingent of his supporting fleet, or on those vessels incorrectly ordered to defend the Thames estuary. The town's defences were in poor repair. In those days citizens had, generally, to build and maintain walls and other defences at their own expense. This was hardly a top priority when so few men were available and taxation to achieve it would have been highly unpopular except under extreme threat.

The threat was perceived too late and the enemy fell upon the town with little resistance and with disastrous results for those unfortunate enough to be there. Popular tradition, arising from the accounts of chroniclers, has it that the inhabitants were surprised while at mass in the church. Since warnings had been issued all over southern England this seems most unlikely. What is much more likely is that the church, in this case probably St. Giles's, a major stone-built structure, was being used, woefully unsuccessfully, as a defensive position by those who had not already fled. Many churches were not only used for such a purpose in medieval times, but designed with defence in mind. The crenellated and embattled appearance of Westham church provides a good local example. However, in this case, any defenders brave enough to take up arms were hopelessly outnumbered. Large numbers were slaughtered. No mercy was shown. 'A gang of French soldiers raped and murdered the most attractive young woman present ... Nine women were carried off never to be heard of again.' All others, men women and children, who could be found, in the church or elsewhere, were butchered 'or exposed to even more hideous atrocities'.[9]

The attack was merciless, although quite in accordance with normal practice on both sides at the time, and left Winchelsea and its population virtually destroyed. The attackers did not, however, get away without some retaliation. The French were initially in no hurry to leave and had set about looting, including the ships which remained in, or rather on land near, the harbour. This allowed time for the Abbot of Battle, responsible for the defence of Winchelsea's part of the coast, to gather 'about 300 horsemen of the Sussex county levies'[10] and mount a counter-attack. On receiving warning of this the French commenced a withdrawal and suffered considerable losses in the process. Some invaders were killed while still in the town, others while attempting to board their ships. 'The French lost about three hundred of their men and two ships which they had beached and were unable to refloat.'[11]

The retaliation may have been provoked by an urgent message sent to the county of Essex and eleven other counties on the day following the initial landing requiring them to prepare for war 'as the said enemies landed at Winchelsea on Sunday last a great host of armed men with their horses, took the town, barbarously slew the men therein found, and are riding over the country, slaying, burning, destroying and doing other mischief, and greater damage unless they be speedily and manfully opposed'.[12]

The precipitate withdrawal of the French might have provided comfort to those not involved who received reports at a safe distance; for Winchelsea's inhabitants it provided no comfort beyond the cessation of the awful events. To add to the devastation, the town, and the remaining ships, were set on fire by the departing enemy.

W. M. Homan produces some evidence of the extent of the destruction by noting that, in 1358, two years before the raid and following the Black Death, 94 properties in Winchelsea were recorded as 'waste and uninhabited', with another 90 also in ruins. In 1363, this figure had risen to 409 properties in ruins with the owners 'unable to pay their quitrent'.[13]

The initial 1360 figure, had a schedule been prepared, must have been much higher. By 1363 men returning after the attack, some from serving their country and some from fleeing their town, would have had three years to rebuild and re-occupy their homes, a perfectly adequate time. Homan also suggests that the only Winchelsea ships to escape would have been those not in their home port,[14] a further major blow to a community relying on maritime activity for such prosperity as it could muster.

And so to the evidence which leads us to believe that violence against Winchelsea's citizens was, on this occasion, most prevalent at St. Giles's Church. 'Following the French raid a patent was issued for the enlargement of [St. Giles's] Churchyard due to the consequence of burial of those slain in the conflict.'[15] Modern archaeological examination of the churchyard area leads David and Barbara Martin to report that 'although only a small area was examined a heavy concentration of burials was encountered.'[16] However, in discussion of this point, David points out that this concentration was no greater than might be expected in an urban churchyard, that these were prepared individual burials and not multiple ones and that he is by no means convinced that the churchyard was ever enlarged.

Legend nevertheless has it that burials took place in the top part of what is now called Hogtrough Lane but also, recalling this disaster, Deadman's Lane. Douglas Seward comments: 'A path next to the vanished church of St. Giles where these were buried is still known as Deadman's Lane, and is haunted; no birds will sing there'.[17] My experience precludes me from confirming the last part of this statement; have any readers seen, at this sometimes rather spooky place, the ghosts of Winchelsea's slaughtered?

While this attack had such appallingly direct results for Winchelsea, it also had extensive indirect disruptive results in the country. Large numbers of men were ordered away from their agricultural employment to defend the coasts, ships were diverted from trading to a war footing and supplies of food were requisitioned to feed the conscripted soldiers and seamen, thus depriving the areas where the food had been produced.[18] The threat had departed almost as soon as it had become apparent but the subsequent defensive measures made the counties acutely aware of the danger of French incursions and, indeed, invasion. They therefore released to the exchequer the funds they had collected for this purpose and made financing the war much easier. The official view might well have been that Winchelsea had not suffered in vain. 'For the ministers at Westminster the incident was an unmitigated boon.'[19]

(46) Hogtrough or Deadman's Lane,
legendary site of burials after the 1360 French raid on Winchelsea

The most immediate use of this money came with the raising of a fleet to mount a revenge attack on the French coast. Cinque Ports ships were included but there is no record of which ports contributed. About 160 vessels took part in a raid which, as at Winchelsea, landed a considerable force at Leure on the north of the Seine estuary. A fort on the beach was captured and the English marched on the important town of Harfleur, about three miles inland. 'It was the mirror image of the French raid on Winchelsea in March, and proved to be equally fruitless for much the same reasons: the follow up was too slow and too little thought out.'[20] The panic caused was similar to that in England but this force, too, had to withdraw. Within a few days negotiations opened which led to the Treaty of Bretigny.

The agreed terms failed totally, for technical reasons, to resolve the conflict although King John was released on payment of the first instalment of a reduced ransom. Payments had still not been completed in 1414![21]

For Winchelsea, though, the Treaty of Bretigny at least provided a nine-year respite before further demands upon the town were provoked by the resumption of hostilities.

27. DETERMINED DEFENCE

During those nine years the town's condition remained poor. W. M. Homan amply illustrated this poverty by discovering that 'the farm of the town manor and marsh in these days hardly amounts to twenty pounds yearly'.[1] The farm was the income generated by rental payments to the King's Bailiff. Homan infers from this that the town and the surrounding marshland which its citizens cultivated 'were in a very bad way' and presumes that any income generated for the town probably came from the fishing and trading activities of the Winchelsea ships which had survived, through their absence, the 1360 attack.[2] Homan also demonstrates that by 1370 only thirty-six out of the 409 properties in ruins in 1363 had been rebuilt.[3]

Despite its poor condition, Winchelsea continued to exert an influence in other ways. In 1365 the Mayor and Barons of the town were called upon to arbitrate in a dispute between Poole and Wareham about Poole Harbour. It appears that an inquiry ordered by the king the previous year had resulted in Wareham laying claim to part of Poole Harbour. Outraged at the injustice of this the Mayor and Burgesses of Poole appealed to Winchelsea for support. Why Winchelsea we do not know, but Poole must have been gratified by the response. The Mayor and Barons of Winchelsea issued what is known in Poole as the Winchelsea Certificate. Carefully avoiding making things worse by naming the culprits, this stated that 'our very dear friends and allies the Mayor and Burgesses of the Town of Poole have given us to understand that certain people suppose that the water between Redclive Attewell and Northaven Orde [Sandbanks] should appertain to some other place than the said town of Poole'. The document goes on to state that the men of Winchelsea and their ancestors 'from time beyond reckoning' have known that area to be part of Poole Harbour and that the town of Poole has always collected the customs duties due there.[4] This appears to have been decisive.

The Winchelsea Certificate is remembered in Poole to this day. In 1993 the former Principal of an Education Centre in the town wrote to me: 'The Winchelsea Certificate is a landmark in the town's not inconsiderable history and is always "a must" in schools' local studies'.[5] One of those schools perpetuates it through its name – Winchelsea School. For many years the Certificate was proclaimed at various stopping points during a 'Beating the Bounds of Poole Harbour' ceremony. Sadly this delightful tradition was marred in 1984, and previous years, by 'the yobbish behaviour of a few yuppies in their high speed power boats' who sped along the harbour at between 20 and 25 knots and 'spoilt the ceremony by throwing water, soot and flour over participants including the mayor'.[6] The dispirited organiser gave up and for nine years there was no ceremony. However, he agreed in 1993, following representations from the Society of Poole men, to try again. 'On 28 April the mayor will lead a procession of boats which will include pleasureboats, lifeboats, workboats and yachts to the boundary stones and the Jurymen, dressed in the uniform of Nelson's navy will see there is fair play.'[7] Let us hope that all went well and that this celebration of Winchelsea's influence continues.

It was in the following year, 1366, that Winchelsea's influence was further extended by the granting, in common with the other head ports of the Cinque Ports Confederation, of two seats in the House of Commons. This grant was as of right and lasted until 1832 with only a brief break in the time of Oliver Cromwell. Individual members will appear in this story occasionally and chronologically but it is worth noting here something of the character of the House of Commons to which they were sent, at the expense of the town, from this date. Most power lay, of course, with the king and the lords but 'Under Edward III [the Commons] assumed a position

(47) The ancient campanile tower which stood in St. Thomas's Churchyard long after the nave was destroyed was eventually demolished in 1790.

distinct, vital and permanent. They had their own clerk who drafted their petitions and their rejoinders to the crown's replies.' The separation of the houses became more clearly defined and 'the figure of the Speaker emerged'.[8] Winchelsea played its full part in this development of democracy. It is also worth noting at this point that these members and others were consulted on matters of national importance beyond the scope of their parliamentary duties. A few years later, at what is known as the Queenborough Inquisition, Winchelsea seamen were 'asked to give expert testimony on the maritime customs of the realm'. Those appearing were Robert Londeneys, Robert Passelawe, Henry Passelawe and William Passelawe.[9]

The members sent to Parliament and summoned to attend inquiries in those days were ordinary leading citizens. By 1369 such men, however, would have been turning their attention again to the threat from overseas for the truce ended and the Hundred Years War with France resumed. There were many reasons, particularly including the French invasion of Aquitaine, which, under the Treaty of Bretigny, had been allocated to the English crown with full sovereignty. In the weeks leading up to the renewal of hostilities and those which followed, many edicts reached the ports of the south coast.

The mayor and bailiffs of Winchelsea were ordered to prevent the export of corn, gold or silver, bows, arrows or other arms and to arrest and imprison the culprits 'because this exporting continues daily and is to the great detriment of the country'.[10] A later Roll cancels the reference to corn because it was badly needed in Calais, but adds that a watch must be kept for 'aliens, particularly clerks and men of religion,' who may be bringing, 'bulls, instruments, letters etc.' into the country to the 'prejudice or hurt of the king or any of his subjects'. The carriers were to be arrested and the offending documents sent to the king.[11] Shipping was once again requisitioned for war service and men were required to muster for the defence of the coasts.[12] The Commons 'asked that all castles, abbeys, priories, cities, towns and boroughs should be surveyed and put in order ... and that walls, ditches and gates should be duly repaired'.[13] There is no doubt that Winchelsea's members would have voted for that but unfortunately they did not receive any money to help! What is worse, additional taxes on the export of wool and leather were imposed which would 'naturally damage the manufactures and trade of a town like Winchelsea and hamper its recovery which was in any case proceeding very slowly'.[14]

The sluggishness of that recovery did not, however, prevent the town becoming, in 1370, the centre, jointly with Rye, for frenetic activity leading up to the dispatch to France of a formidable force under Robert de Knolles. Once more Winchelsea's harbour at The Camber was the gathering place for the English fleet. Instructions were sent to admirals all over the country requiring them 'to detain ships for the expedition and hasten and take them to Winchelsea and Rye'. A courier was sent by the king to Winchelsea to find out how many ships had turned up. The admiral of the fleet and others were to recruit 'as many armed men and archers as were necessary to secure the safe passage of the ships'. The Steward of the King's Household was sent to make sure everything was proceeding smoothly and received £25 in expenses. I note with some regret but little surprise that he took up his quarters at Rye rather than Winchelsea! A certain John de Thorp was sent with £4000 towards the wages of both seamen and soldiers. He did go to Winchelsea! The mustering of this expedition was a very major undertaking. Quite apart from footmen and archers, almost 8500 horses were embarked and a sum of five thousand marks was sent from London to pay the expenses. It took four horses to carry the money.[15]

When the expedition had sailed, the people of Winchelsea must have breathed a sigh of relief and hoped this fleet and army would keep the enemy busy on the other side of the Channel. Unfortunately there was little hope of relief for long because the vital mastery of the narrow seas lay with the French and Castilians. There was no way that this problem could be overcome without a permanent navy. Armed merchant ships like those of the Cinque Ports, called into service as the need required, simply could not cope.[16] The worst example of this weakness came in 1372 when a fleet of 'all ships of 20 tons burden', including those of Winchelsea, was seized by 'the Constable of Dover and Guardian of the Cinque Ports', a man, according to Homan, of extremely dubious character. This fleet was sent, manned by impressed Portsmen to join the Earl of Pembroke at Southampton and sail with him to La Rochelle. Disaster ensued. The Black Prince's unfortunate involvement in Castilian politics had given the Castilians an enhanced reason for joining France to defeat the English and on this occasion their ships under Admiral Bocanegra did so mercilessly. 'The English fleet ... was utterly defeated and destroyed by the Spaniards. Those on board were either killed or taken to Spain as prisoners.'[17]

The ability of the English to defend their shores was again weakened. Hastings and Rye were soon to suffer as a result, although, on the next occasion Winchelsea, remarkably, escaped.

Warnings were plentiful. Rye was directed, as early as May 1376, to 'put all the able-bodied men in arms and to fortify the town that they might be able to resist their enemies'. No-one must leave the town or take away his property.[18] Cooper accepts the account of a chronicler who says that, when this threat became a reality in the following year, after devastating attacks on ports further west, the men of Rye, in cowardly manner, did just that – fled the town and took away their property. Other accounts are less critical, reporting that, in 1377, the French, under Admiral

Jean de Vienne, 'sailed for the Port of Rye which they burnt ... putting to death the inhabitants, not sparing man or woman',[19] which makes it sound much more like the attack on Winchelsea seventeen years previously. L. A. Vidler, provides a convincing and balanced account. He accepts that the French overcame Rye 'owing to the poor spirit of the defenders' and decided to use it as a base for ravaging the surrounding countryside. However they were put off by reports that the Abbot of Battle was raising a major force against them and, 'hearing this, decided to evacuate Rye after loading up their ships with 42 hogsheads of wine and much rich booty, including the church bells, they took four of the richest men as hostages, slaughtered sixty-six people of both sexes, who doubtless attempted to defend their property, set the town on fire and got safely away'.[20] The removal of the church bells was an appalling insult.

Two things are not in dispute. The attack followed only five days after the death of King Edward III and was intended to probe the perceived weakness of a country now with a regency and a boy, Richard II, on the throne and Winchelsea's hero of the hour was Hamo of Offington, Abbot of Battle. Here we must concentrate on how the abbot's actions affected the town. There are two versions. The first is that, after sacking Rye, the French did not depart with their booty as Vidler describes but demanded that Hamo of Offington who was responsible for the defence of Winchelsea, should pay a ransom to save the town from destruction. This he refused to do so the French attacked, 'fighting from morning till vespers' but the abbot had gathered such a considerable force that they failed and were beaten off.[21] The second version is that Abbot Hamo gathered together such a formidable force to defend Winchelsea and the area round Rye that the French were deterred from moving further afield 'and action there was limited to shelling from the sea'. The French then turned their attention back to Rye in frustration, setting about their looting and burning and eventually departing with their booty and the bells.[22]

Whatever the true course of events, the abbot certainly ensured that Winchelsea did not suffer as it had in 1360. Hastings, like Rye, suffered grievously and was ruthlessly fired. J. Manwaring Baines describes an archaeological excavation carried out in 1952 in Hastings High Street which revealed the effect of the intense heat of this raid and an earlier one on the town's medieval buildings.[23]

The men of Rye, supported by Winchelsea, responded to this attack with vigour. There seems to be no evidence that they were joined by the men of Hastings. In the following year, 1378, 'they gathered together a large number of men and ships and sailed for Normandy. Having arrived by night off a town called Peter's Haven [Portus Petri] they landed and slew all who resisted'. Hostages from among the wealthy were taken for ransom; there was much looting and the town was set ablaze. The attackers then 'proceeded to a place named Wilet [Wylet] not far away, treated that in the same fashion and returned home well pleased'.[24]

They may indeed have been pleased for their choice of towns to attack had been the result of good intelligence; among the spoils carried proudly back to Rye were the town's recaptured church bells.

28. ATTACKED AGAIN

The men of Winchelsea no doubt fully shared the pleasure of those of Rye at this successful riposte but the elation of revenge cannot have lasted long. Both the status of their town and its very survival were soon to be threatened again.

Abbot Hamo's defence in 1377, however brave and resourceful, could not save Winchelsea from a severe blow to its pride. 'The decline of the town had become such that in 1378 Chichester supplanted Winchelsea as the chief Sussex port.'[1]

Worse was to follow. The problem was foreseen but this time too late. In 1379 the Abbot of Battle was instructed to hold an inquiry into reports that the Dinsdale Marsh and a nearby road had been inundated by the sea. Those responsible for this neglect must be identified. Houses, too, were under threat. If this was not quickly remedied, assistance and supplies would be very difficult to obtain should the town again come under attack.[2] This must have been the road beyond the New Gate towards Icklesham and Pett. Almost exactly a year later a further Patent Roll addressed to the abbot and also to William Batsford and Edward Dallingridge said that the king (by which it actually meant the regent, John of Gaunt, and his ministers) was very concerned about the possible effect on the country of the loss of Winchelsea in those troubled times, the town being 'situated on the coast facing their enemies. The fortifications ... are insufficient without the king's assistance against hostile aggression for the security of the town and the barons inhabiting it'.[3] The recipients of these instructions were influential men. William Batsford was Lord of the Manor of Buckholt near Bexhill and about to be appointed Constable of Pevensey Castle;[4] Edward Dallingridge, like the abbot, was much involved in the defence of the area and was soon to receive permission to fortify his castle at Bodiam.

When the blow fell it came, principally at least, not from the French but from their Castilian allies; revenge for defeat in the Battle of Winchelsea perhaps. N.A.M. Rodger states that, in 1380, 'the Castilians, with only one French galley in company, burnt Winchelsea and Gravesend and threatened London.'[5] P.E. Russell confirms the presence of the single French galley which he says joined, among other Spanish vessels, 'seventeen galleys based on Seville and two from Santander' at Harfleur before sailing across the Channel to Winchelsea.[6] This was a formidable force. We do not know that it needed to broach any defences which may have been in place for this is the occasion when tradition has it that the attackers were treacherously admitted through the New Gate.

There is little direct evidence of the nature of the damage done to Winchelsea on this occasion. Homan quotes Thomas of Walsingham, when writing of the wars about 1380 as saying, 'Amongst the dreadful damage which befell our country, was that they took the town of Winchelsea and put to flight the Abbot of Battle and all his followers when they tried to assist the town'.[7]

So it seems that on this occasion the abbot failed in his task. We must have sympathy for him if he was, indeed, betrayed by those who admitted the enemy. The results were so devastating that 'there can be little doubt that what was left of the original houses was wiped out when Winchelsea was sacked and temporarily abandoned in 1380'.[8]

Following the raid the Lord Warden of the Cinque Ports, under royal instructions, held a meeting 'of the mayors, barons and leading seamen, [to] point out to them the dangers to be feared if the command of the sea was not regained, ask their advice as to the measures expedient, and induce them to contribute towards the cost'.[9] These worthies could certainly advise, most of them could probably contribute, but the task was far beyond the Cinque Ports acting alone.

Unlike the original houses, two stone buildings which are presumed to have suffered most in this raid, the Pipewell Gate and St. Thomas's Church, survive in their reconstructed form. The rebuilding of the Pipewell Gate will feature later. With regard to the damage to St. Thomas's and the resulting works, W. M. Homan makes most interesting points based on a close study of the building. Presuming that the church, like St. Giles's in 1360, was used as a defensive point, he thinks it highly probable that the nave was burnt and largely destroyed and that the original central tower was 'levelled to the ground ... by undercutting the two west piers'.[10] Homan observed that a strong wall once existed closing the west side of the transepts and that there is evidence of the transept area having been roofed over. He dates these changes from this time, as he does the construction of entrance doors in the south and north transepts. These doors, now archways, he points out are of 'inferior local stone', suggesting that they were constructed at a time when Caen stone could not be obtained from Normandy'.[11] The date of the abandonment of the transept area as a used part of the building, resulting in the present ruins, remains a matter for speculation.

The Spanish seem to have taken some pride in the havoc they wrought in Winchelsea at this time for the raid is commemorated by a plaque in Luarca which depicts men and ships of the Spanish fleet with the legend, 'Ships from Luarca with the Spanish fleet under the command of Admiral Sanchez Tovar sailed up the Thames and set fire to Winchelsea and parts of London'. The name of the admiral apparently fixes the date as 1380. There is much about the admiral and the background to the war at that time in the Municipal Archives of the Council of Valdes. The

(48) The Pipewell Gate, badly damaged in the 1380 attack on Winchelsea and later rebuilt or repaired under the supervision of mayor John Helde.

municipal authorities admit that there is no direct evidence that their ships took part in the raid but the existence of the commemorative plaque is not in doubt. It was spotted twice during the twentieth century by visitors from Winchelsea and these sightings led to interesting investigations by Freemen J.B.L. Clark and D.R. Bourne.[12]

Long before their misfortune was commemorated by the Luarca plaque the men of Winchelsea had to attempt some return to normality within their town, but this was not easily accomplished. It was made more difficult because the need for war finance and the resultant ever increasing taxation, at least temporarily de-stabilised English society. In 1381, just one year after the Winchelsea raid, came the Peasants' Revolt. John of Gaunt's government made the mistake of introducing a poll tax which took no account of individual wealth but, for everybody, was levied at 'a shilling a head per household'.[13] The perceived injustice of this brought the country to the brink of a successful major revolution. One of the underlying causes concerns us more here. Citizens, particularly those of the south-east, felt great resentment that the government was not doing enough to protect the coasts from raids such as that on Winchelsea. The innate loyalty and responsibility of those who supported the revolt is demonstrated by the peasants' leaders, 'patriots first and rebels second'. They issued instructions that those supporters who dwelt in the ports of the south-east coast should not join the march on London but should remain to mount whatever defence was possible against any French attack.[14] This particular complaint was emphasised by the Speaker of the House of Commons at the subsequent inquiry when he reported, 'The common people have not been succoured against the enemies of the realm for they and their homes have been pillaged and robbed and burned ... for which no remedy has been or is yet provided'.[15] The common people of Winchelsea had suffered as much as any.

And not only the common people. Following the 1380 raid, although the exact date of the letter is not known, John of Gaunt, no less, issued a circular addressed to 'Archbishops, Bishops, Abbots, Archdeacons etc.' in which he drew attention to the plight of 'the Master and Brethren of the Hospital of our lady of Nazareth and St. Bartholomew the Apostle in Winchelsea'. Their premises had been 'lately burnt and destroyed by French enemies'. The fact that the enemies were mostly Spanish does not reduce the deprivation! The community could only continue to exist if the clergy urged on their parishes the provision of substantial financial support through the appeal of one Richard Lacock who was touring the country seeking funds for St. Bartholomew's. Sheriffs, mayors and bailiffs were also urged to respond generously to this appeal.[16]

This interest in Winchelsea's impoverished and desolate state was reflected in 1384 by a petition to the king from the House of Commons asking 'that some steps might be taken towards the defence of Rye and Winchelsea "because if these towns be taken, which God forbid, the whole country would be destroyed"'.[17] This parliament was held at Salisbury and it would be nice to think that the petition received the wholehearted supported of Rye and Winchelsea's fellow portsmen. Unhappily it is recorded that after the parliament had been in session for a week 'no elected 'barons' from the Cinque Ports had arrived'![18] Perhaps, like their fellows during the Peasants' Revolt, they had stayed behind for fear of enemy attack.

There can be no doubt of Winchelsea's poor condition at this time. So many buildings had been razed to the ground that there was confusion over identifying plot boundaries and the names of owners. The reduced income of Winchelsea landowners made it very difficult for them to pay the rents due to the crown and to provide the ship service which was their traditional duty.[19] 'Refugees from Winchelsea, rich and poor alike, were living semi-permanently in Battle.'[20] Simon de Burely, Warden of the Cinque Ports, and the Bailiff of Winchelsea were ordered by King

Richard II to seek out absentee Winchelsea landowners and demand that they take steps to rebuild and re-occupy their homes or at least ensure that they were properly tenanted. If they failed to do so their property would be forfeited.[21] Eventually it had to be accepted that a town of the size originally laid out was no longer sustainable and that building should be concentrated in an area not much larger than the present built-up area.[22] Plans were prepared for the secure enclosure of this reduced area but another thirty-five years were to pass before action was initiated.[23]

This impoverishment is well illustrated by the condition of the bailiwick. In 1384 Roger de Wigemore, King's Bailiff of Winchelsea and the Manor of Iham, perhaps overwhelmed by the above task, asked to be relieved of his duties. This application was granted and Simon Colred was appointed bailiff 'for life during good behaviour without his rendering ought therefor'.[24] That the bailiff should be required to make no return to the crown was a startling development. Winchelsea was clearly in a bad way and can hardly have been expected to recover.

The order requiring re-occupation of plots seems to have had some effect for by 1388 the town, even in the reduced area, was much better populated 'to judge by the town accounts and the money available for expenses at that date'.[25]

However, even as things began to improve slightly, the fear of invasion was never far away.

(49) John Helde's name, now almost weathered away, appears on the north-west face of the Pipewell Gate

29. TROUBLED TIMES CONTINUE

In 1385, for example, there was 'information of an imminent invasion of the ports by the French with a large army'.[1] To support defensive measures large numbers of south-east ports, Winchelsea and Rye heading the list, were authorised to make 'a levy of threepence on every boatload of fish landed'.[2] Whatever may have been Winchelsea's use of this additional income, Rye took its preparations to repel attack very seriously, mounting a permanent watch in the Ypres Tower and training its inhabitants to prepare 'a fearsome mixture of molten lead and boiling oil ... which would be poured through holes in the ceiling on any intruders who broke into the ground floor of the tower'.[3]

Winchelsea seems to have had neither the manpower nor the will similarly to prepare but, in the following year, it received assistance from an unexpected source. The French, clearly demonstrating the accuracy of reports of an imminent invasion, had constructed a remarkable piece of medieval prefabrication, an enormous wooden palisade twenty feet high, '3000 paces long', with, at regular intervals, towers 'capable of holding ten gunners'. This elaborate and expensive structure was intended to be quickly erected at any point where a successful landing was made on the English shore 'so that the lords could withdraw there for a night to avoid the danger of alarms and disturbances'.[4] It was also portable and could, no doubt with considerable effort, accompany any advance. Fortunately for Winchelsea these plans went considerably awry when ships carrying parts of the palisade were captured, together with its master carpenter, by Sir William Beauchamp, Constable of Calais, Calais being, of course, at that time held by the English.[5] The palisade was triumphantly transported across the Channel and erected round Winchelsea.

The authorities thus demonstrated some willingness to defend the nation where local action was lacking. As far as the people of England were concerned, though, the appointment of the Earl of Arundel to defend the coasts of Kent and Sussex was a much more positive step. He not only achieved 'a brilliant victory off Margate over a combined French and Spanish fleet' but also destroyed the defences of Brest and returned home with vast quantities of captured wine 'which was sold off cheaply at home'.[6] No wonder he was popular!

The real responsibility for defence, though, continued to lie within the town. In 1388-1389 Winchelsea was assisting with the maintenance of a beacon at Fairlight, the lighting of which would warn of an enemy approach. During the same accounting period 'fifty-five shillings and fourpence,' was paid to the men (probably eighty-three of them at fourpence a day) 'who came for the salvation of the town'.[7] Winchelsea was on the alert again.

Evidence of the town's poor condition after the 1380 raid is considerable and the palisade no doubt increased its confidence if not its prosperity. However there was never any proposal at this time which would alter Winchelsea's leading position of responsibility within the western Cinque Ports. Rather the contrary; in 1392 the situation was clarified and formalised anew. Any ship service requirement was 'to be discharged in the old proportion of five ships from Hastings and its members [notably Seaford and Pevensey], ten from Winchelsea and five from Rye'.[8] These figures only made the proportions of financial responsibility clear for the actual number of ships provided by the Cinque Ports, now that they were much larger, had been agreed in 1387 as ten, with six hundred men.[9] The Cinque Ports were providing a smaller proportion of the national fleet but Winchelsea's relative contribution remained undiminished.

Quite apart from this contribution, there were other expenses involved in membership of

(50) The Old Malthouse, The Strand, stands on the original frontage of Winchelsea's harbour on the River Brede

the Confederation, particularly attendance at meetings. A large part of the expenditure recorded in Winchelsea's accounts of the time was to pay for the mayor and jurats' attendance at Cinque Ports meetings. They sometimes travelled on horseback and sometimes by sea. The former method throws more light on the circumstances of the day; it included paying twopence per horse for use of ferries at Winchelsea and Oxney.[10] Another interpretation of these accounts assumes that the Winchelsea representatives, in order to reach New Romney, had to take a boat 'via the Camber to Snargate and [continue] from there on horseback'.[11]

The withdrawal of the Castilian fleet from hostilities in 1390 and a truce with France in 1396 greatly improved the safety of trade and travel in the Channel. Winchelsea benefited but its men took advantage of the situation for personal gain. In 1400 the new king, Henry IV, was forced to issue instructions to Winchelsea, among others, that 'no one should carry out of the port any ship or armed vessel to go against the French or any of their allies except the Scots, contrary to the present truce'.[12] The exception is an interesting one. Clearly the men of Winchelsea had permission to attack and harass Scottish vessels whenever they could!

The reduced population and prosperity of Winchelsea brought about further assistance in 1400 when 'the arrayers of men-at-arms, armed men and archers for the counties of Kent and Sussex,' that is those responsible for finding troops for the local levy, 'were specially ordered not to meddle with Hastings, Winchelsea, Rye and their members'.[13] The defence of the town and the provision of sailors for the Cinque Ports fleet was as much as could be managed.

A further entry in the town's accounts makes clear that it was involved in extremely early imports of beer. In 1400 eight barrels came through Winchelsea harbour, valued at 21s 8d each. The mayor bought a considerable amount, 'four measures at thirty-one shillings a measure'.[14] It would be fun to assume that this was for his consumption and for civic entertainment. However, it is much more likely to have been as a public duty for in 1399 John Helde, then serving as Mayor of Winchelsea, '[took] an active part in buying beer and other provisions for the crews of the five ships supplied by Winchelsea for Richard II's expedition to Ireland'.[15] Leaving the country for this expedition was to be a major factor in Richard's loss of his throne.

Imports of all kinds, including beer, would have been potentially affected by the continued silting of the harbour on the River Brede. King Henry IV was not amused. He had been informed that many sailors, both English and foreign, had been responsible for emptying 'stones, sand and other ballast' into the river channel. The king noted that, 'vessels laden with merchandise have been unable conveniently to enter the port as formerly, which tends to the destruction and danger of our town and its adjacent haven'.[16] One of the principal reasons was that, as we have seen, Winchelsea's main export was wood, a heavy cargo; ships arriving to collect it had to be in ballast for stability unless carrying a different substantial load.[17] Such dumping, of course, had an insidious and increasingly disastrous affect on the tidal flow of the river and its ability to scour the harbour and keep it free of silt. Four commissioners were appointed to conduct an inquiry, supervise the port, allocate sites where ballast could be left without the tidal flow being affected, and make sure those sites were used. They cannot have been very successful for twenty years later major works, equally unsuccessful, were commenced with this same purpose in mind.

At this point, with the harbour declining and the population unable to ensure the defence of their town, it is worth pausing to examine the activities of a strange assortment of Winchelsea parliamentarians. Two representatives to the House of Commons were elected by the freemen of the town on receipt of the Lord Warden's summons. The result of the election had to be taken to the Lord Warden at Dover by messenger. The Lord Warden compiled a full list of those returned by the Cinque Ports and informed the parliamentary officials.[18] At this time Winchelsea, very properly, elected its leading citizens. We have seen that this was not necessarily likely to make them all upright and law-abiding!

Among those whose indiscretions are recorded was Robert Arnold. Arnold was the second of three Winchelsea men of that name who are presumed to have been father, son and grandson. The father served five terms as mayor between 1351 and 1359; the son held the same office between 1391 and 1394. He was elected to parliament in 1393, during his mayoralty, but had also been member for Winchelsea in 1377 and must have been much respected within the Confederation of the Cinque Ports for in 1389 he was engaged by the Confederation to represent them in claiming confirmation of their customary exemption from national taxation, a privilege resulting from their ship service duties. Arnold's recorded indiscretion? 'In 1397 the new parson of Winchelsea complained to the chancellor that Arnold and others had attacked and wounded him while he was saying mass in his church on 24 June and had carried off his service book and the offertory.'[19] We do not know what provoked the violence or the theft.

Among Arnold's successors at Westminster was Vincent Finch who had formerly been discredited for owing money to Arnold's father and others. At that time borrowing money at a rate of interest was not permitted for Christians and special arrangements were made for repayment, to avoid that situation.[20] Robert Arnold senior and his colleagues were not the only local worthies to whom Vincent Finch at one time owed money but his fortunes greatly increased when he inherited substantial land in the area and he became MP for Winchelsea in 1395, 1397 and 1402.[21] Finch's family had been 'merchants of importance at the founding of New Winchelsea'.[22] Instead of borrowing money illegally, Finch was later donating it for in 1413 a grant was made to the Franciscans providing for 'a mass [to be] said for Vincent Finch and his wife Isabella on their death and their names [to] be written in the gilt book of the convent amongst the chief benefactors'.[23] The Finches were to have a long and distinguished history of parliamentary service and eventually to become the Earls of Winchilsea.

Quite apart from his early financial mismanagement this Vincent Finch also had the misfortune, along with John Helde, Winchelsea's MP in 1397, to become involved with Benedict Sely of Winchelsea. Sely was a strong supporter of Richard II and served at Richard's court. Unfortunately for him he was a bit too strong a supporter for he took part in what is known as the Epiphany Plot to assassinate Richard's successor, King Henry IV. Sely received the usual medieval treatment for such a crime – he was hanged, drawn and quartered. It has even been suggested that a bit of him was sent to Winchelsea to be displayed as a warning.[24] Unaware of his connection with Sely, King Henry appointed Vincent Finch escheator for the county of Sussex, a prestigious royal appointment. Two months later the king found out and the appointment was hurriedly withdrawn![25]

It took much longer for royal officials to find out about John Helde's similar association with Sely. Helde was Sely's executor and continued to administer his Winchelsea lands until 1404 when the Exchequer eventually discovered that they should have been forfeited to the crown.[26] I hope that Helde profited from this administration. He might even have used those profits for the benefit of the town because he is the mayor who is credited with overseeing the rebuilding of the Pipewell Gate after its destruction when Winchelsea came under attack in 1380. Helde's arms and name are displayed upon it, although now much eroded. It has always been assumed that the date of Pipewell Gate's restoration was 1404 when Helde was mayor, although his mayoralty is listed on the Court Hall boards as commencing in 1405. We do not know how this occurred. Perhaps the calligrapher engaged to inscribe the names realised that he had made an awful mistake and hoped no one would notice! 1404 is the correct date.

When writing about this W.M. Homan comments with some prescience that the year 1404 is presumed to be the date for what he describes as 'the patching up' of Pipewell Gate because of Helde's mayoralty 'but he probably held the office at other times as well'.[27] Indeed he did. The publication of *The History of Parliament - The Commons* since Homan's time has shown that Helde was also mayor in 1399 and 1401. The gate's restoration may therefore have taken place as much as five years earlier.

The last of our indiscreet or unfortunate members during this period was Thomas Bette who represented Winchelsea in 1383, 1384 and 1393. Bette was a wine importer about whom 'certain unspecified allegations' regarding the propriety of his conduct were made to Sir William Fiennes, Sheriff of Surrey and Sussex. The Winchelsea authorities obviously thought this an injustice for they sent a representative to speak on Bette's behalf.[28]

As we leave these brief accounts of Winchelsea residents' activities and move into the fifteenth century, troubled times and the need for further defensive measures will continue to be a preoccupation.

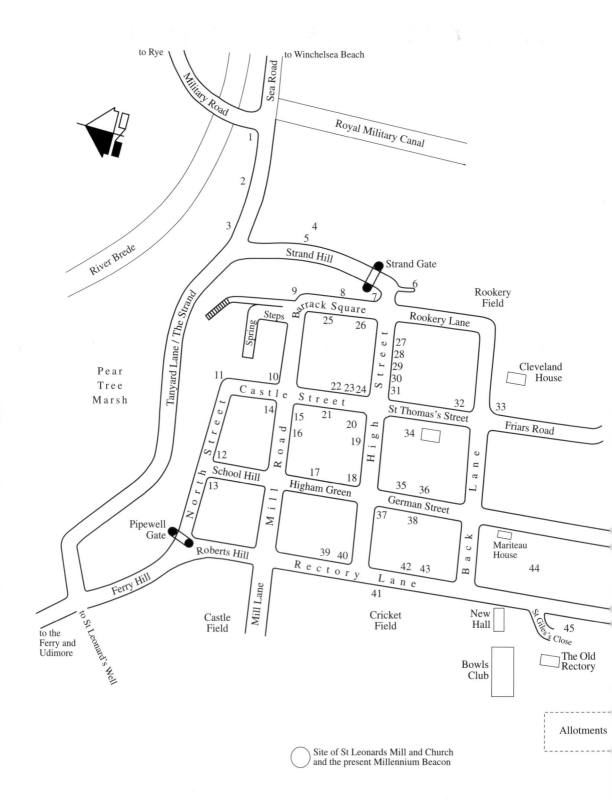

to Rye

to Winchelsea Beach

Military Road

Sea Road

Royal Military Canal

1

2

3

River Brede

4
5

Strand Hill

Strand Gate

6

Rookery Field

9   8
7

Tanyard Lane / The Strand

Barrack Square

Spring   Steps

25   26

Rookery Lane

Pear Tree Marsh

Street

27
28
29
30
31

Cleveland House

11   10

Castle   Street

22 23 24

32   33

North Street

14

15   21

20

High

St Thomas's Street

Friars Road

Mill   Road

16

19

34

Lane

12

School Hill

17   18

German Street

35   36

13

Higham Green

Pipewell Gate

Roberts Hill

39   40

Rectory   Lane

37   38

Back

Mariteau House   44

Ferry Hill

42   43

41

to the Ferry and Udimore

to St Leonard's Well

Castle Field

Mill Lane

Cricket Field

New Hall

St Giles's Close

45

Bowls Club

The Old Rectory

Allotments

Site of St Leonards Mill and Church and the present Millennium Beacon

WINCHELSEA TOWN

1	Strand Garage	23	Town Well
2	Bridge Inn	24	Periteau House
3	The Old Malthouse	25	The Barrack Houses
4	Strand House	26	Stone House
5	Crowsnest	27	Nesbit
6	The Lookout	28	former Post Office
7	The Retreat	29	The Tea Tree
8	Cooks Green	30	Wren Cottage
9	Alards	31	Firebrand
10	Five Chimneys	32	Glebe
11	King's Leap	33	White Cottage
12	The Five Houses	34	St Thomas's Church
13	Saffron Gardens	35	Town sign
14	Salutation Cottages	36	Wesley's Tree
	(formerly Inn)	37	New Inn
15	Three Kings	38	Balladers Plat
16	New Cottage	39	Westway
17	Chapel Plat	40	Firin
18	Court Hall	41	Blackfriars Barn
19	Bank House	42	Wesley's Chapel
20	Magazine House	43	Evens
21	Old Castle House	44	Truncheons
	(formerly Castle Inn)	45	St Giles's Church (site of)
22	The Armoury	46	St John's Hospital surviving gable

Chapel ruins

St Thomas's School

Greyfriars (The Friars)

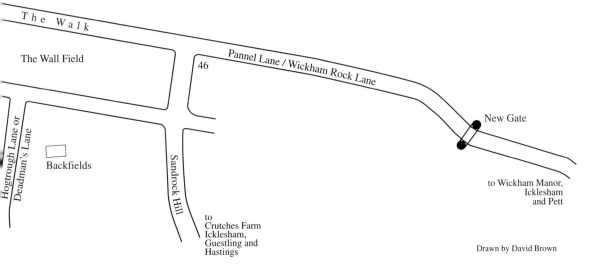

The Walk

The Wall Field

Pannel Lane / Wickham Rock Lane

46

Hogtrough Lane or Deadman's Lane

Backfields

Sandrock Hill

New Gate

to Crutches Farm Icklesham, Guestling and Hastings

to Wickham Manor, Icklesham and Pett

Drawn by David Brown

30. TOWARDS NEW WALLS

In no aspect of the life of the town were times more troubled than for the church, no fewer than five of Winchelsea's religious establishments being adversely affected during the early 1400s.

Things seemed to be going well at St. Thomas's in 1401 when Hugh Setour, rector, was granted, along with his successors, the dues from the town's fishing fleet which had earlier been payable to the king's bailiff. This was worth little in time of war (when the fleet wasn't fishing!) but in peacetime brought in as much as 100 shillings annually, a worthwhile sum. W. M. Homan assumes that this grant was part of the monarch's attempt to gain the support of local clergy in challenging the supremacy of the church of Rome. For Henry IV to gain control of the English clergy and their appointment would be a great political coup and would also prevent much money leaving the country for Rome as the papal levy.[1]

Such a reformation had to wait more than another 130 years and this particular extra income seems to have done Hugh Setour no good at all for he was soon excommunicated by Bishop Robert Rede of Chichester, appealing twice in 1404 and 1405.[2] Sadly we have no details of the reason for the action against him but he probably defaulted in payment of church dues. Whatever Hugh Setour's fate, the fishing income was not lost to his successors for the grant to the Rector of St. Thomas's of 'a tenth of the fishery [in Winchelsea] called Christ's share' was confirmed by King Henry VI in 1426.[3]

Perhaps it was disgruntled sailors, part of whose income was being lost, who were responsible for an attack on one of those successors, William Tyrrell. E. F. Jacob comments that there were many serious cases of violence against the clergy at this time 'none, perhaps, worse than one on the Rector [of St. Thomas's] who was assaulted while reading the gospel at mass. His opponents who beat and wounded him, took away the book that was before him and the oblations and carried them off'.[4] This sounds suspiciously like the previously mentioned attack perpetrated by Robert Arnold but, as such incidents were common, was probably different.

The Blackfriars were in even more serious trouble for in 1402 their prior was accused of high treason. The prior had been a supporter of the deposed Richard II and the royal sergeant-at-arms was sent to arrest him. He was remanded by the privy council to the Tower of London. No documentary evidence survives of the prior's fate but it can readily be assumed that he shared that of many 'whose lives were forfeited by their opposition to the new dynasty and whose quartered limbs rotted at the gates of the chief cities and towns of the kingdom'.[5]

The Franciscans, too, were severely dealt with for similar sympathies. 'Early in 1402 the first execution of a Franciscan for treason occurred when a lay brother of the Aylesbury convent laid information against a priest of the house.' The order considered that Henry IV was entitled to be Duke of Lancaster but not king and even offered to join a force raised against him.[6] If any of the Winchelsea Greyfriars were known within their community to be King Richard's supporters, they must have looked about them with deep suspicion for fear of betrayal.

St. Leonard's Church at Iham, although never within the Liberty of Winchelsea, demonstrates for us the deprivation being experienced among the people of the area at the time for in 1404 'it was one of the benefices so impoverished as to be excused taxation'.[7]

Nine years later a severe blow fell upon St. Giles's Church for, on 28 December 1413, it 'was struck by lightning and burnt down.' The Victoria County History presumes that no attempt was made to rebuild it 'the living becoming a sinecure and no new appointments being made after 1500.'[8] We must not accept the failure to rebuild too readily for, had St. Giles's been in a ruinous

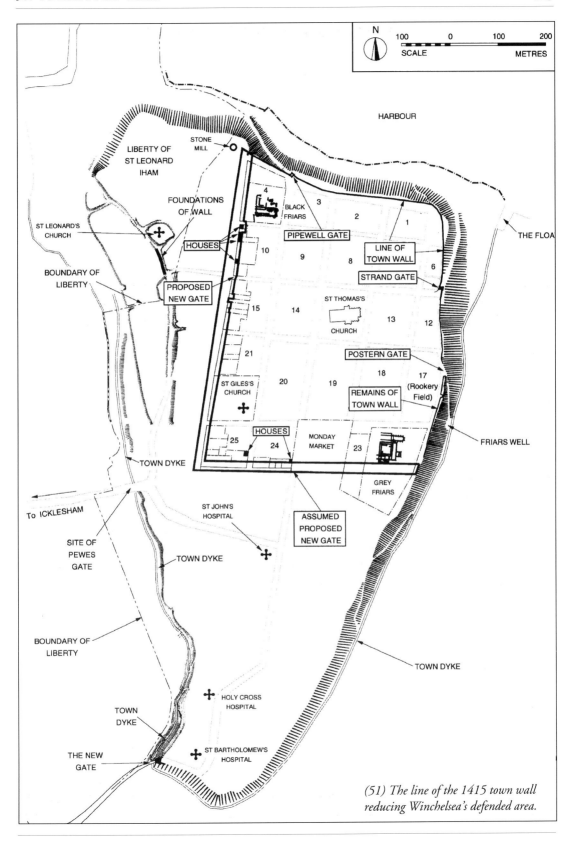

N

100   0   100   200

SCALE   METRES

HARBOUR

LIBERTY OF
ST LEONARD
IHAM

STONE
MILL

FOUNDATIONS
OF WALL

BLACK
FRIARS

ST LEONARD'S
CHURCH

PIPEWELL GATE

LINE OF
TOWN WALL

THE FLOA

HOUSES

STRAND GATE

BOUNDARY OF
LIBERTY

PROPOSED
NEW GATE

ST THOMAS'S

CHURCH

POSTERN GATE

ST GILES'S
CHURCH

17
(Rookery
Field)

REMAINS OF
TOWN WALL

FRIARS WELL

HOUSES

TOWN DYKE

MONDAY
MARKET

GREY
FRIARS

To ICKLESHAM

ST JOHN'S
HOSPITAL

ASSUMED
PROPOSED
NEW GATE

SITE OF
PEWES
GATE

TOWN DYKE

BOUNDARY OF
LIBERTY

TOWN DYKE

HOLY CROSS
HOSPITAL

TOWN
DYKE

ST BARTHOLOMEW'S
HOSPITAL

THE NEW
GATE

*(51) The line of the 1415 town wall
reducing Winchelsea's defended area.*

condition, this is highly likely to have been mentioned in the 1415 town wall inquiry.

While such misfortunes assailed the religious communities of Winchelsea, Thomas of Walsingham was providing us with a delightful snapshot of its position and particularly the problems facing those entering or leaving the town via the harbour. '[Winchelsea] stands on a hill very steep to the sea and overhanging the port; the road from it to which is not straight lest its great declivity should make people stumble headlong as they walk down, or oblige them rather to go up on all fours, but slopes downwards, turning sometime on one side and sometimes to the other.'[9] It would seem that since those days there has been much navvying to make the gradient of Strand Hill comparatively less formidable.

Such natural defences as the steepness of the hill of Iham which Walsingham describes were, however, proving inadequate in protecting the town against foreign incursion. With King Henry V on the throne and making belligerent threats against France, this problem became all the more acute.

The people of Winchelsea therefore petitioned to be allowed to reduce the size of the walled area of the town which enemy attack, the Black Death and consequent depopulation had made much too large. The king's permission was needed. The townsmen pointed out that there were now so few inhabitants that they could not hope to defend Winchelsea without outside help. Some property would be lost if the proposal were put into effect and the monarch was asked to accept that this would result in a reduction of the rent due to him which remained at £14 11s 5¾d as in 1292.[10]

The king commissioned Roger atte Gate and Thomas Oxenbridge to conduct an inquiry into the proposal. The full text of this inquiry survives.[11] Eventually the plans were approved with the exception of the suggestion that the king's income from town rents should be reduced!

The new walls would be of stone and lime and would enclose twenty-one of the original thirty-nine quarters. The parish church of St. Giles would be near the south-western corner and the land of the Greyfriars on the south-east. Sufficient land, more than two-thirds, would remain for Monday's Market to continue operating and the nearby administrative centre would be removed to a site central within the newly walled area near St. Thomas's Church. It would be possible to site the new wall in such a way that only five dwellings would have to be demolished, 'a clear indication of how few houses then stood in these suburban areas of the town'.[12]

There was to be a new town gate at the western end of the continuation of what we call the High Street, thus implying the reduced importance of goods arriving first at Monday's Market. The route to that new gate (never built) would climb the hill gently from the site of the present Motel towards the former site of the mill and turn eastwards towards the town. 'Alternatively, if required, traffic could continue ... passing through Iham and down into the marsh to the ferry, thereby by-passing Winchelsea altogether.'[13] However, this latter route soon fell into disuse as the circumstances of the time made it commercially more valuable to encourage all traffic to pass through the town. Winchelsea has waited in vain nearly six hundred years for the replacement of that by-pass! How many hundred more?

The fact that the road from St. Leonard's Church into Winchelsea would be blocked presented no problems, thus suggesting that the church was already little used.[14]

These plans also provide us with some insight into the circumstances of the Blackfriars at the time, half a century after their final settlement in Quarter 4. Their land was 'largely built upon' but they would lose only one house; 'their church buildings and garden would be unaffected'.[15] The existence of a gate to the Blackfriars site almost opposite Pipewell Gate is implied by the inquiry text. In early twentieth century photographs this stood 'to above the height of a man'. It has since, as already mentioned, been destroyed during road widening.[16]

With his plans to invade France in mind, the additional security for Winchelsea arising from these new walls clearly appealed to the king for 'liking such places to be strengthened and considering that the town was on the sea coast and facing the king's enemies' he authorised a grant of £400 towards the costs. A licence 'to build a wall, and to crenellate, tower and embattle it'[17] was issued. Associated deep-ditching was also authorised. Apart from requiring that his income from the town should not be reduced, King Henry also placed on the Winchelsea authorities the responsibility for negotiating with those whose holdings would be affected.[18]

The work was never completed but some evidence survives. There is an upstanding fragment in what would have been the north-west corner of the town and the ditch into which I recall scrambling on numerous occasions to retrieve cricket balls was also part of the work. It is also possible that the extant remains of the turreted town wall along the eastern side of Rookery Field date from this period.[19]

While wall-building was starting, shipbuilding was continuing. Considering the deprivations we have seen the town suffer, the size of the ships built at Winchelsea at this time is astonishing. Perhaps the most important of these was the carrack *Jesus*. A carrack was a multi-masted vessel, a vast improvement on the cogs which were so important in the earlier Cinque Ports fleet. The *Jesus* was a vessel of 1000 tons equipped with cannon.[20] This was an exceptional size for the period. She is believed to have been the second largest ship in the country[21] and was designed and built, along with many others, to be part of Henry V's fleet in the renewed Hundred Years War. David Howarth writes: 'Between 1410 and 1418, shipyards at Winchelsea and Southampton built ships for King Henry V up to 1400 tons – almost 200 feet in overall length and 50 in beam, ships of nearly the size of Nelson's *Victory*'.[22] Tonnage has been measured in various ways and that recorded for the *Jesus* is way below that of *Victory* but the length and beam are remarkably close. The extraordinary enterprise and craftsmanship needed by the shipwrights of

(52) The surviving north-western corner of the 1415 wall which reduced the defended area of the town.

Winchelsea to construct a vessel of this size in the early fifteenth century is perhaps further illustrated by noting that, 160 years later, when Martin Frobisher set out to seek the north-west passage he did so with ships of 25 and 20 tons.

After his death King Henry's fleet, no doubt including the *Jesus*, had to be sold to meet his debts. The precedent he created of building his own vessels at ports like Winchelsea was, however, followed by his successors. When those ships were not needed for action against an enemy, later monarchs often leased them out to trading merchants.[23] It is strange to record here that this was an almost exact reversal of the origins of the Cinque Ports' ship service.

Winchelsea men were not only active as shipbuilders in support the king, but also as owners. In 1415 the king owed Thomas Walsh, master of the *Gabriell de Wynchelse*, the sum of £12 1s 6d 'for the wages of himself and his mariners, sailing with the said ship with the king in his voyages beyond the sea'.[24] Walsh was allowed to draw that sum from the king's London customs income. Some writers have inferred from this that the *Gabriell de Wynchelse* was King Henry's flagship. It is more likely that she was just part of his fleet. Christopher Allmand, however, states categorically that King Henry, when he sailed with his army for France in 1417, had a Winchelsea flagship, not the *Gabriell* but the *Jesus*. He describes her as 'a great new clinker built ship of 1000 tons and representing something of an experiment in shipbuilding'.[25]

Winchelsea merchants would, undoubtedly, dearly have loved to be involved in providing for this expedition. In some ways they may have been but the vintners missed out. Orders were given to those responsible for victualling the fleet that wine was to be obtained at Winchelsea but 'by this time the trade had dwindled and it never recovered'.[26]

The Winchelsea man most to benefit, however, was William Catton who on three occasions represented the town in parliament. Catton was highly favoured by King Henry and his considerable income as Keeper and Clerk of the king's ships made the payment to Thomas Walsh look insignificant![27]

King Henry's army eventually left Southampton carried in about 1500 ships, mostly small. I believe that this fleet, much of which had been mustered at Winchelsea,[28] was the largest to carry an invading army across the Channel until the night of 5th/6th June 1944 when more than five thousand vessels performed the Cinque Ports' former task.

And so, briefly, to the invasion of France which followed all this frenetic activity. Only two glimpses of events which led to the victory at Agincourt and those which followed it are relevant to us. On its way across northern France from Harfleur the army passed Fécamp, a place which, through its abbey, featured earlier in these pages. One French chronicler claims that the soldiers stopped long enough to burn the town.[29] With his principal battle won, King Henry 'crossed with the chief prisoners from Calais ... He was met and carried ashore by the Barons of the Cinque Ports'.[30] It would seem that this landing was at Dover. I am sure that the barons of Winchelsea, having played so important a part, would have gained all the kudos they could by being associated with the triumphant progress which ended with the king's entry into a rejoicing London.

31. EXTRAORDINARY ORDINANCES

In the short term few benefits accrued for Winchelsea as a result of King Henry V's successes.

The French fleet continued to be a menace to shipping in the Channel and was of sufficient strength severely to delay a large expedition led by the Duke of Bedford which set out to relieve the blockade of Harfleur. Even a counter-invasion remained a possibility for a time. In this connection the system of invasion warning by beacon signal was expanded. Whether Winchelsea established its own beacon as part of this expansion is not known but it was certainly contributing towards the maintenance of one at Fairlight.[1]

Winchelsea may have suffered attack in 1418 while this major threat existed but the specific evidence is sketchy. A number of sources do, however, mention revenge attacks on the south coast after Agincourt and record the infliction of major damage and the entrapment of English vessels in their home harbours.[2]

King Henry's campaigns in France nevertheless gained momentum and threats to the Channel ports were consequently reduced. Eventually the Treaty of Troyes (1420) achieved Henry's ambition to claim the throne of France. He was to be regent for Charles VI during his lifetime and succeed him on his death. Meanwhile he would marry Charles's daughter Catherine.[3] Winchelsea featured in these arrangements only as the port of departure of Archbishop Henry Chichele for France, presumably to officiate at the wedding.[4]

Of the king's premature death, W. M. Homan, a persistent and consistent critic of the belligerent attitude of English monarchs towards France, writes: 'On 31 August 1422, fortunately for the peace of England and western Europe, Henry V died in his 34th year. His ambition and vanity had caused much bloodshed and misery both to the English and the French. The unjustifiable renewal of the wars with France was a catastrophe to the prosperity of western Europe and in the end brought England nothing but loss. Commercial towns such as Winchelsea, largely depending on shipping and trade with other countries, were naturally among the first to suffer from prolonged hostilities'.[5] This last point is telling. While the reasons for Winchelsea's decline are generally accepted as the withdrawal of the sea, the silting of the harbour, the French raids, and the Black Death, the constant detrimental effect of the Hundred Years War on Winchelsea's trade is an often neglected factor.

During King Henry's later years Winchelsea was struggling to reduce the effect of one of the above causes, the silting of the harbour. The principal effort went into major engineering works in the Brede Valley. The old channel of the river was abandoned and a new one cut. The extent of the project and the work involved is illustrated by the length and width of this newly dug channel. It was 4½ miles long and was 'enclosed within banks some 165 yards apart'. This enormous effort must have been designed to increase the ability of the tidal flow to scour out the accumulating silt from Winchelsea harbour. In the process it made the river navigable as far as Brede Bridge.[6] It remained so until the early twentieth century but the resulting scouring was ineffective.

Among Winchelsea's leading residents of the time was Thomas Thunder. Thunder's family followed the habit, confusing to the modern researcher, of repeating the same Christian names. His father and his son seem also to have been Thomas Thunder. The middle of the three, with whom we are concerned here, served as mayor on at least nine occasions and was elected as one of Winchelsea's MPs four times between 1421 and 1435. Thunder was a merchant trader in herring, Winchelsea's principal catch of the time. He had served as a member of the jury summoned to

(53) In earlier years Winchelsea assisted in the maintenance of the Fairlight beacon; whether it had its own is not known. The present beacon stands close to the site of St. Leonard's Mill. It was first fired on 4 August 2000 in celebration of the one-hundredth birthday of Her Majesty Queen Elizabeth the Queen Mother

report to the inquiry into the reduction of Winchelsea's walled area and reported during his mayoralties on the progress of the work and accounted for such grants as had been made available. As a leading shipowner he recognised that by 1436 threats to shipping in the Channel had re-intensified and was among those licensed to 'fit out their ships to safeguard the Channel against the king's enemies'.[7]

It was in 1427, while Thomas Thunder was serving as the town's MP for the second time, that a series of Ordinances were issued by the mayor and corporation for recording existing laws and adding new ones for the proper government of the town. It would be more relevant to know who the mayor was rather than the MP but, frustratingly, 1427 is one of only three years between 1404 and the present day for which we have no mayoral name. Whoever he was, the mayor must have been a busy official bearing very considerable responsibility for the supervision of the many statutes included in these documents, some new and some part of Winchelsea' traditional laws.

The ordinances for the implementation of which he and his successors were answerable provide a fascinating insight into life in a medieval town and well repay some attention here. The document, or rather the nineteenth century transcription which I am able to use, is in two parts, one headed 'Ordinances of the Town of Winchelsea, 5th Henry VI Anno Domini 1427 and the other, with the same date, 'Proclamation of the Mayor and Jurats of Winchelsea'.

The early clauses lay down rules for merchants like Thomas Thunder but particularly for merchants who are strangers. The whole document, indeed, is extremely suspicious of the activities of strangers which, in view of what Winchelsea had suffered at the hands of the French, and the continuing threat, is understandable.

It is made clear that the maltote, or bad tax, on wool imposed by King Edward I was still being levied despite his promise that it should be withdrawn. Apart from this, all masters bringing vessels containing goods for sale into Winchelsea harbour were required to report to the mayor and, upon oath, state exactly what their ships contained and to whom the contents belonged. These declarations had to be recorded by the town clerk. Failure to comply brought a fine of twenty shillings and the mayor was empowered to raise the money by confiscation of merchandise to that value, or, if necessary, of the ship itself. If any merchant was fortunate enough to bring into the town, by either land or sea, goods whose value exceeded 100 shillings, everything above that value had to be offered for sale to the 'mayor and commonalty' and if they refused it everyone was entitled to bid. It seems it did not pay to import in large quantities!

Restrictions on strangers included complete bans on selling to each other, on landing wine and then re-exporting it, on selling wine without the mayor's permission, on selling anything anywhere except at the market place, and on conducting any trade or business in the town for more that a year and a day without applying for the freedom. By then they would hardly be strangers anyway, particularly as any person running 'any hostelrye or otherwise' was to be imprisoned if he or she allowed, without good cause, a stranger to stay more than one night and one day, unless the mayor had given permission. Strangers from Picardy received particularly short shrift. Any 'fisher boat' from that region had to pay five shillings on first entering the harbour and on each subsequent visit must provide for the mayor three mackerel 'if so many be in the boat'.

Importing through the harbour was further controlled and supervised by rules laid down for the porters who carried the goods up the hill into the town. They were required 'truly and duly' (a phrase which survives in the oaths of the chamberlain and sergeant-at-mace taken at the mayoring to this day) 'to certify [to] the mayor and common clerk' how much wine, oil, honey, wax or any other merchandise they brought into the town whether it be 'tonned, pyped, barelled or bayled'. The punishment for failure to comply was a fine of six shillings and eightpence and any offender lost his job. The removal of a man's livelihood in medieval times would have been quite enough of a threat to ensure that these rules were meticulously kept unless bribery by a merchant ensured the porter's future employment.

Citizens who kept a shop or shops paid taxes according to the extent of their sales. If they bought corn either in the town or outside and re-sold it anywhere in England they paid one penny for every horse-load. Preventing goods entering the town was punishable, too, by a fine of three shillings and fourpence and the confiscation of anything acquired in that way.

Users of the harbour were charged wharfage according to the nature or value of the merchandise. Each tun of wine landed at the quay cost one penny; other goods were charged either by assessable weight, or by noting how they were carried. Anything two men could carry cost one farthing, the same charge as for 'every horse load'. Sometimes the horses counted as goods rather than carriers. The charge 'for every horse or great beast shipped or unshipped' was one penny. Even though they could hardly be described as 'great beasts,' sheep were charged at the same rate. Vessel-masters had to pay extra fees if they took too long unloading and prevented the use of the wharf by others.

Controls upon the day to day lives of the citizens were just as restrictive as those upon merchants. 'Common women' came in for particular attention. They might not dwell in the principal streets of the town but only on the outskirts. There was a quarterly fine for disobeying this rule. Six shillings and eightpence was payable to the town and twelve pence to the town sergeant. If this officer found out about such a transgression by a 'common woman' and failed to enforce the fine he must pay it himself. These women were also banned from walking anywhere in the town after curfew and if they were seen wearing a hood it would be confiscated.

Nobody, including the butchers who seem to have been regular offenders, must throw 'gore ne filth' beside the walls. Butchers were imprisoned if they permitted the sale of any 'unholsum' or bad meat. A similar punishment awaited them if they discarded any blood or 'other corruption' of beasts slain at Monday's Market in the streets of the town or on its pendants (the steep slopes on the north and east sides). Anyone reporting the throwing of 'dong into the haven' and giving evidence against the culprit, would be rewarded. It seems it was not uncommon for dung and other offensive matter to be thrown over the town walls. Similar punishment ensued.

No one was allowed to let their pigs loose in the streets. Any pigs found would be killed. Sheep similarly loose, however, were more leniently treated; the owners were fined one halfpenny per animal caught.

It illustrates the stench which pervaded the town that it was necessary to legislate against those who made dunghills in the streets or in front of their houses. If such dunghills already existed they were to be removed 'by Whitsuntide next coming'. As we have no exact date for the documents it is not clear how much time was allowed before a fine was imposed. It is unlikely that there was any great improvement. If this requirement was complied with at all before summer heat made it worse, it would probably be by throwing any offending sewage over the walls or into the harbour at night, both actions being already listed as offences.

Miscellaneous further provisions include that bakers were required, at least once a week, to bake fourth class bread, the only kind which could be afforded by poor citizens; that no man might carry any unlawful weapon; this, surprisingly, included a sword; and that it was forbidden to dig 'any sand of the pendaunts' for fear of undermining the walls.

Perhaps most surprising, to the modern reader, of all these provisions is a complete ban on the playing of 'tennis, dice, cards, quoits or bowls or any other unlawful game' in the streets or on the town green. The fine imposed by the mayor on those who transgressed was twelve pence.[8] It is not clear to me why so many games were illegal, at least in public places, although monarchs of this period discouraged the spending of time on such amusements so that men would have more time for practising the vital use of the longbow.

Despite its citizens being hedged round by all these regulations, life in Winchelsea proceeded in its frequently lawless way with no activity illustrating this lawlessness better than the piracy in which the town's masters and seamen, along with those of the other Cinque Ports, regularly took part.

32. PIRACY PERSISTS

In order to explore the kind of piratical activity, already mentioned in these pages, in which the mariners of Winchelsea were constantly involved we must take examples from the wider Cinque Ports context. Captain of the Cinque Ports fleet in the early fifteenth century was Harry Paye of Faversham, a man of notorious reputation who hailed from Poole. Paye led the Cinque Ports fleet when, on ship service at the king's command, 'it sailed to assist in the crushing of the Welsh rebellion in 1405'.[1] The following year Paye and his Cinque Ports ships surprised and captured one hundred and twenty French ships laden with salt, iron, oil and wine. The profits from ventures like this were considerable and a leader who could provide rich pickings for his men was loyally followed. The spoils of such attacks were often taken to the Camber, Winchelsea's outer harbour;[2] an area much more convenient for off-loading and distribution than a return to Faversham.

William Longe of Rye was another who took advantage of official authority to indulge in piratical activity. Longe, a seaman representing Rye in parliament, was given the job of maintaining an anti-piracy patrol in the Channel. While on this duty he seized a Florentine carrack laden with wine from La Rochelle. Having escaped before an order for his arrest could be executed, Longe later captured eleven Flemish wine ships. This time he was not so lucky and arrest by the then Admiral of the Cinque Ports fleet led to eighteen months' incarceration in the Tower of London. No such punishment could, however, reduce William Longe's reputation in his home town where he was elected to parliament on another four occasions![3]

The audacity and enterprise of such men is further illustrated by a later escapade of Harry Paye, known by his French and Spanish enemies as 'Arripay'. Again on official service, this time with a fleet under the command of the Duke of Somerset, Paye's own vessel was taken by the enemy who imprisoned him and his crew below decks. The prisoners were, however, soon able to break out and overcome the French prize crew who had looted and enjoyed the wine on board! 'Paye then sailed his ship, as well as the escorting French vessel which he managed to capture, up the Seine flying the French flag and doing much damage ashore before returning to Poole.'[4] Such exploits were greatly admired by his English colleagues if not by the French!

Some piracy, of course, was not illegal at all if it could be included under the official description of privateering. Harry Paye would have used such an excuse even if William Longe failed to do so. Any private citizen who owned a ship could become a privateer by obtaining a 'Letter of Marque'. Many Winchelsea masters no doubt did so. Ships sailing under such an authority were supposed to bring their captures before the Prize Court to be assessed. If this procedure was correctly followed the master might expect to receive ninety per cent of the value. However, many by-passed such regulations by ransacking at sea any vessel they could overcome and avoiding the time and trouble of bringing it to port.[5]

The vessels of Winchelsea and the Cinque Ports 'were in an especially advantageous position to reap corporate profits from privateering'.[6] They were used to sailing as a squadron which gave them greater power and their geographical position provided immediate access to what were, even then, the busiest shipping lanes in the world. However, the general strength and influence of the ports of the south was moving west. Southampton, Dartmouth, Plymouth, Fowey and Bristol could each, when called upon, send a greater tonnage for the king's service than could the Cinque Ports.[7] Problems which the prevailing south-westerly winds caused for the Cinque Ports ships heading west are emphasised by Margery James when she describes how five of the king's ships which set out from London in 1414 'to seek the vintage wines at Bordeaux' managed to reach the Isle of Wight but were then driven back to Winchelsea 'and eventually returned to London without making the voyage that year'.[8]

The national influence of Winchelsea and the Cinque Ports may have been declining but it was far from finished. In the same year, King Henry V sent ambassadors to France to claim large areas which had once been part of the Angevin empire. Such an embassy had to be demonstrably powerful and well equipped. The king therefore ordered all suitable vessels to report to Winchelsea 'in order to convey the ambassadors with their company and 500 horses'.[9]

It was Henry V's Leicester parliament which in 1415 made a serious attempt to control piracy. The king knew from first-hand experience what was going on because he had served as Lord Warden of the Cinque Ports during his father's reign. John Hawley junior of Dartmouth was a senior and able captain within the fleet. Hawley's arrest and use as an example was followed by the introduction of regulations which required an anti-piracy officer to be appointed in every port. He was to be a man of standing who owned 'at least forty librates of land' and was to preside over a court entrusted with all the powers of the admiral 'except for questions involving capital punishment'. A register was to be kept of all vessels sailing from the port with details of the crew and the cargo and of all prizes captured at sea. No record survives of any attempt to establish such an authority at Winchelsea. If it happened it was ineffective in dealing with the problem and 'like many other attempts to harness piracy had no lasting success'.[10]

Of the Winchelsea mariners who indulged in piracy and took advantage of privateering opportunities in the fifteenth century we know most about William Morfote. Morfote, like William Longe of Rye, had achieved the distinction of representing his home port in parliament in 1428, 1429 and 1431. In those days an element of popular democracy survived in such elections and we must therefore assume that Morfote was admired and respected by Winchelsea's electors. He was not, however, admired and respected by the authorities attempting to control

(54) This beautiful row of Winchelsea houses on the west side of Friars Road dates, partly at least, from the late fifteenth century. Nos. 2/3 were the home of William MacLean Homan

piracy who imprisoned him in Dover Castle for this activity. When the formidable nature of Dover Castle is taken into account we must assume Morfote to be a man in Harry Paye's mould for he successfully escaped!

Unfortunately for Morfote, following his escape, a complete ban was placed on his being allowed to land at or trade through any south coast port and understandably this proved a considerable problem. In 1435 he therefore submitted a petition to parliament explaining that he was sailing at his own expense in command of vessels with crews totalling one hundred men 'for to withstand and depress the king's enemies and his rebels and of this worthy realm'.[11] As Morfote was a wanted man, this must have been a self-appointed form of privateering! His petition went on to explain that as a result of his escape from Dover Castle he was prevented from victualling at many places and 'dare not come to land'. Only if he was granted a pardon for his escape and, presumably, for the crimes causing his imprisonment, could he successfully serve the country in the way he claimed to be doing. The parliamentary committee which considered this petition was both grateful and gullible for it recommended the king 'to inflict an easy fine on him for breaking prison and to grant him the desired pardon'.[12] The king complied.

Eight years later Morfote, fully forgiven, was included within a major privateering fleet recruited to attack foreign shipping in the Channel. Eight ships with crews of 150 were to be at sea from February to November, each ship supported by two smaller vessels, a barge and a balinger. The men serving in this fleet were poorly paid but had the ever-present privateer's incentive that they would be compensated from the spoils of enemy vessels captured. The eight ships and their accompanying vessels, having gathered at Winchelsea, were sent to use the Isle of Wight as their base but two barges, one the *Marie* commanded by Morfote, were left behind stationed at Winchelsea to guard Rye Bay where their local knowledge would be invaluable.

To refer to a vessel as a barge is misleading to the modern ear for medieval barges of this time carried a crew of eighty and must have been substantial in both size and fighting capacity. William Morfote endears himself to me not only because of his piratical activities but also because he chose as his associate vessel in defending Winchelsea on this occasion, the *Trinity* referred to in surviving documents as 'that other Pratte barge'.[13] The name Pratt has been common in Sussex for centuries. Its use entered this country with the Vikings; its misuse, albeit with only one 't', came from the USA in the 1960s! The original meaning was 'cunning, crafty, wily, artful and astute',[14] terms which would have been taken as considerable compliments in medieval England and would have been readily lived up to by the owner of Morfote's accompanying barge.

Unfortunately the barge owner's Christian name has not come down to us but since he was from Winchelsea and was clearly a person of some substance it may well have been John. John Pratt was appointed a jurat at the annual Easter Hundred Court five times between 1441 and 1455.[15] In 1439 he is listed as commanding the *Grace Dieu* of Winchelsea, 50 tons, in the service of the Earl of Shrewsbury.[16] John Pratt's activities as a pirate, a privateer, or both, clearly later went beyond the law for in 1464 he, or someone of his name, was 'stigmatised', that is severely censured, as a pirate.[17] This punishment, however much disgrace it involved, probably very little, was considerably lighter than that imposed on another Winchelsea pirate name Pratt – we can't even guess at his Christian name – who was hanged in the town in 1572.[18]

Although I do not come originally from Sussex, I should love to think that these Winchelsea pirates were my ancestors!

The successors of Morfote and Pratt were to persist in piracy and revel in privateering based at Winchelsea for another hundred years after Pratt's 'stigmatisation'. In 1483 a Hamburg master complained bitterly that his ship had been 'seized and brought to the town of Winchelsea'.[19] In 1542 Thomas Fouglar and John Bell of Winchelsea obtained royal licences for a privateering expedition.[20] Two years later it is recorded that the vessels used by privateers such as Fouglar and Bell were only of twenty tons each.[21] In 1564 Queen Elizabeth I, following vehement complaints from the French and Spanish ambassadors, sent 'a sharply worded letter' to the Lord Warden demanding action against men of the Cinque Ports who were harbouring, victualling and maintaining pirates'.[22] It would seem that in 1571 Winchelsea was guilty of this offence for the Mayor and Jurats of Rye reported that they had arrested pirates 'whose boat rideth at anchor in the Puddle within the Liberties of Winchelsea'.[23]

Perhaps the most interesting Winchelsea pirate of this later period was Francis Bolton, one of my predecessors as town clerk. On 30 November 1578 the Lords of the Council sent to the Lord Warden a list of Cinque Portsmen on whom fines for piracy were to be levied. These included Robert Perse and Francis Bolton of Winchelsea.[24] Bolton was at the time serving as town clerk and continued to do so until 1585. He was removed from office on the orders of the Privy Council without any specific offence being mentioned.[25] Bolton may have been a member of a privateering syndicate but his removal at Winchelsea did him little harm for he was appointed town clerk of Rye in 1590 and served until his death in 1600.[26] There can have been little animosity within the Confederation towards piratical activity.

This conclusion is reinforced by the reaction of the men of Rye when Queen Elizabeth I withdrew all privateering licences in 1588 because she so desperately needed seamen for her expanding fleet to face the threat of the Armada. The barons of Rye protested that the queen was infringing their time-honoured right to 'the licence for the men of war to go to the seas'.[27] By that date Winchelsea would have been little involved, its maritime activity having been almost completely ended by the withdrawal of the sea and the silting of the harbour.

When, in 1619, the Barons of the Cinque Ports were required to support the merchants of London in raising money for a fleet to repel from the Channel pirates of Algiers and Tunis who were creating havoc among English merchant ships, Winchelsea was assessed to raise funds but would not have been able to contribute otherwise.[28]

Just once more Winchelsea, in name at least, became involved with piracy and then only through *HMS Winchelsea* in 1723. In that year the Governor of St. Kitts reported that this ship had taken a notorious pirate, Captain Finn, and eight of his pirate crew on the Island of Tobago. This seems to have been a major achievement in putting down the piracy of the time. Captain Orme of *HMS Winchelsea* was highly commended. As a result of his action 'the captured pirates were put on trial and six of them were hanged "at the high water mark in the town of St. James in Antigua"'.[29]

A violent note on which to end this account of Winchelsea's involvement with a violent activity.

33. PRINCIPALLY OF PILGRIMAGE

In the fourteenth and fifteenth centuries, to which we now return, Winchelsea pirates like Morfote and Pratt would have further supplemented their income by using their ships to take pilgrims abroad.

Only one Winchelsea reference to pilgrims and pilgrimage pre-dates those centuries.

Miss Maud Peel, owner of The Armoury in the early twentieth century, claimed that, in her garden, she had found the site of a preceptory of the Knights Templar,[1] a fighting order of crusaders pledged from as early as 1118 to protect pilgrims. She believed that the Templars purchased from the heirs of Richard Hethe the land in Quarter 7 on which her home stood.[2] How Miss Peel came to assume this we do not know, and there is nothing to confirm it. However, the medieval features which she so lovingly recorded are still there.

When shown round by the present owner, Tony Jasper, I saw the seat beneath which Miss Peel thought were the remains of the apse. On the stones forming that seat there is an inscription of more than four hundred words describing her findings.[3] A few feet away is a stone set above ground level and engraved 'This is the floor level of the Chapel'. Corbels spring from a boundary wall nearby and, recovered from the footings of another now ruined wall, is a damaged (headless) figure of the Madonna and child.

In what seems to modern experts the unlikely event that Miss Peel's deductions were correct and the Knights Templar sailed from Winchelsea as pilgrim escorts, their destination would have been the middle-east for their charges sought to visit Jerusalem. In later years the principal route from Winchelsea was much shorter, taking those who travelled to the shrine of St. James of Compostela at Santiago in northern Spain.

Santiago may have been much nearer than Jerusalem but the journey by sea was nevertheless, as we shall see, both hazardous and uncomfortable.

The pilgrim trade between Winchelsea and Santiago has been shown to have been under way by 1356 when the crown was taking a tax of twopence from every pilgrim returning from abroad through Winchelsea. In that year twelve pilgrims who had travelled to the shrine of St. James were charged under this statute.[4] Restrictions other than such taxation were also imposed on pilgrims, especially during the Hundred Years War. They were forbidden from taking any gold, silver, armour or horses with them.[5]

Although these numbers were to increase enormously in the fifteenth century, while the Hundred Years War progressed visitors to the shrine must have been further discouraged by events such as the presence of the Black Prince and his army. They used the overland pilgrim route to Santiago on the way to Spain in 1367. In 1386 things were even worse for John of Gaunt's soldiery 'plagued by sickness and sodden with drink' captured Santiago de Compostela where Gaunt set up his headquarters.[6]

Nor can it be assumed that many pilgrims would have had the slightest interest in taking along 'gold, silver, armour or horses'. The vast majority were ordinary folk, usually unused to travel, motivated by their religion, the need to seek a cure, or both, and in many cases no doubt sufficiently gullible to be overcharged by the shipmasters of Winchelsea, Sandwich or Bristol, the principal ports of departure.

The names and experiences of the vast majority have, by the very nature of things, long been lost to the records. However, we know a little about Margery Kempe, an illiterate woman who, remarkably, dictated her experiences to her priest and father confessor. Her account has

(55) This scallop shell, a 'pilgrim sign' collected as a souvenir and proof of pilgrimage. It includes the head and shoulders of St. James

survived.[7] Two things make this remarkable document disappointing for us – she did not sail from Winchelsea but from Bristol, and she was not interested in providing an account of her journeys but concentrated only on 'her immediate difficulties and the visions and meditations experienced during her visits to the holy places'.[8] The immediate difficulty on her journey to Santiago was her fear that such was her reputation for religious fervour and as a mystic that, should they encounter storms, her fellow travellers would be likely to blame her presence on the ship and throw her overboard. When no storms interrupted the voyage, 'those who were against her when they were in Bristol were now very nice to her'.[9]

Thus we hear of one somewhat alarming hazard which a pilgrim might face. We hear of many more in a poem dating from the sixteenth century which is preserved among the Trinity College Manuscripts. This is entitled *The Pilgrimage to Saint James of Compostela* and makes it clear in the opening verse that, as already noted, Winchelsea was among the principal points of departure.[10] The poem describes how, when the time of departure approached, the pilgrims' 'hearts begin to fail'. And well they might for life aboard is revealed to have been almost unbearable. The passengers, despite their inexperience as sailors and, much worse, their chronic sea-sickness, were, regardless of their protests, required to take a turn at the demanding tasks involved in manning the ship. The master, having already saved money on crew through this requirement which was rigidly enforced, then rejoiced that the sea-sick pilgrims would not require as much food! At the end of the poem we are told:

> 'For when that we shall go to bedde,
> The pupe was nygh our bedd hede,
> A man were as good to be dede
> As smell thereof the stynk!

Two versions which I have seen translate the word 'pupe' as pump.[11] It may be otherwise!

However appalling the conditions there was no shortage of takers.

In 1431 licences were issued for the transport of no fewer that 2433 pilgrims to St. James.[12] We do not know how many of these left from Winchelsea but slightly later records are more specific. In 1434 Robert Porter, Winchelsea master of the *Trinity* was permitted to carry sixty pilgrims on the aforementioned conditions and 'that they would not reveal the secrets of the kingdom to any one abroad'. The same master, but then in command of the *Katherine*, carried a further forty pilgrims later in the same year.[13] We are entitled to presume that Robert Porter profited considerably from these voyages and Ford Madox Ford comments that the trade was sufficient to revive Winchelsea's fortunes for a time and that its ships 'forestalled the [Thomas] Cook of today in the service of the Galician saint'.[14] One hopes that Thomas Cook's holidays never provided conditions like those the pilgrims suffered. Nevertheless many such travellers seem to have approached the experience with optimism for 'however harrowing they may have been for pilgrims in search of a cure, pilgrimages also engendered an atmosphere of carnival'.[15]

In 1445 the traffic was still considerable for more than two thousand pilgrims were carried, some as much as one hundred per vessel. In noting this Gordon Taylor presumes that such large concentrations of people travelling with a strictly religious aim would necessarily be accompanied by priests and that this provided a boost to the profession of sea chaplain which prospered so greatly in the reign of Elizabeth I.[16] If that is correct it certainly does not seem to have given Margery Kempe any confidence that priests on board would have been able to prevent her being thrown overboard if the weather turned bad!

The last known recorded grant of a licence to a Winchelsea man for carrying pilgrims to St. James was in 1456 when Simon Farnecombe, owner of the *Helen*, carried eighty persons to St. James. W. MacLean Homan reinforces the view I have given of the conditions the pilgrims suffered, mentioning in addition that the ships of the day were 'mostly open without decks and such cabins [as] might be provided were erected by the ship's carpenter while under way'.[17]

(56) The cathedral of St. James at Santiago de Compostela

Ford Madox Ford's account of this trade included the observation that 'the cult of St. James lived on well into this [the nineteenth] century.[18] It has lasted a great deal longer than that for my friend Dennis Williams made the pilgrimage in 2002. Understandably, like Margery Kempe, he did not sail from Winchelsea! He took the overland route, known as the Camino, which was followed by John of Gaunt's army as noted above, or, to be strictly accurate, he took part of this route. This pilgrimage has become increasingly popular in modern times and those taking part are supported by an organisation known as the Confraternity of St. James. There is full provision for travellers. The route is clearly waymarked, there is accommodation in fairly basic pilgrim hostels and small hotels and a great cameraderie develops among pilgrims of many nationalities. Dennis has written of the history which provoked vast numbers of his predecessors to travel so dangerously in medieval times and thus give Winchelsea sailors ample opportunity for profit:

'Santiago de Compostela is a small provincial city in Galicia, in NW Spain. It has been one of the major Christian places of pilgrimage since relics claimed to be those of St. James (hence Santiago) were discovered there in 813AD. Only Jerusalem and Rome achieved greater acclaim. Initially the relics were entombed in a primitive wooden church. The shrine quickly became a rallying point for Christian Spain, the Moors having forced the Christian community into a narrow strip at the northern end of the Iberian peninsula. In 1078 the construction of a magnificent cathedral began. And, during the Middle Ages, Santiago thrived as millions of pilgrims arrived from throughout Europe to pay homage.'[19]

Apart from this historical background, Dennis Williams has also kindly provided my photographs of the cathedral and a pilgrim depicted upon it.

What, now, of the Winchelsea which medieval pilgrims left behind?

We can assume that despite the increasing problems created by the silting of the harbour the town was still playing an important part in the life of the country. In 1430 a large amount of money was taken from Winchelsea to Dieppe to pay the 'ships, archers and mariners' supporting the army in France and later in the same year a certain Roger Minster travelled to Dieppe and Rouen via Winchelsea to deliver the then enormous sum of £2500 to John, Duke of Bedford 'to pay the wages of the men at arms'.[20] W. M. Homan suggests from this evidence of regular transfer of funds through the town that the money which was used by the Duke of Bedford to purchase Joan of Arc and thus facilitate her trial and execution 'had passed this way'.[21]

Despite the silting, the vessels which carried the couriers with this money could still have been substantial for 'although the port became increasingly choked and less serviceable, it was still able to receive vessels of up to 200 tons in 1433'.[22]

(57) A medieval pilgrim depicted on the façade of the cathedral of Santiago de Compostela.

The men of Winchelsea who served their king by providing such ships for transport from their port remained in a position of strength and were not averse to standing on their dignity when their independence was challenged. In 1432 the Lord Warden, Humphrey Duke of Gloucester, complained that the Mayor and Jurats of Winchelsea, had held 'a certain trial touching life and limb' in their town and ordered their appearance at Dover to explain themselves. We have already seen how sentences of death were well within the compass of Winchelsea's courts and the complaint received a very frosty response to the effect that the Mayor, Bailiffs and Jurats were perfectly entitled to deal with such cases in Winchelsea and the Lord Warden could intervene only if they failed in this duty. Even then he must travel to Winchelsea to deal with the case.[23]

It is significant in studying Winchelsea's history to note that it is from the year of this complaint, 1432, that the full records of the Confederation of the Cinque Ports and the courts attended by its members remain available through *A Calendar of the White and Black Books of the Cinque Ports*. It can be no surprise to us in view of the family's importance in Winchelsea that one of the town's two representatives at the first recorded Court of Brodhull on Monday 20 July 1433 was William Alard. However, on that occasion it was the other Winchelsea delegate, William Werthe who was appointed to serve as Bailiff to Yarmouth for Winchelsea and Rye.[24] Nor is it surprising that William Werthe and his fellow Bailiffs complained bitterly to another Brodhull on 7 December 1433 about the insults and injuries which they and their officers had received at the hands of the provost and others of Yarmouth![25]

We do not know exactly how Winchelsea representatives to Cinque Ports courts were chosen or whether any voting was involved. It certainly was in appointing the Mayor each year and there must have been problems at this time on at least one occasion about this vital decision for the rules had to be clarified. On 10 July 1434 it was decreed 'that if the community cannot agree in the choice of a Mayor, it shall be referred to the Common Council [a body of thirty-six freemen] with the advice of the Jurats to choose one of the candidates and if the Jurats and Common Council do not agree and when the voices are equal, the former Mayor to determine the election'.[26] Whatever may have provoked this resolution, the surviving records continue to detail the annual Easter mayoring but do not tell us whether the mayor, in following years at least, ever had to exercise his casting vote.

34. A LONG WAR'S END

With this elaborate electoral system available to be brought into play if needed, leading citizens continued to emerge with major responsibilities for the life of a town of piracy and pilgrimage, a town which had, within living memory and beyond, been in almost permanent fear of attack.

These responsibilities, typically for a medieval community, included, as we have seen in the case of the fate of pirate Pratt, the power of enforcing capital punishment. Winchelsea's gallows was used at this time 'by virtue of Edward IV's act to the Cinque Ports'[1] and stood on the marsh to the north of the town. Other responsibilities which applied to Winchelsea and its fellow Cinque Ports proved considerably more arduous for the town's mayors and bailiffs and the difficulties arising from them were among the factors which heralded Winchelsea's major decline.

The Cinque Ports' traditional ship service of fifty-seven ships for fifteen days was met fully for the last time in 1444-1445.[2] Thereafter considerable problems were experienced in supplying even a reduced number of larger ships. '[The Cinque Ports'] ships, so far from providing the permanent nucleus of the navy were used only to reinforce a fleet of ships drawn from other sources'.[3]

The privilege of sending members to parliament was also proving a headache for those responsible for the government of Cinque Ports member towns. For some considerable time there had existed an unofficial arrangement whereby, if parliamentary proceedings dragged on, one member remained to cover for two ports and the other went home. As early as 1388 Edward Martham of Hastings had also represented Winchelsea during part of what is known as the Merciless Parliament.[4] It would seem from this that it was also general practice that one of a town's two members was an adequate representation and that the attendance of both was not necessarily required. Records of Winchelsea's representation after the February 1388 elections are not complete, but William Skele, John Pulham or Robert Harry enjoyed some time off thanks to their Hastings colleague. The perk for Martham was that he was paid by both towns. This arrangement was regularised by a Court of Brodhull held at Romney on 21 July 1444. The resolution lays down four weeks as the time after which this double representation may come into force and refers to the practice as 'olde custome'.[5]

There is no direct evidence for a final debilitating blow to Winchelsea during the Hundred Years War but if it in fact took place, Skele, Pulham and Harry might well have witnessed it. Source for this suggested attack is Samuel Jeake's *The Cinque Ports* which states that 'both Winchelsea and Rye were burnt in the time of Henry VI about the 26th or 27th year of his reign'. The twenty-seventh year of Henry's reign began on 1 September 1448.

I have not been able to reach a definite opinion as to whether this attack on Winchelsea actually happened but W. M. Homan felt that the evidence suggests it. He comments that all Rye's charters before this date are lost and therefore may well have been burnt in the raid and feels it clearly significant that Tenterden was incorporated as a limb of Rye in 1449, to provide assistance to her Head Port which 'by burnings of the town by the enemies ... had fallen into devastation, destruction, waste and impoverishment, not only of lands and tenements but also of inhabitants'.[6] Homan also found evidence in the Rye Town Accounts of repairs to the town's walls at this time and a payment of fifteen pence 'for watching two nights when a ship was being looked out for off the Camber with Frenchmen'.[7]

Professor Burrows, while acknowledging that there is no direct evidence of the attack, accepts it more forthrightly and assumes that the Tenterden Charter under which the town was incorporated 'so that it may contribute towards the Service due from that "Ancient Town"'[8] is the clinching evidence. The modern reader may not be aware that in those days the sea reached Tenterden and that its ships were built at Smallhythe. Bringing us close in this story to the Wars of the Roses which were in progress at the time, Burrows adds that, Winchelsea and Rye having been 'unprotected and unavenged', this attack 'put an end to all respect for the Government which had in fact fallen to pieces'.[9]

The Victoria County History is far more sceptical about the 1448 raid and dismisses Jeake's assertion on the grounds that 'burnings' was merely a general term for attacks which might have taken place long ago. Other contemporary documents which do survive would certainly have mentioned the attack had it happened.[10]

Even these arguments, such as they are, do not help us about Winchelsea and my only conclusion is that if the town was, indeed, attacked in 1448 or 1449, the damage done, either physical or moral, was insufficient to prevent the appointment of Commissioners to take a muster of men-at-arms at Winchelsea in 1449. Most relevant to us among the Commissioners was Thomas Thunder, Mayor of Winchelsea on several occasions, whom we have met before, and their number also included Richard Dallingridge of the Bodiam Castle family. The purpose of the muster was to reinforce the army under the Duke of Somerset in Normandy. W. D. Cooper assumed that this muster was to defend Winchelsea against further attack but the Patent Rolls make it clear that the troops gathered were to proceed to France.[11] The Duke was under considerable pressure because the French, taking advantage of 'the discord in England' had successfully attacked the English presence in Normandy and had little trouble obtaining the surrender of many of its towns which were 'only too glad to throw off the foreign yoke'. The Commissioners were instructed to 'seize all necessary ships for the transport of the troops, and to gather them with their masters and crew at Winchelsea'.[12] Other instructions were issued for similar action at Southampton, Portsmouth and Poole.

The Winchelsea commissioners reported that 55 men-at-arms and 508 archers had been despatched, fully armed for war, to France under the command of Sir William Peyto. A full list of these men is extant and some of them who had names common in the town probably came from it.[13]

Despite this reinforcement, the Duke of Somerset's position in Normandy was untenable. He was forced into retreat and in November 1449 had to surrender Rouen.

Winchelsea, however, remained reasonably alert and ready to do what was needed. In *The Paston Letters* most disparaging comments are made about 'the neglect of the sea' and how as a result the country's mariners had suffered grossly. In 1451 ships were simply not available when needed for the defence of the country and those available were manned by sailors who were 'unskilled for want of exercise'. The writer, with feeling, prays, 'May God take away our reproach and raise up a spirit of bravery in the nation'![14] However, Winchelsea was able to help overcome such a dire position for the section following this heartfelt plea notes that some ships were available for the king's service 'in the Thames and at Winchelsea and Sandwich'.[15]

This unreadiness and the defeat of the Duke of Somerset were two of many factors which led to the end of the Hundred Years War, from England's point of view an ignominious end. Churchill records: 'By the end of that year [1453] through force or negotiation, the English had been driven off the continent. Of all their conquests they held henceforward only the bridgehead of Calais'.[16]

(58) Five Chimneys, Mill Road, a Wealden hall house rebuilt in the fifteenth century over an existing cellar.

W. M. Homan views this conflict, over the previous century and a quarter, as an unmitigated disaster and 'a setback for civilisation not only in France but also in Great Britain'.[17] The effects on Winchelsea's buildings and population were certainly vast but it is reasonable to assume that they only accelerated the town's gathering decline, the major cause of which was the withdrawal of the sea and the silting of the harbour.

Perhaps we should note one last, extraordinary, incident in the war because of its indirect effect on Winchelsea. The Battle of Castillon took place on 17 July 1453. The English forces were led by John Talbot who had given his pledge on earlier release from French captivity that he would 'never again wear armour against the King of France'. Talbot was clearly a man of his word for, in fulfilment of this promise, he encouraged his troops into battle while riding a white pony and entirely without a weapon or armour. His astonishing valour bore no fruit for his pony was killed by a cannonball, trapping him beneath it and 'a French man-at-arms leapt over the parapet to finish [Talbot] off with a battle-axe'.[18] A rout followed, the English retreated to Bordeaux and even that city, held by the English for centuries, was soon lost. Bordeaux, of course, had been the principal port from which the wine trade with England and particularly with Winchelsea had been conducted.

From that time forward the trade was subject always to French co-operation. Safe conducts were issued and frequently not honoured. Where a safe conduct was confiscated its non-return was followed by a piratical attack or it was returned only on payment of a large sum. 'The merchants and mariners,' no doubt with Winchelsea men among them, 'who were victims of these seizures contested the validity of the actions of the French officials' but they were not brought to book. The volume of the vital wine trade consequently shrank to the detriment of Winchelsea and of England.[19]

Enmity and rivalry over six generations meant that even the end of the Hundred Years War did not bring about much reduction in Winchelsea's fear of threatened attack. This fear applied not only to the French for in 1455 the Commons made representations to the monarch about Italian merchants who were travelling in England selling particularly wool and gaining intelligence about the country in the process. They were to be prevented from trading in this way and should not be permitted even to make purchases at ports 'unless driven by stress of weather into the ports of Fowey, Falmouth, Plymouth, Dartmouth or Winchelsea'.[20]

This type of alarm was reinforced in 1457 when orders were issued in Winchelsea that the inhabitants should be 'mustered and arrayed' to defend their town and, if necessary, other parts of Sussex.[21] Not only men but sailors and their ships were called to arms during this same year. The

French had made several raids on the Sussex coast. Two French fleets divided their attentions, one sacking Fowey and the other landing 4000 men at Sandwich 'and plundering the town'. Ships were ordered to sea to resist the French who, by the time the order was issued were in the North Sea. Much frenzied activity took place including payments to two men to keep watch on the steeple of Lydd Church, and for two sledges to carry guns across the shingle at Dungeness. These guns were being locally manufactured and the gunmakers' expenses were to be met 'when they went to buy metal in Winchelsea and Hastings'.[22]

The examples we have seen in this section of how Winchelsea was still being consistently mentioned as the equal of other well-known ports, and frequently in preference to other Cinque Ports convinces me that the town's seamen can in no way be excluded from the unreliability that the men of the Cinque Ports displayed at this time in their loyalty to their country and their monarch.

For example, in 1450 the king's instructions were received by the 'bailiffs, burgesses and commonalty of Winchelsea' banning all 'gatherings and assemblages except such as were by the king's proclamations justified'.[23] This refers to the Cinque Ports' known enthusiasm for Jack Cade's rebellion which had many supporters among the portsmen.[24]

In 1460 the monarch's suspicions about the Cinque Ports would have been even greater. In that year, with the Wars of the Roses at their height, they supported the Earl of Warwick's invasion and facilitated his capture of the royal fleet and its leaders at Sandwich. Warwick went on from that victory to install King Edward IV on the throne.[25] Later, and even more impertinently, when Thomas of Faucenberg, in support of the Lancastrian claim, landed to raise an attack on London he was able to recruit large numbers from the Cinque Ports. This attack was one of the earliest examples of shore bombardment by naval guns which by that time the Cinque Ports ships were carrying. These rebellious activities lead N. A. M. Rodger to conclude that, at this time, 'the Ports do not appear as providers of valuable naval services but as dangerous troublemakers willing to sell their geographical advantages to the highest bidder.'[26]

Winchelsea must take its full share of this censure.

It was not only in matters seafaring that Winchelsea continued to exercise influence. Christopher Dyer illustrates the somewhat strange phenomenon that distinguished late medieval purchasers tended to buy from large towns rather than much closer smaller communities. One of his examples is that while the Duchess of Buckingham was staying at Writtle in Essex during 1465/6, instead of buying fresh fish for her household from the many little ports on the nearby coast, she ordered it from Winchelsea and its despatch involved a journey of more than sixty miles. The same applied much nearer home for Battle Abbey, a major consumer within the area, did not order its 'supplies of fish, spices and other goods' from the increasingly significant town which was growing up around it but from Hastings, Winchelsea, Canterbury and London.[27]

Thus, as in this story we approach the later years of the fifteenth century, we observe Winchelsea as a major player in the seafaring and commercial life of the country; a status which many commentators would expect us to believe the town had lost much earlier. Cooper tells us that in 1475 Winchelsea contributed 'its quota' to the fleet when Cinque Ports ship service was required.[28] We must assume that this was a full quota. The Winchelsea ships which joined this fleet went in support of Edward IV's army which landed at Calais to renew the English monarch's claim to the throne of France. Loyalties had changed again!

The serious and subsequently near-fatal decline of Winchelsea was, however, not to be much longer delayed.

35. BEER AND BUILDINGS

The major factor in that decline during the latter part of the fifteenth century was the rapidly deteriorating state of the inner harbour on the River Brede at the foot of Winchelsea's hill. Gertrude Leigh in a much heralded 'New Illustrated Edition' of the Winchelsea Town Guide published in 1927 stated that 'The harbour became more and more shallow and more difficult of approach and, at length, by the year 1475, we find all ships unlading at the Camber or Rye and the port of Winchelsea practically closed for craft of any size'.[1] Unfortunately the authors of town guides do not refer to their sources but although I have not discovered where she might have obtained such precise information, it is likely that she was right. Her finding would be supported by figures quoted at a 'Special Brotherhood' of the Confederation held at Romney on 21 November 1475 when an assessment for some form of national taxation the purpose of which is not clear to me, divided the responsibility of the head ports, calculated to the nearest pound as follows: Sandwich £140, Dover £92, Romney £30, Hastings £22, Rye £19, Hythe £14 and Winchelsea £1![2]

Miss Leigh's mention of the Camber which was in Winchelsea's Liberty and was available as an alternative to the inner harbour although nowhere near as convenient for trade, allows us to reconcile the discrepancy between commercial decline and ship service importance. In 1491 the Confederation was required to provide its traditional ship service to carry horses to France for Henry VII. It would seem that the fifteen days was exceeded for the king made a grant of £500 to the Cinque Ports and this was distributed in proportion to ship service responsibility. Winchelsea received £80, representing the provision of ten ships. Only Dover which provided twenty-one ships, received a larger grant of £168.[3] In contrast, in the later years of the century with the inner harbour 'no longer approachable ... it was reported that all merchants were quitting the town'.[4] This is supported by Cooper who draws attention to a return made in 1498 which stated that no person remained within the town who was worth £40 per annum in goods.[5]

One merchant who did not 'quit the town' was Maline Farnecombe and it is to her story that we now turn. Maline, the daughter of John Godfrey of Winchelsea and his wife Alice, was born about 1425. Her father was a leading citizen who was mayor in 1431, 1432 and 1438. Intriguingly he had to remain in office from Easter until 11 June 1433 because there was a dispute among the freemen about who was to succeed him.[6] Godfrey also represented Winchelsea in parliament in 1441 and 1448.[7] So far as we are aware Maline was his only daughter and she eventually became part of another leading Winchelsea family when she married Simon Farnecombe, mayor in 1457 and 1458. Simon Farnecombe has already been mentioned in these pages for he was one of the shipowners licensed to carry pilgrims to St. James of Compostela. Unusually for the times, Maline went into business on her own account and is believed to have been the owner of two hostelries in the town, The Salutation and The Three Kings, both names which survive to this day, although no longer as inns.[8]

We have already noted that Winchelsea was an extremely early importer of beer in 1400 and the town's medieval custumal refers to the absolute right of the freemen of Winchelsea to sell and buy beer 'throughout the whole kingdom of England' and makes provision for any freeman to be protected against this right being challenged.[9]

It may be that The Salutation and The Three Kings were at one time the property of Flemish beermakers. Early in the 1400s Burgundy and England were allies against France and trade between them flourished. However in 1432 the Duke of Burgundy transferred his allegiance to the French and the property of the Flemish who had taken advantage of good relations with

(59) The present appearance of Periteau House gives absolutely no indication of how it might have looked in the fifteenth century ...

England to settle and establish breweries in Winchelsea was confiscated. Two of the Flemings who forfeited buildings on The Strand, to the west of The Bridge Inn, and among them possibly The Old Malthouse, were Cesse and John Beremaker. These breweries would have been popular with Winchelsea residents and innkeepers for the Flemish developed their beer by using hops.[10] The beer including hops must have been taken up by those brewers succeeding the Flemish because 1466 is recorded as a year in which hop imports were considerable, and, more relevantly for us, 1488 was a year in which Winchelsea was exporting beer.[11]

By that time Maline Farnecombe had undertaken her most notable contribution to the life of Winchelsea. She established two chantries in St. Thomas's Church. The first in 1478 employed a priest or priests to say prayers daily for King Edward IV and his queen, Elizabeth (Woodville) 'while they live, and for their souls when they go from this light'. Similarly to be remembered were Maline herself, her late husband, her parents, Simon Godfrey and his wife Joan 'and the souls of all faithful dead'. The dedication went further to commend all 'who in future times give support to this Chantry and assist the foundation of the said Maline to be kept in perpetuity'.[12] Employing priests cost money, of course, and the permanent income for this chantry was raised by transferring to the first chaplain, John Hunte, the income from four houses and a windmill within the town.[13] This mill was not St. Leonard's Mill, fondly remembered by many present residents, which was destroyed by the 1987 storm, but another which probably stood in the field known as Great Millbank, where the town's allotments are now situated.

There is no disputing Maline's right to these properties which were part of her much greater estates, but when, three years later, she established another chantry, the Farnecombe Chantry, in the same 'chapel of the blessed Mary' at St. Thomas's, the grant was considerably more dubious. Those to benefit from the prayers to be offered were the same as for the Godfrey Chantry, with her parents rather noticeably no longer included and with the addition of four more family members. The problem was that the buildings which were to provide the income to pay William Farley, the first priest, and his successors did not belong to Maline at all but to the crown. They were the same buildings earlier confiscated from the Flemish beermakers and then granted to William Pope as tenant. He later relinquished the tenancy and they reverted to being crown lands. How Maline came to be in occupation of them we do not know except through her obvious interest as a publican, but she sought to cover herself against future discovery of the deception by appealing for authorisation to the king. His commissioners, knowing that the monarch and his queen were included among the beneficiaries, authorised the grant and said that he would not suffer if it were allowed.[14]

The deception was not discovered until the dissolution of the monasteries by which time 'the said Maline' was beyond having to answer for her sins. At that time the Godfrey/Farnecombe Chantry was still operating.[15] The land and buildings which she had misappropriated were eventually confirmed as the property of Winchelsea Corporation by the 1586 grant of Queen Elizabeth I.[16]

It remains only for us briefly to ask which part of St. Thomas's Church Maline Farnecombe acquired for her exclusive use in this way. We have already seen it established with some certainty that the St. Thomas's side chapels were mistakenly assumed by W. D. Cooper to have been the opposite way round to the actual medieval dedications. If that is correct then Maline Farnecombe was setting up her chantries in the south aisle where stand the famous, if only reputed, tombs of Gervase and Stephen Alard.[17]

(60) … but this three-storeyed jettied house in Lincoln gives a better indication.

During the early years of prayer in Maline Farnecombe's chantries life in Winchelsea for the ordinary citizens would have been little affected by an order placing restrictions on the election of the mayor, but the freemen and jurats observed it and it was only when King Edward IV intervened that its terms were broken. This dated from 1462 and decreed that no man might serve as mayor in less than three years from his previous term.[18] There seems to have been a particular concern for Mayor John Sylton here. He served a second term in 1463, apparently in contravention of the requirement, and when he came up for re-election in 1481 the king wrote 'recommending John Sylton, one of the Yeomen of the Crown, to be continued mayor'.[19] Understandably the freemen agreed to this royal exhortation but they added that, except in this case, 'the decree was to continue in full force'.[20] We do not know why Richard Davy (see Appendix 1) had been allowed to break this rule in 1474 and by the end of the century it had fallen into disuse.

Any townspeople who, for whatever reason, had been worshipping at St. Leonard's Church, Iham, outside Winchelsea's walls, or what remained of them, were soon to lose that opportunity for Thomas Bate, inducted to that parish in 1484 following the death of John Grafton, was the last rector and 'from this time the church was allowed to fall into decay'.[21] This can hardly have caused comment for we have already seen that when new walls were planned the blocking of the road to St. Leonard's was not seen as a problem.

Such Winchelsea ships as might still be operating from the harbour, or, more likely, from the Camber remained under threat from enemy or piratical action. In 1487 the *Peter* and the *John of Fole* both of Winchelsea were ordered to sea by Henry VII 'to guard his fleet sent out to fish'.[22] In the following year further more elaborate arrangements were made for the protection of the fishing fleet off the south coast.[23] At about this time English merchants, acting in the style of Portsmen, hired a Genoese carrack with a crew of one hundred and fifty to escort and protect a convoy of ships. When the merchants thought danger had passed they tried to give the Genoese the slip without paying them![24]

It is symptomatic of the propensity of Winchelsea men to become involved in major projects that a member of Columbus's crew, listed as Tallarte de Lajes, English seaman, may well have been an Alard of the Winchelsea family, Tallarte being a Spanish form of the name. He was not an officer but served Columbus as an ordinary seaman and Kenneth Clark suggests that perhaps he was anxious through taking part in this expedition to revive the fortunes of his family who, having had such importance in medieval times, were now associated with a Winchelsea in decline. I like to think that this assumption is correct but the story does not have a happy ending. Tallarte was 'among those left behind on Hispaniola, and when Columbus's second expedition reached Hispaniola the following year they found the garrison had been wiped out by fierce Caribs.'[25]

Mention above of The Old Malthouse as possibly one of the properties inappropriately acquired by Maline Farnecombe leads me to mention, as my story reaches the end of the fifteenth century, the other buildings remaining in the town which survive from, say, fifty years either side of that date. Just as we have found it anomalous that a Winchelsea which was being deserted by its merchants maintained its full ship service responsibilities, there is a similar anomaly in the survival of so many buildings of this period. The merchants were leaving, the harbour was silting and the fleet was greatly depleted and yet a good deal of private building was going ahead within the town.

Archaeological work undertaken on the site of the public conveniences and adjoining Blackfriars Barn produced clear evidence of 'major phases of modification and enlargement carried out during this period'.[26] Of the buildings which residents and visitors can see today no fewer than thirteen contain major work of construction and extension carried out at that time. In at least two of them, Periteau House and 2/3 Friars Road, the work was of high quality. 'All this suggests that, despite the town's problems, for some an acceptable, if not a good living could be enjoyed.'[27]

While there is, in the present day, little external evidence of their age and importance, all these houses were timber framed and four of them had the open halls popular at the time. Of those four, Five Chimneys and The Retreat were Wealden hall houses standing on important corner sites above medieval vaulted cellars and built with their principal façade facing the street. Both these properties and Crowsnest, which stands behind Strand House at the foot of the hill, had 'what appear to have been very standard plan forms which would not have been out of place in any small town, or even a rural situation'.[28] By contrast, on the south side of the High Street, now incorporated within Nesbit, there are two buildings turned gable end to the street. The more important of these, at the eastern end of the present eighteenth century façade, certainly had an open hall, one room back from the street, together with a first floor gallery. This type of 'end-on' construction was 'a classic design found in densely built up urban centres'.[29] The survival of so many old buildings on the south side of the High Street suggests a reason for this further anomaly.

The last of the four buildings of this period known to have had open halls is of particular interest to us here because it was the home of Maline Farnecombe, innkeeper and chantry founder, who has already featured in this chapter. Glebe stands on an important plot in Quarter 13, now the corner of St. Thomas's Street and Rookery Lane. The building incorporates a fifteenth century crosswing. It seems that Maline's site was not quite big enough for her requirements as in 1477 she purchased from the rector a piece of land measuring only seven feet four inches by three feet three. On this plot it is presumed that she built the chimney to heat her crosswing and a chimney of about the right size still projects from the northern wall of the house.[30]

The most spectacular of all the Winchelsea buildings constructed or rebuilt between the mid-fifteenth and mid-sixteenth centuries was Periteau House. This, too, is on a major corner plot at the junction the High Street and Castle Street. Its present appearance gives almost no clue as to the magnificence of the late fifteenth century structure. At that time it was of three storeys with continuous jettying along the northern and western frontages. Nothing is known about the nature of the top storey which was removed in the eighteenth century. 'The ceilings incorporate heavy, neatly finished joists, moulded crossbeams and board panels set in grooves cut into the sides of the joists.' Clearly this building had a wealthy owner and a known name is that of Richard Barkeley whose heirs held it in 1529 and whose daughter sold it to Thomas Hinxstead of Winchelsea, merchant, in 1541.[31] Like the Court Hall, this building has an unvaulted cellar accessible from the street. Although presumably very early in these cases, such cellars are difficult to date. Periteau House is the only building of this period in Quarter 7 which was at that time the home and workplace of many Winchelsea tailors.[32] If Richard Barkeley had been one of them it would have indicated enormous prosperity for at least one of that trade in the fifteenth century. Unfortunately I have not been able to find any evidence that he was.

Perhaps second in importance to Periteau House as far as the prosperity of its owner at the time is concerned is 2/3 Friars Road. This has a similar boarded ceiling to Periteau's, indicating its high status. Although it does not occupy a corner site, this building was close to the highly valued Monday's Market of New Winchelsea and within what remained an important commercial area. What is now Friars Road was the Butchery at this time and a recent archaeological excavation at St. Thomas's School where new classrooms were to be built revealed considerable evidence of discarded animal bones. 2/3 Friars Road had a commercial area on the street frontage. 'Despite the comparatively small size of the building the finish is good and a reasonable suite of rooms is included.'[33]

Understandably there is only room here to mention very briefly the other Winchelsea properties which date from this period. Strand House, 'a small rectangular building of c.1500 with later repair and a big chimney stack inserted early in the seventeenth century,'[34] later became Winchelsea's workhouse and was extended when the number of paupers outgrew the accommodation; it is now a Guest House. Strand House and 7/8 High Street (Bank House) may once have had open halls but are now too altered to be certain.[35] The Salutation, once an inn and now three cottages, 11/12 High Street (The Tea Tree Restaurant and the former Post Office) and Wren Cottage are the others in this group.

This quantity and quality of building activity was supplemented by fairly major alterations and improvements to the Court Hall, Firebrand and The Armoury parts of which, as already shown, survive from medieval times.

36. HOSTILITIES RENEWED

During the early sixteenth century, with work on these buildings completed, continuing or planned, Winchelsea's St. Giles's Church followed St. Leonard's into obscurity. Lawrence Pike was inducted as Rector of St. Giles in 1500 on the resignation of W. Wightman. After that time there are records of no further rectors and the parish was eventually held with St. Thomas's from 1543. [1]

King Henry VIII now begins to dominate Winchelsea's story.

His influence commences from his coronation when the town was represented by its barons under the Confederation of the Cinque Ports' ancient right to honours at court, the ceremony being to all intents and purposes the same as in the time of Richard I. Winchelsea's special privilege on this occasion was that it was allowed to keep the canopies, staves and bells which were used for the king himself. [2] What wonderful artefacts they would be were they still to be seen in the town!

The records of the Confederation show that on 24 July 1509, exactly one month after Henry's coronation, Robert Sparrow of Winchelsea 'brought the charter of Henry VII to the Brotherhood'. Unfortunately the members attending could not find the keys to the chest in which the charter should be stored so it was handed to a Romney representative to be kept safe until legal consultations about its confirmation were completed. [3] In those times the Cinque Ports Charter was renewed at the commencement of every reign. Robert Sparrow was present at that meeting as a Winchelsea jurat and, although his career was to be a distinguished one, it is not clear how he came to be delivering the charter of the previous reign. He was 'a Winchelsea merchant who imported wine, raisins and other commodities'. Sparrow had first served as mayor in 1501 and was to represent Winchelsea in parliament between 1510 and 1523. [4]

Comparatively peaceful activities like coronations and charter deliveries were soon to be shattered in Winchelsea and the Ports by King Henry's aggressive ambitions towards the traditional enemy, France. In 1513, in advance of a campaign in Normandy, the Court of Brotherhood decreed, when their ship service was required, 'That every man that goeth in the navy of the Portes shal have a cote of whyt cotyn with a red crosse and the arms of the Ports undernethe, that is to say [as it is today] the halfe lyon and the halfe shippe'. [5] We know that Winchelsea fulfilled its ship service on this occasion [6] but whether through a financial or a practical involvement is not clear. Any Winchelsea men who went, wearing this new uniform, are unlikely to have been involved beyond the army's port of disembarkation. However, the campaign is relevant to us because it was conducted in a way which indicates that, only sixty years after the end of the Hundred Years War in which Winchelsea had suffered so grievously, hostilities were renewed on an similar basis. Simon Schama, entertainingly and cynically: 'This [campaign] was a huge success; farms were indiscriminately ransacked and burned, towns put to the sword. Henry thoroughly enjoyed the whole thing, especially the skirmish dignified as the Battle of the Spurs in which the French cavalry, finding themselves ambushed, turned and fled, leaving nobles behind as lucrative prisoners'. [7]

As in the previous conflict, such aggression did not go unreturned although fortunately Winchelsea does not seem to have suffered. In the following year, 1514, the vulnerability of the south coast to French attack was amply demonstrated when Admiral Prégent, with considerable artillery power at his disposal, set fire to Brighthelmstone, now Brighton but then 'a poor village in Sussex', and plundered all that his men could lay their hands on. On this occasion, once they organised themselves, the Brighthelmstone community seems to have responded creditably for, firing so rapidly that the galleys had to move seaward, they chased the French back to the shore whereupon many including the admiral were wounded wading to their ships.[8]

This form of warfare came to a temporary halt in 1520 for Henry VIII's famous visit to King Francis I of France on the Field of the Cloth of Gold. This was really little more than another war, but one to determine who could put on the most elaborate display of opulence. The fleet, containing only 'a token force of Cinque Ports ships',[9] gathered at Dover to convey the king and his vast retinue to France. They transported '700 quarters of wine, 150 tuns of French and Gascon wine, six butts of sweet wine, 560 tuns of beer, 340 'beeves' at 40 shillings, 4200 muttons at five shillings, 800 veals at five shillings, eighty hogsheads of grease, salt and fresh fish'[10] etc etc. And well might they take those vast supplies for 'the greatest transportation exercise since the campaigns of Edward III ... shipped over the entire ruling class of England, about five thousand of them, earls, bishops and knights of the shire'.[11] When the logistics involved are considered, their horses should not be forgotten. Responsibility for this massive exercise fell on Sir Edward Guldeford as acting Lord Warden. Much of his property lay within the Liberty of Winchelsea and his name, with others of his influential family, is permanently remembered through the present East Guldeford.

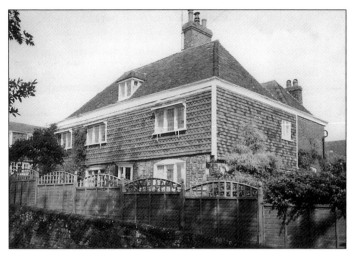

(61) The Retreat stands at the top of Strand Hill. It was rebuilt over its existing cellar in the fifteenth century

Despite its continuing decline Winchelsea may have made a contribution to the 'token force of Cinque Ports ships' on the way to the Field of the Cloth of Gold for four years later it is recorded as fulfilling its commitment when four ships totalling ninety-six tons sailed with the fleet and fifteen Winchelsea mariners were among their crews. The Victoria County History of Sussex considers that this was Winchelsea's last service save for 'six hoys' twenty years later.[12]

The Field of the Cloth of Gold is important to Winchelsea in another, quite striking, way. Among the ladies attending Queen Catherine of England was Lady Finch of the family long connected with Winchelsea; among the ladies attending the queen of France was Ann Boleyn.[13] King Henry may well have spotted her there. Their later relationship created a major impact on the history of England, an impact severely felt in the ancient town as we shall see.

The false and forced friendships apparent on the Field of the Cloth of Gold did not last long and within two years England and France were again at war. In 1522 and 1528 enemy ships entered Winchelsea's outer harbour at the Camber.[14] In the former year 'a French corsair' attacked English ships which were supposed to be protected by 'a new tower and bridge in the Camber'.[15] This structure became important later as the central tower of Camber Castle. In the same year the Cinque Ports were ordered to mount a defensive patrol in the Channel when war with France and Scotland was expected. Winchelsea is not recorded as contributing to this patrol and the problems the town was facing are illustrated by the growing inadequacy not only of the inner harbour but also the outer. 'There was some intention of laying up the *Henry*, a first-class ship, in the Camber for the winter but when soundings were taken it was found that there was not sufficient depth of water.'[16]

King Henry VIII's influence on Winchelsea was soon to be felt in another way. In 1526 he ordered a change in the method of choosing Winchelsea's mayor. Any chance that the men of Winchelsea should show some democratic independence must be snuffed out and the right to elect the mayor was therefore transferred from the citizenry at large to a selected number of twenty-four freemen who could be relied upon to support a candidate favoured by the king. The excuse for such an action was that the elections had been plagued with riot and disorder in the past. Nevertheless this decree remained in operation until 1550 when the rioting and disorder resumed![17]

It was not only the king who was deeply concerned about the problems experienced in electing mayors and bailiffs at that time. At a Cinque Ports Court of Guestling, held a year before the king's instructions to Winchelsea, reports were received of 'great dissentions' over such elections, not only on the appointed day but beforehand when unlawful gatherings and unruly behaviour had resulted in riot 'to the great abusing and unquietness of the well-disposed people ... [and] to the great slander, rebuke and decay of the said towns'.[18] Orders were given requiring that a certain number of worthy citizens should be nominated to carry out the election, thirteen of them at Winchelsea, a number increased to twenty-four by the king as we have seen. The mayor was responsible on election day for naming the electors who must be 'of the wisest and discreetest persons there present and that everyone of them be a freeman, householder and indweller'.[19] The proclamation which it was decreed at that meeting should precede the calling of the names of these worthies and their election of the mayor, required that 'every man lay from him his weapon and keep the king's peace, and that no man disturb this election nor give no voice in choosing here the king's head officer other than be assigned'. The penalty was forty shillings or imprisonment. Those requirements, with slightly different wording, are included in the proclamations still read by the town clerk at Easter Monday mayoring ceremonies in Winchelsea. However, these possible punishments now include 'losing their uppermost garments and twenty-two pence in money without any favour,' a delightfully anachronistic phrasing included when the town's custumal was confirmed in 1557.

It is clear from the above that by that time the townspeople were allowed to appoint their principal officers, both mayor and bailiff, the bailiff earlier having been nominated by the monarch.

The history of the development of the Cinque Ports courts lies generally outside the scope of this book but here it becomes relevant to us because, during Henry VIII's reign, they were often held in Winchelsea. The 'Guestling' at which instructions were issued about elections was held at Dover and attended by representatives of all the head ports. The Guestling has, since 1857, been subsumed into the Court of Brotherhood and Guestling. However, before that such gatherings were described as 'General Brotherhood *or* Guestling' and sometimes 'Special Meeting or Guestling'. Where such special meetings were to consider only matters of concern to either the eastern or the western ports they were held separately. It was those attended by the western ports which were often in Winchelsea.

For example, in 1517 the Abbot of Battle refused to return a criminal wanted in Rye. The mayor and jurats of Rye wrote to Winchelsea and Hastings requesting a Guestling at Winchelsea to consider what legal action could be taken as a result of this breach of the ancient Cinque Ports right of outfangthef, that is the right to detain and execute felons who were outside the ports' jurisdiction. The head officers and two or three jurats from each town attended. In the case of Winchelsea and Rye the head officer was, of course, the mayor but in Hastings it was still the bailiff. The dispute had arisen over John Burrell, 'a painter', of Lydd who had stolen, in Rye, a horse worth thirty shillings and fled with it to Alfriston which was then under the jurisdiction of the abbot. The abbot, instead of returning Burrell, transferred him to the King's Bench Prison in Southwark 'contrary to the liberties of the Ports'.[20] The outraged representatives at the Winchelsea Guestling demanded his return and nominated solicitors to appear at Southwark on their behalf. The plea was successful and a further demand was made of the abbot to return the horse! This he did. When Burrell came before the Rye justices he pleaded that he was in holy orders and therefore came only under the jurisdiction of church courts. This was admitted but before he was handed over for the second time he was 'brent in the brawne of the left thombe',[21] that is he was branded as a thief.

Accounts of the proceedings of other Guestlings held at Winchelsea during this period do not survive in such detail but they clearly involved matters of great concern to the Portsmen. In 1526 Guestlings were called, at Dover for the eastern ports and at Winchelsea for the western, to deal with Cinque Ports fishermen who had committed offences at the Yarmouth Herring Fair. The matter was considered so important that the representatives were to be of the same number as would be required for a Court of Brotherhood.[22] This importance was emphasised by the personal attendance of the Lord Warden, Sir Edward Guldeford, although he presided at the Dover court, not the Winchelsea one much nearer his personal estates.[23] In 1529 the western Portsmen again gathered at Winchelsea to discuss what action they could take to prevent the traditional enemy, the French, from fishing 'on this coast'.[24]

Legal proceedings of quite a different kind were affecting at least one Winchelsea resident at this time. He was Nicholas White who, together with eight men of Rye, was arrested in 1525 for holding what were then heretical Protestant beliefs about purgatory, confession and the sacraments.[25] In those days, under the direction of Cardinal Wolsey, a fanatical zeal operated in attempting to suppress such ideas. In pursuit of this zeal, Winchelsea was one of the ports watched in 1528 for any attempt at escape from the country by Thomas Garrett, a fellow of Magdalen College, Oxford who had been imprisoned for 'trafficking in imported Protestant books,' and had escaped from prison.[26] The watch at Winchelsea was in vain – Garrett was apprehended in Bristol.

In 1529 White was forced to recant his views.[27] This may well have been an expedient for, as the movement towards Reformation grew in strength, a unanimous vote to lease part of Winchelsea Court Hall to a Nicholas White was made by 'the whole Assembly' of Winchelsea in 1538.[28] Assuming that it was the same person, the document makes clear that White was already in possession of the part of the building he was permitted to lease. The agreement was for a period of twenty years at an annual rental of three shillings and fourpence, with liability for paying 'the king's rent'.[29] By that date the Corporation Court Hall was within the present site but White's part was in the northern wing, now demolished.[30] Had White still been out of favour, as he was earlier, such a grant would have caused much more of a stir.

Another man closely connected with Winchelsea who shared White's views was Alexander Welles, a Rye lawyer. He, too, came back into favour. In 1538, having served as deputy town clerk of Winchelsea, he was appointed to the senior post, later serving in the same capacity in Hastings and Rye.[31] Eventually he became Mayor of Rye in 1557 and 1558.[32]

The then heretical ideas and beliefs of White, Welles and many others were to become orthodoxy but Winchelsea suffered in the process.

37. DISSOLUTION

In fact Winchelsea was already suffering because its religious houses which had for centuries been providing much of what we would call social service to the community were, like their home-town, in decline. The immediate cause of the Reformation was Henry VIII's wish for the English Church to break from Rome so that he might defy the pope and obtain his divorce from Catherine of Aragon in order to marry Ann Boleyn. A century or two earlier he might have found it impossible to achieve this break but by the 1530s the communities of the friars and the hospitals, not only in Winchelsea but generally, were in poor condition.

We must not, however, underestimate either the ruthlessness of Henry's attack on the church or its impact in Winchelsea.

Frank Jessup in his *History of Kent* makes the point about ruthlessness forcefully when he stresses that 'The king's motives and those of his henchmen [were] of the basest, their methods dishonest and their lack of humane consideration for the inmates of suppressed houses sometimes deplorable'.[1] The enabling legislation was, in its implications and in its excuses for action, terrifying enough to those affected for, among other things, it referred to, 'manifest sin, vicious carnal and abominable living' being rife in the small communities where, the monks and nuns were guilty of 'spoil[ing], destroy[ing], consum[ing] and utterly wast[ing] their churches, monasteries, priories, principal houses, farms, granges, lands, tenements and hereditaments'.[2] Simon Schama, somewhat extravagantly, claims that tens of thousands of people were 'cast out into the world' and 'the property distribution was on a scale that no other English revolution ever approached ... the former residents were soon forgotten or reduced to family legends of headless nuns or spectral monks'.[3] In the face of such a royal and legislative indictment how could the smaller communities stand any chance of resistance? Of course they could not and in 1536 the destruction of the '374 lesser houses', among which were Winchelsea's, began, to be followed two years later, by the 186 'great and solemn monasteries'.[4] Mark Taylor, writing in *The Historical Atlas of Sussex* describes this as 'an unparalleled act of vandalism'.[5]

The property distribution which resulted will exercise our attention later. At this stage we must move from the general to the particular and examine the actual condition of the Greyfriars and the Blackfriars in Winchelsea.

The Greyfriars had certainly remained influential within the community during the early part of the sixteenth century. In 1521 the will of James Marshall desired 'a taper to be kept before Saint Barbara in the Friars Minors' for a year after his death. The chapel of the Greyfriars, part of which survives, was dedicated to St. Barbara.[6] Five years later Gregory Wylgate went a bit further. He wished to be buried in 'the church of the Greyfriars' and to establish a temporary chantry there in which the warden of the Greyfriars, Thomas Man, was required to 'sing for my soul and for my father and mother in the chapel of Saint Barbara for the space of one whole year'. The warden was to be rewarded with the sum of £6 12s 4d.[7]

Thomas Man ceased to be warden in 1530 when he was succeeded by Robert Benyngton.[8] No doubt Benyngton was gratified to receive, in that same year, a legacy of twenty shillings from the distinguished Sir Goddard Oxenbridge of Brede for 'the reparations of the church and house of the Greyfriars of Winchelsea'.[9]

The evidence gathered in 1538 by the Bishop of Dover and reported to Thomas Cromwell at the king's command suggests a very rapid decline in the situation of the Winchelsea Greyfriars since Benyngton's appointment. One possible reason for such a decline appears in the White and Black

Books of the Confederation of the Cinque Ports which, recording the attendance at a General Brotherhood held at Romney on 11 September 1536, notes that 'because of the sickness and visitation of God which was at Rye and Winchelsea [the representatives of those towns] did appear by their attornies'.[10] Such 'sickness and visitation of God' was liable to affect close-knit communities such as monasteries particularly badly. The bishop noted that the Greyfriars were very poor and not able to continue and comments that if the warden had been at home he 'would have given it up'. Later in the year the bishop again visited Winchelsea, presumably for the surrender of the land and buildings. He then stated that he had 'sold the stuff', meaning the ornaments and furniture, and informed Cromwell, 'The house is at the king's command and yours'.[11] The tenancy of the site was, in 1542, formally allocated to Philip Chowte who, as we shall see, was serving as Captain of Camber Castle which had undergone major development in response to the renewed threat of invasion and attack by the French.

Chowte was a man of considerable influence, a former yeoman of the guard and, valuably for him in those days, a relation of Sir Thomas Cheyney, the Lord Warden. He was one of Winchelsea's members of parliament, certainly from 1542 and possibly three years earlier and was to have a distinguished army career.[12] Chowte used his occupation of the land of the Winchelsea religious houses as a quarry for Camber Castle's later further development, with the Blackfriars suffering more than the Greyfriars. When his interest in the Greyfriars ended, Chowte's twenty-one year tenancy, for which he was charged only £1 per annum,[13] was foreclosed in 1545 and the site sold to 'George Clifford, gentleman and Michael Welbore, gentleman,' for the considerable sum of £736 11s 0d.[14] The king was reaping his reward for the acquisition of church land. Interestingly the sale to Clifford and Welbore was endorsed with a memorandum stating that 'all the bells and bell metal and lead upon the premises' were excluded.[15]

There seems to have been no lead at the Blackfriars site to be excluded from any future sale for the Bishop of Dover's report, also submitted in 1538, on that community was as follows: 'At Winchelsea the stuff of the Blackfriars is sold for about ten pounds. The house has no lead but slate and tile and is falling down. There is a close let for twenty shillings a year but the rent for four years to come was taken five years ago. The rest is not worth ten shillings a year'.[16] With his ready eye for scandal, W. M. Homan thinks the bishop's officials were not given reliable information for this statement is not compatible with the land and property formerly owned by the Blackfriars which is mentioned in Queen Elizabeth's grant to Winchelsea Corporation in 1586. Although there may be double entries for some sites, the grant includes Castle Field, slopes and several areas of land, a stone mill, a windmill, a maximum of six houses, etc. etc.[17] Homan comments: 'One cannot help thinking that either the Friars hoodwinked the expropriation officials or that they succeeded in bribing them, a risky proceeding, but no doubt sometimes resorted to'.[18]

Whatever they may have secretly held elsewhere, available evidence suggests that the Blackfriars' principal site near Pipewell Gate was, indeed, in a very poor state. The premises remained unoccupied for more than three years 'after the religious were driven out'. Nobody could be found to take a lease of the site, buildings and one acre of land even at the low rental of five shillings a year. Eventually, in 1542, Philip Chowte took the tenancy 'at that fixed rent'[19] and set about plundering the site of stone even more effectively than at the Greyfriars.

St. Giles's, now derelict, was also used as a quarry at this time. Rye was busily improving its defences in response to the invasion threat. One major aspect of the work was the rebuilding of the town wall east of Landgate 'for which over 200 tons of dressed stone was brought in from Winchelsea and Camber Castle, at least 150 tons of it from the remains of St. Giles's Church'.[20]

It would seem that St. Thomas's Church did not entirely escape the wrath of the king for its dedication was to a man who had defied his monarch. 'The statue of St. Thomas Becket was removed from its bracket c.1538 and at the same time the church's dedication was altered to St. Thomas the Apostle.' Becket's tomb at Canterbury was destroyed at this time and he was declared to be not a saint but an ordinary bishop.[21]

Other events closely associated with the dissolution would have affected St. Thomas's' income, resources and appearance. In 1547 an Act of Parliament required that, as with the monasteries earlier, all chantries be dissolved[22] and in the same year 'pots of limewash were brought into the churches of England to obliterate the wall paintings.'[23] At St. Thomas's only a tiny fragment survives this deprivation and later ones.

(62) Crowsnest, a small fifteenth century hall-house, stands behind Strand House and now provides additional accommodation for Strand Guest House.

Rather to my surprise it seems that King Henry's ire did not extend so forcefully to Winchelsea's hospitals for at least one of them survived, although not for long. Holy Cross had already ceased to exist. Its last master was appointed in 1501 and by 1570 the mayor and jurats declared formally that they had no knowledge of a hospital or chapel of the Holy Cross and that the present, secular, owners of the land had been in possession of it for fifty years.[24] 'In 1559 the corporation appointed a master and mistress to the hospitals of St. John and St. Bartholomew, probably combined on the St. John's site by that date.' This worthy lady and gentleman were instructed 'to live in the Chapel of St. John and build up the houses and chapel of St. John within three years'.[25] They might just have succeeded in fulfilling that requirement but, if so, their success was not sustained for, although a master was appointed to St. John's Hospital in 1565, within as short a period as a further three years from then it seems the land was being granted to 'a private individual'.[26] That had been the situation with St. Bartholomew's land since 1543.

What, then, of the effect of all this on the ordinary townsfolk of Winchelsea. To find out we have to rely largely on general evidence rather than that specific to the town. The dissolution of the monasteries destroyed 'a large institutional charitable framework' and some system had to replace it. It soon became clear that the ecclesiastical parish would be required to undertake this responsibility and legislation categorising poverty and demanding action proliferated. Between 1531, when an act distinguished between beggars able to work and those incapable, and the Poor Law Amendment Act of 1834 there were no fewer than fifty-one statutes requiring parishes to respond in various ways.[27]

These demands and the great weight of poverty which was to pervade the town would, before the end of this volume's remit, bring Winchelsea almost to its knees.

Most important to us here is the act of 1536 in which Thomas Cromwell laid down the basis for parish reaction to the problem of poverty. Parishes such as St. Thomas's, by now, as we have seen, combined with St. Giles's, were required to keep and look after the 'impotent' poor, that is those unable to work, by collecting 'voluntary and charitable alms' so that such people would not have to resort to begging. As for the 'sturdy vagabonds' who were capable, they must be forced to work 'in such wise as they may get their own living by the continual labour of their own hands, on pain that every parish making default shall forfeit twenty shillings a month'.[28] Presumably this fine applied to each able-bodied pauper. The act went on to place responsibility for raising the 'voluntary and charitable alms' on the head officers (the mayor in Winchelsea's case) and the churchwardens, together with two others 'who may serve for only one year', to collect the alms and keep them 'in a common box in the church'. This was recognised as being a difficult task in which all types of clergy should assist at every possible opportunity by exhorting parishioners to contribute.[29]

Quite apart from punishing the parishes for permitting the able-bodied poor to resort to begging, the act laid down severe consequences for those individuals who did so. A first offence was punished by whipping, a second by cropping of the right ear and a third by imprisonment until the next quarter sessions where, upon conviction, the culprit was to be sentenced to death as a felon. The nineteenth century commissioners inquiring into the operation of the Poor Laws commented, with unconscious irony, 'It appears that the severity of this Act prevented its execution'.[30]

This legislation, and all that followed, demanded a whole new layer of local government the provision of which fell upon Winchelsea and similar communities without financial support from outside. The similarity between this situation and the effect of national legislation upon local councils in the late twentieth and early twenty-first centuries is undeniable.

In assessing the impact on Winchelsea of the dissolution of the monasteries I find myself readily able to accept the conclusions put forward by the anonymous author of a Guide Book to the town published in 1915. He or she wrote: 'Few places can have suffered more than Winchelsea by the dissolution of the religious houses which took place during the reign of Henry VIII. The dispersal of the Greyfriars and the Blackfriars, and the monks and nuns belonging to the religious houses of St. John's, St. Bartholomew's and Holy Cross, meant the disappearance from the town of an influential section of the inhabitants. Round the monasteries was centred a particular group of trade interests and their destruction meant ruin not only for the very poor but to many of the middle classes'.[31] This type of structure in the Winchelsea community was not re-established until the late nineteenth century when wealthy incomers purchased the larger houses, bringing a great improvement in the economic welfare of the town and its ordinary inhabitants through the provision of services for and within these houses.

Throughout the time of the immediate effect of the dissolution and its impact upon the king's enemy, the papal church, Winchelsea's insidious enemy, the silting of its harbour, steadily progressed. In 1533 Thomas Cromwell's attention to poor law legislation and plans for the dissolution might well have been interrupted for a few moments by a petition beseeching him to intercede with the king 'to improve the harbour at Winchelsea which was being choked by gravel'.[32] This document was drafted by Rev. John Thompson who took a great interest in harbour engineering. Knowing this the mayor and jurats of Winchelsea had obtained for him 'the benefice of St. Thomas' in the hope that this would encourage him to support them. Mr Thompson's petition, in eliciting a grant of £500 from the crown, was successful; the resulting works, insofar as they were carried out, were not.[33] The mention of gravel suggests that this may refer to the Camber and the eastern drift of the shingle but it might equally apply to the inner harbour for, between 1537 and 1562, no fewer than 730 acres of land to the south-west of Winchelsea in the Brede Valley were 'inned' by landowners[34] and the effectiveness of the scour of the tides was consequently further greatly reduced.

But also throughout that time, close-by, development was being hurried forward to prepare defence against an enemy other than the papal church and the inning of marshland – the French.

38. WINCHELSEA'S CASTLE

A confirmed Winchelsea Castle existed only during the sixteenth and seventeenth centuries when it was the acknowledged name of Henry VIII's great defensive fort since known as Camber Castle. That castle was only accessible from Winchelsea and was partly constructed from materials scavenged from the town. Whether there was ever a Winchelsea Castle on the hill of Iham is a matter of doubt.

There has been a Castle Field or 'Castell Land' to the north of the site of St. Leonard's Mill and within the former Liberty of St. Leonard since at least 1500 and almost certainly much earlier but how it came to be known by that name is a mystery. A certain General Elliott once claimed, as a result of dowsing, that a Roman Fort had been constructed on the site. A resistivity survey in 1989 revealed nothing to substantiate this claim and Edward I would not have built any form of fort there for it remained within the Liberty of Iham under the influence of the Abbey of Fécamp and was not included as part of New Winchelsea.[1]

Therefore we have to look to a much later period for the story of 'Winchelsea Castle' which, for the sake of convenience, I shall refer to by its later name.

The origins of Camber Castle are believed to lie in a grant made in 1486 of the lordship of the Manor of Iham to Sir Richard Guldeford. In return for the rights and income from which he benefited as a result, Guldeford was required to build 'a tower ... within two years at his own cost near the port called the Camber'. The purpose of this tower was to defend the coast against 'any rebels, transgressors and enemies coming sailing there by sea'.[2] There is no firm evidence that Sir Richard fulfilled this requirement and, if such a structure resulted, it was probably of wood with all evidence therefore now lost.[3]

However, in 1506, Sir Richard's influence in the area and, indeed, his income was further enhanced by his becoming Bailiff of Winchelsea and it was only six years later that his son, Sir Edward Guldeford, Master of the Armoury for Henry VIII, commenced what we know as the first phase of the construction of Camber Castle. It stood close to the harbour and now forms the lower part of the castle's central tower but, on its own, it was of limited effectiveness, was never armed and played no part when hostile ships entered the Camber in 1522 and 1528.[4]

Henry VIII's break with Rome vastly increased the threat of action against England by the combined forces of France and Spain. There was frantic activity to prepare the defence of the country. The king was not short of support, great numbers of the population had 'a positive passion to shoulder a weapon and – even more – put on a uniform'.[5] This enthusiasm needed physical support and Camber was one of the castles Henry built or extended between 1538 and 1540 to provide for the defence of the south coast. The building was modified under the direction of Stephen von Haschenperg, a distinguished Flemish castle designer and builder, using no fewer than 1300 labourers and craftsmen. The central tower was strengthened and raised. Five D-shaped bastions with walls to resist the strongest sixteenth century artillery were built around it. They formed an octagon and were connected by vaulted passageways.

Also involved with von Haschenperg as one of the commissioners overseeing the work was Philip Chowte whom we have already met becoming tenant of the land of the Greyfriars and Blackfriars in Winchelsea. He was to make good use of that tenancy. Chowte was a paid commissioner and obviously took his work extremely seriously for his signature appears on every page of the accounts. I cannot resist mentioning that Chowte's fellow commissioner, John Fletcher, ancestor of the playwright, signed these same pages with a cross against which a clerk

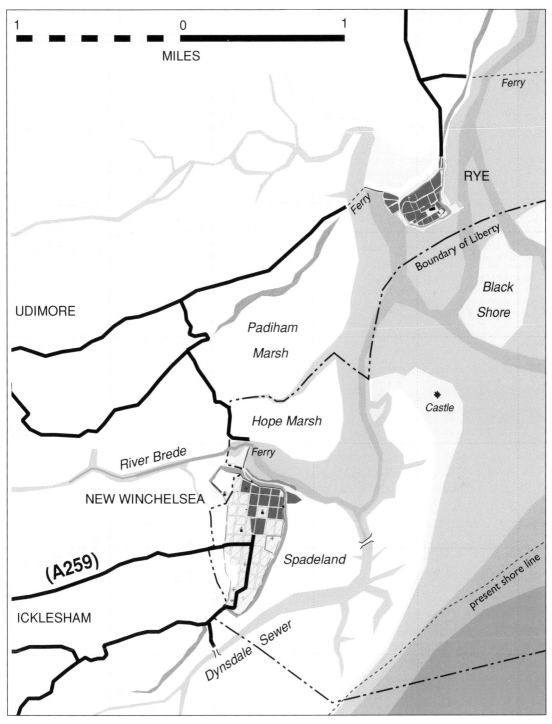

(63) This plan shows clearly how the only land route to Camber Castle was from Winchelsea and includes the bridge which was essential for access.

wrote 'Fletcher'.[6]

In order for supplies to reach these works it was necessary to build a new bridge across the Dinsdale Sewer for the only land access to the site was from Winchelsea. Across that bridge 'wagonloads of stone could be brought from the local quarries at Fairlight, Hastings and Playden. Caen stone (paradoxically provided by the potential foe, the French) came in by sea and was exchanged for billets. Timber for the floors and scaffolding was prepared in the woods of Udimore, Beckley and Appledore. Bricks and lime, on the other hand, were manufactured on site, with clay, straw and chalk brought from Dover'.[7] It is not difficult to imagine the urgency and intense activity involved.

Nevertheless the threat was so great that results were considered to be inadequate and a further period of development was begun within only a few months. It has been suggested that the king himself, having been brought up knowing the more traditional form of castle building, may have instigated this last addition to the structure. It involved the building of four massive semi-circular bastions at the four points of the compass, in front of the D-shaped or 'stirrup' towers, and the heightening of the internal walls.[8] The immense cost of £10,000 hardly seems justified for it has been argued that this third phase potentially weakened the castle's defences by creating 'dead ground' around the bases of the bastions 'that could not be swept by the fire of its guns'.[9]

Philip Chowte must have benefited greatly by this additional building for he was not only tenant of the Winchelsea religious houses but had been appointed Captain of Camber Castle in 1540. John Steane concludes his account of the building supplies quoted above with the words, 'All this material was topped up with second-hand stone and hardcore from one of the religious houses of Winchelsea'.[10] For this work the Blackfriars Church and buildings in Quarter 4 near the Pipewell Gate would have been considerably more convenient. Stone from them could easily be carted down Ferry Hill, loaded onto barges on the River Brede, and shipped quite close to its destination.[11] Perhaps that is why the only Blackfriars remains are below ground while at least part of the Chapel of the Greyfriars survived.

Philip Chowte's position was strengthened even further when he was appointed Captain of the Castle for life in 1544 with the added title of Superintendent of the Camber and the Puddle Creek. His salary was two shillings a day and he had 'the power to appoint eight soldiers and six gunners to be paid sixpence a day out of the treasury'.[12]

Considering the enormous expenditure involved the castle was never an effective form of defence. It was built on what was then the edge of the Camber, commanding the anchorage. Within a few years the harbour's silting and the sea's withdrawal became increasingly pronounced so that now the castle stands lonely among the fields.

It was not long before Camber Castle's decline set in and it never fired a shot in anger. Philip Chowte is last mentioned as captain in 1565, a long term by the standards of the day and he was succeeded the following year by Thomas Wilford, a staunch Protestant who had been in exile during the reign of Queen Mary I. Wilford became a Freeman of Winchelsea in 1569, a jurat by 1571 and mayor in 1571-2.[13] He was still captain in 1599, another very long term of office, but by that time the castle was falling into serious disrepair.

As early as 1584 attempts to maintain gun platforms of wood and lead were abandoned. A massive programme of in-filling then began in the north and south bastions so that guns could stand on these new earthen ramparts, or rampires.[14] For the castle it was the beginning of the end of any possible effective use in war.

The first abandonment proposal dates from 1623. Three years later local dignitaries were told of information reaching the king that 'our Castle of Camber in our County of Sussex is grown into great decay, being forsaken by the sea and left distant from the water two miles at least so that the same is now of no further use for defence'.[15] King James had most certainly not been misinformed. Those local dignitaries may well have included the Captain of the Castle who was among those complaining to the Lord Warden that they had not been paid because the arrangements had ceased on the death of James I.[16] Instructions issued in 1636 to demolish the structure were, fortunately, not carried out. The garrison was disbanded the following year 'and the ordnance later removed, but the castle remained in use as a weapon store'.[17] Whether all those weapons were included when, in 1642, during the civil war, the House of Commons ordered that the 'muskets, powder and other ammunition' should be removed to Rye[18] we do not know.

The great present archaeological interest of Camber Castle is that its ineffectiveness discouraged all attempts at developing or altering it as the years progressed and therefore what survives is prime evidence of the castle-building methods of Henry VIII's time and the circumstances of those who served there.

Dr. Barry Yates, Warden of Rye Harbour Nature Reserve, whose organisation is now charged by English Heritage with general supervision of the Castle and its surrounds, was kind enough to escort me there one afternoon in October 2003. I had not visited since the early 1980s and an enormous amount has been done by way of investigation and restoration since that time. The forbidding boundary fence and the unsightly buildings it enclosed are gone and the external view from ground level must again be much as it was four hundred and fifty years ago. The interior has been made safe for public visiting supervised by volunteers and at the time of writing this is allowed at weekends during July, August and September. The necessary walk from Rye is well rewarded.

Barry Yates took me first to the central tower or keep, the massive scale of which comes as a considerable surprise. As we stood on the restored floor beside the well from which the men of the garrison drew their water, I was amazed that such an enormous building, let alone all the stirrup towers and bastions could, if ever the castle had come under attack, have been defended by so small a garrison. We have already seen that Philip Chowte was authorised to engage six gunners and eight soldiers at the public expense. Surely an inadequate force. 'When wages were paid for 1 October to 31 December 1540 there were sixteen gunners, a porter and the captain. By January 1542 this had been increased to twenty-nine men.'[19] Such a tiny force, faced with a concerted attack from troops and guns landed nearby by an enemy would, however strong their fortress, have been justifiably petrified.

If such an attack had ever taken place these men would hardly have been fortified for action by the comfort of their living conditions. The ground floor of the central tower would, in most Henrician castles of the period, have been used as a communal mess hall, kitchen and barrack room with storage in the basement. The upper floor provided accommodation for the captain and there were additional sleeping quarters in the bastions. This applied generally at Camber except that money was saved by putting the kitchen in a bastion where 'the smoke vents in the firing chamber also served as chimneys for the baker's oven'! Making this observation, Norman Longmate goes on to point out that, while earlier medieval castles were places for sheltering civilians and retainers, 'Henry VIII's forts were designed solely for fighting, cramped, low-roofed, and immensely strong, they subordinated the occupants' needs to operational necessity as much as any fighting ship'.[20] I feel relieved for the garrisons at Camber that they never had to fight.

The accuracy of Longmate's use of the term 'low roofed' is amply demonstrated for anyone attempting to negotiate the excavated passage which surrounds the keep, a passage containing sixteen gun ports with neatly constructed smoke vents. I was surprised to find such a raking slope of stonework at these gun ports. This made it look as though only an enemy coming over the outside walls would be within the range of fire but later I discovered that these apertures were for hand-guns and that soldiers manning them could have commanded the courtyard.[21] That is, of course, if there had been enough men present to undertake such a duty.

From the mid-seventeenth century until the late twentieth century when restoration work and archaeological investigation began the castle lay abandoned in the fields and open to all who might wish to visit and play there. Ford Madox Ford, when living in Winchelsea, visited frequently. His account evokes particularly well the castle's condition during this time. He wrote, with particular reference to the underground passage already described:

> 'Perhaps Henry VIII had not in mind the provision of hiding places for those young in years or mind, but he has provided splendid ones. As such the place is educational. One understands the use of castles and fortresses when one has employed them in this way; one sees the kings and queens and personages of history so much better after one has breathlessly crouched in a half earthed-up tunnel, whilst the footsteps of a pursuer [bring] down fragments of stone around one.'[22]

By the second half of the 1940s I was just such a person, young in years, often visiting the castle to play while on holidays in Winchelsea. By that time access to the tunnels which set Ford's imagination racing had been further restricted and by far the most evocative moments of my visit with Barry Yates came when we climbed the rampire of the south bastion. Here, unlike the north bastion which has been archaeologically excavated and restored, the in-fill has been left undisturbed and the climb reveals a wonderful view of Winchelsea and of the surrounding fields and lakes, all of which are either part of the Nature Reserve or are managed in co-operation with it. This was the castle as I remember it from my boyhood, a peaceful and yet exciting place for idling away the hours, scrambling around the surviving walls, or for enjoying the almost unparalleled distant view of Winchelsea which, even then, I had learnt to cherish. Since then my memory has played tricks with me. I do not recall a steep drop from the battlements to the ground. I have the firm impression that the soil had built up against the walls, carried by the prevailing winds so that there was, certainly against the south bastion, an, albeit smaller, natural rampire on the outside to match the man-made one within. An aerial photograph taken in 1948[23] shows the well-worn paths around which my friends and I would run but fairly conclusively fails to confirm my impressions of long ago about the exterior slope.

And so back to the Winchelsea of the sixteenth century, contemporary with the later phases of Camber Castle's construction. When Henry crossed to Calais with an army in 1544 after war with France had again broken out, hoys (not full-sized merchant vessels but more modest sea-traders[24]) were used to carry the troops. Eight of them came from Rye and six from Winchelsea.[25] This is believed to be the last time that Winchelsea was able to make any practical contribution to the ship service which had been its duty for centuries. In the following year a further expedition was mounted against France and plans were laid that, in the event of bad weather, the vessels of the fleet 'proposed to avail themselves of the roadstead at the Camber, under cover and protection afforded by the new Castle.'[26] If that had happened no Winchelsea boats could have provided leadership but the masters of the nine from Rye would have known the waters well.

Winchelsea's outstanding prowess at sea, apart from a few acts of piracy and privateering already noted, must now pass from this story. We are entering the time when debilitating decline became irreversible and the town relied on being sustained by its surviving traditions and increasingly strident appeals for help.

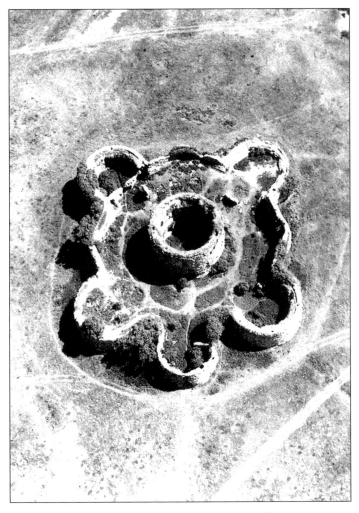

(64) Camber Castle from the air, 1948

39. WINCHELSEA'S CUSTUMAL

We turn next to those surviving traditions. They were contained within Winchelsea's custumal. The custumal, as the name suggests, set down the customs of the town. In fact they were more than just customs; they were laws regulating the government of Winchelsea. Within the Confederation of the Cinque Ports the custumals contained marked similarities because these were originally ancient traditions dating from long before written versions existed. Those of Winchelsea and Rye were modelled on that of Hastings, originally their head port. The Hastings custumal was probably first put into writing in 1356.[1] There was a close correlation with the other ports but variations developed over the centuries. For example, Winchelsea, when criminals were sentenced to death, hanged them while Dover and Hastings threw theirs over cliffs.[2] The Winchelsea custumal features at this point in my story because in 1557 the town clerk, Thomas Hooker, produced a written version which was supposed to remove any doubts about the various laws and their interpretation. There had been some concern in the Confederation about the way these laws were being used, a concern which seems to have been strong in Winchelsea for in 1550 the jurats examined 'the Custumal brought in by George Lowes [and instructed] that Winchelsea should send the book to Romney to be copied and sent on to Hythe for copying and so forth until it reaches Sandwich'.[3] Lowes was a leading citizen who had seven times been mayor and was to serve again the following year.

Thomas Hooker's version was translated by W. MacLean Homan, assisted by his record agent, Miss Gwyneth Wise, and they helped the ordinary reader to understand it by attempting 'to eliminate legal phraseology as far as possible'.[4] Although there are other versions which contain variations[5] I rely here on Homan/Wise for my extreme summary of a few interesting clauses.[6]

The best known of these is the one regulating the election of the mayor. 'The people of the Commonalty' (that is the Freemen) were to gather at the Hundred Place on Easter Monday 'and by common consent elect a mayor'. If the proposed mayor refused to serve 'the people of the Commonalty shall go and break down his principal dwelling house'. The mayor is still appointed at a Hundred Court on Easter Monday but the latter provision would not be enforced in the twenty-first century! The mayor's oath, still in use, is laid down in the Custumal, as is his duty to appoint twelve jurats 'from among the wisest of the town'. The number of jurats was greatly reduced during Winchelsea's later years as a rotten borough and the exact number of twelve, while desirable, is no longer a firm requirement.

To all intents and purposes those are the only parts of the 1557 Custumal which have any relevance to the unique survival of Winchelsea Corporation to the present day. The mayor's duties as coroner, however, remained in operation until 1886. In the event of an accidental or suspicious death within the Liberty, the mayor must view the body and hold an inquest. The regulations which we have already seen applied to Robert Alard, Vincent Finch and others, still applied in 1557. If anyone was suspected of murder he was arrested and the charge announced at three successive Hundred Courts. If no one came forward to prosecute, the accused was freed. If there was a prosecution and thirty-six men would came forward to state the accused's innocence he was also freed and the prosecutor or plaintiff was 'arrested and all his belongings forfeited to the King'. If any of the thirty-six did not so declare the accused was 'hanged on the gallows'. At that time the gallows was 'above the Salt Marsh on the North side of the town'.

Provision was made for any person guilty of lesser crimes to seek sanctuary by 'flee[ing] to holy Church'. In those circumstances the mayor as coroner must question him. If guilt was admitted and he, 'the felon', agreed to leave the country, then arrangements were made for his safe conduct to a port which he might name. Some specific crimes bore punishments before the perpetrator was allowed to go. For example, if anyone snatched a purse or was caught with 'silver stolen from a pouch in the market or elsewhere', the owner could demand that one of the thief's ears was cut off. In that case, having suffered already, he only had to agree to leave the town rather than the country. For a second offence he lost his second ear, and for a third, his life.[7]

Certain offences were not eligible for trial by the mayor and jurats of Cinque Ports towns but were reserved for the Lord Warden's courts or for hearing by his commissioners. One of these was counterfeiting money. Three counterfeiters were tried in Rye by commissioners in 1551. It was a show trial and the judges were entertained at considerable expense. This was a capital charge. The men were found guilty which involved further expense. The town chamberlain's claim read: 'Paid to the executioner the 10th of April for making the pit, burying and for poles to set their heads on. And bearing one of their heads to Winchelsea and setting it up – four shillings'.[8]

If anyone 'of evil reputation' enters the town the mayor 'shall have him arrested and hand him over to the bailiff to be put in prison'. That is quite regardless of whether or not he commits any crime in Winchelsea. The clauses dealing with this go on to state that the bailiff may not arrest anyone or release anyone from prison without the consent of the mayor and jurats. This is important because it confirms the precedence taken by the mayor who is the people's representative over the bailiff who is the king's representative.

The custumal lays down the medieval conditions under which a new resident might apply to become a freeman. These are as follows: 'If any stranger comes to Winchelsea and dwells there following his lawful vocation and is of good behaviour for a year and a day ... he shall come before the mayor and jurats met in full Assembly and request the franchise'. This clause was already, in the mid-sixteenth century, being overlooked and the mayor and jurats had taken fairly firm control of who may and who may not become a freeman. As we shall see, the phrase 'of good behaviour' was being used to exclude existing freemen who did not meet with approval.

Perhaps somewhat unexpectedly as we look back four hundred and fifty years, there is much in the custumal which protects married women who own or inherit property in their own right. In many cases the courts require, where land or property is to be sold, that the woman concerned shall appear without her husband so that her personal agreement may be confirmed. How often women in those circumstances would refuse agreement is not clear.

In this mention of a few of the custumal's provisions I conclude with examples of the considerable duties of the mayor. He has to take responsibility and make arrangements in cases where the heir of a deceased person is under age. The mayor must ensure that the child is placed in the care of 'the nearest blood relation to whom none of the inheritance can descend', a very precise definition which might well involve much investigation. That person becomes the child's guardian and guardian of 'all the goods and chattels' until the child comes of age. In the event of no relation being available then 'some worthy man in the community' must accept the same responsibilities.[9]

We have already seen how the mayor also at one time took responsibility for admissions to the town's hospitals and for ensuring that the hospitals were properly run. Following the Reformation the hospitals were, like the town, in decline but not entirely extinct for as late as 1564 William Harman was appointed Master of the town hospitals, almost certainly St. John's and St. Bartholomew's combined, and in the following year he was succeeded by Thomas Spruce.[10] The hospital of Holy Cross seems to have met its demise long before the Reformation for, as we

(65) Camber Castle in the eighteenth century

have seen, in 1570 the mayor and jurats declared that they had no knowledge of its existence except that the land had for more than fifty years been in the ownership of the Guldeford family.[11]

In 1557 when Thomas Hooker's version of the Custumal was made, Winchelsea's most powerful resident was one William Egleston. Egleston was mayor four times[12] and was twice elected to parliament as member for the town. Thomas Egleston, possibly his brother and certainly a relation, was also a member of the corporation at that time and served as mayor in 1556/7 and MP in 1586. Both had Thomas Hooker as their town clerk and William actually purchased land from Hooker in 1549.[13] The Egleston family seems to have originated in Hastings for William is mentioned there five years before his name first appears in the Winchelsea records.[14] William's election to parliament was recommended to the electors of the town by the Lord Warden, Sir Thomas Cheyney. In those days the Winchelsea freemen would readily accept such a nomination for at least one of their seats and they would initially have approved warmly of William Egleston regardless of the Lord Warden's influence for the mayor and jurats sent him as their representative to London 'to sue for the relief of this town of Winchelsea', and they paid his expenses.[15] However, William later blotted his copybook in the eyes of the mayor and jurats and became one of those excluded from the franchise for what they viewed as unacceptable behaviour. In 1561 'various charges were brought against him and he was fined £100 and disfranchised.' Apparently he had taken home the town's records and documents and allowed Sir John Guldeford to see them. Sir John was the king's bailiff and had inherited the Manor of Iham adjoining the town. The mayor and jurats looked upon this as a betrayal of trust but officialdom viewed it quite differently and the Lord Warden wrote three times asking for Egleston to be reinstated. Winchelsea eventually relented and he was re-admitted in 1567.[16]

This was not the end of the matter. William Egleston was the only freeman I know of who was threatened with banishment from the franchise on two separate occasions for different reasons although the action was only implemented once! In 1568 there was a disputed election for mayor. Edward Middleton was elected but 'in view of the weak support of this election, other freemen have elected William Egleston'.[17] A great fuss ensued; the perpetrators of the illegal subsequent election were fined and Middleton's mayoralty confirmed. The most interesting point about this particular dispute was that among the sanctions used against the 'ringleaders' of the alternative election of William Egleston as mayor is that they were 'ordered to lose their uppermost garments which they wore on that day'.[18] This particular sanction is still read each Easter Monday that a new freeman is appointed as being applied against anyone other than a freeman who tries to take part in the election. It remains part of Winchelsea's ancient tradition and the fine quoted is 'twenty-two pence' in money. Other fines which were charged following the 1568 dispute are also listed in the records but 'the entry disfranchising William Egleston for a second time is struck out'.[19]

There must have been very good reason for sending William Egleston to London seeking assistance on behalf of the town because of Winchelsea's impoverished state. In 1548 the corporation had been forced to raise funds by selling 'the Great Chalice and the bells of the Great Cross in order to defray debts'.[20] It may be that Egleston was involved in the drafting of a parliamentary bill for in the same year legislation on behalf of the towns of Rye and Winchelsea sought permission to construct a number of sluices designed to increase the scouring action of the tides. Reasons cited were the unhelpful actions of landowners who released water from sluices when the tide was out and 'the damage done by the castings of ballast into the harbour'. The subsequent legislation included penalties for ballast dumping but nothing about the sluices.[21] Since Rye and Winchelsea were both involved this harbour would have been the one at the Camber. It is noted in the bill that this was 'so choked, and filled up that there cannot lie in the same harbour above thirty or forty sail of ships and yet [the] same ships cannot come into the same harbour without great danger'.[22]

Perhaps the most dramatic example of Winchelsea's declining fortunes in the mid sixteenth century lies in the customs returns made to Chichester. These show a comparison between the dues collected from Rye and Winchelsea in 1490/1491 and in 1559/1560. The contrast is stark. In the former year Winchelsea paid £88 16s 7¾d and Rye £12 8s 1¾d. In the latter Rye paid £573 1s 7d and Winchelsea £1 5s 5d.[23]

It is therefore hardly surprising that the town turned for help to the queen herself.

40. A PLEA TO THE QUEEN

Before considering how a personal appeal became possible, we must return to the subject of Winchelsea's two parliamentary seats, an election privilege which was the principal, possibly the only, factor which kept external interest alive in a rapidly declining town. With the mayor and jurats generally becoming less happy to undertake the parliamentary duties involved and, more importantly, increasingly unable to find the necessary funds, the influence of the Lord Warden spread. In 1553 there was, however, considerable disquiet among the portsmen when Sir Thomas Cheyney sought to nominate all the members due for election in the Cinque Ports. This led to 'an uneasy compromise whereby the Lord Warden was usually granted one nomination and individual towns the other'.[1] Sir Thomas on that occasion wrote to Winchelsea saying that Captain Chowte would be one member if he wished or otherwise his brother could take his place; Sir Thomas would nominate the other.[2] Winchelsea obviously shared the disquiet of its fellow towns for the members elected on this occasion were William Egleston and Michael Blount.[3] As Egleston was a leading Winchelsea citizen he is unlikely to have been Sir Thomas's nominee although that influence may have resulted in Blount's success.[4] The reason for Sir Thomas's mention of Philip Chowte, whom we have already met as Captain of Camber Castle, is clear for they were related, but, despite the Lord Warden's recommendation, Chowte's brother Anthony was never to be Winchelsea's MP.

Six years later the post of Lord Warden was vacant. The mayor, Goddard White and the deputy mayor, John Pecke, were elected for Winchelsea 'but for some reason Henry Fane, a Kent gentleman, was substituted for the latter'.[5] Fane had a little property in Winchelsea but no other qualification other than being held in strong regard by William Brooke, Lord Cobham. Although Cobham was yet to become Lord Warden he is likely to have been behind this change.[6] The list of Winchelsea members suggests that, at least during the period under consideration, the town managed to continue to control the election of one of its two members.

The most interesting of these, Thomas Wilford, would have been well known to the queen. He, like Chowte, served as Captain of Camber Castle as well as being jurat and once mayor. In the later part of the century national rather than local affairs took his interest and he became adviser to the government about England's relationship with the Netherlands where he advocated 'whole-hearted intervention' in a way which rather scared his colleagues. However by the time of the Armada threat Wilford was felt to be 'the only person left in the Netherlands capable of giving good advice and the queen considered sending him to arrange a settlement of all outstanding differences'.[7] Wilford was therefore another Winchelsea man, if not by birth, whom the town could claim as exerting national influence.

The Confederation of the Cinque Ports' concern about external intervention in parliamentary elections is clear in a resolution passed at a General Brotherhood held at New Romney on 22 July 1572. This, in essence, ordered 'that in future only freemen resident in the Ports shall be chosen as barons for Parliament'.[8] However, the records show that this requirement was easily circumvented in later years by any newly elected member taking the oath of a freeman quite regardless of whether or not he was properly qualified.

Winchelsea Corporation's concern about the cost of sending members to parliament and its resulting willingness to allow others to bear that expense is reflected in its dealings with the Confederation. In that case the expense was in sending bailiffs to Yarmouth to regulate and administer the annual herring fair over which the Ports retained control despite Yarmouth's strong

(66) The Castle Inn, now Old Castle House, contains many internal medieval features.

objections. In 1563 John Pecke of Winchelsea, he who had been discarded as an MP, was to take the town's turn as one of the two bailiffs and it was minuted that 'Winchelsea is to be considered at the next Brotherhood for mitigation of the charges of the bailiff to Yarmouth'.[9] Sadly there was little sympathy for the town's plight for at the next meeting it was decreed that if Winchelsea did not pay the £5 7s 3d it owed, the mayor would be placed under house-arrest.[10] Fortunately in 1567, when it was again the town's turn to provide a bailiff, Winchelsea's delegation nominated Goddard White. They also 'brought in a letter from the Lord Warden regarding the poverty of [Winchelsea] and seeking relief in the charge of the bailiff to Yarmouth'.[11]

Quite apart from seeking help elsewhere, the mayor and jurats of Winchelsea were attempting to put their own house in order. Unfortunately they chose to do so in an extremely unpopular way. Various returns of this period make the poverty of Winchelsea's fishing capability, previously so numerous and profitable, abundantly clear. In 1561 there were 'ships, boats and crayers – none' and only four mariners.[12] Two years later there were again no fishing boats. Very slight improvements are noted in 1565: 'ten sailors and two fishermen'[13] with 'five lighters operating from Winchelsea,[14] and, in 1572, 'two coastal trading vessels'.[15] There is, however, no evidence of any real return to profitable fishing despite the corporation's contentious requirement that every freeman should twice a year 'venture unto the seas £10 at a time'.[16] The effect of this was that they had to invest £20 a year in some maritime trading activity from the port. There was an awful row which was not sorted out until a Confederation Court of Brotherhood in 1580. Two jurats, Goddard White and Thomas Fane, are referred to by name as having been involved in 'diverse and sundry strifes, debates, controversies and displeasures [which have been] of late stirred up between them'.[17] Arbitrators had been appointed and they required that all conflicts between the two men, 'from the beginning of the world until 27 July 1580 shall cease' and that they shall become friends and pay their own expenses in the matter.[18] The arbitrators recognised the injustice of the cause of this dispute and ordered the mayor and jurats of Winchelsea to call a meeting to nullify the decree.[19] As the brotherhood also ordered the oath of a jurat to be administered to Mr Fane, it would appear that he had disobeyed the decree and Goddard White had been attempting to enforce it.[20]

The anxieties felt by the mayor and jurats about the condition of the town would have been further enhanced by the frequent demolition of Winchelsea properties. An order was made 'forbidding building materials from any buildings within the town from being removed from the Liberty.' Cynically, however, having introduced this regulation, the corporation was able to charge for granting licences allowing residents to disregard it. This they frequently did.[21]

Demolitions, however, still exceeded repairs and, in 1565, only 109 inhabited houses remained in the town.[22] Such evidence as exists suggests that the trend would continue rapidly downwards.

During the period leading up to Winchelsea's plea to the queen there was, however, a positive development for Winchelsea trade which is in evidence to this day. There was at least one successful clockmaking business in the town for the Rye Church clock was made between 1560 and 1562 by Lewis Billiard of Winchelsea. This clock is believed to be the oldest clock in England working regularly and retaining, for the most part, its original mechanism.[23] The Rye Churchwardens' accounts show that Mr Billiard was paid £33 18s 6d for his work.[24] A letter from the Rev. Oscar Brooks, then Vicar of Rye, points out that the internal workings of the clock have been made visible to public view by the use of glass screens but states that the most famous part of the clock, the external face and the Quarter Boys, were not Billiard's work but date from 1760.[25]

Another positive for Winchelsea was its reputation as a healthy place. Frederic Inderwick wrote: 'The chief attractions of [Winchelsea's] site were its strategic position, its abundance of excellent water ... and its general reputation for healthiness ... When the great plague broke out in 1563 and again in 1586 Winchelsea was selected as a sanatorium for the troops and others during the time of pestilence'.[26] No doubt the mayor was attempting to protect that reputation when the corporation agreed that no sheep or pigs should be allowed at large in the town. The pigs were further restricted by having to be 'yoked and ringled' (they must wear a bell) and no citizen might have more than four of them.[27]

And so, in 1573, Queen Elizabeth I visited a town where she need not fear infection and where she would see no sheep or pigs in the streets. She must have been well aware that she would be asked for help because three years previously the town had addressed an urgent appeal to the Privy Council which set out to show 'why the town of Winchelsea is worthy to be advanced and raised up out of the present poor and most lamentable state it is in'.[28] Through the Council the queen was told about Winchelsea's regular layout, its surviving cellars, its former excellent harbour and its previous prosperity. The document's perhaps exaggerated claim was that 'there was in the narrow seas no place so fit to have a good haven made'. Reasons given were that it lies in the middle of 'a fair bay' between Rye and Hastings, that rocks are available 'to make piers and jetties' and that 'there were three fathoms at low water without any sand, flat bar, or any other danger near.' The mayor and jurats proposed a surprisingly simple solution, namely that if a channel five hundred and fifty yards long were cut through 'good firm marsh ground', the sea could be admitted to a depth of two fathoms to the great benefit of the fishermen of Hastings and Rye and of the queen's navy. They concluded, a bit pointedly, that 'such a place of defence was more necessary since the loss of Calais'.[29] The Privy Council took neither notice nor action. Saving

Winchelsea was not high on the national agenda as it had been in the time of Edward I.

There is only one account of Queen Elizabeth I's visit to eastern Sussex in August 1573 which includes what happened when she came to Winchelsea. That account is by Samuel Jeake and, although no other contemporary writer refers to it, we must accept it here. Cooper suggests that the visit was in compensation for the town's disappointment at receiving no help. That may be so but the queen can hardly have expected to be spared further representations. Anyway, Winchelsea put on a good show in an attempt to make a favourable impression. Her Majesty, 'beholding the goodly situation, ancient buildings, grave bench of a mayor and twelve jurats in their scarlet gowns, and city-like deportment of the people (there being then several gentry) ... she gave it, as she thought deservedly, the name of Little London'.[30] Well! That is a bit difficult to take literally – it seems most likely that she was being sarcastic although the kindest interpretation is that she was commending the effort that had been made to impress her. Winchelsea's real situation is described in Lambard's *Topographical Dictionary*, published only two years after the event. According to Lambard there were fewer than 'sixty households standing and those, for the most part poorly peopled'.[31]

The town must have been extensively smartened up for the queen's visit and the gowns purchased. The corporation, being frugal, made sure that the gowns were not used only on a single occasion, however important. They later issued an order that the mayor and jurats were to wear gowns in court.[32] Considering the town's state of impoverishment, it was fortunate that the queen visited only briefly and did not stay three days as she did at Rye. There the visit cost £150 of which the mayor, Henry Gaymer, had to lend the council £100. Those costs included providing uniforms for sixty members of the local militia who escorted the queen.[33]

What exactly was said to the queen in Winchelsea we can never know but, probably by coincidence, the town was to receive favourable treatment thirteen years later.

41. RESIDENTS AND REVENUES

It was while Her Majesty was causing Rye Corporation so much expense that a Rye mariner, William Fyrrell, had his vessel requisitioned to carry the English ambassador's gelding to Dieppe. Fyrrell agreed to take Thomas Green, a merchant of Winchelsea, as a passenger. During the voyage across the Channel, Green hailed and boarded a passing vessel from whose crew he acquired five barrels of herrings. The gullible Fyrrell, persuaded by Green's smooth talk that all this was quite legal and that he would be in no danger, agreed that the herrings should be loaded into his boat. The pleas in mitigation, eventually made by Fyrrell to the Lord Warden, state plaintively that 'Your Honour's Humble Servant, being a simple, plain man, gave credit unto the sayings of Thomas Green'.[1] Fyrrell was unwise to do so for when they landed at Dieppe the rightful owner happened to be present, recognised the markings on the barrels and had Fyrrell arrested for piratically robbing him of herrings to the value of more than four hundred pounds. The poor man was committed to prison. Meanwhile 'the said Thomas Green conveyed himself away and came over into England'![2]

Prison conditions for the unfortunate Fyrrell were harsh. For sixteen weeks he was confined in irons, sometimes 'in the dungeon and sometimes more at large'. Eventually he had no option but to pay 'four hundred crowns' for his discharge. The outraged letter which he addressed to the Lord Warden claimed recompense from Green, not only for the money but also on account of the loss of his time and the great distress caused to his wife and family. The Lord Warden was asked to appeal to the Mayor and Jurats of Rye to arrest Thomas Green whenever he might come to Rye and order him to pay Fyrrell for his loss.[3]

There is an intersting sidelight on Fyrrell's imprisonment which suggests that he may have had crew members arrested with him. George Sandon, also imprisoned at Dieppe, heard that there were other English prisoners and asked to be allowed to see them. The gaoler agreed, provided Sandon paid a fee 'according to the custom of the said prison'. Conditions do not sound as bad as earlier described for the English prisoners, including Fyrrell were brought to Sandon and 'they all made merry at dinner'. The sailors sought Sandon's support and told him that they were held because 'one Green of Winchelsea bought five barrels of herrings out of a pirate, for which herrings they were now put in prison, and the said Fyrrell requested him [Sandon] to take note of their words'. This he did and later gave evidence for them.[4]

The Lord Warden must have responded to Fyrrell's pleadings for Green was arrested in Winchelsea and locked up in the town gaol from which, like many after him, he escaped. When Green thus avoided justice, at least temporarily, the Mayor and Jurats of Rye initiated an action of withernam against Winchelsea.[5] This meant that any Winchelsea freeman going to Rye could be arrested and held until the debt was paid.

Whether Green repaid Fyrrell, whether repayment came from elsewhere, or whether no recompense was made, we do not know. There must, however, have been some resolution of the matter because the dubious Thomas Green continued trading in Winchelsea and is shown as entering into an agreement to deliver 'six tons of bar iron to John Love of Winchelsea at Bodiam Bridge by 25 July 1575'.[6] I hope Love did not pay in advance! It seems he did not but there was still a dispute because Green was late delivering the consignment and used the appalling condition of the roads as an excuse.[7]

This reference to Thomas Green's transporting a consignment of iron gives me the opportunity to refer briefly to Winchelsea's involvement with the iron industry. Through the development of iron-working technology there was, in the Weald of Kent and Sussex, a major industrial revolution more than two hundred years before the developments which are normally accorded that name. The town's initial reaction was distinctly negative. In 1540 an ironworks was established at Robertsbridge Abbey. This addition to others in the area was 'looked upon with much disfavour by the Ancient Ports of Hastings, Winchelsea and Rye'. The export of wood was an important part of the western Cinque Ports' economy and this was being affected by the ironmasters' use of 'vast quantities amounting to 1500 loads of great wood made into charcoal annually'.[8] They demanded an inquiry which was not held until 1548/9. A jury of responsible citizens was appointed to give evidence to the inquiry and they concluded that any ironworks which were 'above ten miles off from the seaside and six miles from the downs may best be spared to stand'. Those closer to their towns despoiled the countryside, robbed them of vital exports and caused a general increase in prices.[9] This seems to us to be balanced and sensible evidence but the portsmen adhered to their old adage that actions speak louder than words and did not wait to hear the outcome of the inquiry. Before that was announced, 'a rude company appeared at [Robertsbridge] Abbey and proceeded to put down the forge'.[10] The damage must have been repaired for the business was profitable and continued during the remainder of the century bringing Winchelsea some benefits.

Winchelsea in fact benefited not a little from the important industrial activity of its hinterland. The Victoria County History of Sussex notes that 'the mineral wealth of Sussex was always confined to its iron, though it may be noticed that in 1570 Sir Thomas Smith endeavoured to remedy this by some experiments made at Winchelsea in the transmutation of iron into copper'.[11] Sir Thomas was unsuccessful but later in the century there is evidence that Winchelsea managed reasonably successfully to export iron. Towards the end of the sixteenth century Rye, like her sister town, was suffering a general decline in exporting activity. 'Only iron, down by a quarter, and horses which alone showed a minor increase, showed any signs of maintaining their earlier levels.'[12] The fall in iron exports from Rye continued in the 1590s but Winchelsea partly took over. It was Winchelsea's proximity to the iron works which, even though the town had earlier protested about the loss of timber, allowed it to benefit most. The extent of the town's liberty gave it jurisdiction over what became known as 'The Puddle' at the mouth of the Rother. Here it was possible to load and unload with lighters even if larger ships could not come alongside and from this point Winchelsea's iron exporting temporarily flourished.[13] The ironmasters who operated in the area must have been grateful for this outlet for only through Rye or Winchelsea could they move their product without an extremely hazardous and expensive journey by road.

Mention of journeys by road prompts me to record a proposed visit of the Lord Warden, Lord Cobham, to Winchelsea in 1583. Unfortunately Winchelsea had been involved in a dispute with his lordship about the jurisdiction of his courts as opposed to that of the individual towns and a summons to attend at Dover had been disregarded. Lord Cobham was not pleased. Winchelsea, with due deference, gave instructions that preparations were to be made for the visit when His Lordship was due to travel by road from Hastings. A feast was to be ready at the town's expense at the home of Mr Love. When the Lord Warden and his retinue reached Winchelsea, Lord Cobham 'rode past through St. Leonard's' although Lord Buckhurst and Lord Montague did come into the town.[14] I hope thay partook of the feast! The mention of St. Leonard's must not confuse us. The Lord Warden travelled along a road which then existed to the west of Winchelsea through the parish of St. Leonard and was thus able to by-pass the town. How badly such a facility is needed in the twenty-first century!

(67) Nos. 3-5 The Five Houses, built in the eighteenth century for Winchelsea's cambric manufactory

As this story progresses we find that the many surviving records provide an insight into the lives of Winchelsea residents which was perhaps less readily available earlier. We have already noted the miscreant Thomas Green. Another who belongs to the period under consideration is Christopher Mockett. Intriguingly there survives within the archives of Winchelsea Corporation a list of Mockett's possessions dated 1569, considerably before he became prominent within the town. As this document[15] is unintelligible to my inexperienced eye, Roger Davey kindly agreed to examine it for me. He assures me that when the list was drawn up Mockett's possessions included: a cloak bag of motley (i.e. many colours), one pair of shoes and a pair of slippers, two handkerchieves, one pair of linen hose, a pillow coat [case], a pair of Spanish leather buskins dyed with velvet [calf-length boots], a Spanish leather jerkin, a doublet of fine canvas striped with a green silk with white sleeves and one ell of coarse canvas. Not all the items can be included because the page is defaced by a large blot but the total value was thirty shillings. Whatever may have been the purpose of this list, some items suggest a certain opulence and, if that assumption is correct, it is confirmed by Mockett's later lifestyle when he is invariably referred to as Christopher Mockett, 'gent'.

The minute books of the corporation[16] provide numerous references to Mockett's holdings within the town which included a field, orchard and garden called Savery's Field, Tinker's Garden (now part of Rookery Field), at least two further houses and part of 'the pendents of the hill' (that is the cliff) on the eastern side of the town. Most specifically and interestingly we know that his 'mansion house' was in Quarter 12[17] which adjoined those pendents and is now principally occupied by Rookery Field. Mockett was heavily involved in building work for he was at various times authorised by the corporation to sell the stones from the walls of a house which he had purchased from the corporation, to remove building materials from a small property adjoining his home and to take slate out of the town. We know nothing of Mockett's marital status but there was certainly room in his home for him to take a lodger. This was a yeoman by the name of Robert Morrell who was inconsiderate enough to commit suicide in his bedroom.[18]

Mockett was a leading member of the corporation but his colleagues seem to have been somewhat wary of him. This is evident towards the end of his career when it was suspected that he had 'long occupied the pendents east of his mansion house wrongfully',[19] but even more much earlier when he was 'deprived of the freedom on insufficient grounds'[20] and when it was suggested that he should be made mayor. This latter recommendation came to the mayor, jurats and freemen from no less a source than the Privy Council who urged, in 1587, 'that an able and sufficient man be chosen to that place of mayor among them, whom they shall know to be good and sound in Religion and fit to govern there and forasmuch as Christopher Mockett and John Love are noted unto their lordships' they recommend the election of whichever the corporation prefers.[21] Perversely, but not uncharacteristically, the electors chose Adam Moyle! This mistrust was apparent again later when Winchelsea was ordered by a General Brotherhood of the Confederation to produce books to answer charges made by Mockett and to make him a jurat.[22]

Perhaps the problem was at least partly engendered by an incident in 1589 when Mockett, while serving as Overseer of the Poor, to which post he can be shown to have been appointed under the will of Goddard White,[23] stole or otherwise acquired the town drum; the corporation seemed to think they were not going to get it back and demanded it.[24] The town drum had a purpose associated with Mockett's work as overseer for it was used to call out a work force to repair the highways. The problem of transporting iron and the poor condition of Sussex roads is mentioned above. Mockett might have been trying to enforce an act of 1585 which 'stipulated that for every six loads of charcoal, or every ton of iron, a cartload of slag, gravel, stones, sand or chalk must be laid down. But the foul highways and byways of Sussex grew steadily fouler'.[25]

Christopher Mockett is one of the many Winchelsea residents mentioned in 'Queen Elizabeth's Charter' which, in 1586, confirmed the ownership of land in Winchelsea, much of it the corporation's. It would be a happy thought that this resulted directly from the appeal made to the queen when she visited Winchelsea, even if it took thirteen years for her to respond. Not so! The corporation, after the dissolution of the monasteries, came into the possession of a large amount of the former property of the Greyfriars, the Blackfriars, the chantries and the hospitals. Exactly how this was managed is not clear but there was much judicial inquiry into the matter and in 1584 an order was issued that all the evidence produced for examination in consultation with Mr Edmund Pelham, the town's legal adviser, 'concerning the title to town lands' should be 'put into three baskets or caskets and returned to the town chest'.[26] In 1585 Thomas Talbot and Peter Smith of London obtained a crown lease on these properties which they, probably rightly, claimed were concealed lands acquired by stealth. The corporation had to pay £150 to buy out the interest of Talbot and Smith and were then eager to ensure that some way was found of confirming their right to the properties, some of which they may already have sold to pay the £150.[27] When they heard of the forthcoming grant, a number of Winchelsea residents asked that their lands should be included in it in order to secure their titles. Perhaps, as with the corporation, there was room for doubt!

The grant was duly made in the elaborate form of the day with all the properties listed, together with the names of their occupiers. The first page is embellished with an original portrait of the queen, 1586 being before the time when standard illustrations were used on official crown documents. W. D. Cooper lists all the properties involved[28] as does the official entry of the grant in the Winchelsea Corporation Records.[29] Twenty-first century Winchelsea residents wishing to find out whether their own property was included will, however, be disappointed. There is only mention of the quarter in which a property stood or of 'The Strand'. The former owners do feature, however and the large amount of property 'formerly part of the Dissolved Monastery or House of Blackfriars or Friars Preachers'[30] seems to confirm W. M. Homan's contention that when the Bishop of Dover's officers were told of the Blackfriars' poverty they were being hoodwinked.

Christopher Mockett's 'mansion' in Quarter 12 is not included but he is shown, in addition to the property listed above, as being in occupation, jointly with Richard Breadman of two houses and two gardens in the fourteenth quarter, and, solely, of two acres of land in the seventeenth quarter.

Largely from this grant stems the quaint and possibly unique survival of the annual collection of 'The Queen's Dues' in Winchelsea when amounts ranging, in modern terms, from 3p to £4.11p per annum are collected by or on behalf of the town chamberlain.[31] The total is £19.33; sufficient to provide quite generously for the corporation's day-to-day expenses when granted by Queen Elizabeth I as £19 6s 6d but hardly adequate in the twenty-first century. If only she had made the grant inflation proof! It may be, however, that the origin of the Queen's Dues dates back much further to the original grant of land for the construction of New Winchelsea and that the 1586 grant merely caused the modification of the sites and the amounts. This possibility, suggested to me by Christopher Whittick, Senior Archivist at East Sussex Record Office, whose knowledge of the Winchelsea archives is second to none, is supported by an entry in the corporation record of 1580, six years before the grant, which refers to 'the collection of the queen's rent or rent of assize'.[32]

What, then, of the original of this vitally important Winchelsea document? For many years it was lost and the corporation knew nothing of its existence. In 1816 it was produced at the annual Easter Monday Hundred Court, rather to the surprise of those present, by George Stace. Stace had served Winchelsea in many capacities over fifty years, starting as sergeant-at-mace and finishing as mayor. How he came by it without the knowledge of his colleagues remains a mystery. After proper authentication an order was made that the 'Charter' should be produced each Easter Monday to ensure that it was not lost again. This did not happen during the twentieth century but after many years in the vaults of the corporation's bank it was transferred to East Sussex Record Office for proper permanent storage and care. There it is available for inspection.[33] Winchelsea readers and visitors may also see a framed photograph of the first page including the royal portrait. This was presented by Jurat Knightley Chetwood during his mayoralty and hangs in the Court Hall Museum.

The Winchelsea where, to many residents' relief, their rightful entitlement to land was settled by the 'Charter' was soon, however, to be badly unsettled by the threat of Spanish invasion.

42. ARMADA ALERT

Before negotiations were completed about the terms of Queen Elizabeth's 'Charter' and the land it would include, rumours of a threatened Spanish invasion were rife in England. There was much justification for such rumours and, as always when a foreign invasion on the Channel coast was a possibility, Winchelsea was prominently featured in the defensive preparations. Particular urgency was felt when, after intelligence received during his attack on Cadiz, Sir Francis Drake sent a message home warning: 'Look well to the coast of Sussex'.[1]

Citizens of the town were constantly required to be on the alert for strangers and, if they spotted anyone, would immediately act as a constable and bring him before the magistrates for questioning. In those days of static communities where newcomers were instantly recognisable, this was much easier than it would be today. Spying consequently became infinitely more difficult and the expelled Spanish ambassador, de Mendoza, who was directing operations from Paris, complained that 'not a man, not even a fly, could approach the naval ports without being seized'.[2]

The magistrates were involved in other cases which highlight the grave concern about invasion. In April 1585 a Winchelsea man, John Black, was convicted of pulling down a fort which stood on the King's Green to the east of Quarter 39. Black and others involved with him who seem to have escaped prosecution are likely to have looked upon the available building material of a badly maintained structure as fair game to remove for construction elsewhere. However, the magistrates took a much more serious view and said that 'the exercise of martial causes had been much hindered' by the damage to the fort.[3]

Somewhat to the embarrassment of the town officials, Winchelsea's ancient duty of ship-service was called for as the Armada threat grew. In 1586 they wrote to the Constable of Dover Castle, Sir William Brooke, and the Lord Warden of the Cinque Ports, the same Lord Cobham who had earlier been so displeased with Winchelsea, pointing out that Winchelsea had no 'ships, barques or vessels nor yet any masters or able mariners, but only one sailor, William Buxton,' who was at the time on a voyage to La Rochelle.[4] It is possible that this return was an attempt to dodge the column and that the Lord Warden discovered the subterfuge because in October of the following year he compiled a certificate which listed a barque, the *John* of 20 tons, as Winchelsea's only ship. The certificate goes as far as to name the crew who were Nicholas Penbough and John Lovell, masters, with Robert Pevenshe, John Brown, James Lever and Nicholas Barnonfield, 'able-bodied mariners'.[5] There are constant uncertainties about the accuracy of such listings – for example the brothers Jessup have the *John* as a Romney ship.[6]

Those uncertainties multiply when numerous variations in the naming, tonnage and home port details of the Cinque Ports contribution to the fleet raised to combat the Armada are taken into account. I have preferred the annals of Rye Corporation. The Rye representatives who had attended a meeting at Dover to allocate the required 'five ships and a pinnace' from the Cinque Ports reported that Hythe was to find the pinnace, Dover was to provide one ship, Sandwich another, Romney and Lydd one, Rye and Tenterden one, and the last was to come from Hastings and Winchelsea. The members would help their head ports where necessary.[7] This seems convincing and entirely contemporary with the events of the day. Despite its lack of shipping Winchelsea made a financial contribution of £66 13s 4d towards the costs of the Hastings ship.[8] This was the *Anne Bonaventure* of 70 tons with a crew of 49.[9]

The Cinque Ports ships, at this very late stage of the requirement of their ship service, appear to have acquitted themselves honourably. 'They were for a considerable time anchored [with that part of the fleet which was under the command of the acting Admiral of the Cinque Ports] in Dover Roads ... and when the enemy sailed up the other side of the Channel ... took part under Lord Howard [of Effingham] in that action off Gravelines which thoroughly discomfited the Spanish.'[10] Winchelsea's monetary contribution which must have been quite a problem to find can, I hope, be counted as honourable support!

The town's geographical position meant that there were other urgent considerations to be dealt with. A survey of Sussex's defensive preparations was made by two of the county's deputy lieutenants who reported that 'Winchelsea is strongly seated and a dangerous place if the enemy should possess it'. The town should therefore be provided with 'one demiculverin and two sacres at least'. A demiculverin was a 4½ inch cannon, a sacre a rather smaller one of 3½ inch bore. The extreme shortage of manpower at Camber Castle is also commented on in this report. Although the castle was in good repair and 'well furnished with ordnance and munitions' including nine guns, only three men formed the garrison.[11] The number of defenders was increased.

It was no good, of course, being able to identify spies easily, having an adequate fleet, or being as well armed as possible if there was no early warning of the enemy's approach. Such warning was provided through the beacons which, standing at high points on the coast, had been in place for two centuries. They were hurriedly repaired where necessary, watch-rotas compiled and watchmen recruited. It is claimed that within a few hours news of the approach of a hostile fleet could be relayed to the government in London and to vulnerable points whence orders would be given for the militia to mobilise.[12] The signalling devised was sufficiently sophisticated for the watchmen on the Isle of Wight to be able to send a message warning Sussex to send forces to guard the coast.[13] Keeping watch duty at one of the beacons was a responsible and boring task.

(68) John Norden's map of Sussex was drawn in the late sixteenth century and augmented by John Speed in 1616.

There always had to be two men on duty day and night and they were not allowed to sit or lie down for fear they would go to sleep. Even when a hut was provided it was so small that the occupants had to stand up![14] There can be little doubt that men of Winchelsea had to undertake this unenviable work but we do not know whether Winchelsea by then had its own beacon or whether the town was still helping in the maintenance and manning of the Fairlight beacon as before.

In Winchelsea all this preparation led to something of an anti-climax. The Armada passed up the Channel on 27 July 1588,[15] apparently not within sight of the town. No doubt the people of Winchelsea kept anxious vigil with the demiculverin and sacres ready, and the beacon watch keenly awake.

Two short footnotes to this episode are required here. The traditional piratical activity of the men of the Cinque Ports, particularly through privateering was threatened when Queen Elizabeth I, with complete justification, temporarily withdrew all licences to privateers in order to obtain sailors for such a vital fleet. 'The barons of Rye protested loudly that the queen was infringing upon the mariners' time-honoured right to "the licence for the men of war to go to the seas."'[16] It may be this incident which provoked N. A. M. Rodger to state categorically that 'with great reluctance [the Cinque Ports] put some ships to sea in 1588.'[17]

Winchelsea had no privateers, does not seem to have complained, even when asked for money, and finally paid off its debt to Hastings in 1596. After some adjudication which suggests that the whole amount may not have been forthcoming, the mayor and jurats of Hastings issued a receipt for £10 'concerning a ship set forth against the Spaniards in 1588'.[18]

Throughout the Armada crisis Winchelsea's leading citizen, serving both as mayor and member of parliament, was Adam Moyle. Moyle was one of those who fell foul of the regulation requiring all freemen to invest £10 in a trading venture at sea.[19] When this demand was repealed as both impracticable and largely unenforceable, Moyle was reinstated on payment of a twenty shilling fee. That was exactly the same sum that the corporation voted to pay 'towards his charges' when he was elected to parliament in 1586![20]

Moyle's career in Winchelsea provides an interesting insight into the corporation's relationship with the Privy Council. Such a direct contact seems surprising to us but the layers of government were spread more thinly in those days. Before the 1584 parliamentary election the Lord Warden wrote to Winchelsea and the other ports indicating that the Privy Council wanted him to ensure the return of 'suitable persons'. Winchelsea responded by ignoring the Lord Warden and sending the Privy Council eight names direct. One of those names, Giles Fletcher, was approved and elected, together with Herbert Pelham, 'a Sussex gentleman who had recently become a jurat.' This particular Lord Warden, towards whom Winchelsea's attitude seems always to have been abrasive, was considerably annoyed at being sidelined in this way but the town made no move to reconciliation and went on to ignore his lordship's claim to influence selections at the next three elections.[21]

It was while Adam Moyle was mayor that the Rector of St. Thomas's Church, who was also by then responsible for the disused and dilapidated St. Giles's, was granted a licence to sell stones which were lying in St Giles's churchyard. It was, however, a condition of this licence that the standing remains of the church should be left untouched.[22] It seems quite surprising that anything remotely like a substantial part of the church was left at that time for forty years earlier there had been a major reconstruction of the Rye town wall east of the Landgate. For this work, as we have seen, 150 tons came from the ruins of St. Giles's Church; the remaining fifty tons came from

(69) Nos. 11/12 High Street, now the former Post Office and the Tea Tree Restaurant, dates from the fifteenth century. To the left is Nesbit, probably older and containing the remains of two medieval houses built end-on to the street.

Camber Castle'.[23] The amount of stone in St. Giles's churchyard, through which the rector could increase the church income, must have been limited. Four years later, in 1591, things were financially easier for St. Thomas's because by that time the tithes of both St. Giles's and St. Leonard's 'had been annexed.'[24]

The following decade produced something of a boom in map-making for the area. From those maps I have selected two which will help provide information about the Winchelsea of those days.

John Norden came to Winchelsea in 1595 and served the needs of this book well by writing about his visit. Recounting Winchelsea's early history he wrote that, 'the streets lay so direct that view might be had in every of them from one end of the town to the other'.[25] As Winchelsea's highest point is at the New Inn/Court Hall junction whence it drops away to all four points of the compass, I think Norden may have been looking at a plan rather than carrying out observation in the town. Others of his observations, though, convey to us something of the impression Winchelsea gave the visitor at the end of the sixteenth century. 'It is now a very poor town wholly in manner decayed, but the ruins of the stately decayed houses, vaults and cellars in every street to be seen seem to yield tears, even out of the hard stones that so pleasing a [place] so well contrived should so suddenly sustain desolation.'[26] As we progress through hundreds of years of Winchelsea's story we may not be convinced of the suddenness with which the desolation struck, but the picture which Norden evokes is clear.

His map, as later amended by John Speed, gives a good idea of the topography of the area as the vast anchorage at the Camber shrank and shallowed through constant inland inning. What appear to be four islands in the lower Brede Valley should be taken as representational. That area was marshland, occasionally flooded at high tide and ripe for more inning. The odd position assigned to Bulverhythe suggests some further misinformed assumption.

Another map of the period, prepared for an inquiry into 'the acreage and boundaries of Camber Beach and salts',[27] provides important information about the rights and claims of the Guldeford family. Camber Beach was part of the Manor of Iham which they held, together with the bailiwick of Winchelsea. This map is now in the possession of All Souls College, Oxford.[28] Details included state that the current Lord of the Manor, Sir Henry Guldeford, had ancient rights of anchorage, could claim the benefit of acquiring the contents of wrecked vessels, owned the parsonage house and received rent from lighthouses on his land.[29] A tiny plan of the town from the corner of this map has been skilfully enlarged by the staff of East Sussex Record Office, enabling us to add to John Norden's observations of the Winchelsea of those days. With the most westerly quarters missing it would be misleading to assume that this can be taken literally but it clearly shows that the walls and gates along the top of the eastern cliff were still in place and suggests that the centre of population was almost as it is today. What are now the High Street, Castle Street and Mill Road are particularly built up with a clear gap where the Barrack Houses stand; they were not to be built for another one hundred and fifty years.

Within three years of the inquiry which provoked the drawing up of this map, Sir Henry's rights were challenged by Cinque Ports seamen. John Boddy of Hastings complained bitterly to a General Brotherhood that he had had a topsail confiscated in lieu of payment of 'boomage and fierage' when he had entered 'the creek of Winchelsea,' part of the Manor of Iham.[30] This, he claimed, was contrary to the rights granted to Cinque Portsmen. The Brotherhood agreed. Francis Bolton, formerly both a pirate and Winchelsea's town clerk, but now working for Sir Henry, was ordered to return the topsail pending a further meeting of the Guestling which Sir Henry was invited to attend. If he failed he was to be fined by the Mayor of Rye.[31]

The final decade of the sixteenth century from which these maps date saw the Cinque Portsmen once again called upon to provide ship service 'to suppress Her Majesty's enemies'. This was required in waters both near home and far away. Comparatively close at hand were continued attempts to suppress the marauding Dunkirkers but the Cadiz expedition in 1595 was quite a different matter. The confederation provided vessels from Rye, Romney, Hythe, Dover and Sandwich. The voyage was expected to last five months and cost £1600.[32] Cooper notes that Winchelsea 'could not offer any part'.[33] However, Winchelsea's record books, unavailable to Cooper, show that the town was expected once again to make a financial contribution towards the ship provided by Rye, this time of £80.[34] That seems a considerable commitment and, as raising the complete amount would have been difficult, an attempt was later made to avoid full payment.[35]

And so, with Winchelsea continuing to struggle to meet its responsibilities, we move towards the end of a long and memorable reign.

43. GRIEF FOR THE GODFREYS

When, in 1603, the old queen's death heralded the accession of the Stuart dynasty in England, one of the knights of the canopy at her funeral was Sir Moyle Finch, Member of Parliament for Winchelsea.[1] This is the only reference I have found to canopies being carried at royal funerals; canopies at coronations feature here and frequently elsewhere in these pages. Sir Moyle had been elected for Winchelsea, his family's home-town, in 1601, having represented other constituencies earlier. He died in 1614. Members of the Finch family had long served the town, not only in parliament, but also as mayors and bailiffs. Sir Moyle's principal relevance to this story is that it was his widow, 'the richest widow in England',[2] who was, in 1628, to be created Countess of Winchilsea in her own right and paid his home town the compliment of adopting its name for her peerage. Elizabeth, Countess of Winchilsea's wealth stemmed principally from her inheritance from her father, Sir Thomas Heneage, and her title, granted by Charles I, specified that it should continue through 'the heirs male of her body lawfully begotten'.[3] Spelling was extremely variable in those days and her version has remained in use by the Earls of Winchilsea to this day.

Sir Moyle's canopy-carrying skills were not, however, required for James I's coronation. On that occasion Winchelsea appointed leading citizens. There was somewhat nervous preparation for this ceremony, probably in the hope of avoiding embarrassment. Henry Brooke, Lord Cobham, had succeeded his father as Lord Warden. Readers may remember that Lord Cobham senior, William Brooke, had been in dispute with Winchelsea and it seems he must have been a generally combative personality for he died of wounds received in a duel.[4] Henry Brooke wrote to the ports urging them to select 'men of the meetest and comeliest personage among you and of the best sufficiency otherwise'.[5] Presumably they had to look good and to be able to afford at least some of the expenses. They certainly had to dress up to make an impression. The Confederation decreed that each baron should wear 'one scarlet gown, down to the ankle citizen's fashion, faced with crimson sateen, gascoigne hose, crimson silk stockings, and crimson velvet shoes and black velvet caps'.[6] Quite a get-up and certainly expensive! Strangely, when the Lord Warden wrote to the Ports seeking their choices he said that, although this privilege was customary, 'No precedent of a Privy Seal' for these services could be found.[7] The Cinque Ports submitted their claim to the 'Grand Seneschal and the other Commissioners' who made up the Court of Claims and received their approval that the ceremony should include 'Barons of the Cinque Ports to carry the Canopy over the King'.[8] As Winchelsea appointed four barons, it seems that a canopy was carried over the queen also. It was not only the Lord Warden who was nervous about the Cinque Portsmen doing the Confederation credit; the barons were nervous about their stay in London. They had received a report that 'the sickness is much more increased this week and is dispersed in all places about the city and therefore it will be fit that those chosen to do this service should be provident where they lodge'.[9]

It is worth noting that on this occasion there was, for Cinque Portsmen, a privilege beyond canopy bearing. Orders were issued to the Lord Warden to summon all of them 'worth forty pounds a year to be knighted at the coronation'.[10] There were unlikely to be any Winchelsea qualifiers. However, the financial restriction did not apply to what leading Winchelsea citizens were entitled to wear on formal occasions other than coronations. In that case 'the mayors and bailiffs of the Cinque Ports and the barons of the same' were authorised to dress as would 'esquires and gentlemen having possession of the annual amount of forty pounds'.[11]

The Confederation of the Cinque Ports, despite its own decline, was kept surprisingly active by government demands in the early years of the seventeenth century. In 1605 instructions were

received to 'muster and train soldiers about the Cinque Ports'.[12]
This was in response to the Gunpowder Plot. Other precautions
were later required of the member ports in keeping a check on
travellers crossing the Channel. In 1608 Dover, Rye and Sandwich
were designated the only Cinque Ports from which such travel was
permitted.[13] The following year Winchelsea was urged to ensure
that this requirement was met. A letter addressed to 'The Mayor,
Minister and Jurats' appointed them to examine anyone who
attempted to embark or land near Winchelsea in defiance of the
order and 'to bring such as they shall find suspicious before Sir
Thomas Waller, Lieutenant of Dover Castle'.[14] Rather to my
surprise, soon after this, Winchelsea and Pevensey were added to
the ports from which continental travel was permitted.[15]

*(70) The ninth Earl of
Winchilsea is probably the best-
known of his dynasty. He gave
financial support to Thomas
Lord in the establishment of
Lord's cricket ground. This
portrait hangs in the Long
Room there*

Although Winchelsea was no longer able to contribute ships
when service was required, in 1608 the Confederation put a vessel
to sea 'against irregular French fishermen' and the following year
complained bitterly that 'the Netherlanders drive them from their
fishing and sell fresh fish in England contrary to the laws'. They
urged the king to retaliate with a tax of fifteen shillings upon every
'last' (boatload) of fish which was what the English had to pay in
the Netherlands.[16]

Life in Winchelsea may not have been affected too greatly by such problems for its fishing
fleet was tiny at that time but there are other sources which enable us to consider the situation in the
town.

The position at St. Thomas's Church does not seem to have been too bad. During the general
visitation of 1603 the report on St. Thomas's stated that there were one hundred and eighty
communicants. The rector was Robert Poole who had no other living and paid twelve pounds a year
towards the salary of a curate. How much of the work was undertaken by Mr Poole himself is not
clear. The patron was Sir Henry Guldeford, Bailiff of Winchelsea and Lord of the Manor of Iham.
The annual worth of the living was thought to be about £30.[17] David and Barbara Martin assume
from the figure given for communicants that the number of houses in Winchelsea had fallen 'little if
at all' since 1575.[18]

However much or little he may have been personally involved, Mr Poole would, through his
parish officers, have had a growing overall responsibility for the care of Winchelsea's poor. It was in
1601, two years before this visitation, that all earlier provisions regarding the treatment of the poor
were collected into one of the last great legislative acts of Queen Elizabeth's reign. This established
the office of overseers of the poor and made them responsible, with the churchwardens, for
collecting and administering the poor rate and for distributing relief to paupers in workhouses and
almshouses and in their own homes where appropriate.[19] The Justices of the Peace, in Winchelsea's
case the mayor and jurats, would sign all related documents and would supervise and hear appeals.[20]
It was a responsibility which would weigh heavily upon the parish throughout the remaining period
of this book and on into the nineteenth century.

The majority of members of the corporation would probably have been too preoccupied with
their own responsibilities and internal feuds to play an effective leading part in administering the
poor laws. In 1609 complaints about their conduct were lodged by some aggrieved inhabitants with

the Privy Council and the Lord Warden. The Privy Council responded with a long letter referring to 'many defects and disorders crept into your corporation by a strong combination of a few factious persons that had ingrossed the government [of Winchelsea] into their own hands'.[21] This clique had prevented the admission of new freemen and declined to appoint as mayor the Privy Council's recommended candidate. To put this situation to rights, it was proposed by the Council that in future the senior jurat should always succeed as the next mayor. This, it was felt, would be 'the best means to establish peace'. They went even further by pointing out that Paul Wymond was a senior and respected jurat and that he should be the next mayor, to be followed by others according to the unbroken seniority recorded in the town's annals.[22] All this was to no avail, the 'factious persons' clearly held sway for, although Paul Wymond, whose troubles in office will feature later, had already been four times mayor, he was not appointed again for another six years.

Some clues as to how this faction operated can be gleaned from an account by Thomas Godfrey who must have been in favour with them. He tells how, on 30 April 1609, even though, as we shall see, he was not living in the town, he was made a freeman of Winchelsea unopposed and almost immediately had his expenses paid to go to London to 'make intercession' to the Lord Warden as to why the Privy Council's instruction had been disobeyed by the appointment of William Bishop as mayor rather than Paul Wymond. Godfrey was then installed as a jurat and rapidly promoted up the list for future preferment.[23]

This considerable favour came as a result of the active support of Robert Butler, William Bishop's successor as mayor. Thomas Godfrey was a Londoner who moved to Winchelsea after marrying Margaret Lambard at St. Catherine's by the Tower on 5 May 1608. Why he should choose Winchelsea to set up home with his new bride is not clear but it may be a family connection for he was possibly a descendant of Maline Farnecombe née Godfrey, innkeeper of the town and founder of two chantries in St. Thomas's Church a hundred and fifty years earlier. Thomas and Margaret Godfrey did not buy a home of their own but 'lay for one year at sojourn with Mr Robert Butler.' It was at Butler's home that their first child, a son, was born. In his recollections of his time at Winchelsea, Thomas Godfrey included a note: 'My son was nursed by Mr Butler's son's wife in the Camber Castle'.[24] This comes as something of a surprise until we note that Camber Castle was still occupied, was Robert Butler's home for he was currently Lieutenant of the Castle, and that the Godfreys had moved in with him. Camber Castle seems a wild and bleak place to start a marriage but surviving evidence suggests that the private apartments were comfortable. They included, for example, an imported, smokeless ceramic tile-stove; a luxury so far discovered on military premises only at Camber.[25] However, it was not long before the Godfreys took a house in Winchelsea itself.

Godfrey claims that he was not only preferred by the corporation but also elected as one of Winchelsea's MPs in 1614. Only one name, that of Sir Edward Barcit, appears in the list of parliamentarians compiled by W. D. Cooper[26] and, if Godfrey should fill this gap, the appointment was of little significance for 'the parliament was dissolved and nothing done, and concluded to be no sessions'.[27] Another son, Thomas, was born to the Godfreys in 1610. The chosen godfathers were John Egleston and Thomas Isted, the town clerk, 'who gave him his name'. They must have been members of the corporation clique which so readily drew in Thomas Godfrey to join them.

Sadly tragedy was soon to strike the Godfrey family. Thomas junior died aged only five months and he was followed by his mother two years later. They lie buried 'in the south aisle of the church of St. Thomas … just under the great window of the east end.'[28] Their short association with the ancient town can still be seen commemorated by a plaque on the wall above their tomb.

The Godfreys had planned to move to Canterbury where they had bought a house but,

(71) Nos. 7/8 High Street (Bank House) may have incorporated a medieval open hall but is now too altered to be certain.

following his wife's death, Thomas sold it. He later remarried and moved to Kent.

Thomas's reminiscences of Winchelsea are accompanied by the accounts he kept while living there. These show, among considerable detail, that he paid the corporation two pounds to become a freeman and had his sheep washed for two shillings and his bow mended for the same amount. He paid to 'the collectors for the poor of Winchelsea for half a year three shillings and fourpence' and contributed a pound towards a levy for the purchase of a bell. Cooper comments: 'The new bell for which [the levy] was made in 1610 yet remains'[29] which would be in 1850 but the location or purpose of the bell are unknown to me. Godfrey also had the misfortune to lose four shillings playing bowls.[30]

While Thomas Godfrey was living in Winchelsea, John Hobjohn was attempting to revive the trade of Godfrey's ancestor by operating a brewing and malting business which he had started in 1606.[31] Sadly it was to be an unsuccessful attempt. By 1612 he was in considerable difficulty. When serving as town chamberlain with responsibility for collecting corporation rents, he failed to pay his own for the tenancy of the brewhouse. This caused a loss to the corporation of £6 13s 4d. Hobjohn had also tried to pay the brewhouse's king's dues out of the town's assets. His punishment was to be removed from the list of freemen and thus to forfeit the franchise. Things must have grown even worse for him for in 1613 he and his wife Elizabeth sold their house, an orchard and land in the Strand (the traditional area for brewing in the town) to Richard Mills of Rye, a shoemaker.[32] We know nothing more of what happened to them.

The Hobjohns are unlikely to have been alone in such failures.

44. THE CORPORATION IN CONFUSION

Anyone attempting to establish a Winchelsea maritime business at this time, as John Hobjohn had with brewing, was certain to have extreme problems. An inquiry was held into the general situation of the harbour at the Camber in 1619. Those who gave evidence said that fifty years previously access had been possible to Lydd for flat-bottomed vessels of up to six tons, that as many as sixty ships of eighty to one hundred tons could anchor 'between Camber Point and Guldeford' at the mouth of the Wainway which provided the access to Lydd, and that twenty ships 'of good burden' could anchor near Camber Castle. 'By 1619 none lay in any of these places.'[1] Winchelsea was not alone. In the same year the Confederation of the Cinque Ports reported to the Lord Warden that they had only one ship trading any distance overseas (to Malaga and Bordeaux); the rest were usually engaged only in coastal trade to other English ports although a few made journeys to France, Holland and Flanders.[2]

The situation was soon to grow even worse for in 1630 Sir George Curteis inned about two thousand acres of land adjoining the Wainway Channel, resulting in the loss of tidal scour and consequent silting.[3] It should be added here that, while Winchelsea had always controlled the great natural harbour at the Camber because it lay within the town's liberty, Rye's growing importance and greater trade meant that, throughout the period covered by the remainder of this book, the availability of acceptable harbour facilities for the two communities was to become an expensive and eventually insoluble problem.

In 1623, between the time of the harbour inquiry and Sir George's major inning, there occurred one of the more notable scandals associated with Winchelsea's right to elect members to the House of Commons. This was caused by the mayor, Paul Wymond, who gave notice of a forthcoming election only the night beforehand and without telling two electors by the name of Tilden. Somehow the Tildens heard what was happening and turned up at the Court Hall, whereupon the mayor disqualified them from voting on the grounds that they had not been living in the town in recent months and that a by-law excluded them from voting for that reason. The Tildens protested but eventually left, saying that, if allowed to do so, they would have voted for Sir Alexander Temple. Sixteen electors remained to hear the precept for the election read, eight of them voting for Sir Alexander and eight for Sir John Finch. Mayor Wymond thereupon exercised a casting vote in favour of Sir John and declared him elected. The defeated candidate, informed how he had been deprived of the Tildens' votes, appealed to parliament for the election to be declared void. There followed a parliamentary inquiry which concluded that the mayor had conducted the election without due notice and that by 'threatening and terrifying the Tildens and Martin, three of the electors, unlawfully excluding the Tildens from their voices, seeking to draw Sir Alexander Temple into scandal touching his religion without cause, [the mayor] had committed an offence against the liberties and privileges of the Commons in Parliament.'[4]

Paul Wymond was ordered to kneel at the bar of the House 'as a delinquent' and, after questioning by the Speaker, was committed to prison in the custody of the Sergeant-at-Arms. After again appearing before the Speaker during his sentence, Wymond was ordered to admit his faults and apologise, on his knees, to the House before being released. On his return to Winchelsea he was to admit his guilt to the jurats and freemen before another election was held. When it was, Wymond, who clearly disapproved strongly of Sir Alexander, again disqualified electors who would have supported Sir Alexander and declared Sir John elected. This time, no doubt much to Wymond's relief, a further inquiry accepted Sir John's election.[5] The loser's further appeal failed.[6] Perhaps Wymond's determined support of Finch was because he was one of many members of the ancient Winchelsea family who appear from time to time in these pages. If Wymond was also a royalist, that support, was, as we shall see, fully justified.

Paul Wymond's career was controversial in other ways. The year after the election scandal, he was appointed as one of the Confederation's bailiffs to the Yarmouth herring fair. When he made his report of this service to a meeting of the General Brotherhood, his fellow bailiff, John Herbert of Sandwich, complained bitterly about Wymond's 'undecent and unseemly carriage' which had been to the great discredit of the Ports. Wymond was fined five pounds.[7] Sadly we are not told how he had been 'undecent and unseemly'. This was not Wymond's only spat with the Confederation. In 1628 Winchelsea sent no delegation to a General Brotherhood. Wymond compounded this offence by refusing to appear to explain why this had happened and on this occasion was fined £30.[8] Winchelsea Corporation may well have paid; it was probably cheaper than the cost of attendance! The mayor continued to offend by refusing payment of a ship service tax, and towns which had lent Winchelsea money were permitted to sue him personally for its return.[9] Eventually Paul Wymond relented, apologised, and 'promises reformation of himself henceforth.'[10]

It was a good thing that he did for when he was next mayor, in 1633, Winchelsea held the Speakership and Wymond was therefore required to preside over the Brotherhood's deliberations. He, not untypically, used his new status to obtain the support of the Lord Warden for major reductions in Winchelsea's liabilities on account of the town's ' poverty and decay'.[11]

That poverty and decay was not sufficient to deter Winchelsea from sending its barons to the coronation of King Charles I in 1626 but it did induce a certain meanness when two of those representatives were not needed. Here Paul Wymond features again, together with his brother George. They had been provided with £20 to cover their travelling expenses and the purchase of their 'scarlet robes' to be worn when carrying the canopy over the Queen Henrietta Maria. However, the queen was not crowned and the corporation demanded the return of the robes or the sum of £10, being half their payment. The Wymonds were considerably offended by this decision and the matter was sent for arbitration.[12] The town annals do not record the outcome.

This information that the queen was not crowned led me down one of those fascinating by-ways which are often suggested by a study such as this. Why was the queen not crowned? Although very young and not getting along at all well with her husband at the time she was married to him and she was in this country. By far the most likely reason seemed to be her devout Catholicism but everybody knew about that so surely the canopy-bearers need not have been called at all. It transpired that it was indeed her Catholicism which led the queen to refuse to attend the coronation even though a place well out of public view had been reserved for her. Instead she and her ladies 'chose to peer down from a window in Old Palace Yard as ... Charles walked to the Abbey'.[13] The queen's French entourage included, as its chief ecclesiastical member, the Bishop of Mende who forbade her to receive the crown from the Protestant Archbishop of Canterbury.[14] It would seem that for Winchelsea's representatives the bishop's decision came too late to prevent unnecessary travelling and expense.

The records of this coronation provide an insight into the physical requirements for canopy-bearers which had often occurred to me. Even though poles were used, did not their dignity and general appearance require that they were of similar size? Dover appointed 'Mr Prinsell, Mr Eaton, Mr Kemp and Mr Monings.' The unfortunate Monings was objected to not only for political reasons, 'having been the cause of Sir William Beecher losing his election,' but

(72) Mariteau House has been much extended since the central block was built for M. Mariteau of the cambric manufactory

also because he was 'too low of stature.'[15]

Quite apart from appointing coronation canopy-bearers, the towns of the Confederation of the Cinque Ports, despite their reduced trading activity, had plenty of other concerns to deal with. In 1625 a meeting of the Brotherhood had to be postponed until a new summons could be issued because 'it pleased God then to visit this kingdom with a great plague which was dispersed much in the Ports, Towns and Members'.[16]

There is no evidence that this outbreak of plague affected Winchelsea but another Cinque Ports preoccupation of the time certainly did. In 1625 the Duke of Buckingham, Lord Warden, was instructed that three hundred mariners from the Cinque Ports towns were to be pressed into naval service. A proviso was added that they must be capable and reliable 'and not loose and unskilful poor men'.[17] In the same year the duke was ordered to call a muster of the Cinque Ports trained bands and report to the Privy Council the names of all defaulters.[18] The cause of all this urgency was the threat posed by 'the dreaded Dunkirkers' who were terrorising the east coast and ports, having attacked and burnt King's Lynn 'like modern Vikings' and, with great effrontery, landed in Lincolnshire to dry and mend their nets[19] as though they had the same rights that the Cinque Portsmen had at Yarmouth. There were other examples of this continuing piracy in the Channel, particularly by the Barbary pirates whose ruthlessness was legendary and whose presence caused the Cinque Ports to report themselves 'miserably oppressed'.[20]

I suspect that when it came to pressing mariners or calling out the trained bands, Winchelsea was not much help. However, the emergency provoked a call for ship service from two Cinque Ports vessels of two hundred tons each. These were provided, saw active service, and returned with prizes.[21] Those prizes would not have come to Winchelsea which in its difficult financial circumstances had, nevertheless, had to pay its share of the cost of the two ships. This it did by demanding contributions as widely as possible from those within the jurisdiction of its liberty. Sir Henry Guldeford and Henry Peck, owners of land on its eastern boundary, complained bitterly to the Privy Council that this was unprecedented and should not be allowed.[22] Winchelsea Corporation protested equally loudly to the Lord Warden that if they had to find the very considerable sum of £270 towards the cost of these two ships they would seek payments from the owners of all land 'within the town'[23] by which they meant the liberty. The corporation won!

Throughout these difficult times the corporation was hampered in its decision making by constant bickering over who was and who was not entitled to take part in its deliberations and vote on important matters. An early example of this came in 1620 when the Lord Warden asked that Robert Butler should be reinstated as a freeman and jurat. We have met Mr Butler before and it was his service as Lieutenant of Camber Castle which put him out of favour with the corporation. They said that he was not entitled to be of their number because he had, for more than a year and a day, been living at Camber Castle which was 'within our liberties but not of them'.[24] A fine point. What they really meant was that they did not like him and that his duties at the castle prevented him taking a proper interest in their affairs and, if he was reinstated, he might find some way of laying his hands on their precious funds.[25] Robert Butler further inflamed the situation by saying that he was jolly pleased not to have the burden of corporation membership any longer.

The following year the Confederation was told that such disputes meant there were only two Winchelsea jurats left in office, one of whom was Paul Wymond, and, 'great differences have arisen between the mayor, jurats and freemen over the election of new jurats.'[26] The Lord Warden, in arbitration, recommended individuals who were rejected by the corporation. The Confederation eventually arbitrated on this arbitration and ordered Robert Butler, Giles Waters and Thomas Bigge to be made jurats, the punishment for non-compliance being £50. In future if the mayor interfered with the carrying out of appointments according to custom, he would be fined £20.[27]

Another appointment was proving difficult. In 1636 great efforts were made to persuade Washington Reynolds to continue as town clerk despite his age and infirmity, there being no other person available.[28]

The corporation's apparent bankruptcy, its inability to repay loans and its mismanagement of its appointments and property led to the Confederation taking firm action. The editor of *A Calendar of the White and Black Books of the Cinque Ports* comments, 'This small town seems to have been especially refractory and there is hardly a meeting after 1633 when some aspect of its affairs or some inhabitant was not brought before the Brotherhood and Guestling'.[29] Moving beyond the chronological scope of this chapter we note that in 1647 the Confederation became so frustrated by the whole problem that 'it took upon itself to act as a superior authority licensing the actions of the Corporation of Winchelsea so far as leases of town lands were concerned'.[30]

Into this somewhat turgid turmoil came, in 1635, an observant and interesting visitor. He was Lieutenant Hammond who, in the style of the time, entitled his account *A relation of a short survey of the western counties starting 4th August 1635 by a Lieutenant and Ancient of the Military Company in Norwich*. Quite how Winchelsea and Rye came to be in 'the western counties' is not clear. The lieutenant was not overly impressed by Rye which he said was known at that time as 'ragged Rye' because of the appearance of both its inhabitants and its streets. To stay there for a week would tax a man's patience and to march up and down (on the cobbles) for two hours would be 'sufficient to founder a soldier'. No such strictures are passed about Winchelsea, which he reached from Rye by using two ferries, but the town clearly caught his interest as well as his sympathy. He notes that in its heyday Winchelsea would have had a 'stately decorum of buildings, and thirty-six [actually thirty-nine] quarters each measuring two acres'. He observed that the streets were laid out 'so if you had marched any way in her, in the distance of a stone's cast, you had been sure to meet with a cross way'. Of the situation which he found in 1635 he said that there were 'ruins of some old Towers still standing' but he could not work out whether they were defensive structures or the remains of former monasteries. They were some of each.

Lt. Hammond noted that the cellars were in use as stables and for tailoring. Perhaps most interesting for us are his assumptions about the ancient tombs which he saw in St. Thomas's Church. In the south aisle he thought there lay 'two old warriors of the family of the Oxenbridges' while in the north aisle his attribution was that these were 'two ancient bishops in their habits and by them another old man o' war'. Clearly this is hopelessly wide of the mark but, writing of the north aisle tombs, he was told that these three effigies were 'taken out of the old church long since eaten up with the sea'.[31] We can therefore assume that Lieutenant Hammond and his seventeenth century informants were the source of the long held belief, now disproved, [32] that these tombs came from St. Thomas's in Old Winchelsea.

The lieutenant tells that his interest in Winchelsea delayed him so long that it would be night-time before he reached his intended lodgings. He therefore hurried away towards Hastings, passing on the way 'a fair house and park of an ancient gentleman's' [Broomham] and climbing a 'very high commanding hill' [White Hart Hill] from which he observed 'a great deal of the county I was in and of the other that I last came from'.[33] If he could see as far as Kent it could not have been very dark!

I have tried, as this book progresses, to draw attention to surviving relics from the past which can be observed by residents and visitors in the early twenty-first century. One example Lieutenant Hammond would not have seen when he visited St. Thomas's. Margaret Jordan died in the following year, 1636. The brass inscription on her tomb lay originally in the choir; it has since been removed and can now be found displayed on the north wall of the sanctuary. It is a touching tribute:

> Here lieth the body of Margaret Jordan, late wife of Jeremy Jordan
> of Winchelsea, who had issue by him three daughters, Margaret, Alse
> and Martha. She departed this life the 24th April 1636 at the age of 63.
>> 'Tis not (dear saint) a stone can deck thy hearse
>> Or can thy worth lodge in a narrow verse.
>> No (pious matron) this engraven breath
>> Is not to speak thy life but weep thy death;
>> And is here laid by the ingenious trust
>> Of a sad husband, in honour to thy dust.

45. CIVIL WAR AND COMMONWEALTH

The first man with close Winchelsea connections to become, unfortunately and unwittingly, involved in the dispute between Charles I and parliament was Sir John Finch whose election for Winchelsea, as we have seen, had received the determined support of mayor Paul Wymond. By 1629 Finch had been elected Speaker of the House of Commons. At that time he was member for Canterbury but, as he was to serve Winchelsea again later, we need not lose sight of him.

Sir John was faced with a demand from the king that parliament should be adjourned to prevent the questioning of royal officials and the passing of resolutions critical of his government. The Commons interpreted this as an attempt to close them down. When he tried to follow the king's instructions the Speaker was told by angry members that he was their servant not the king's. Finch responded: 'I am not the less the king's servant for being yours. I will not say I will not put the question but I must say I dare not'.[1] His fear of the king's reaction to being defied was understandable but he was given no option. While a resolution condemning taxes raised without parliamentary authority and 'innovations in religion' was enthusiastically passed, the Speaker was forcibly held in his chair by members. Their interpretation of Charles's intentions was correct. Parliament was not to meet again for another eleven years at which time Finch was again returned for Winchelsea.

During those eleven years Winchelsea was seriously affected by both types of royal 'legislation' about which the Commons were complaining.

Of the taxes raised without parliamentary authority, the first and probably the best known was ship money. Initially this raised little protest. It was levied on the ports and coastal towns with the purpose of reinforcing the navy sufficiently to protect the coasts against piracy in the Channel and North Sea. Those subject to this tax could provide ships and men, as the Cinque Ports had traditionally, or the equivalent in cash. When it later became clear that Charles was going to obtain funds by levying ship money across the whole country rather than just on the maritime communities and, even worse, was going to require it regularly rather than in face of a specific threat, resentment greatly increased.

In 1635 Winchelsea received a demand for its share of £50 which remained unpaid 'of the tax assessed on the above-named towns towards the ship lately charged on the counties of Sussex and Kent'.[2] The 'above-named' towns were Hastings, Winchelsea, Rye, Pevensey and Seaford, the last two mentioned being at that time important limbs of Hastings. On that occasion we do not know how much was Winchelsea's share. In the same year Charles was also issuing instructions designed to reinforce the militia. Winchelsea received a stern reminder that it was supposed to have submitted to the lieutenant of Dover Castle, 'by a day now past', lists of the names of all men in the town between the ages of 16 and 60 who were not already members of the trained bands, and details of available arms and ammunition.[3]

Two years later the Cinque Ports were 'begging some remission' from what they clearly saw as excessive demands for ship money, pleading that 'there was not a single fishing boat at New Romney or Lydd and only a few at Hythe, beached a mile from the town'.[4] Clearly Winchelsea was not alone in its decline.

At this point in the story Sir John Finch reappears. The king seems to have recognised that the 1629 Commons resolutions had been passed only under duress and rewarded Finch's loyalty by appointing him Chief Justice. This post proved just as uncomfortable as the Speakership! He had to preside at the high-profile trial of John Hampden for non-payment of ship money. Finch, fairly obviously but with consistent loyalty to the king, said: 'For us islanders it is most necessary to defend ourselves at sea'.[5] The twelve judges found Hampden guilty by a majority of seven to five, declaring that this tax, 'even when charged annually, on inland towns and by the king's authority alone,' was legal. Crucially Sir John voted with the majority.[6]

This verdict did nothing to defuse the situation. Opposition rapidly increased and when the fourth ship money writ was issued in 1639 the amounts were greatly reduced as a result of the protests. In contrast with the 1635 levy we know here the amounts required from the Sussex Cinque Ports. They were as follows: Hastings £29, Rye £18, Winchelsea £18, Pevensey £32, Seaford £5.[7] Considering their relative prosperity at that time, Winchelsea seems to have had cause for complaint. Nationally, even at the reduced rate, of the £70,000 required only one-third was collected, in comparison with 100% received from the first levy.[8]

Alarmed at the growing rift with his people, Charles turned his attention to land as well as sea defences. Camber Castle was still accessible only from Winchelsea and was within the Liberty although not governed by the town. The king noted that this potentially useful stronghold was by then 'quite inland, being a mile from the sea'.[9] The situation there had been declining for a long time. By 1626 the castle was seriously decayed and the guns out of range of the harbour. The following year its demolition was proposed but not implemented because 'the materials would not sell for much while the towns could think themselves in danger if it was pulled down'. Rye, Winchelsea and Hastings did, indeed, petition against its destruction.[10] In 1637 the garrison was finally disbanded. By 1642 it was not the king but the parliament which was in control of the situation. Parliamentary commissioners discovered that the departing garrison had left 'divers pieces of ordnance, with powder and other warlike provisions,' behind in an altogether unguarded structure and, 'exposed to the surprise of any ill-affected or malignant persons' who might terrorise the countryside or, of course, oppose the parliament. Captain Richard Cockeram, formerly Mayor of Rye, was made responsible for arranging the removal of these weapons to safe storage in Rye.[11] The castle was left open to the sky and available as a quarry for stone and lead to anyone who might wish to help themselves.

During the years in which the ship money conflict and the abandonment of Camber Castle were taking place Winchelsea was also being affected by the second type of legislation to which the House of Commons so strongly objected when Sir John Finch was forced to remain in the Speaker's chair. This was 'innovations in religion'. Arminianism was a line of religious thought strongly supported by King Charles and Archbishop Laud but strongly opposed by Protestants and particularly Puritans. It specifically required the placing of the communion table at the east end of the church like the Roman Catholic altar, 'and the return to other ceremonial practices [which] seemed to some like a half-way house to Popery'.[12] The placing of the communion table caused the rector and churchwardens of St. Thomas's a considerable headache because the mayor and corporation had taken the opportunity of the Reformation to emphasise their own importance by having an elaborate pew, exclusively for their use, built across the sanctuary facing the congregation. Representations were made in 1639 that, 'there was not even an ascent for the altar since the seats for the mayor and jurats stood between it and the east end of the church.'[13] Perhaps the expense of this enforced change was made more difficult by the contemporary undertaking of other necessary work, for in 1640 a certificate was issued at East Grinstead Assizes authorising the repair of the church and four years later it must have been in progress for records survive of the engagement of masons from Dover and Rye and of the burning of lime for use at St. Thomas's.[14] The church authorities were not allowed to avoid their responsibilities for, in the same year, 1644, the mayor and jurats' pews were removed and reconstructed on either side of the sanctuary where they then obstructed, not the communion table but the sedilia and the vestry door![15]

(73) The sanctuary of St. Thomas's Church with the mayor and jurats' pews long gone. The picture features the millennium altar table and, above the two chairs, the Margaret Jordan plaque.

To move to the war itself rather than the theological dispute, it was in 1642, the year that the arms from Camber Castle were transferred to Rye, that a powerful blow for control of the south-east coast was struck by the parliamentary capture of Dover Castle. The royalist garrison of such a vital stronghold was only twenty men. As few as twelve townsmen were able to scale the wall and take control. Treachery is implied by the fact that the castle's royalist commander was soon to be found on the Parliamentary County Committee of Kent.[16] Domination of the south-east gave the parliament, which had always possessed more artillery than its opponents, the opportunity to extend that advantage through access to 'the whole iron industry of the Weald of Kent and Sussex with its 27 furnaces and 47 forges'.[17]

Actual fighting came near to Winchelsea only in 1648 during the Second Civil War when a certain Major Anthony Norton tried to take control of Rye for the king. The details of a 1651 inquiry into the forfeiting of Major Norton's estate show that he had recruited in the area, had threatened the lives of parliamentary supporters and had intended to seize the keys of the Rye magazine where arms, no doubt including those of Camber Castle, would be obtained for the king. He and his sixty men would oppose any addition to parliamentary forces in Sussex and encourage assistance for the contemporary royalist rising in Kent. He stood no chance and was easily routed by Major Gibbons for the parliament. It is something of a surprise that Major Norton, although he lost his property, both escaped with his life and failed to learn his lesson. He was later accused of declaring that there were none but rogues who fought against the king and that Cromwell and all that followed him were rogues.[18] Incredibly dangerous words in 1654. It is perhaps symptomatic of the nature of the times that Anthony Norton's accuser kept quiet about what had been said for twelve months because Norton owed him money and he wanted to get his money back before betraying him!

The fortunes, or rather misfortunes, of Winchelsea Corporation during the years of the Civil War and Commonwealth must now briefly take our attention. They were years of constant conflict with the Confederation of the Cinque Ports on the grounds that the corporation's affairs were being grossly mismanaged. After a quiet start in 1641 when the Confederation insisted on the reinstatement of William Joy as town clerk after his removal, the matter escalated to a mayoralty dispute over the election of Hugh Beresford, on which occasion the principal trouble was caused by Richard Marten and George Sampson. Sampson was accused of 'wilfully in an outrageous manner in the presence of the Assembly break[ing] the then mayor's staff in pieces and plot[ting] with Mr Beresford to make a disturbance'.[19] This is the only mention I can recall of Winchelsea's mayor carrying a staff; some

Confederation mayors still do so and, as this quotation suggests, each mayor has his own, it is not handed to his successor.

Whether the authority of a mayor's staff did him much good in those days is a matter for conjecture. Much of his jurisdiction had been taken over by the Confederation's Committee for Winchelsea because Winchelsea was adjudged not competent to manage its own affairs. Among other charges, Winchelsea's chamberlain was threatened with prison if he did not keep proper accounts, the town was declared bankrupt, and it was alleged to have appointed the wrong bailiffs to Yarmouth, the appointed ones defaulting anyway. To make some amends every member of Winchelsea Corporation was to pay twelve shillings towards the cost of sending bailiffs to Yarmouth. The chamberlain would impound the cattle of any member who did not pay up.[20]

(74) Sir John Finch

Perhaps the most dramatic of all the incidents during the disputes between the corporation and the Confederation came on 27 July 1647 when 'Winchelsea refused to pay their part of the common charge'. Five Winchelsea men attending the General Brotherhood were to be imprisoned until the money was paid. The imprisonment did not last long. 'Winchelsea presently after paid and were freed.' Among the gaoled five was George Sampson, he who had broken the mayor's staff. He was not only then serving as Winchelsea's mayor but also presiding over the Brotherhood as Speaker of the Confederation![21]

The Winchelsea mayors and jurats so mistrusted by the Confederation nevertheless continued to fulfil their duties as Winchelsea's justices. Ben Eggleston has drawn my attention to an extraordinary incident in Winchelsea's court records of this time. His ancestor, Elizabeth Ecclestone, appeared, in 1644, before the Winchelsea Court complaining bitterly that George Rockley, 'one of the residents in the house where she was dwelling at the time,' had been heard beating his wife and turning her out of their room. She was not allowed back for half an hour, during which time Rockley was joined by a certain Anne Hedge. The language used in court was robust to say the least. When Mrs Ecclestone reproached Rockley for this unseemly behaviour he called her 'toade face and whoor'. In response to her threat to report him to the mayor he retorted that 'he did not care a turde what shee or Mr Maior could do.' Elizabeth Ecclestone told the court that Anne Hedge 'laid in the said Rockley's chamber by the space of a quarter of a yeare'. Having complained in this way, Elizabeth 'goeth in feare of her life of the said Rockley'. It is difficult to judge whether the justices dealt with such cases appropriately for there is no record of any sentence. All we know is that when Elizabeth's husband appeared to deny absolutely that he had spoken maliciously about Rockley, the court believed him and discharged him. Rockley was said to have been a baker and alehouse keeper in the town. I am sure the Ecclestones bought bread and beer elsewhere.[22]

We gain a glimpse of the Winchelsea of Rockley, the Ecclestones, George Sampson and his colleagues through the eyes of the formidable diarist John Evelyn. Evelyn went to Rye in June 1652 to meet his wife who was due to land there from the continent. There was a long delay for passengers at sea caused by the proximity of the warring English and Dutch fleets. Becoming bored with passing the time in Rye, about which he is not very complimentary, Evelyn walked to Winchelsea. There he thought that what remained suggested the one-time existence of 'a considerable and large city'.

Surviving to catch his eye were 'vast caves and vaults, walls and towers, ruins and monasteries, and a sumptuous church'. However, his impressions were dominated by his amazement that Winchelsea 'now all in rubbish, and a few hovels and cottages only standing, hath yet a mayor'.[23] We must assume that the mayor and jurats lived in some of the 'hovels and cottages'.

John Evelyn and his wife were lucky that the first sea action of the war with the Dutch which came close to Rye and much of the route of her passage had happened the month before Mrs Evelyn made her journey. On 17 May the Dutch Admiral Tromp had anchored off Dover and exchanged fire with the castle, now strongly garrisoned on behalf of the republican government. It so happened that the English fleet was anchored in Rye Bay, readily available to answer an urgent summons. On sighting the enemy Admiral Blake demanded the customary salute and received a broadside instead. The fleets were engaged for four hours at which time, despite outgunning Blake in terms of the number of his ships, Tromp withdrew leaving behind two captured vessels.[24]

The large discrepancy between the size of the fleets reflected King Charles's earlier failure to raise enough ship money to build the navy he and his country so badly required. Action was already being taken to rectify this and it was now stepped up. Between the year of the king's execution and the Restoration no fewer that 218 ships 'were built, bought or taken for the Commonwealth'.[25]

Those already in service were pressed into action in November 1652 by which time Mrs Evelyn was safely at home. On this second occasion, the engagement took place even closer to Winchelsea, off Dungeness and Admiral Blake, although still outnumbered, commanded forty-two ships rather than the thirteen he had earlier. It was not enough. The Dutch undoubtedly came off best, sinking three English ships and capturing another two before sailing on down Channel with the convoy Tromp was escorting.[26]

One undoubted bonus of these actions for Winchelsea and the Cinque Ports was that frantic naval building work continued and the eventual existence of a vastly stronger navy made the Channel a much safer place for English fishing and trading.

For Winchelsea generally the impact of the government of Oliver Cromwell and the Commonwealth had been limited. The town's right to elect two members of parliament was removed and the places allocated to unrepresented larger towns, an action which long predated the 1832 Reform Act. However, these places were restored before the return of Charles II with Robert Fowle and John Busbridge serving for Winchelsea during the brief 'reign' of Cromwell's son Richard in 1659.[27] An act was passed in 1660 recognising and legalising the appointment and the executive decisions of mayors who had served during Cromwell's time. Of Cromwell himself there is but a solitary mention in the annals of Winchelsea Corporation. The preamble to the record of the annual Easter Monday Hundred Court in 1654 reads: 'The Hundred for His Highness, Oliver Lord Protector of the Commonwealth of England ...'.[28]

At the time of the Restoration Dover Castle was surrendered by General Monk to the Earl of Winchilsea, who assumed the duties of Governor, for the new king. Monk then joined Winchilsea to welcome King Charles II and witness the general rejoicing which accompanied his arrival. The earl is listed as being appointed Lord Warden in 1669,[29] presumably as a reward for his loyal service to the monarchy.

This chapter must end, as it began, with Sir John Finch. Re-elected as Winchelsea's member when parliament met in 1640 after the eleven-year 'personal rule', he later went into exile. He returned to England in 1660 as Baron Finch of Fordwich. In October of that year he was one of the commissioners for the trial of the regicides, but took little part in the proceedings.[30] Baron Finch died the following month, deserving more time to relish the return of the monarchy he had served so loyally.

46. RESTORATION AND RESPONSIBILITIES

The Earl of Winchilsea, whom we have just witnessed assuming the governorship of Dover Castle for the king at the time of the Restoration was Baron Finch's kinsman Heneage Finch. Like the baron, the earl had a distinguished career in support of the monarchy. During the civil war he provided auxiliary troops at his own expense; during the Commonwealth he supplied 'with great hazard' Charles II's 'necessities in foreign parts'.[1] One wonders what that might have involved!

Unlike the former Sir John, Heneage lived long enough to enjoy his reward, becoming Lord Lieutenant of Kent and, for twenty years, Lord Warden of the Cinque Ports. The earl's steadfast support persisted. When James II's first attempt to flee the country ended ignominiously with his 'arrest' by the fishermen of Faversham, Winchilsea interceded on James's behalf. However, after James's second successful flight, Winchilsea, possibly finally exasperated by his master's conduct, joined the Earl of Sandwich, whom we shall soon briefly meet, and many others in offering the throne jointly to William and Mary.[2]

King James II, as Prince James, Duke of York, was the earl's predecessor as Lord Warden and Winchelsea's representatives attended his Court of Shepway. A Court of Shepway is a very grand affair, now, and I think then, used only for the installation of a new Lord Warden. Ivan Green quotes a contemporary account of that seventeenth century grandeur. Unfortunately it is too detailed for much to be made of it here but it includes the information that the mayors of the five ports and the two ancient towns were 'all in black gowns and on horseback'.[3] This must have been a uniform required just for the event for it is the only reference I know to Winchelsea's mayor wearing a black gown. Hopefully he, William Pelham, was an experienced horseman.

The splendour of the Court of Shepway would nevertheless have been far exceeded by that of the coronation of the Lord Warden's brother in 1661. On that occasion Winchelsea's representatives, present, of course, as Barons of the Cinque Ports, became caught up in the most amazingly undignified scenes. The barons, dressed in 'large cloaks of garter blue satin with slashed arms of scarlet and red and stockings of dead red,'[4] had, despite the probably uncomfortable nature of that form of dress, conducted themselves properly in carrying canopies over the king and queen and escorting them to the foot of the steps in Westminster Hall. At that point, their duties completed, they turned towards the table at which they were to dine but before they could reach it they were set upon by the king's footmen who, 'most insolently and violently' attempted to obtain the canopy. The barons clung on. Unfortunately they were outnumbered and the struggle continued until they had been dragged to the lower end of the hall. There the footmen, later disgraced and dismissed by the king, were stopped by York Herald who, seeing what was happening, had shut the door. The barons' triumph at the recovery of the threatened canopy soon turned to dismay when they discovered that, during the melee, certain judges and bishops had seized the opportunity to take the barons' privileged places at the king's right hand. Tactfully avoiding another conflict and most unwilling to forego their dinner, the barons ate at a lower table.[5] L. A. Vidler asserts that there was more indignity for the barons to suffer as the canopy was, despite the king's firm action against the footmen, ordered to be put 'in [the] charge of Sir R. Pye, until the matter could be settled by the Court of Claims'.[6]

Five years after Winchelsea's barons were involved in this fracas important instructions were issued to move the town's Court Hall. The year of this change was 1666, often thought to be 1665 because of calendar confusion. The order was promulgated on 15th February in the eighteenth year of the reign of Charles II. Charles II's reign was calculated from the day of his father's execution so his eighteenth year lasted from 30 January 1666 until 29 January 1667. At an Assembly it was, 'ordered, concluded and agreed upon that the Court Hall of the Town of Winchelsea shall be taken down and a new Court Hall made in the chambers over the [here there is a tantalising gap in the record]'.[7] What almost certainly happened was that the Court Hall was the building of which the walls survive as the present garden walls and that, as a cost-cutting exercise, it was moved to part of the upper room of the surviving building, in those days known as the Freeman's Hall. It is from 1666, then, that we can assume all the corporation's responsibilities being exercised within the present building. The Court Hall and the Freeman's Hall were both on the upper floor. David and Barbara Martin assume that the lower floor was already a prison by that date.[8]

Once the order for the Court Hall to be moved had been issued, no delay was to be permitted. A corporation committee of five jurats was appointed to supervise the work with financial inducements to ensure the job was completed by the next Easter. Committee members were to be fined five shillings each if it wasn't. They were further instructed to keep costs down by selling the materials from the demolished building.[9] We must be grateful that they did not carry this too far and that we still have the garden walls.

The successful completion of this change meant that the first parliamentary election to be held in the present building was a by-election in October 1666, caused by the death of one of Winchelsea's sitting members in the 'Cavalier Parliament', Sir Nicholas Crispe. The by-election provoked extraordinary scenes. We have seen how Lords Warden carried considerable influence over election nominations and the Duke of York nominated Baptist May. May had been, like Heneage Finch, an attendant of the duke, the future James II, in exile, and was currently Keeper of the Privy Purse to King Charles II in which capacity he enjoyed 'the greatest and longest share in the king's secret confidence of any man at that time'.[10] It was hardly politic to object to someone with such influential backing but the Winchelsea electors did just that. Their favoured candidate was Robert Austen of Heronden in Tenterden who had local influence and interests. Nine votes were cast for Austen and six for May. Samuel Pepys records the incident memorably when writing: 'Bap[tist] May went down in great state to Winchelsea with the Duke of York's letters, not doubting to be chosen, and there the people chose a private gentleman in spite of him, and cried out that they would have no court pimp for their burgess: which are things that bode very ill'.[11] Baptist May at least travelled to Winchelsea 'in great state' for the election, a courtesy extended by few candidates nominated as he was. After the indignity he suffered he may well have travelled back in *a great state*!

As with almost all disputed Winchelsea elections there was an appeal to parliament. The parliamentary committee which inquired into the matter discovered that the Mayor of Winchelsea conducting the election, Thomas Gostrey, had 'not within one year next before his election taken the Sacrament of the Lord's Supper according to the rites of the Church of England,' and used this very convenient failure to observe the Test Act to declare the election void. The sitting members of parliament, like the Winchelsea electors, were more robust. When the matter came before them on the floor of the House they rejected the committee's recommendation by 138 votes to 63 and declared Robert Austen duly elected.[12]

Perhaps it was the local gentry who, as voting members, encouraged their colleague jurats and freemen to take this defiantly independent action. After the Restoration such men were certainly exerting a growing influence. 'They owned about half the land in the country and when they served as justices of the peace they exercised an even greater degree of local power between 1660 and 1685 than they had done before 1640.'[13] They may well have encouraged the

(75) Strand House, formerly Winchelsea's workhouse and now a guest house, may have incorporated a medieval open hall but is now too altered to be certain.

corporation to show greater financial prudence than we have already noted by such methods as the Court Hall move. One responsibility mercifully removed from the corporation at this time was the need to appoint, in their turn, an expensive bailiff to Yarmouth. The Confederation had finally become fed up with putting on a show to demonstrate its rights and, in 1663, abandoned its annual Yarmouth Herring Fair. The banner they carried for the last time was made in 1632 and now hangs in the Council Chamber of the Maison Dieu in Dover.[14]

No cost-cutting could remove from the mayor and jurats the responsibility, as magistrates, for conducting the town's courts. In addition to that, as leading citizens, they would have kept an anxious eye on national events, particularly as the south coast was again under threat during the Anglo-Dutch Wars. Reports of sightings of the Dutch fleet came from towns as far apart as Dover and Plymouth. 'The maritime counties were kept in a state of alarm.'[15] In 1667 the Duke of Albemarle ordered English ships to be 'run aground and [have] holes bored in their hulls so that the Dutch could not take them'.[16] Such panic had not been seen since the French raid of 1360.

An ancestor's involvement in these wars leads us to turn at this point to the Winchelsea family of Fuller. The first Fuller to arrive in the town is reputed to have come during the civil war. He had served as Captain of a Troop of Horse under Prince Rupert for the king and, on the disbanding of the prince's army, took flight by ship, landed within Winchelsea's liberty at Rye Harbour, and made his way originally to Brede. Intriguingly Fuller family tradition has it that during this journey the family plate was lost at sea with only one or two pieces surviving.[17] The family's association with Winchelsea lasted until the mid-twentieth century. Most of its earlier leading members were called Thomas. One was mayor in 1692, another was churchwarden of St. Thomas's in 1726, a position which entitled him to sit in the pews constructed in the sanctuary.

The same Thomas purchased the Greyfriars in 1731. Another committed some serious indiscretion and after spending time abroad, drowned as purser of the *Royal George* when it sank at Spithead in 1782. The only Fuller indiscretion that I have discovered came too late to cause that exile; in 1797 Thomas Fuller, gentleman, appears in the parish records acknowledging his financial responsibility for 'the bastard child' of Margaret Clarke.[18] The most relevant association with the Fuller family for those presently associated with the town is that in 1763 Arnold Nesbitt engaged Walter Fuller to build the row of manufactory houses now known as 1-10 Barrack Square.

Captain (later Sir) Richard Haddock was a Fuller ancestor by marriage. A distinguished mariner, he commanded the *Royal James* at the battle of Sole Bay off the Suffolk coast in 1672. Aboard Haddock's vessel and in overall command of the fleet was the Earl of Sandwich. The earl was a cousin of Samuel Pepys and had, despite earlier service in the navy under Cromwell, played a leading part in the restoration of Charles II to the throne. In this action the English fleet destroyed numerous enemy vessels but eventually the *Royal James* was set on fire and the situation on board became hopeless. There are varying accounts of what followed. We know that Sandwich, who had led the fleet with great distinction, was drowned and the Fuller family records show that Richard Haddock must have survived for on his return to London, wounded, he was presented by King Charles II, in gratitude for his gallant service, with 'a satin cap which [the king] took from his own head and placed on Sir Richard's.' This cap was preserved by the family for many years.[19]

The Thomas Fuller who bought the Greyfriars in 1731 must have died eight years later for the property was sold by trustees of whom one was Samuel Jeake. Jeake's father, also Samuel, was historian of the Cinque Ports and sole source for the story of Queen Elizabeth I's visit to Winchelsea. Jeake senior was himself a previous owner of the Greyfriars and much other property in the town which he bought from the corporation when they were desperately trying to balance the books. His interest to us here is that in 1674 he made a hazardous journey from Hastings to Rye via Winchelsea and left an account of it. He and his party had sailed from Dieppe. They left Hastings on horseback in pouring rain and a gale force winds. Things became so bad that they left the horses in Winchelsea and attempted to make their way on foot to Rye. 'When we came to the ferry, the tide being up, we could neither get over nor make the ferryman hear, but were fain to go back to Cadborough House almost a mile.'[20] The fact that they had to return to Cadborough suggests that the ferry they wanted was over the Tillingham. It is interesting that Jeake makes no mention of a ferry at Winchelsea thus confirming David and Barbara Martin's finding that a new ferry bridge over the Brede had been built in 1658. The work accompanied the adjoining construction of a sluice where a ferry had operated until at least the 1640s. It would seem that the fourteenth century bridge had long decayed and been removed.[21]

The population of Winchelsea which would have used that new bridge was small. A religious census taken two years after Jeake's journey shows the town to have had ninety-one communicants, probably living in about thirty houses the majority of which were clustered round the present-day High Street.[22] Nevertheless the responsibilities assigned to St. Thomas's Church where the people worshipped were, as we have seen, very considerable. Social services, particularly the administration of the Poor Laws, were required by statute of the vestry meeting, the churchwardens and the overseers of the poor. At that time the complications created by the law of settlement had been in operation for more than a decade. Under this infamous legislation the justices, when requested by the churchwardens and overseers were empowered 'to remove any stranger who settled in the parish unless he rented a house worth £10 or found security to indemnify his new parish from any expense it might incur on his behalf'.[23] Thus the whole, very considerable, population of the poor were treated as only 'rogues and vagabonds' had been treated previously.[24] As a result demands on the parish in administrative time and money vastly increased. In 1676 St. Thomas's was so poor that it no longer had any bells. The 'Little Watchbell' was taken from the Strand Gate and lent to the parish officers so that the congregation could be summoned to church.[25]

While the church and the residents who contributed alms for the poor were being impoverished in this way, some inhabitants, the freemen who enjoyed the parliamentary vote, were doing very nicely. The only occasion for which we have actual figures of the amounts involved in the bribery and chicanery which often accompanied Winchelsea elections was in 1678. It was another by-election. While recording Winchelsea's history during the seventeenth century it is difficult to keep the Finches out of the story for long. This by-election was caused by the death of Francis Finch a representative of the constituency where the Kentish Finches had begun their parliamentary career in 1337.[26]

Sir John Banks stood with admiralty support, bypassing the Lord Warden's influence. Banks was an incredibly unpopular candidate among the aforementioned gentry who held sway in the town. He was a self-made man who would these days be described as nouveau riche. Strong words were used. The Lord Warden, still the Earl of Winchilsea, was urged not to use his influence in support of Banks, 'his person and principles being so obnoxious to the whole country'.[27] Against him Robert Austen nominated Creswell Draper who was known to him as a neighbour of his brother Sir John Austen. There was a third candidate, Sir Nathaniel Powell, who also opposed Banks. In view of what happened it is worth noting that Banks had influential support particularly from Samuel Pepys, another who had risen, as it were, through the ranks and was currently in the service of the future James II. Pepys sent Banks an encouraging letter implying that if no-one of greater quality, or resources, appeared, he would win the seat.[28] At this point strong words became reinforced with strong money. *The History of Parliament – The Commons*, while acknowledging that things improved later, describes Winchelsea Corporation at this time as, 'a small and notoriously bribarious body'.[29]

When the election took place things had polarised to such an extent that Banks received six votes, as did Draper, and Powell received none at all. The mayor, William Smith, having already disqualified non-resident voters then claimed his 'traditional' right to use a second and casting vote and declared Banks duly elected. It was at the subsequent and inevitable parliamentary inquiry that actual figures of the money involved appeared. Col. Robert Austen was alleged to have offered Francis Sampson, one of the electors, thirty guineas to vote for Draper. When this seemed insufficient he later, 'at Mr Marten's house' [Firebrand] offered Sampson one hundred guineas, to which would be added two hundred and fifty guineas and, a nice touch, fifty pounds for his wife, these later sums to come from Draper himself. In desperation he said that, if none of this was acceptable, Sampson could have £150 to absent himself and not vote.[30] Banks's accounts were examined and he was shown to have spent £4500, some of it, no doubt, paid to mayor Smith. Years later it was alleged that Draper had spent as much as ten or eleven thousand pounds. On this occasion it seems that justice was not done for the investigating committee found in Draper's favour and the House of Commons, after a vote, accepted this decision.

This chapter has touched upon the responsibilities of the mayor and corporation and of the parish authorities. Finally we return to the responsibilities of the bailiff. Readers may recall that originally the bailiff was the king's representative who, while conceding precedence to the mayor, represented the monarch in the town and collected rents due to him. By the mid-seventeenth century the bailiwick, rather than being a direct royal appointment, had become a saleable commodity along with the Lordship of the Manor of Iham, a more profitable adjunct. Soon after the Restoration, Edward Guldeford Esq., descendant of the long-time bailiffs, acquired from the new monarch 'a grant of these estates to himself and his heirs and assigns without the limitation to his heirs male'.[31] With the hereditary principle established, Guldeford sold the manor, with the exception of Camber Farm, and the bailiwick to John Caryll of Harting. The Carylls were to fulfil the function of bailiff, such as it was, for almost exactly a hundred years. They are an interesting family whom it is unusual to find in such a position for they were devout Catholics unwavering in their loyalty to the faith. Through almost all of the seventeenth century this was a dangerous path to tread. The Carylls seems to have trodden it with considerable success, harbouring priests disguised as servants, using a secret chapel, building priests' holes, and surviving searches of their home without ever getting into serious trouble. They would perhaps have viewed as the most serious happening in all this an occasion when the sixth John Caryll (as with the Fullers a single name recurred in many generations) took the oath of conformity with the rites of the Church of England. He soon recanted and, in penance for this departure from the family tradition, gave an endowment of £600 so that the family home at West Grinstead could become a dwelling place for three priests.[32]

Here we meet another supporter of King James II to join Samuel Pepys and the Earl of Winchilsea. This one, however, the seventh John Caryll, did not, like the other two, eventually transfer his allegiance to William and Mary. He followed James to France, became secretary to James's queen and was rewarded by being made the first Lord Caryll but his peerage is not recognised in his homeland. Sadly he was never able to return to England.[33]

There are two surviving reminders of the Carylls' Winchelsea connection. One we shall deal with later, the other is the appearance of the family arms on an artefact still in Winchelsea Corporation's possession, known as the Water Bailiff's Sergeant's silver oar. This is a badge of office carried by the sergeant on behalf of the bailiff who was ex-officio also the water bailiff. It is not in fact an oar at all but a short mace extremely heavy for its size for it has an iron core. The sergeant would produce it as his authority when he went to sea to collect dues from passing ships.

The story of the Carylls must briefly continue as we consider Winchelsea's, albeit peripheral, involvement with the notorious Titus Oates.

47. SEQUESTRATION AND SHIPS

The Caryll family's long-lasting loyalty to the Catholic faith can never have been more dangerously threatened than by the so-called Popish Plot which 'revealed' a plan to assassinate Charles II. Titus Oates's totally unfounded allegations led to the deaths of at least thirty-five innocent Catholics. The authorities seem to have had little inclination to challenge Oates's testimony. Had they done so they might well have discovered that he was already a convicted perjurer. In Hastings where he served as curate to his father, Samuel, Rector of All Saints, Titus twice brought false charges before the local bench. One case was against a young schoolmaster, William Parker, the other accused one of the churchwardens of All Saints. The mayor and jurats of Hastings found that Oates had 'corruptly committed perjury and bound him over to appear at the next sessions'.[1] He did not turn up. Instead he went to sea, claiming to be serving in the navy (he had earlier been, briefly, a naval chaplain) but actually as a passenger. The voyage ended in further disgrace. Titus was severely punished on board ship for 'perverted behaviour' and put ashore at Tangier in disgrace.[2]

The Oates family's local connections were not only with Hastings but also with Winchelsea. Samuel Oates, while still a respected clergyman (he was later expelled from his Hastings living for 'improper practices')[3], was entrusted with the sequestration of the parish of St. Thomas, Winchelsea in the early 1670s. He would have preached at St. Thomas's during that time and W. M. Homan considers that his curate son would most likely have done so as well.[4] The sequestrator's duty was to administer the income of a benefice, to clear an incumbent's debts or to accumulate funds for an incoming incumbent. The surviving list of St. Thomas's seventeenth century rectors may well be deficient. It certainly has a long gap. The Rev. Martin Fist was inducted in 1639 and the Rev. Richard Acton was appointed, after Samuel Oates's management of the parish, in 1672.

Direct evidence of Oates senior's Winchelsea activity comes from an inspection of St. Thomas's carried out on behalf of the Archdeacon of Lewes by Messrs. Thomas Brian and William Williams in 1686. After fourteen years any improvements which the Rev. Samuel might have made were certainly no longer in evidence. The inspectors were not impressed. They reported that the two side aisles were, 'much dilapidated, especially the pavements', and that the church was 'endangered by the want of gutterheads'. All the bells except one had been sold. Many items which the church should have possessed were missing. These included 'the carpet for the communion table, a linen cloth and napkin for administration of the most blessed Sacrament, a poor box, a Common Prayer Book, the Book of Homilies, a book of articles and canons, [a] table of degrees, [a] book to set down strangers' names that preach and a surplice'. Pigs were kept in the churchyard. Most tellingly for us the report concludes, 'The parsonage house pulled down, and the materials all sold by the Salamanca doctor's father while he had the sequestration'.[5] Clearly Oates made some attempt to obtain money for the parish in this way; whether leaving it without a rectory, or, indeed, whether the parish ever benefited, we shall never know.

Titus Oates was 'the Salamanca Doctor' referred to by the inspectors. While ingratiating himself with the Jesuits to obtain corroborative circumstantial evidence for his anti-Catholic assertions, Titus spent time at a Jesuit college in Spain from which he was expelled for scandalous behaviour after five months. Thereafter he styled himself D.D. of Salamanca. The title stuck, eventually as a term of derision.

We should note here that the electors of Winchelsea were, at that time, quite prepared to believe Titus Oates unquestioningly. In 1668 they petitioned one of their Parliamentary members,

Creswell Draper, seeking the utmost official attention to exposing 'that most hellish and damnable Popish plot', hoping for the unification of Protestant Englishmen 'against the common enemy at home and abroad' and urging that the Catholic Duke of York, later James II, should be excluded from the succession.[6]

After the executions which followed the Popish Plot the death penalty for being a priest was removed. Instead fines and taxes on Catholics were doubled and civil rights were taken from them. Nearly all the local Catholic families conformed at that stage but not the Carylls who stayed faithful to their religion and the Stuart monarchy. As a result they were continually harassed and eventually became impoverished.[7] They sold the Bailiwick of Winchelsea to the Earl of Egremont in 1762.

Long before these events led to the impoverishment of the Carylls the Corporation of Winchelsea was continuing its efforts to stave off its

(76) Titus Oates

own financial ruin. In 1689 the two rooms then on the first floor of the present Court Hall, The Court Hall and the Freeman's Hall, were let to Edward Marten for twenty-one years at an annual rental of one pound. He was permitted to move the access stairs and it was decreed that during the period of this lease, 'the said chambers shall be used and employed as a place for religious worship ... and not [for] longer.'[8] The lease's terms seem generous and as Marten was mayor at the time we do not know whether he was trying to help or exploiting the situation for his own advantage.

Another transaction in the same year seems less likely to have been public spirited. The same Edward Marten and George Head were granted a 101-year lease on 'a piece of roadside verge opposite and about midway between their houses ... so that they might dig a well and build a well-house *for their own use*'.[9] This must have been part of what is now the grass verge on the church side of St. Thomas's Street. Marten lived at Firebrand and Head probably at Glebe. There was no well for public use in the main part of the town until 1851. All the public wells were at the foot of the hill.

Marten and Head paid sixpence a year for their lease which seems very reasonable compared with a fine of ten pence proposed shortly afterwards by Marten and his colleagues for 'anyone refusing to remove "dung, sulledge, straw and other stuff" from the streets.'[10] From what knowledge we have of conditions in the town at the time, the corporation may have benefited considerably.

Other ways of recovering funds were tried. In the same year a bill of charges for suits, that is legal expenses, was submitted by Winchelsea to the Confederation of the Cinque Ports' Court of Brotherhood and Guestling. In that case the ancient town received short shrift. 'This Assembly will not meddle any further with the said charges.'[11] There was, however, some minor success in this direction for, later in the same meeting, Fordwich was ordered to pay three pounds owed to Winchelsea.[12]

Winchelsea's membership of the Confederation brought perks as well as problems. We have noted in these pages numerous times when the town's representatives were present at coronations. They attended King James II, to whose succession, as we have just seen, they had so strongly objected. Perhaps it was the opulence of the occasion and the vast amount expended which encouraged them to set aside these scruples. The Barons of the Cinque Ports' ancient right to dine at the king's right hand was here allowed for the last time.[13] And what a meal it was! The Jessup brothers comment: 'There is little wonder that the barons were anxious to secure their proper seats'. No fewer than 1445 dishes were prepared and served with 'the variety of fish alone includ[ing] lamprey, salmon, cold lobster, cold pickled oysters, anchovies, cold "souc'd" carp, "souc'd" trouts, marmoted fish cold, crayfish, periwinkles, cockles, mullet, prawns, crabs and collared eels.'[14]

The flight of King James who had emphasised his power and influence by providing such a ridiculously expensive meal led again to war with the French, the enemy with whom Winchelsea had so often previously clashed. This war, too, came dangerously close to the town but it is a surviving souvenir rather than further devastation which serves to remind us of the incident today. In 1690 the English and Dutch under the command of Lord Torrington fought the French off Beachy Head and suffered a major defeat. W. D. Cooper records what seems to be the last use in action of the great harbour at the Camber at some time before during or after this battle when he writes, reporting evidence later submitted about the harbour's poor condition, that at the time of the Battle of Beachy Head 'Captain Stone came into the harbour with a fire-ship which drew eleven feet of water and two or three other fireships', that 'the *St. Andrew* [rode] there in twenty-one feet of water' and that 'a Dutch man of war of forty guns [rode] afloat with loaded guns'.[15] The need to obtain help must have led to some exaggeration!

The *Anne,* an English ship badly damaged in the battle was run ashore at Pett Level and set on fire by her captain to prevent her capture. The crew hurried to assist in the defence of the area. Guns were set up, protected only by deal boards, near Camber Castle.[16] This action was part of a panic reaction to defeat at Beachy Head. John Evelyn, in typically pessimistic style: 'The whole nation now exceedingly alarmed by the French fleet braving our coast to the very Thames Mouth ... God of his mercy defend this poor nation'.[17] Any Winchelsea residents who knew about what had happened to their town in the fourteenth century must have shared Evelyn's fears.

It is a gun like the ones set up near Camber Castle which remains of interest in Winchelsea today. The *Anne* was built at Chatham in 1678 as part of a fleet expansion ordered by Charles II. She carried seventy guns and had a crew of about four hundred and fifty. After her demise she lay derelict, rotting and sinking into the sand at Pett. In the early 1940s it was said of her, 'portions of the wreck were to be identified at low water within living memory'.[18] The letter from which this quotation comes contains the earliest mention I have found of the gun, believed to come from the *Anne,* which is displayed in the garden of Winchelsea Court Hall. Hugh Whistler of Battle writes to W. M. Homan, 'Not only am I glad to have saved it but have also been successful in making the mayor interested in it and he tells me that he will have a carriage made for it'.[19] How Mr Whistler came to save it, unless it was to prevent it

(77) The gun believed to have come from the Anne is a feature of the Court Hall garden.

being taken for the manufacture of armaments during World War II, I do not know. Nor do we know when it was brought to Winchelsea from Pett Level. Nevertheless it remains, with the carriage the mayor had made, an important reminder of the last sea battle fought in the area.

Winchelsea's connection with the sea and the navy could no longer persist in practice but instead it continued through the town's name. Only four years after the Battle of Beachy Head the first *HMS Winchelsea* (spelt *Winchelsey*) was built and launched specifically for service in the war with the French. She was a 360 ton, 32 gun frigate known from her size and armaments as a Fifth Rate. She served out her short time as part of the fleet on blockade and escort duties in home waters. On 6 June 1706 she was attacked off Hastings by four French privateers and taken after a gallant defence in which her captain, John Castle, was killed.[20] There is a certain irony that the first *HMS Winchelsea* and her crew should suffer the same fate and in the same waters as had so many ships and men of the town in centuries past.

Six more naval vessels were proudly to carry Winchelsea's name. The last, a destroyer, served escorting Atlantic convoys during the Second World War. The duty for which she is best known, however, is that she was ordered to assist in the evacuation of the British Expeditionary Force from Dunkirk. She took from those beaches 4,957 troops, (was anyone really available to count that accurately in such chaotic circumstances?) carrying as many as 1,200 on one occasion. She was the last destroyer to leave the port with British troops embarked, shortly before midnight on 2/3 June 1940, surviving numerous air attacks mercifully undamaged.[21]

I cannot resist adding here a sidelight to this story, an example of the delights of local history research. I was contacted in January 2001 by Barbara Leighton, the daughter of one of those almost five thousand men, Driver Albert Ellis RASC. Mr Ellis was picked up 'on Friday 31 May at 8.30 p.m. just as the jetty was bombed'. He went on to see service in North Africa, Egypt and Italy and landed on the Normandy beaches on D-Day plus one. A remarkable record. Throughout his long life he has, understandably, been profoundly grateful for what he describes as, 'the gallant efforts of the captain and crew of the *Winchelsea*'.[22]

We must now hurry back from the twentieth century to the end of the seventeenth and to Edward Marten who featured earlier in this chapter. He it was who perpetrated another of Winchelsea's parliamentary election scandals. By 1700 the Winchelsea Borough had fallen entirely under the patronage of the Treasury, for whom Edward Marten was the agent. The candidates whom Marten supported at an election held on 7 January 1701 were his superior officer in the customs service, the Hon. Thomas Newport, who was unknown to the electors, and Robert Bristow who had also been the town's member earlier. This sudden introduction of an unexpected candidate caused considerable resentment. An alternative faction within the corporation put up another former member, John Hayes, whom Marten was trying to displace, together with Robert Austen who had earlier represented Hastings.[23] The electors (not many of them!) gathered at the Court Hall and the votes were publicly cast (the secret ballot was not introduced even by the Reform Act of 1832). In favour of Newport and Bristow were Edward Marten, Matthew Seager, Thomas Jenkins and John Hawkins. Votes were cast for Hayes and Austen by Richard Ashdown, Robert Symonds, Philip Drinker, Thomas Bottle and John Hopper. By a process of extremely simple arithmetic it can be seen that Hayes and Austen had won.[24] Marten nevertheless declared Newport and Bristow elected, 'ignoring the protests of the jurats'.[25]

Hayes and Austen petitioned parliament and the subsequent inquiry revealed that Marten had not only retained his mayoral office illegally while serving as a customs officer but had also threatened one freeman employed by the excise with dismissal for refusing to vote for Newport and

Bristow.[26] On the floor of the House the election of each of the four was declared invalid. Edward Marten was stripped of his customs post and, together with Robert Bristow's agent, John Dunmall, committed into the custody of the Sergeant-at-Arms, Dunmall having been found guilty of bribery. Winchelsea's appalling record of such goings-on and the House's frustration with them were evidenced by an order that no new election should be held and the town should remain for the time being unrepresented.[27] It was not until 3 May that Marten was able to submit a petition expressing his sorrow for 'having incurred the displeasure of the House', begging members' pardon and seeking his release. Two days later he was brought to the bar of the house and, kneeling, 'received a reprimand from Mr Speaker'. He was discharged upon payment of the appropriate fees.[28] I regret not knowing how expensive the fees were or what happened to Dunmall.

By pure coincidence the page of the House of Commons Journal which records Marten's petition for his release also records a petition from the mayor, jurats and freemen of Rye about the poor condition of their harbour.[29] This problem, also deeply affecting Winchelsea, would become the hot topic in the area throughout most of the eighteenth century, resulting eventually in a vast waste of effort and money.

Rye's petition had been long preceded, in 1692, by one from Winchelsea seeking the reopening of the harbour. This was addressed directly to the king. The monarch's advisers marked it: 'Nothing to be done'.[30]

We can gain an introduction to the state of the harbour at this time through the observant eye of Celia Fiennes who, five years later, gazed out from the top of Rye Hill to view the sea with 'a great tract of land on each side that is choked up with sand, which formerly was a good haven for ships; the sea does still come up to Rye town as yet but it is shallow and the Castle which stands a little distance a mile is also left of the sea ... this is Winchelsea Castle but all between it and Winchelsea is nothing but quagmire and marshes drained in some places by ditches'.[31] Celia Fiennes continued her journey on horseback along the Udimore Ridge and crossed the ferry bridge to Winchelsea. There she remarked that it had once been a large place with, 'Thirty-six [sic] large squares of buildings'. Now she saw mostly remains of walls, churches and halls. She rode up a main street, saw the regular intersections, and commented, 'But else[where] the grass grows now where Winchelsea was, as was once said of Troy'.[32] There were very few houses and she thought the mayor, jurats and freemen must make up the majority of the inhabitants. 'Mr Mayor's house' and 'the parsonage' receive favourable comment so action must have been taken since 1686 to house the rector.

My account of Winchelsea in the seventeenth century ends, then, with the parliamentary petitions designed to deal with Celia Fiennes's pessimistic view of the condition of the harbour. The later Rye petition, referred to above, came in the face of a damning assessment of the position by Commissioners who visited in 1698. They concluded that there was no way the harbour could be made useful for the navy and gave detailed reasons, drawing attention to the eastward drift of the shingle, the sandbars, the extreme shallowness of the haven, etc. etc.'[33] If only notice had been taken! Cooper comments that, 'Notwithstanding this unfavourable report, the inhabitants of Rye and Winchelsea made vigorous, though fruitless effort to obtain the sanction of the legislature to an amendment of the haven'.[34]

It will come as no surprise to those cognisant of the history of the harbour that all suggestions to dredge inland and increase the scour of the tides, thus improving things for the seafarers, were firmly opposed by the landowners.

48. VISITORS AND THE CONTROL OF VOTES

At the very beginning of the eighteenth century there came to Winchelsea a visitor just as observant and interested as Celia Fiennes, James Brome. Brome was a clergyman, Rector of Cheriton in Kent, who journeyed widely through England and Wales and left diaries which reveal much about conditions in his day. He travelled through Sussex from Hampshire and after finding Hastings pier 'quite gone to decay' he proceeded to Winchelsea where he wrote of 'a Castle built by King Henry VIII, now [also] quite gone to decay, and large marshes which are defended from violence of the sea with great earthen walls and banks which are preserved and repaired with no small charge and trouble'.[1] This is an aspect of the area's story on which I have spent little time but Brome makes it clear that the landed interest with which the last chapter closed, was, as on Romney Marsh, devoting great effort and expense protecting the reclamation and inning which had characterised preceding centuries.

The Rev. Mr Brome comes closest to home for us when visiting the sites of Winchelsea's three churches and his observations about St. Leonard's are particularly interesting. This church, which had once served Petit Iham and had never been within the Liberty of Winchelsea, had been so poor three centuries earlier that it was excused all taxation and in 1414 no protest was made when the direct route to and from Winchelsea was blocked by the new wall. Nevertheless at least one wall of the church still stood to a good height.[2] Brome was told of a legend regarding this old church which he re-tells as fact: '[In St. Leonard's] was formerly erected a picture of St. Leonard, the patron of the place, holding a fan or aeolus, his sceptre in his hand, which was movable at the pleasure of any who would turn it to such point of the compass as best fitted the return of the husband or other friend whom they expected.' From that direction the wind would blow. This pointing of the picture was accompanied by offerings of which Brome, showing a clergyman's scepticism of such matters, comments neatly, 'without offerings these idols would be idle'.[3]

Frederic Inderwick believed that the picture referred to by Brome reappeared when the Court Hall was refurbished in 1890. This piece of medieval art still hangs in the museum as a prominent exhibit. It was pieced together after its separated boards were found as part of the dais on which stood the former magistrates' bench when it was dismantled, but it is not the St. Leonard picture. Inderwick, repeating the legend told to Brome, tells us that 'the tradition of many ages ascribed to this Norman saint a miraculous power ... over the winds and the waves' and says that the picture was connected to a weather vane on the church steeple.[4] The great weight of the two large panels which form the depiction makes the story seem somewhat less than likely. W. M. Homan, who also claims to have been told that the more incomplete section of panelling was found separately forming part of a pig-sty, was the first to doubt Inderwick's attribution.[5] This doubt has recently been confirmed. The painting has been examined by David Park, Director of the Conservation of Wall Painting Department of the Courtauld Institute of Art. Mr. Park's report[6] reveals that the panels are late medieval and that they depict not St. Leonard who was a hermit and would not be dressed as a bishop but St. Peter and St. Paul. There is no evidence that the painting came from a church and, if it was originally painted in connection with the dispensation of justice in an earlier Court Hall, as well might be the case, it is a rare survival. Further examination and inquiry will be needed if the investigation is to be carried further.

Readers will recall that St. Leonard's Church, where Mr. Brome was told the legend about its patron, stood on the same site as the mill so tragically destroyed in the great storm of 1987. A predecessor of that mill was sited nearby in 1713 and the original lease shows that Samuel Newman, then owner of The Friars and much other Winchelsea property, let a small site to Thomas Taylor of Hastings, miller, on which a windmill formerly stood and on which the lessee intended to erect another.[7] This early eighteenth century mill was actually about two hundred and twenty yards to the north-east of the St. Leonard's remains and its successor, so well known to Winchelsea residents of the nineteenth and twentieth centuries, was built (the remaining St. Leonard's walls were destroyed for the purpose) in the early nineteenth century. This perhaps explains but does not excuse the inaccuracy of the explanatory plaque currently in place. This reads: 'On this site stood St. Leonard's Windmill, destroyed in the great storm of the 16th October 1987. The windmill was built in 1703 on the site of the ancient Saxon church of St. Leonard on which you are now standing'.[8]

In the early eighteenth century, when James Brome visited, the residents of Winchelsea would warmly have welcomed the exercise of St. Leonard's alleged powers over the winds and the waves. The year 1703 saw a storm over Sussex which was likely to have been even worse than that of 1987 and arguably the worst in history. Although there are no records which show precisely its effects in Winchelsea, it must have caused much damage and great distress to a poor population still suffering, among other factors, from the deprivations brought about by the doubling of bread prices during the last decade of the previous century.[9] Accounts elsewhere show that 'sea spray driven far inland by the wind left fields coated with salt and the sheep would not feed'.[10] Incredibly this sea-salting reached Cranbrook, 16 miles inland.[11] 'The wind began to blow at midnight on 27 November and raged continuously for eight hours. As far as records for those days could be made it was estimated that eight thousand people in Britain perished.'[12]

That great storm would have brought only a very a temporary halt to the smuggling which was, at that time, endemic within the local community and vitally important to its economy. Ford Madox Ford writes of the difficulties faced by the preventive officers. In 1703 there were elaborate anti-smuggling provisions in the eastern part of Sussex and in Kent. Fifty officers received £60 per annum, with another £30 spent on a servant and a horse to assist each in night duty. In that same eventful year, 'were added the whole force of dragoons then stationed in Kent. They were made to do duty throughout the marsh from Folkestone to East Guldeford and were supplemented by a number of cruisers'.[13] Against intimidation and bribery they frequently found themselves helpless. Ford quotes the case of an excise officer called Carter who captured a group of New Romney smugglers only to see them released on bail by the local magistrates, whereupon the smugglers chased Carter all the way to Rye Harbour seeking revenge. Only a few years would pass before the mayor of Winchelsea was similarly accused of quite unjustifiably releasing a suspected smuggler. The dragoons

(78) Salutation Cottages, formerly the Salutation Inn c.1950s. Below is a remarkable three-bay cellar, all the bays having quadripartite vaulting.

were apparently just as susceptible to back-handers as were the local judiciary.[14]

We know that a detachment of the excisemen was based in Winchelsea at this time and for the greater part of the eighteenth century. They lived particularly in the south-east corner of the town. W. M. Homan notes that, 'The initials T. W. and the date 1714 may be seen on the outside of the chimney of Glebe.' This was Thomas Walsh. Sadly, when I visited the present owner, John Parry, we were unable to find these initials. In the early twentieth century a riding officer's diary was found, during redecoration work, inscribed on the walls of White Cottage opposite.[15]

The Carylls, bailiffs of Winchelsea, were clearly not immune from receiving the benefit of the area's smuggling activity for in 1717 the poet Alexander Pope wrote to one of the many John Carylls, 'I beg you do me a familiar or rather domestic piece of service. It is, when a hogshead of good French wine falls into your hands – whether out of the skies or whatever element pays no custom – that you would favour me with about twelve dozen of it at the price you gave'. The authors who provide this insight into the attitudes of those days add, 'This letter was to John Caryll, a Sussex squire of known Jacobite sympathies.'[16]

It is those sympathies which are alleged to provide another way in which the Carylls are still remembered in the town, the first being the Water Bailiff's Sergeant's mace as already described. There are, alongside Rectory Lane, a number of Scots Pines. Some of them have, in recent years, fallen or decayed and been replaced. An anonymous note within my collection of Winchelsea papers indicates that it was the belief of the late Miss Edith Holmes of Alards that landowners who were secretly followers of the Old Pretender would indicate their feelings by planting fifteen Scots Pines on their estates as a silent and anonymous affirmation of that support. The number fifteen reflects the first Jacobite rebellion of 1715. As a pine tree lasts between two hundred and two hundred and fifty years and almost three hundred years have now passed, the surviving originals seems to have done well. I do not know whether the writer or, indeed, Miss Holmes knew anything about the Carylls but the note ends, 'It would seem that the "squire" of Winchelsea in the 18th century was a Jacobite and showed his loyalty to the Stuarts by planting our Scots Pines'.[17] I am convinced.

In returning to the subject of Winchelsea's parliamentary seats and the corruption involved in its elections we remain with the Carylls. The same John Caryll who was urged by Alexander Pope to provide him with smuggled wine had, nine years earlier, written to a prospective purchaser of some property near Winchelsea. Caryll explained that when he bought the Manor of Iham he had been confident of being able, through his land ownership in the area, to influence the outcome of elections. Since that time he had had very little to do with such things but, 'as corruption daily spurred itself more and more through every Corporation in England, so you may conclude that this [Winchelsea] became proportionately infected; yet I question not but a stranger may be chosen there at any time for £300 and as the market runs I believe few boroughs are cheaper'.[18]

When last we dwelt on that corruption we found that in 1701 parliament became so aggravated with Winchelsea that it declared an election void and ordered that the town should, for the time being, remain unrepresented. That exclusion lasted only eight months and when the authorities relented the two members who had won the vote but been declared defeated, Robert Austen and John Hayes were, at last, returned as Winchelsea's members. As such they were accorded the honour of representing the town at the coronation of Queen Anne. The official record states that on 13 April 1702, 'At this Assembly John Hayes Esq. and Robert Austen Esq. are elected barons of the said town to bear the canopy over Her Majesty Queen Anne at her royal coronation to be held on the 23rd instant and their commission is sealed accordingly'.[19]

While Hayes and Austen enjoyed this temporary eclipse of their opponents, the influence of the Bristow family lasted much longer. The Robert Bristow who felt such shame and dismay at the failure of his election and the imprisonment of his agent was succeeded by his son of the same name. This Robert Bristow was a man of considerable influence. He owned much property in or near Winchelsea, later shown to have included Cadborough, and it was he, I am sure, who was purchasing from John Caryll. If so he was reassured by

(79) Among these trees are two of Rectory Lane's remaining Scots pines.

Caryll's comment on the apparent cheapness of buying a seat at Winchelsea and he was elected for the town in the year of Caryll's letter, 1708. Bristow became (as far as my researches have led me) Winchelsea's longest-sitting member between that year and 1737 when he was succeeded by his son, yet another Robert Bristow.

The Bristow family's fortune was originally made by the first Robert Bristow (father of the one excluded from Winchelsea membership) as a merchant in the American colonies. He returned to this country and continued trading with Virginia at an enormous profit. The Bristow with whom we are now concerned, elected in 1708, was a director of the Bank of England and of the East India Company, eventually obtaining a position in the household of George I.[20] Such a man quickly exerted his power over those in authority in the town and by 1715 had obtained, through his influence, control of the Winchelsea seats in partnership with a certain George Dodington.[21]

Before this appropriation of a Treasury Borough was quite improperly achieved, however, there had been a classic example of how such influence could operate. In 1710 Robert Bristow stood, officially as a Treasury candidate, with Francis Dashwood, a family connection he had nominated. Bristow and Dashwood received ten votes each. Their opponents, William Penn and Richard Jones, polled twelve votes each. The votes of all but two of Penn and Jones's supporters were disqualified by the mayor. Bristow and Dashwood were declared elected. Although the mayor, John Parnell, was acting in support of a couple of very shady operators, he actually had, in terms of Winchelsea legislation at least, a considerable amount of right on his side. In 1704 Winchelsea Corporation had resolved to exclude from the franchise all freemen living away from the town and this remained in force until external pressures led to its being rescinded in 1730.[22] As always happened in these cases Penn and Jones appealed to the elections committee of parliament who found in favour of Bristow and Dashwood, taking no notice whatsoever of unchallenged evidence that they had paid their voters £30 a head![23]

A further attempt to limit the franchise within Winchelsea was made in the same year as this election, 1710. That resolution, passed while John Parnell was still mayor, decreed that no freeman could be, 'a victualler, innkeeper, alehouse keeper or person that should retail any beer, brandy, distilled water or any other liquor whatsoever'. The requirement went on to state that any person admitted to the freedom should undertake not to indulge in any of these occupations while a freeman.[24] The freemen hurried to sign such undertakings and the papers which they signed remain in Winchelsea's archives.[25] It would seem that any attempt to enforce this ended at the same time as the rules about absentee voters were relaxed for the last of these documents is dated 1730.

John Parnell remained in office for the 1711 mayoral year and was elected again in 1713 but, sadly, died of smallpox during that period of office. He was replaced by Thomas Jenkin, senior, although the research which led to the inscription of the Court Hall mayoral boards missed this change. I should probably be referring to John Parnell, the elder because, in the way of the times he was to be followed as mayor in 1718 and subsequently, by his son, yes, of course, John Parnell! However, down that route lie many pitfalls. The History of Parliament overcomes the problem by calling the Robert Bristows I, II and III. Since no similar genealogical researches accompany the Winchelsea mayoring lists it is almost impossible to deduce how many mayors of the same name there were and at what point one became another!

The appointment of Thomas Jenkin to replace the deceased John Parnell involved a curious incident. Samuel Newman, owner of the Greyfriars and lessor of the mill site, was the only jurat present and he absolutely refused requests from the new mayor and the freemen to administer the mayoral oath of office.[26] How this was overcome is not clear. Nor, in view of it, is it absolutely certain that there was a mayor until Thomas Jenkin was elected the following Easter Monday, but it was impracticable and probably illegal to be without one so I have assumed that some way of overcoming Mr Newman's obstruction must have been found.

The same Samuel Newman is listed as the most extensive landowner in the earliest surviving list of payments due for the King's Dues and Town Rents. This is dated 1716. It is far too detailed to permit us more than a passing glance but of the men who have recently featured in this story, those registered as liable included Samuel Newman, paying on no fewer than thirty-seven buildings, outbuildings, fields and pieces of ground, the heirs of John Hayes Esq. (22) the heirs of Robert Bristow Esq. (10), the heirs of Edward Marten (8), and Thomas Jenkin, tanner, (8). It must have taken an awfully long time to sort out the estates of the deceased in those days. Perhaps Newman objected so strongly to Jenkin because he was a tradesman. The balance of property ownership in the town is indicated by the fact that John Parnell appears only as a tenant and a further seventeen entries account for the whole of the rest of the landowners who had to pay.[27]

We conclude here, as this chapter began, with a visitor, or in this case visitors. James Petiver and James Sherard were on an intriguing mission. Petiver was 'apothecary to the Charterhouse and demonstrator of plants to the Society of Apothecaries'. His colleague was another apothecary and they were making a tour of Sussex and Kent in search of botanical specimens. In this area they first stayed at Brede Place with John Tilden, almost certainly ancestor of John Tilden, the saviour of Winchelsea Corporation.[28] Like James Brome they visited Hastings where they collected specimens, 'from the Castle Walls, by the Bourne Stream and on the beach'.[29] By the time they reached Winchelsea they were tired and more interested in accommodation and refreshment than their collection. They were not disappointed. Petiver and Sherard stayed at the Salutation Inn which was kept by the mayor, Thomas Jenkin, who must have been not only doubling as tanner and innkeeper but also ignoring the resolution excluding innkeepers from the franchise! I would not know how well he was doing as either mayor or tanner but he was certainly doing well as innkeeper for he 'produced so excellent a punch that every bowl was better than its predecessor'.[30]

We must now return to the involved and controversial story of the Harbour of Winchelsea and Rye but it is a pleasure to note first that by the time these visiting apothecaries proceeded, happily by the sound of it, on their way to Kent they had recorded 'about thirty-five specimens, many of them for the first time in Sussex'.[31]

49. THE NEW HARBOUR STARTS AND STALLS

Complaints about the effects of inning or reclamation of land had been growing in volume since the middle of the sixteenth century and with them a developing feud between the maritime and landed interests. It was in 1719 that this inning, so detrimental to the tidal scour of the former great harbour at the Camber, was dramatically reinforced by Sir Robert Guldeford. He built a dam across the mouth of the Wainway, formerly part of the Camber and the route by which shipping reached Lydd. Cooper gives a very precise figure of 187 years since the reclamation of the marshes began and laments, 'thus ... was the ancient haven called the Camber, alias the Wainway Creek or Channel, totally stopped and destroyed, and a new church and parish erected on its ruins'.[1] Thus, too, was Sir Robert's family name perpetuated – East Guldeford. The cartographer John Norden shared Cooper's dismay at this vandalism but seems to have gone a bit over the top when, in 1724, he claimed that 'within the memory of many yet living there have been anchored above 400 sail of the tallest ships of all nations in a place called the Camber near Rye, where now sheep and cattle feed'.[2] The reader will realise from information earlier in this book or just from looking at the following paragraphs that, unless the 'many yet living' had lived an unbelievably long time, Norden was exaggerating for effect.

The old harbour which had made first Winchelsea and later Rye so dominant in national maritime service and trade had, under Sir Robert's direction, finally turned into a shallow creek. The natural reaction was to strive to replace it. At the end of the first quarter of the eighteenth century it was the Ryers who had the energy to press for such a development for they stood a reasonable chance of re-establishing profitable trading, the men of Winchelsea did not. One feels it must have been, even initially, with some desperation that the mayor and jurats of Rye, with official support, re-activated a scheme which their predecessors had firmly rejected almost a century and a half earlier.

In 1591 an Italian engineer called Gedevilo Gienily, well aware of the problems even then, proposed to the citizens of Rye a plan to rejuvenate their harbour. For this service he demanded an initial payment of £4000, £2000 of it on account and a pension for twenty-five years. In return he would develop and maintain an anchorage far more serviceable than it had been 'for forty years past'.[3] Rye was exultant and enthusiastic but only until the details became known. Gienily, whose name was anglicised to Frederick Genebelly by the locals and even in some official documents, intended to make a new outlet to the sea 'from Dinsdale Bridge beside Winchelsea' to what we now know as Winchelsea Beach. This might have pleased those wishing to undertake further land reclamation but Rye's maritime interests were seriously threatened. This would not benefit Rye at all, it would benefit 'others', meaning Winchelsea. Rye's mayor and jurats ordered that, 'Frederick "Jenebell" hath most treacherously abused this township by his false illusions in promising to amend the Harbour of Rye and [we] will no longer meddle with [him] nor with any of his devices'.[4] When the engineer, quite reasonably and modestly, submitted a bill of £85 9s 0d for his expenses payment was refused!

The story of this New Harbour will be of import in these pages because, although Rye was pleading for aid and initiating proposals, Gienily's sixteenth century plan for a western solution was, surprisingly and eventually disastrously, largely followed. As a result the main construction work took place in the Liberty of Winchelsea, under Winchelsea's gaze and jurisdiction; the remains form an important feature in the landscape of Winchelsea Beach to this day.

In 1720 Rye succeeded in achieving a quick, if ineffectual, riposte to Sir Robert Guldeford's dam. An Act of Parliament condemned, unspecifically, the innings which had taken place in the area of the Camber and provided that no new walls, banks or stops were to be erected which interfered with the flux and reflux of the tide.[5] Two years later Rye Corporation wrote to other seaports urging them to support a further Act for the regeneration of their harbour. The letter included the observation that, unless a harbour could be retained at Rye there would be nowhere between Dover and Portsmouth 'to receive shipping in distress or give them shelter in time of war from ships of the enemy'.[6] Perhaps Newhaven should have replaced Portsmouth but an important point was made.

All this seemed to bring success. On 12 May 1724 newly appointed Harbour Commissioners met for the first time. By an Act of 1723 they were empowered to do everything necessary to construct 'any New Cut or Channel from Winchelsea Water to the sea.'[7] Winchelsea Water meant the River Brede. This was, indeed, Gienily's plan resuscitated. Only a very brief mention is possible here of the works proposed at the Rye end. There the plan, frequently varying in its method, was to direct the Tillingham and the Rother towards the new harbour. At the Winchelsea end the flow of the Brede would be redirected and instead of going north towards Rye would, through a new canal, head south-westwards to the sea. It is perhaps a bit cynical, having already indicated that the whole thing was eventually to be a disaster, to point out that many of the Commissioners were riparian landowners.

A Captain Perry was appointed engineer and, in order to provide proper access to his works, he first built a drawbridge across the Tillingham and later a road alongside the Brede. Winchelsea residents would no doubt have been delighted by these developments but the nearby ferry owner was greatly incensed by the threat to his livelihood. This gentleman, Mr Hounsell, complained bitterly that many pedestrians and horse riders were using the bridge instead of his ferry. Locals had to be prevented from taking advantage in this way so a fierce-looking gate was erected 'with spikes of iron on the top and on each side'. Only the Commissioners, their agents and their workmen might cross the bridge. Lady Doneraile also suffered losses at the Winchelsea ferry, presumably later as a result of the road construction. Both Hounsell and Her Ladyship were paid compensation.[8]

There is just one intriguing contemporary account by a visitor who had no personal interest in the project, Jeremiah Milles. Milles saw the work in progress in 1743 and immediately recognised the reason that Rye's elders had so unceremoniously condemned Gienily's proposals in the late sixteenth century: 'If the new cut which they are making towards the sea succeeds there is some hopes that Winchelsea may

(80) Remains of the New Harbour, including stonework from the east pier head and the wooden pier head extensions. Very little of these features is currently visible.

survive, it lying nearer and having more conveniences for a merchant than Rye by the number of its vaults'.[9]

By 1748 work had progressed very slowly at various points of the development. The road, the pierheads at the sea end, and the sluice which would control water levels in the channel were completed and part of the channel had been excavated. At this point all work stopped as the Commissioners had run out of money and were £11,000 in debt. The money should have been coming in perfectly adequate amounts from a toll, partly shared with Dover, of three pence per ton on all shipping passing Rye. John Collard points up one reason for the

(81) Wren Cottage, High Street; a small medieval house which did not originally incorporate an open hall.

Commissioners' problems when he states, 'It seems that the agents entrusted with [collection of the toll] – including one Mayor of Rye – were, to say the least, somewhat lighthanded with the proceeds'.[10] Sadly he doesn't provide a name! Paul Kléber Monod is less reticent, he attaches the blame firmly to James Lamb and his family.[11] However, regardless of any misappropriation, income from that toll was reducing because of war with France and Spain and authorisation for it was limited to a few further years. At this point it was decided to close the bridge (local protests led to separate funds to keep it open), and sell off timber and materials which were deteriorating.[12]

With work stopped, assets sold and debts owed, we must leave the story of the New Harbour until later. It will not go away!

What of life in Winchelsea while harbour work proceeded at a snail's pace? We have seen how pleased the townsmen would have been with access via a new road from Rye. Their route to Hastings via Icklesham was more direct and secure and was indicated by seven milestones.[13] I wonder whether any of them have survived.

Within Winchelsea the roads were, however, in a very poor state. Although they had been 'well paved' they were, in 1730, overrun with grass.[14] These grassy streets were also littered with rubbish according to Commissioners appointed to survey the coast of Great Britain. They came to Winchelsea and observed that it had 'lost even the very appearance of a city, except in the rubbish of it'. They could not refrain from commenting on a phenomenon frequently noted in these pages, that 'where the ships lay with their broadsides to the shore, you now see the green marshes'.[15] A good deal of the rubbish in the streets may well have been created by the mayor, jurats and freeman who had 'immemorially enjoyed the liberties and advantages of turning out and feeding horses, cows and cattle in the streets and waste ground belonging to the corporation'.[16] I suppose this privilege might at least have led to some of the grass in the streets being eaten! Anyway these worthies actively sought to protect their privilege by issuing a decree seeking to 'prevent persons enclosing those areas and thus preventing those rights being exercised'.[17]

The retreat of the sea from the town was only a minor irritant to Winchelsea's smugglers who continued to indulge freely in their 'trade' along the extensive piece of coast which came under the jurisdiction of the town's magistrates. They just had to go a little further to do so. It would seem that the receipt of smuggled goods by such distinguished associates of the town as the Caryll bailiffs, already noted, may have been shared by leading residents. In 1734 the mayor, John Parnell, whose father of the same name had died of smallpox, received a stern rebuke from the Commissioners of Customs in London for acquitting and releasing a known smuggler, Thomas Darby.[18] The Commissioners must have been informed of this by John Collier, Surveyor General of the Riding Officers for the County of Kent, who had carried out an investigation. Collier's title is a bit misleading because he lived in Hastings and obviously included the eastern part of Sussex in his area of responsibility. His papers show that Parnell was not only mayor at the time but also Supervisor of the Riding Officers. Whether this was an ex-officio duty or a separate one is not clear to me. Apparently Darby had been accused of 'assaulting the Officers of the Customs'. In response to being faced with a resident accused of this extremely serious charge Parnell is reported to have excused his conduct by feeling that the witness to the event was 'a paltry fellow and his affidavit ought not to be regarded, or words to that effect'. Darby was freed. Parnell received a reprimand from Collier but no worse.[19]

Mayors, including Parnell, jurats and freemen whose stock could graze the streets were at this time having not untypical problems in administering the town's affairs. In 1739 the then mayor, John Jenkin, suspected that Winchelsea's ancient record books 'had been taken out of the chest and carried away or otherwise embezzled'.[20] At an assembly he required the chamberlain, William Garland, to open the chest so that Garland could take the documents into his own safe-keeping. Garland refused and, equally determinedly, declined to hand over the key. Frustrated by this obstinacy the mayor demanded that those present, himself, two jurats and five freemen, take a vote as to whether the chest should be physically broken open. Six voted in favour of this and allowing the mayor to keep the books safely elsewhere. Garland and John Knight voted against.[21] Garland was a freeman as well as being Chamberlain or he would not have been able to cast a vote. Garland's motives for this obstruction, unless he was in some personal dispute with the mayor, are not clear. No lasting action was taken against him for he continued to be elected each Easter Monday into the office of Chamberlain with its responsibility for the corporation's finances.

The Confederation of the Cinque Ports was also trying to keep its affairs in order. Rather earlier than the Winchelsea Court Hall chest was smashed the Confederation had been 'conscious of its special duty to maintain a proper tradition' in calling sittings of its courts, particularly the Brotherhood and Guestling.[22] It was decided that after taking office on 21 May each year the Speaker would send a circular letter to each member town asking whether a meeting was required. It seems that meetings were likely to be held only 'when some special question arose, when officers were to be appointed or accounts were to be passed'. Felix Hull, editor of the *Calendar of the White and Black Books of the Cinque Ports* comments that 'it was essentially the circular letter that kept the Confederation alive for a century and a half'.[23] That view must be accepted for from the time of this decision, 1726, until the beginning of the twentieth century the Confederation met an average of only once every eighteen years. In 1902 a Brotherhood and Guestling decided that 'the mode of calling these courts is dilatory and cumbersome' and it was agreed to set up a Standing Committee comprising the mayor, town clerk and one other member from each port, to meet annually and conduct normal business.[24] Even this arrangement had long fallen out of use by 1985 when it was proposed by the Speaker, Jurat Charles Croggon of Winchelsea, and his successor, Councillor Roger Breeds of Rye, that the Standing Committee should meet automatically on 21 May, or as close to that date as possible, each year, the business to conclude with the installation of the new Speaker.

That is the present practice.

In considering the third and fourth decades of the eighteenth century (except for the story of the New Harbour which carried us a bit further) we turn last to St. Thomas's Church. This was a busy time, partly provoked at least by the submission in 1724 of a derogatory report by officers of the Hastings Deanery. They noted that the patron of the living was Sir William Ashburnham and the incumbent, instituted the previous year, was Mr William Wills. The only good comments were about certain artefacts, the Bible and Book of Common Prayer, a pewter flagon, a silver cup and a surplice. The presence of other items was merely noted. They included a linen table-cloth and napkin for the Communion, a chest, a poor box and one bell. The fabric and furnishings were in poor condition with the parish authorities responsible for doing something about it. The rectory pulled down by Samuel Oates had still not been replaced. The parish contained 'about 35 or 40 families. One Anabaptist, one Presbyterian.' This population provided only about twenty communicants. A service was held each Sunday by the rector with communion, 'three times a year in the past but the incumbent intends for the future to administer it four times.'[25]

Following the comments about the fabric and furnishings some action was taken. Within seven years box pews had been installed and the roof retiled.[26] In a further attempt to improve the church's appearance, 'the whitewash was repeatedly renewed from 1726 onwards.'[27] Thus was perpetuated the covering of St. Thomas's original wall paintings, probably first whitewashed over at the Reformation. Later the plaster on which they had existed was stripped off to expose the stonework. W. M. Homan laments, as I am sure do we all, that all but a tiny painted fragment above the central effigy in the north aisle, showing an angel swinging a censer, was lost to us.[28]

The parish, of course, had concerns and responsibilities far beyond the maintenance of the church itself. Two instances must suffice here for they demonstrate how these responsibilities had proliferated in almost two centuries since the Reformation. Funds must be raised locally to support the poor. We have an example of one way that this was done in a receipt dated 7 April 1724. It reads as follows: 'Received of John Valentine, the sum of one pound ten shillings for a year's rent for the Court Hall house, due and ending Lady Day last for the use of the Poor of the Parish of St. Thomas at Winchelsea'.[29] Unfortunately I do not know which part of the Court Hall complex, much larger then than now, was 'the Court Hall house'.

One of the ways in which funds raised in this way were spent was in supporting the poor in apprenticeships and employment. All did not always go well. Three years after John Valentine paid the rent noted above a case was brought before the Winchelsea Sessions which involved the employment of a pauper, John Parris. Mr Thomas Isigham had agreed to take Parris into his household as a servant for a year from the previous Lady Day and to pay him thirty-five shillings for his year's work. Unfortunately Parris 'had been very idle and run away from his service for several days'. The master asked, for this reason, to be freed from the agreement he had entered into with the authorities of St. Thomas's and to be permitted, in the language of our day rather than his, to be allowed to sack this servant. After some deliberation the court ruled it to be a reasonable request but the decision did not entirely go Isigham's way. He was ordered to pay John Parris the eight shillings and ninepence due to him in wages to date. Only then could he be discharged.[30]

When the records of Winchelsea's courts are examined, the findings are frequently sensibly even-handed like this one and a credit to the mayors and jurats who occupied the bench.

50. JEREMIAH'S JOURNEY

Such probity, as indicated in these pages, did not generally apply to the mayors' conduct of elections.

Winchelsea's anachronistic privilege of electing two members to parliament did not escape the eye of Jeremiah Milles whose comments on the construction work in progress at the New Harbour we have already noted. By the time that he visited Sussex in 1743 Milles had travelled widely in Europe and been elected a Fellow of the Society of Antiquaries and of the Royal Society; all this at the early age of twenty-nine.[1] He was a traveller whose observations carried much weight. He wrote 'Winchelsea ... sends two members to Parliament, though there are not above thirteen voters, and yet great sums have been expended on this occasion in this poor place'.[2]

While mayors continued to benefit from those 'great sums', in the mid-eighteenth century the increased politicisation of Winchelsea's parliamentary seats and the circumstances surrounding elections created confusing complexities. By as early as 1715 George Dodington and Robert Bristow had acquired much property in and around the town; their influence over those of their tenants who were voters ensured that Dodington and Bristow could then secure the election of their favoured candidates.[3] In 1741 George Bubb Dodington and the next Robert Bristow, who had inherited these estates from uncle and father respectively, defected from the government cause and went over to the opposition. If it was their intention to protect their Winchelsea interests, this was a misjudgement. Prime Minister Robert Walpole arranged, through the Treasury, the candidacies of two potential government loyalists, Arthur Mohun St. Leger and Thomas Orby Hunter; defeat for Dodington and Bristow's nominees followed.[4] Since he was important locally, it is worth noting that one of the latter was Samuel Jeake.

Arthur St. Leger, by then Viscount Doneraile, three years later protected his seat by, in his turn, buying up Winchelsea land and property including the Ferry House and the Salutation Inn.[5] His Winchelsea membership has, for him, a sad ending for by 1747 he had followed Dodington and Bristow into opposition. Although he realised the futility of opposing the Treasury candidates, Hunter and Colonel John Mordaunt, he had fallen out so badly with Hunter that he stood in opposition to him on principle. Mordaunt polled 15 votes, Hunter 12 and Doneraile 3. It was said that nobody took any notice of Doneraile except his two tenants.[6] Where the third vote came from is not recorded!

With these examples of how parliamentary seats could be won by local influence, provided at least that those elected were loyal to the government, it is hardly surprising that the precedent was followed. Two who acquired property for this reason were Albert Nesbitt and William Belchier. Belchier was a London banker whose principal local acquisition was the considerable acreage of the Manor of Iham, formerly owned by the Carylls. Most of the land and property of the manor may, in fact, never have been Belchier's freehold at all. He lent money to John Caryll on the security of the Iham Manor estate and, later, when trying to fend off bankruptcy tried, unsuccessfully, to foreclose on the loan. Deeply embittered, as well as by then bankrupt, Belchier was later to write to Caryll, 'Your unkindness in this very long delay in your clearing up the title to the Winchelsea estate has in great measure been the cause of my ruin'.[7]

The Nesbitt influence, although eventually also terminated by financial ruin,[8] lasted much longer. Albert Nesbitt, a London merchant, was a friend and associate of the Pelham family which had members of great influence both locally and nationally. With their encouragement he bought up Winchelsea property, some of it from the heirs of Viscount Doneraile, and set about 'solacing the worthy gentlemen of the borough'.[9] On Albert Nesbitt's death in 1753, his heir was his nephew, Arnold Nesbitt.[10] With Arnold's entry into these pages we make contact with a major player on Winchelsea's eighteenth century stage; a man whose energy and enterprise must concern us for some time. The Prime Minister, Henry Pelham, virtually insisted that Arnold stood for the seat formerly controlled by his late uncle and he was elected for Winchelsea in 1754. A letter sent later (in 1761) by Arnold Nesbitt to Pelham reveals much about electioneering in those days and Winchelsea candidacy in particular. Nesbitt had been considered, because he already owned land in and near the town, to have the best chance of beating William Belchier. He took a considerable financial risk in doing so and it was agreed that his expense should be limited to £1000. If he was happy to lose such a sum in those days he was pretty well off. Nesbitt saw that the election would probably cost him much more but he entered enthusiastically into the fray: 'We baffled Mr Belchier in all his schemes, both in the Corporation and at law but my expense instead of being £1000 amounted to above £3000 besides a pretty considerable annual expense since'.[11] Despite this complaint Arnold had, in the meantime, happily continued expanding his holdings in the area, the largest of these purchases being the Manor of Icklesham which included Wickham Farm.[12]

(82) Richard Maplesden of German Street was an enterprising grocer and draper who issued his own token coins. The top coin (both sides are shown) has on the edge 'Payable at Richard Maplesden's, Winchelsea'. A similar imprint was used by troops stationed at Brighton during the French war which broke out in 1793 and could be used in Brighton. These tokens were very popular and the lower coin has on its edge 'Payable in London, Lancaster or Bristol'.

When in Winchelsea, as he frequently was, Arnold Nesbitt lived at Periteau House.

Nesbitt's success in, 'baffl[ing] Mr Belchier in all his schemes' led to farcical goings-on at Easter 1753. At the usual Easter Monday Court of Hundred the Belchier interest had managed to secure the election of John Knight as mayor and Charles Stephens as town clerk. This was grossly unsatisfactory for those supporting Nesbitt and must have been in some way flawed because legal ways were found of recalling the court the following day and re-running the elections. The proceedings in the Court Hall on that occasion were reported by one observer to John Collier who had an interest in seeing that his excisemen controlled the corporation as far as was possible. Collier's correspondent:

'Mr Marten is elected Mayor of this Corporation of Winchelsea – Mr Belchier and his party appeared in Court and protested against all the proceedings. Their behaviour was Very Extraordinary. They attempted to carry away the Constable's Staff by force to regain which we had a great struggle in Court. Mr Adcroft's behaviour in this matter was very Impudent and Scandalous. The keys of the Chest were refused to get the Book of Oaths, as also the Oaths of Allegiance etc. and on a person's being ordered to break open the Chest, Mr Belchier and his companions sat upon the same and bid defiance to the Court for to break the same open ... Old Knight came into Court and demanded the mayor's seat and then sent for the Staff and insisted upon the same again but was refused – he sat upon the Bench during the whole sitting of the Court with his Staff in his hand.'[13]

I am much relieved that such goings-on do not characterise the mayoring these days! The outcome of this fiercely and physically contested ceremony was that, the Nesbitt supporters having mustered a majority, John Knight and Charles Stephens were removed from office after serving only one day. William Marten became mayor for the fourth time and Nathaniel Dawes was reinstated as town clerk. Stephens was later to claim, as part of his Winchelsea credentials, that he had served as town clerk. He omitted to mention the brevity of his term of office![14]

It is difficult to appreciate the significance of the factional interests which controlled Winchelsea Corporation in those days. The key lies in the involvement of Edwin Wardroper. Wardroper, who was acting at this time on behalf of the local Treasury agent, John Collier,[15] served as both mayor and town clerk of Winchelsea and as town clerk of Rye. He gathered a significant number of voters to him and could therefore swing elections according to the size of the rewards which he was offered. A list of the Winchelsea voters made in 1747 included Wardroper himself and eight others who were variously described as his friend, his brother (actually his brother-in-law for his sister Catherine married John Parnell[16]), or as being 'attached' to him, or made freeman by him. Of these nine, 'Marten [the friend] is the only one easily to be got off'. Eight other voters are listed, at least four of whom might be expected to oppose Wardroper, but if all these combined in opposition they might not succeed for long as, 'Wardroper can make what number of freemen he pleases'.[17] We can reasonably assume that by 1753, if not later, Wardroper was supporting Nesbitt for the mayor who replaced John Knight (listed earlier as a Wardroper man it must be admitted) was William Marten. Or perhaps he had been 'got off'!

By 1753 Edwin Wardroper's influence extended not just to Winchelsea and Rye but throughout the Confederation for he was appointed Solicitor to the Ports in 1750.[18]

Many of the voters listed in the document referred to above were Riding Officers employed to control smuggling. The Treasury would ensure the security of Winchelsea's seats by appointing men to such posts. If they were legal voters they were genuinely resident in Winchelsea which is one reason why the mostly public Winchelsea cellars are unlikely to have been widely used for contraband storage. However, that did not prevent the men of the town smuggling elsewhere.

Smuggling, of course, was the name by which the evasion of import duties was known. When the traffic operated in the opposite direction, usually the illegal exporting of wool, it was known as owling. The records show that Winchelsea men were also directly involved in this activity for in 1748, 'William Dunk and other labourers of Winchelsea ... were caught stealing 600 pounds of wool in order to ship it to France'.[19] No doubt Jurat John Dunk, a Winchelsea man born and bred and, at the time of writing, about to become mayor, may have an interesting ancestor in William.

Those involved in both smuggling and owling could not assume during the 1740s that they were unlikely, when crossing the channel, to avoid clashes with Winchelsea's traditional enemy, the French. Preparations in 1744 for an invasion in support of Bonnie Prince Charlie's attempt to reclaim the crown (the '45) provoked a threatening enemy presence in the Channel and 'reinforcements were ... poured into Kent, Sussex and Hampshire'.[20] This threat came closest to Winchelsea in February 1744 when Admiral Jacques de Roquefeuil, having found no opposition off the Isle of Wight, sent instructions for the invasion to commence, and sailed with his own fleet to Dungeness. There the English under Sir John Norris were available in strength. No attack was mounted immediately and the French escaped during the night by drifting away down Channel. The weather intervened at this point. A ferocious storm scattered the French naval fleet and of the army transports, caught en-route, 'twelve were sunk of which seven went down with all on board'.[21] The invasion was abandoned and Winchelsea suffered no eighteenth century equivalent of its earlier devastation.

Here we return to the writings of Jeremiah Milles who cast a penetrating, if sometimes jaundiced, eye over the Winchelsea which would within a few years of his visit see the election fraud, smuggling and threats of invasion described above. His facility encourages me to use his view at some length. It is difficult to imagine the Winchelsea of his day becoming eventually the Winchelsea of our day.

Milles noted the continued existence of 'five streets in the length

(83) The Millennium 'Tapestry' is displayed in the north-west corner of St. Thomas's Church where the Rev. Drake Hollingberry's new vestry was built.

way [presumably north-south] and four that crossed them [east-west]'; very close to the present street pattern. The remaining streets were already under the fields. Some lengths of the old town wall survived, probably considerably more than today. Interestingly he saw remains of 'the four gates on the four sides of the town'. As we now have only the Strand (east), Pipewell (north) and New (south) Gates, it is not clear to me where Milles's fourth was sited, probably at what is now the Sandrock Hill entrance. That would be the missing western gate. Here Milles deserves to speak for himself:

> 'Winchelsea at present is reduced to a miserable village consisting of only 10 or 12 houses; the people who live in them are very poor, as they have no manner of trade here, and I am told it is reckoned an unhealthy place and subject to agues on account of the marshes which are to the south of it ... Near the church they have a Town Hall and a gaol, the former of which they say is a handsome room; it might be so for Winchelsea but I did not think it worth my seeing.'[22] What a snub!

While he may not have expected much of the Town [Court] Hall, Milles did marvel at the amazing survival of so many magnificent cellars, 'ribbed across in as elegant a manner as the aisles of gothic churches'. He could not believe that the original buildings above them could have been built to equivalent standards.

Milles was also condescending enough to comment favourably on the remains of the Chapel of the Greyfriars. 'There is a very fine prospect from the eminence where this old monastery stands, which is (as it were) a natural terrace of a great height over the marsh.'[23] At St. Thomas's Church, although misinterpreting the nature of the monuments, he admires them and he confirms that the church authorities have acted on their unfavourable 1724 report already quoted by commenting, 'The Chancel is in repair', adding, most unappreciatively, 'that is as much as one can say of it'.[24]

Finally here we turn to those church authorities and the amazingly varied duties that they were expected to undertake as a result of poor law legislation. In 1748 payment of six shillings was made to Elizabeth Catt for work she had done for pauper Daniel Dungate; this work included making three shirts, knitting a pair of stockings and mending clothes. Thomas Harrod was paid for 150 faggots for the poor at twelve shillings per hundred and a certain John Knightley received one pound seven shillings 'for Physick due to Ann Reeves'.[25]

An even more unusual example of the way in which paupers had to be looked after will set us on our way as we turn to Winchelsea's story during the 1760s.

51. CAMBRIC AND CAUSES

It was in 1761 that the St. Thomas's authorities had to deal with the case of 'a poor parishioner' whose name, unlike those of Daniel Dungate, Elizabeth Catt and Ann Reeves, is not available for us. The unfortunate woman had been sent to Canterbury to the home of Elizabeth Cooper whose ministrations it was hoped would cure 'a most dreadful leg'. The letter which Elizabeth Cooper sent in response to the pauper's arrival is preserved with the day-to-day nineteenth century correspondence of the St. Thomas's Overseers of the Poor. As it is dated well before any others among the collection it was probably kept as a curiosity even in those days. I will let Elizabeth Cooper, like Jeremiah Milles, speak for herself:

For the Gentlemen Parish Officers of Winchelsea in Sussex

Canterbury 2 August 1761

Gentlemen,

Your poor parishioner that you sent me has got a most dreadful leg indeed and will want a prodigious deal of attendance to make a sound cure of it which I hope she will have. If not the trouble I have will be of no charge to you. If I cure her it will cost you four guineas for the same and five shillings per week for her board, Gentlemen. According to your desire I have taken her into the house by reason of the small pox. As to the small pox it has been in Canterbury very little and that a very favourable sort. I have had above three score patients this summer and have not had one of them catch it, but if she should be taken with it she must be put out of the house. I will do the uttermost of my endeavour to get her well and send her home from

Your most humble Servant

Eliz: Cooper[1]

How refreshing to find a woman, practising medicine in the manner of her day, offering to work on a no cure, no fee basis! Quite apart from the mine of information about the circumstances of the day which this short letter provides, there is a postscript which reminds us of the complexity of eighteenth century communication in those days. Mrs Cooper tells the overseers that she will require 'prodigious many' white linen rags which she will not provide as part of the arrangement. She asks that they should be sent to 'Mr Luxford's at Rye and he will bring them to Mr Brown's at Hythe and Mr Brown will bring them to me on Monday next'.[2] The network of services then offered by carriers such as Luxford and Brown was slow by our standards but fortunately reliable.

Jeremiah Milles has given us a glimpse of the poverty of the Winchelsea from which this pauper had been despatched. Fortunately things were about to improve. In 1761, the year of Elizabeth Cooper's letter, a business was established in the town for the manufacture of cambric. This fine linen takes its name from Cambrai, its place of origin. The process was introduced into England at Winchelsea by M. Mariteau whose name will be known to Winchelsea readers through the home in German Street, built for and named after him. Here was hope, indeed, for some revival of Winchelsea's fortunes. A letter from the town waxes lyrical: 'The cambric manufactory here established is like to be attended with great success; we have now already eight looms at work and shall soon have two more. Two pieces have been finished and sent to town, one of which I am told, was presented to the king'.[3] There was an element here of revenge on the French for Mariteau and his immigrant colleagues were Huguenots, Protestant refugees from religious persecution in that country. It was estimated that having cambric manufactured in England rather than imported might save £300,000 a year, an absolutely astronomical sum.

The advantages which Winchelsea provided for this work were several. The even year-round temperature and the humidity of the many cellars were ideal for the delicate process; the local water was exactly right for the bleaching involved and the rich soil of the land reclaimed from the sea and the River Brede was ideal for growing the raw material, flax.[4] So far so good. Here at last was a benefit accruing to Winchelsea from the insidious inning which had been reducing the effectiveness of its harbour and consolidating the retreat of the sea for centuries. However, as readers may have come to expect, all was not to be plain sailing.

The first problem was the legality of the sale of this cambric, 'it being doubtful whether it was consistent with the laws

(84) Arnold Nesbitt

then in existence to sell such articles in England'.[5] To overcome this and regularise the situation it was decided in 1763 to promote the statutory establishment of The English Linen Company and a large part of the initiative for this enterprise came from Arnold Nesbitt who thus returns to our story. Nesbitt and his partners obtained authority through the necessary parliamentary legislation to 'buy land to the value of £500 a year and raise capital of £100,000'.[6] The company took over existing property and built anew. The houses now known as 1-10 Barrack Square bear Arnold Nesbitt's initials and the date 1763 and were then in 'Bear Square'.[7] They formed part of a fifteen property development built for the company by Walter Fuller. The Five Houses, too, date from this time.

At the height of its success the company employed 160 spinners, winders and weavers together with 26 apprentices and had 86 looms at work.[8] A town of the size described by Jeremiah Milles could not provide such a work-force and had to look elsewhere. Many of the skilled workers came with their masters, M. Mariteau and M. Francois-Marie Corbeaux, from France. The apprentices were mostly recruited locally, if not from Winchelsea. Twelve of them, aged between nine and fourteen, came from Hastings. The records there show that these children were 'enabled ... to be disposed of as apprentices at a charge of £88 in premiums and the cost of their clothes'. The parish officers of St. Clement's and All Saints could not afford this amount and had to borrow £100 'from Mr Milward ... one of the great men of the town'.[9]

Further complications were added by the extreme delicacy of the manufacturing process. As already noted, the weaving of the specially grown, very spindly flax into cambric was chiefly done in the town's cellars. Their stillness and regular temperature made them ideal for, as the problems were described by skilled workers, the thread was so fine that, 'it will not before weaving bear the influence of the upper and freely circulating air'. Any disturbance of the air would tend to make the thread brittle and lead to its breaking during the weaving process, 'as if it was rotten'.[10]

It is not clear how the English Linen Company came to cease production; the extreme complication of the process and the heavy outlay required for its establishment must have been factors. Ford Madox Ford is specific in blaming finance. 'After exhausting the greater part of their capital in erecting houses, workshops and two large houses for the principal managers, the proprietors failed.'[11] The proprietors and the workers were fortunate in that it was possible to lease the business to Messrs. Nouvaille, Kirkman and Clay, all merchants from the City of London, whose end-product was Italian crêpe. No doubt the crêpe required less demanding facilities for it to be made successfully.

Nouvaille and Co. were already lessees by 1767. Winchelsea's cambric manufacture, so enthusiastically started and heralded, therefore lasted only a maximum of six years. The investors will have been relieved to continue receiving a return through Nouvaille's payments on the lease. Peter Nouvaille, rather than his partners, was the driving force behind the new business and it was through his ingenuity that 'the manufacture arrived at great perfection'.[12]

That perfection was labour intensive and could not be achieved without the necessary workers. The rules which governed the employment of their staff, both adults and children, were strict. The neighbouring parish of Icklesham was pleased to rid itself of expensive pauper children but the indentures of those children bound them to the company for a very long time. In 1769, the early days of crêpe manufacture, George Dengate, a poor boy aged 'ten years or thereabouts' was apprenticed to Nouvaille & Co for the modest parish outlay of eight pounds. In return for faithful service 'in all lawful business' he was to 'be well and truly trained in the art of weaving as well as being provided with food and lodging'. There is no mention in the document of wages. Astonishingly to us this agreement was to keep him in the company's employment until 'he achieved his full age of twenty-four years'.[13] An Icklesham girl of twelve, Sarah Fuller, was apprenticed in the same year. The terms were similar. She was to learn spinning and weaving and was bound until she was twenty-one.[14]

George Dengate did not serve that full apprenticeship. In 1776 Richard Dengate, perhaps a relative anxious to help, paid eleven pounds to secure George's release and undertook to provide him with employment.[15]

Equally strict rules applied to adult workers. In the same year that George Dengate and Sarah Fuller joined the company, Joseph Lorty ran away from it. An order was issued to the Winchelsea Constables to arrest Joseph and bring him before the mayor and jurats in their capacity as magistrates. Peter Poreau would appear in court on behalf of the company to accuse Lorty of 'leaving his work unfinished and suffering himself to be employed by another master'. The matter was taken very seriously and the constables were told, 'Fail not at your peril'.[16]

We do not know the outcome of that case but the experience six years later of a certain Charles Dean gives us the flavour of the kind of justice meted out to Nouvaille's workers. Like Lorty, Dean and two colleagues, Edward Pankhurst and William Day, were brought before the court accused of 'running away and leaving the service of Peter Nouvaille'. There must have been much to run away from! Pankhurst and Day were sentenced to be discharged; not too serious whatever the consequences. Dean, however, before being similarly discharged, was to be 'stripped from his waist upwards and receive twenty stripes on his naked back in the yard of and belonging to the said Court Hall'.[17] Readers familiar with the tranquil and beautiful Court Hall garden will perhaps not want to remember, when visiting, that it was once the scene of such punishments.

M. Nouvaille and his colleagues continued to prop up Winchelsea's economy, supported in their harsh regime by the magistrates, until 1810 when the business was moved to Norwich.

Perhaps it was the problem of distributing their wares which eventually drove them from the town. The roads in the area were terrible and we have already seen that transporting goods by sea from Winchelsea had become virtually impossible. As late as 1838, when the Duke of Wellington, who was Lord Warden, wanted to travel from Walmer Castle to London, he undertook only a tiny part of the journey by road. The remainder was by such railways as then existed across Kent and by boat up the Thames from Whitstable.[18] Over fifty years earlier such travelling problems of the illustrious were vastly greater for ordinary

(85) Arnold Nesbitt's memorial in Icklesham Church

citizens, particularly those wishing to trade along the inadequate highways. Winchelsea Corporation, as the local authority, was unfortunate enough to be burdened with the responsibility of trying to do something about it.

This applied to all parishes; they looked after their own roads, often at considerable expense and often inadequately despite that expense. F. W. Jessup describes the road between Tenterden and Ashford as 'scarcely passable after rain, the horses plunging into the mud up to the girth of the saddle and the wagons sliding along in their hubs'.[19] Conditions near Winchelsea were frequently very similar.

The parish records of this period show Burford Jeakens as co-ordinating road works in the area. He was reimbursed by the corporation for such projects as providing oak 'waytrees' which I assume to be signposts, for fencing beside roads, for 'brushing' highways, for carrying beach and stone for surface maintenance and paying workers to spread them, for 'wheeling earth at Ferry Road' and 'for the use of wheelbarrows'. Among the workers named are John Hills, William Bragg, Joseph Tree, 'Bennett' whose Christian name is not given, George Suters and William Pollard.[20] These were not just labourers. Some of them were quite important citizens which reflects the fact that every parishioner was obliged to work on the roads for a certain number of days in each year, or to provide materials for mending them, or to lend a cart and horses.[21] Apart from Ferry Road, particular mention is made of 'Strand Road', Tanyard Lane, 'Newer Road', whichever that may have been, and Hogtrough Lane.[22]

Hogtrough Lane appears clearly, although without its name, on the earliest detailed map of Winchelsea, of which various versions survive. The one I have used (see facing page 1) was included by W. D. Cooper in his history of Winchelsea. The cartographer was Charles Stephens. It seems likely that this map was drawn to clarify for future reference the various landed interests in the borough and that the various earlier versions which exist were updated from time to time and the 1763 fair copy which Cooper used was made at the instigation of the Earl of Egremont shortly before his death.[23] This map repays careful examination. We find Barrack Square with its earlier name, Bear Square, from the bear-baiting pit which still exists on private land at the northern end. The great rush of building provoked by the establishment of the cambric manufactory which brought the town Mariteau House, The Five Houses and the Barrack Houses, had not yet taken place. The presumed campanile tower is still in St. Thomas's Churchyard and the Roundel is shown as The Round Tower. The windmill remains well to the north of its later site where are shown the remains of St. Leonard's Church. Among names which are still in use we find the Salutation, Ballad Singers' [Balladers'] Plat, Three Kings, Nesbit, Cooks' Green (which must therefore not, as some assume, derive from the time of later military occupation), Truncheons and Saffron Gardens. There was still a 'Float or Wharf for shipping or unshipping Goods' on the present site of Strand Garage and barges continued to use the Brede as a route inland. Close study shows that the map includes 'between 49 and 52' houses. In 1801 when the first detailed census was taken that number had risen to 105, much of which difference is accounted for by the manufactory houses. Apparently this doubling of the town's size was not unusual for David and Barbara Martin comment that 'the percentage increase in Winchelsea was no greater than that within most local parishes at this time'.[24]

It does not require the same close study to spot the prominent legends along Winchelsea's western and eastern boundaries. Respectively they read: 'Arnold Nesbit Esq. his land' and 'The R^t Honble The Earl of Egremont his land.' These interests provoked Winchelsea's best-known legal case, the Winchelsea Causes. Court hearings to consider the case took place between 1766 and 1769. Charles Stephens, the cartographer, was among those involved. In a deposition dated 1767 he is referred to as 'Charles Stephens, gent. aged about 38 years who has lived in the town fifteen years, paid all public taxes and has been a freeman for 14 years. He has served as the Town or Common Clerk.'[25] We have already seen that his service lasted only one day! The use of 'gent' presumably arises from his position as Supervisor of the Riding Officers. Stephens lies buried in St. Thomas's Church and lived at 2 Friars Road, or so assumed W. M. Homan whose home this was in the twentieth century. Homan opened up 'a salthole in the chimney corner' and found there 'a paper dated 1763, written in a boyish hand and signed John Stephens'.[26]

The Earl of Egremont had, following Belchier's bankruptcy in 1760, set about acquiring Belchier's Winchelsea estate. Egremont's interest was strongly supported, against that of Nesbitt, even after the Earl's death in 1763, by Edwin Wardroper who, as we have seen, carried great influence and virtually controlled elections. Probably not wishing to offend Egremont, the prime minister, the Duke of Newcastle, asked Nesbitt to stand down in 1761. Herein lies the essence of the Winchelsea Causes. Arnold Nesbitt, whose supporters registered the complaint with the courts, stated Winchelsea Corporation's constitution as requiring that all new freemen must be resident in the town and paying scot and lot, (the normal taxes due from residents). The medieval 'a year and a day' length of qualifying residence had long been abandoned as had anyone's right to claim the freedom, with the single exception that the eldest son born to a freeman might so claim. Additonally it was still the custom that the mayor might nominate one freeman during his year of office[27] but the mayor's freeman must be eligible within the rules.

Under the pressures of acquiring sufficient votes to secure the election of mayors and members of parliament, non-residents had been appointed and the court was asked to rule as to their eligibility. Sitting in judgement was Lord Mansfield who pronounced, decisively and helpfully, that if anyone had enjoyed the freedom unchallenged for twenty years his right to that freedom became unchallengeable. Such clarity had not before existed. However, the courts remained liable to inquire into the cases of those who had been freemen for less than twenty years. As the Winchelsea Causes dragged on the court considered many such cases. Two challenged freemen, Edwin

Wardroper himself and Nathaniel Dawes, had been freemen for almost twenty years, Wardroper having also been a freeman before that period. Richard Wardroper and Thomas Marten had served shorter periods. The court confirmed all their freedoms, despite the fact that they had not been resident or rated at the time of their election. One strong reason for this was that the complainants, whom the court referred to as 'the relators', had sat and voted alongside these men without making any objection to them before the Winchelsea Causes arose. In reference to this, Lord Mansfield went so far as to say, 'They come now to complain of their own iniquity'[28] in now objecting to the presence of men who had long been their colleagues.

Nesbitt's real purpose in urging men to bring this case had, in fact, been getting rid of Wardroper who stood in his way. The court was even-handed. It examined the qualifications of men on both sides. In her detailed study of the litigation Janet Stevenson tells how the court threw out the case against the four above but also, 'inexplicably' confirmed the freedom of Nesbitt's non-resident supporters who included his brothers Albert and Alexander;[29] they had virtually no connection with the town at all.

Wardroper, 'driven hard by Nesbitt to incur legal costs beyond his means,' had to declare himself bankrupt and by 1771 had given up his interest and left the town. He died in Boulogne that same year.[30] Nesbitt's finances, too, had been put under great strain by the Causes but his contemporaries were not aware of this and he would have considered himself victorious. His control of one Winchelsea seat was confirmed and he was freed to concentrate his political interests at Cricklade, which borough he had also purchased. His financial problems, however, persisted and he died, insolvent, in 1779.[31] Nesbitt is remembered locally by the use of his name on a house in Winchelsea High Street (although with the alternative spelling Nesbit) and through his memorial in the south aisle of Icklesham Church.

Despite Lord Mansfield's landmark judgement and perhaps because of the inconsistency of his decisions on individual cases, abuses of the freedom continued almost unchecked.

(86) Nos. 1-10 Barrack Square, the remaining continuous section of the houses built for the cambric manufactory and later used as barracks.

52. TWO REVEREND GENTLEMEN

In 1772, the year after Edwin Wardroper's departure from the town, John Wesley visited Winchelsea for the first time. He preached at eleven in the morning on 30 October, in what he described as 'the new Square,' to 'a considerable number of serious people'.[1] Wesley's influence in Sussex was never extensive but in the far east, Rye, Winchelsea, Northiam and Brede, it was considerable.[2] It was quite in character, indeed probably much less than his normal day's travelling, that he returned from Winchelsea to Rye to preach again in the evening. His sermons that day would have included, as they always did when he was in this part of Sussex, his strongest, most persuasive, disapproval of smuggling. In this respect he was disappointed to record that his ministry failed. Of his Rye and Winchelsea hearers he wrote: 'They do many things gladly, but they will not part with that accursed thing smuggling, so I fear with regard to these our labour will be in vain'.[3]

Wesley's visits to Winchelsea were rare but the group in the town who embraced his Methodism were energetic and soon well-established. He may have known many of Winchelsea's Methodists before this first contact for he began visiting Rye in 1758 and they would eagerly have walked there to hear him. Certainly he knew some of them personally and at one time stayed with the Jones family who had two small daughters. He took the girls into the garden and, anxious to illustrate an enlightening point, picked two apples, one large and ripe and the other smaller and green. Wesley offered the choice to the older girl and, understandably, she chose the bigger apple. Wesley then cut it open and there was a maggot in it. "You see, you chose the bigger apple and you left the small green one for your sister and here is a worm." The point was made. Unfortunately, when the other apple was cut open it also had a maggot in it. The Miss Jones who told this story when an old lady was asked, "What did Mr Wesley say then?" With a smile she replied, "Mr Wesley said nothing!"[4]

Undaunted by the failure of this piece of religious education, Mr and Mrs Jones and their friends set about acquiring the land to build a chapel where they could meet; the open air and private houses had to suffice until the work was completed. A sympathetic supporter lived at the house in Rectory Lane now known as Evens. He donated land from his garden and reduced costs by allowing the chapel to have a wall shared with his home. The resulting small building is dominated by the pulpit which stands high on the east wall, probably because the large congregation could only be squeezed in if they stood for the service. It was certainly the type of pulpit which Wesley advocated.[5] The Winchelsea Methodist community opened their chapel in 1785 and four years later the great man himself preached there. He noted in his Journal, 'The new preaching-house was well filled with decent, serious hearers who seemed to receive the truth in the love of it'.[6]

Wesley returned to Winchelsea just the following year (1790) and that visit provoked by far his best-remembered association with the town. After a preaching life during which he travelled 'some 250,000 miles, mostly on horseback'[7] he spoke for the last time outdoors under a large ash tree at the western end of St. Thomas's churchyard. 'He called on his listeners to repent and believe in the gospel and felt that "all who heard were, for the present, almost persuaded to be Christians."'[8] Roy Hattersley, in his exceptionally revealing biography, writes: 'Mortality began to force itself upon him. At Winchelsea ... he preached his last open-air sermon. The heady days of field preaching – competing with wind and weather for the attention of thousand strong crowds ... were over for ever. The last Journal entry – meant like the rest for publication and posterity – was dated [the following month] and ended too suddenly to have any meaning'.[9] John Wesley died in March 1791.

In Winchelsea Methodism prospered for many years. The tree under which he preached was

(87) German Street featuring Wesley's Tree, much as it would have been when John Wesley preached his last open-air sermon there.

blown down in 1927, 'greatly weakened by souvenir hunters'.[10] A scion of the original was planted on the same spot and survives there with a commemorative plaque. As for the chapel, it was eventually superseded by a much larger one in Higham Green but, fortunately no buyer could be found for the original and it became a Sunday School room. As the congregation shrank in the twentieth century the new chapel was closed and sold (Chapel Plat now stands on the site) and Wesley's Chapel came back into use. Sadly, in 1994, it became clear that even this was no longer a viable option. However, all was not lost; the management and maintenance of the chapel was taken over by a dedicated group of local Methodists who formed The Friends of Winchelsea Methodist Chapel. Occasional services and other functions are still held there and those who so lovingly care for it are able to make the proud claim that it is the only Methodist Chapel still in use in the south-east of England where the great man actually preached.

It was John Wesley's avowed intention to influence the reform and revitalisation of the Church of England not to create a separate church. In this particular he eventually failed. That intention makes it seem surprising that Methodism flourished in Winchelsea during the later eighteenth and early nineteenth centuries for during that time the Rector of St. Thomas's was a man much respected in the town who dedicated well over half a century to Winchelsea and its people, the Rev. Drake Hollingberry. Hollingberry became curate at St. Thomas's in 1764, and was Rector from 1767 until his death in 1821. W. M. Homan, drawing attention to the 1724 visitation, noted that thirty-five or forty families living in the town produced only twenty communicants. As they would have been large families he concluded that, well before Hollingberry's time, the inhabitants of Winchelsea had 'long adopted a lukewarm attitude to the established church.' Additionally, the influx of persecuted Huguenot Protestants who fled France and set up the cambric and crêpe manufactories would have found 'Wesley's teaching rather akin to that of their own church.'[11] If Hollingberry was working difficult ground, his achievements and reputation eventually overcame that difficulty.

Drake Hollingberry was historian of his family for which he claimed very ancient lineage and an association dating from pre-Roman times with Hollingbury Camp near Brighton.[12] He wrote of ancestors who went into exile when their estates were confiscated by Henry VII, returned to serve under Cromwell and later provided two mayors of Dover who also served as 'Masters of the Castle'.[13] His meticulous attention to family detail was reflected in his care of the St. Thomas's records. These were beautifully kept in his fine, regular hand and it must reflect his conscientious nature that few, during almost sixty years, are in another hand.

Hollingberry's rectory stood on a site behind the Victorian villas to the east of the Court Hall garden. His home is reputed to have been a fine medieval structure originally the home of one of the Alards. It was pulled down not long after his death. The rector's convenience in reaching the church from the rectory was served by the placing of a gate in the centre of the churchyard's northern wall.[14] That gate is still much in use.

The rector's duties in Winchelsea and the Diocese of Chichester were vast. Not only was he the incumbent of St. Thomas's but for forty years Chancellor of the Diocese, quite apart from being Vicar of Salehurst from 1768-1772 and of Icklesham from 1772-1817.[15] He must, surely, have installed curates at Salehurst and Icklesham but there is no evidence that he did other than devote himself to his church and his people in Winchelsea.

When he arrived in the town the manufactory houses were still being completed; when he died the Napoleonic Wars were long over. Perhaps it was those wars which brought most stress to his Winchelsea duties. This was elegantly highlighted by Miss Maud Peel, owner of The Armoury in the early twentieth century, who wrote of life at the time of the garrison which gave its name to Barrack Square and her home: 'Soldiers with their wives and children, one regiment succeeding another, and all to be cared for; ... the military band playing daily in front of Magazine House; soldiers from the front returning wounded, many to die and find burial in the churchyard. Amidst the anxiety, sorrow, poverty, excitement and reckless living inseparable from a deadly war, the Rector's responsibilities could not have been light'.[16]

As ex-officio chairman of the St. Thomas's Vestry meeting, the Rev. Mr Hollingberry bore much additional burden through the growing poverty faced by Winchelsea's ordinary citizens. It is central to the theme of this book that the Winchelsea which achieved great prominence within England in the late thirteenth and early fourteenth centuries, descended into considerable poverty which was still prevalent at the end of the eighteenth. In 1776 the Vestry meeting made a response to a national investigation about the facilities it provided. This recorded that thirteen paupers had been in receipt of regular relief during the year at a total cost of £78 1s 6d. The workhouse belonged to the parish and had room to accommodate twenty-four persons. The cost of regular payments and all other expenses had to be met from a total assessment of the poor rate at £160 1s 0d.[17] These were considerable sums to be found by a small community. Similar statistics extracted from the surviving books would show that, by the end of the century, the situation had become much worse.

These costs had to be kept down whenever possible and, as happened in parishes all over the country, the easiest way was to get rid of those paupers who could not prove that they belonged in Winchelsea. To this end Mr Hollingberry and the Overseers would take residents who were not known to have been born in the town before the magistrates to be examined as to their legal place of settlement.[18] To attempt to stay in Winchelsea by declining to answer was a criminal offence for which Thomas Bromley and Mary Austin were imprisoned in the Court Hall during Mr Hollingberry's time.[19] If it could be shown that you were the responsibility of some other community, a removal order required that the constables should take you there, regardless of all other circumstances.[20]

This, of course, is a gross over-simplification in the interests of brevity of the problems which any parish faced at that time. I cannot believe that Mr Hollingberry would be anything but distressed by having his parishioners, however poor, imprisoned or forcibly ejected from the town. Sadly, he had no alternative but to follow the procedures laid down by parliament or bankrupt his parish.

Payment of the poor rate was not the only taxation levied upon Winchelsea's landowners at that time. The poor rate was for purely local needs; national government had also to be resourced. Readers may recall that, as a privilege arising from their provision of ship service, the Confederation of the Cinque Ports had, in medieval times, been excused all forms of national taxation, 'an exemption which was sustained until new forms of taxation were introduced in the mid-17th century'.[21] Roger Davey explains that, 'even then ... the Ports retained the right to assess and collect their own taxes independently of the county divisions'.[22] Winchelsea was one of five Cinque Ports jurisdictions in Sussex and here was another responsibility falling upon the parish. As an example, in 1785 the amount of land tax collected for the government was £166 15s 1d.[23] The title land tax is misleading in that other income factors could be taken into account by those responsible. In Winchelsea the assessors seem to have taken advantage of their right to make such variations for, while including taxes on houses, shops, farms, 'the Pear Tree Marsh' etc and, obviously, on land, the list also includes 'Kings and Town Rents' and the salaries paid by the crown to officers of the excise.[24] Heavy taxation brought an increasing burden upon the town.

Drake Hollingberry, who paid land tax in 1785 on 'a garden' and 'Saint Gyles church yard' was Rector of both St. Thomas's and St. Giles's, the latter position being purely nominal as the church was in ruins. At St. Thomas's he did much to preserve and enhance the fabric, presenting, for example a new church clock in 1790[25] and, in 1794, opening up the two important eastern-most windows in the north aisle.[26]

One alteration he made would, however, seem to us controversial. When, in 1779, the lead on the vestry roof was blown off and stolen he declined to carry out the major restoration required, abandoned that vestry which was on the present site and built a new one at the west end of the north aisle. The wall of this new structure divided one of the north aisle tombs in a most unfortunate way and the room was lit by a window made in the west wall to give light from the ruined transept. 'The position of this window may still be seen; the keystone bears the date 1779.'[27]

At St. Giles's he did nothing to preserve or maintain the fabric, in fact he destroyed it. Two years before the construction of the new vestry at St. Thomas's the ruined walls of St. Giles's still stood, rising in parts several feet above the ground on the present site of Nos. 4 and 5 St. Giles's Close. Far from the reverential care which would be lavished upon such remains now, the rector ordered that these walls should be knocked down and the foundations dug up. He availed himself of the opportunity to cover, at least partly, the expense of this operation by selling the stone to the builders of the New Harbour at Winchelsea Beach. After the stone had been removed the land was ploughed with unexpected results. The ploughshare 'struck against something so firm that it became necessary to use a mattock'. On investigation the obstruction turned out to be a bar of lead of which five more were found together with some sheet lead. The rector assumed that these must once have been part of the church roof. He sold them as well, raising a further £23 10s 6d, thus completely

(88) The Wesley Chapel in Rectory Lane, together with that part of Evens which provides its southern wall.

covering his costs. Hollingberry's pride and satisfaction at the success of what we would consider an inexcusable piece of vandalism is reflected in his comment in the parish register: 'The rector is now in possession of a level and pleasant field and garden made from a heap of ruins and a roughter [a rough enclosure] by the indefatigable exertion and perseverance of D. Hollingberry'.[28]

Drake Hollingberry's penchant for removing ancient buildings was renewed in 1790 when he arranged for the ancient tower in the churchyard to be pulled down for it had become roofless and ruinous. W. M. Homan referred to this as 'another piece of vandalism', in which we would feel he was justified if he was correct in his assertion that the structure might have dated from before the building of New Winchelsea.[29] It is generally believed that this was used as a campanile tower although Homan thought that it looked nothing like an ecclesiastical building or any part of one. He claimed that the foundations of the tower, or the excavation from which they had been removed, were still visible in 1940 and he managed to plot their exact dimensions. About 2½ feet wide, they formed a square with 25ft sides which was 'apparently orientated as the present Town Hall and the adjoining streets, and not exactly due east/west as the church'.[30] This would certainly seem to suggest that, whenever the tower was built, it was not as part of the church complex. However, David and Barbara Martin, using the dimensions and siting shown on Homan's original plans[31] rather than the above, think that the tower was attached to the western and of the south aisle and 'may have been one of a pair of attached western towers rather than a detached structure'.[32]

Poor Mr Hollingberry is again accused of making a profit by laying low a building in his care. The present bell tower had been built by 1790 and the stone from its presumed predecessor, 'and allegedly that from the foundations of the original nave, were used for works on Rye Harbour'.[33] If so, they must have been works restoring the original harbour on the Rother for, as we shall see, the New Harbour at Winchelsea Beach had been abandoned three years earlier.

I near the end of my account of Mr Hollingberry's life in Winchelsea with what must have been the most bizarre situation he had to deal with. In the early 1780s there lived at the Greyfriars two apparently wealthy, quiet and decent men known in Winchelsea as William Johnson and Samuel Watson. These were, in fact, the Weston brothers, George and Joseph, seeking a calm retreat from the consequences of a life of crime.

Among their numerous criminal activities the Westons included forgery, bribery, blackmail and, as a speciality, highway robbery. This dubious past eventually caught up with them upon which they fled Winchelsea and sought refuge in an hotel in Wardour Street, Soho.[34] Rewards for their capture encouraged the criminal underworld to inform and the brothers were arrested outside their hotel. The particular charge was that they had robbed the Bath and Bristol Mail as it travelled between Maidenhead and Hounslow on 29 January 1781. Indeed they had, and they were astonished at the value of their haul, approximately £15,000, the biggest highway robbery at that time.[35] While awaiting trial Joseph and George compounded their crime in the eyes of the authorities by escaping from Newgate; they were soon recaptured. At their trial, which began on 2 July 1782, over one hundred witnesses testified against them. The verdict was a foregone conclusion and the Westons were hanged at Tyburn on 3 September, either displaying great dignity or dragged to the gallows kicking and screaming, depending on which version of the story is believed.

Many of those accounts, including that of John Pendragon,[36] claim that George Weston became churchwarden of St. Thomas's while living in Winchelsea. When W. D. Cooper inquired of the then rector, the Rev. J. J. West, whether this was true he was told it was not.[37] Understandably Mr West knew nothing of the brothers' aliases for an examination of the Vestry Minutes shows that, on 3 April 1782, 'William Johnson Esq.' was, indeed, appointed as a churchwarden.[38] No doubt his apparent wealth had made him an excellent potential benefactor. Whether George ever intended to carry out the duties of churchwarden is extremely doubtful. Anyway, his 'term of office' lasted but one month for, on 5 May, no doubt to the considerable embarrassment of Mr Hollingberry, the Vestry Minutes record the re-appointment of John Peters in place of 'Wm. Johnson – absconded'.[39]

The sensation which this caused in Winchelsea can well be imagined. W. M. Thackeray, who knew Winchelsea well, was certainly told all about it. He immortalised the Westons as the villains in his unfinished novel *Denis Duval* which is set in the town.

The Rev. Drake Hollingberry, except when ruffled by intrusions on his life like that of 'William Johnson' and, perhaps, when disposing of unwanted ancient buildings, conducted himself with great dignity during his long association with Winchelsea and was much admired and respected by his parishioners. His memorial tablet in the church is notable both for its simplicity and for its understatement:

'Sacred to the memory of Drake Hollingberry, Clerk, M.A.
Late Rector of this Parish and, for upwards of 40 years
Chancellor of the Diocese of Chichester.
He died in the eightieth year of his age.'

53. THE NEW HARBOUR FINISHES AND FAILS

By 1782, when the Westons were hanged, work on the so-called Rye New Harbour at Winchelsea Beach, for which Drake Hollingberry sold the stone from the ruins of St. Giles's, was well advanced. To that story we must now return. Readers may recall that we left the project, deeply in debt and selling off assets, in 1748. Ten years later work seems to have started again, on the pier-heads and other sections, under new management. An act of 1762 made it lawful for the Commissioners to let the sea and tides into the new channel or cut but only as far as 'Winchelsea Wall' which separated the cut from the River Brede. When this was done, those involved would have looked upon it as a major step forward. However, the problems which would make this such an unhappy story immediately became apparent. The New Cut began to silt up heavily through lack of tidal scour and the relentless eastward drift of the shingle began to obstruct the entrance by turning the constantly extended and modified pier-heads.

The moment of truth had arrived. To allow the sea and tides entry to the New Cut meant nothing until the Winchelsea Wall was removed and access to Rye obtained. Major decisions had to be taken on Rye's three-river system. Expert advice was needed; the source of that advice had to be unimpeachable and inspire confidence. John Smeaton, the well-known engineer, famous for designing and building the Eddystone Lighthouse, was called in. It is unfortunate for him that his name has indelibly stuck to this work. He was never the resident engineer, nor was he the on-going consultant. Had his recommendations been adopted in full, things might have turned out better, although the whole concept was so basically flawed that success could not have lasted long. The most important of those recommendations was that all three of the rivers Brede, Tillingham and Rother, should be diverted to flow through the new channel and harbour, that being the only way to ensure enough scouring action to remove the silt and help keep the harbour mouth open. Smeaton thought that this would best be achieved by taking the Rother to the north of Rye and building a drawbridge for traffic to Playden. It is fair to say, however, that he did not rule out the eventual use of the southern route. By 1764 Smeaton was complaining, on being further consulted, that nothing had been done to implement his suggestions and that urgent action was needed.

Any action taken was certainly not urgent. By 1769 the Commissioners concluded that for a number of reasons which their records do not give, 'there was a great and evident necessity to deviate from [Smeaton's] plan'.[1] Another five years later, and fifty years after the whole project had been commenced, the inhabitants of Rye complained bitterly that the mouth of the New Harbour was filling up with beach and that the great sluice (where Willow Lane now crosses the channel) was ruinous; they pleaded for the dam blocking the Old Harbour to be removed so that they could continue to use it.[2] This was done but another four years later parliament authorised the building of a further dam to the Rother so that its waters should flow as required for the New Harbour. Additional work to clear the entrance was also commissioned.

In 1787 orders were given that no traffic might enter the old harbour past the site of the proposed dam (the work was at the time threatened with vandalism). Michael Tiltman was 'appointed pilot of the New Harbour with responsibility for the lighting of lights by night, and hoisting the flag by day'. A most unenviable job description also required Tiltman to place buoys and beacons as appropriate and, 'at vacant times employ himself in removing the shingle and obstructions in the mouth of the harbour'.[3] The futility of such a requirement was soon apparent.

The Commissioners seem not to have had any control over the long awaited opening of the New Harbour for 'if an opening ceremony was planned for the New Harbour, it did not take place on the appointed day, because a few days beforehand the sea broke through the last remaining barrier and the tides started to flow up the whole length of the New Harbour to Scots Float sluice unannounced'.[4]

The harbour was in regular use for just three months. By November 1787 operational difficulties and bitter complaints from landowners affected by poorer drainage led the Commissioners to conclude that 'the said harbour is now totally inadequate for the purposes of navigation and sewage [i.e. drainage]'.[5] John Collard lists some indirect benefits of this work to the continued use of the old harbour but concludes that 'the intangible assets emerging from the folly of Smeaton's Harbour consisted of bitter experience and practical lessons learned'.[6] Some £200,000, which would be an astronomical sum in our day, had been spent over 63 years. Perhaps the most entertaining comment comes from W. M. Homan writing in 1944: 'Surely the conception and construction of this work must hold a record that is not eclipsed by the incompetence of local public bodies and their engineers in our times'.[7]

In 1802 the bed of the New Harbour was sold to James Jones of Winchelsea for £600. From Jones's successors it came eventually to the family of Sir Stephen Holmes and thence to Icklesham Parish Council. Observed by properties standing on the banks created by its excavation, the New Harbour, now known as Harbour Field and bordered on two sides by Smeaton's Lane, is a successful recreation ground and playground and has a significant place in the topography of Winchelsea Beach.

One tragic incident which occurred during the time that the mouth of the New Harbour was open leads me to return to the subject of the duties of Winchelsea's Mayor as Coroner for the Liberty, a duty he fulfilled until 1886. This was no sinecure. On receipt of the report of a death the mayor issued instructions to the Chamberlain to summon a jury of 'good and lawful men of the town of Winchelsea'. This would be immediately

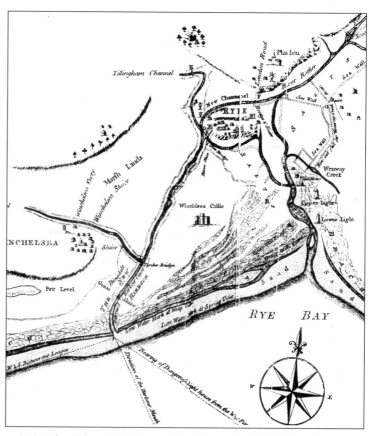

(89) A detail from John Smeaton's advisory plan for the New Harbour

carried out and the jury assembled, usually on the day following the death. This urgency, sensibly designed to ensure that witnesses' recollections were fresh, dated back to the twelfth century reign of Henry II, long before Winchelsea had a mayor, later also to be ex-officio coroner.[8] It was part of the jury's duty to examine the body which was brought to the place nominated for the hearing. All three cases cited here were conducted by Mayor Thomas Marten at the New Inn, noted in the records as 'the house of John Alce'.

On the evening of Sunday 19 November 1780 Robert Haffenden set sail from the New Harbour 'in a Hoveler or Boat bound to Dover'. This raises interesting questions about what Haffenden was up to for the Oxford English Dictionary defines a Hoveller as a boat used by 'an unlicensed pilot or boatman ... frequently applied to a boatman who goes out to wrecks, sometimes with a view to plunder'. If he had any skills as a pilot they did Haffenden no good on this occasion for his vessel was 'by the violence and tempestuousness of the wind overset'.[9] Haffenden was drowned together with his companion Thomas Gasson whose body was presumably not found for there are no equivalent inquest papers for him. John Pierce and Henry Naylor gave evidence to the coroner that they had found Haffenden's body on the beach, 'about twenty yards to the west of the buoy lying at the mouth of the Old Harbour in the Port of Winchelsea'.[10] This was hardly a difficult case. The jury recorded a verdict that Robert Haffenden died by 'Misadventure or Misfortune but not otherwise'.

Thomas Marten had also heard, five years earlier, the sad case of John Gross, a labourer, who when making his way towards Rye, along a path beside a creek, was unlucky enough to fall in. The court records describe exactly what happened to the poor chap: 'In the creek was mud and slub of the depth of five or six inches and the said John Gross being intoxicated with liquor and unable to get out of the said creek remained and continued there until the tide flowed over him and by this means he was drowned and suffocated'. Again the verdict was that death was caused by misadventure or misfortune. It is an amusing irony for us that, in view of the deceased's condition, this tragedy took place 'near the Jolly Boys Dock'.[11]

In the third and last of these inquests, we note something more of the life of the times through the death of a boy of eight, George Suters. On Saturday 25 February 1780 George and his friends were playing near the windmill owned by miller Robert Clarke; that is the one on the former mill site a hundred yards to the north-west of the site well known until the 1987 storm. Despite the fact that this former mill was in the Parish of St. Leonard, and thus outside Winchelsea's liberty, Thomas Marten presided as mayor. The boys played dangerously close to the mill on a windy day for George Suters 'did receive from the sweeps of the said mill a violent blow between his shoulders and bruised him very much ... of which bruise he languished about half-an-hour and then died'. The scene can well be imagined. It is a further curiosity of the duties of the coroner's court of the day that any inanimate object involved in a death had to be valued and the owner identified. In returning a verdict of misadventure the jury added, 'The sweeps of the said mill were the cause of death and the said sweeps are valued at one shilling and in the custody of Robert Clarke'.[12]

Further light can be thrown on the judicial activities of the mayor and jurats in the eighteenth century by the case of George Mugliston, heard in 1788. The surviving records open with instructions to Benjamin Tree junior, 'Sergeant-at-Mace and servant of the Court' to summon 'four and twenty good and lawful men of the said town' to serve as jury at the forthcoming Quarter Sessions. The list of those who appeared shows who was excused and who was sworn to comprise the usual jury of twelve persons. Among the jurors or potential jurors were

(90) Harbour Field as it is now, looking towards the sea. Properties have been built on both sides on the banks created by the excavation of the harbour basin. Some of these can be seen on the left

Benjamin Tree senior, the sergeant-at-mace's father and, of those who have appeared elsewhere in my text, the foreman Charles Stephens (riding officer and cartographer), James Jones (purchaser of the bed of the New Harbour), Robert Clarke (mill owner), and George Stace (custodian of Queen Elizabeth's Charter).[13]

Witnesses were also needed and those for the case of George Mugliston were left in absolutely no doubt about the requirements. They were Burford Jeakens, Robert Woodsell, Thomas Austen and Henry Leadbetter. The town clerk demanded that 'laying aside all pretences, excuses and delays whatsoever' they appear on time before the mayor, Joash Adcroft, and jurats to 'testify the truth according to your several knowledge between us and George Mugliston'. The penalty for failure to respond to this summons was £100 which, when Mugliston's eventual fine is taken into account was positively draconian. The town clerk, like a peer of the realm or a Speaker of the Cinque Ports, signs only with his surname, 'Waterman'.[14]

We do not know what evidence the witnesses gave to the jurors but we do know that Mugliston was found guilty. He had had the temerity to set up in Winchelsea as a butcher, 'for his lucre, profit and gain'. Unfortunately he had never properly qualified, butchery being an 'art, mystery or manual occupation' for which a full apprenticeship of seven years was required within the terms of an act passed in the days of Queen Elizabeth I. The court viewed this offence, undetected for two months, very seriously and fined him four pounds which he duly paid into court.[15] Of George Mugliston we hear no more but he must have been persona non grata in Winchelsea.

We must now return to the privilege which kept external interest in Winchelsea alive for so long, the election of two members to the House of Commons.

Arnold Nesbitt, no doubt supported by freemen of dubious qualification, was elected as one of Winchelsea's MPs for the last time in 1774, five years before his death. Nesbitt is about to leave our story but, before he does so, it is worth pausing to note briefly the strange and eccentric parliamentary career of the man elected with him on that occasion, Charles Wolfran Cornwall. Cornwall was a less than prepossessing character who gained rapid promotion. He had already served six years as member for Grampound. On his election for Winchelsea he went straight into Lord North's government as Lord of the Treasury and, when, subsequently, again returned for the town in 1780, was installed as Speaker. Although he was said to have a good voice and to bear himself well, he really owed these posts to his family connection – he had married Lord Liverpool's sister. As Speaker, Cornwall 'relieved the boredom of debates by fortifying himself with porter'.[16] Perhaps this habit influenced him when, with the House divided 169-169, he exercised his casting vote against Pitt's plan to fortify the dockyards and thus set back the Prime Minister's far-seeing intention to strengthen the country's defences. When Cornwall died it was unkindly said of him that 'Never was a man in a public situation less regretted or sooner forgotten'.[17] The History of Parliament speaks of him in a less jaundiced manner. While commending his earlier parliamentary career, it confines itself to saying that he was 'of no great vivacity' and 'as Speaker he was undistinguished'.[18]

Cornwall's unfortunate vote came during the years between the American War of Independence and the French Revolution. There being no immediate apparent danger at that time perhaps makes it more understandable. However, the former conflict had brought to Winchelsea and its fellow south-coast towns renewal of an oft-repeated threat. The French, supporting the American colonies, were dominating the Channel while 'New England privateers waged a lively and profitable warfare against English commerce'.[19] Winchelsea had no ships to suffer in these attacks but it must have been affected by the influx of troops sent to defend the coast. There were ten thousand soldiers at Maidstone, whence they could be deployed as needed, but the principal area of danger was emphasised by the establishment of advanced positions on high ground at Playden near Rye and behind Hastings.[20]

Four years after Charles Wolfran Cornwall represented Winchelsea for the second time, the town's electoral reputation had become so bad that an inquiry was held. The first sentence of the report says it all: 'The borough is now, it is feared, in a bad state indeed and scarce any good voters in it'.[21] The investigation concluded that the electoral borough had been neglected and the situation would only become clear if a further examination was held in the town. However, the report is optimistic about bringing Winchelsea back into the government's pocket 'though probably with some bustle and expense'.[22]

By the time of this inquiry Nesbitt's property had been inherited by his nephew John who, in about 1790, sold the Winchelsea parliamentary interest to Richard Barwell and Lord Darlington. Their story, in so far as it comes within the remit of this book, belongs, therefore, to the last decade of the eighteenth century.

54. WAR AGAIN

A late eighteenth century account of this sale is, to us understandably, cynical in the extreme. 'Where the right of voting ... depends upon freedom, it is probable that, in the sale ... the voters themselves like so many beasts in a pen at Smithfield, were bartered at the transfer.'[1] It is then suggested that the price per voter might have been as much as £100 for which, most of them being ordinary working men, they would have been truly grateful had they actually received it!

Richard Barwell and Lord Darlington were the last patrons of Winchelsea parliamentary seats, if you prefer the complimentary term, or Winchelsea's last borough-mongers if you prefer the perjorative one. Darlington fits the former and Barwell the latter.

Richard Barwell returned from India at the age of thirty-eight an extremely wealthy man. He had successfully lined his pockets as Warren Hastings' principal supporter during Hastings' dubious control of the East India Company and is reputed, on one occasion, to have lost 'at cards at a single sitting, a staggering £40,000'.[2] With plenty still to spare he purchased Stansted Park in West Sussex where he made extensive alterations and became extremely unpopular by forbidding access to land which had been available for public use for centuries. 'His very name from such conduct was soon held in such detestation that men, women and children hissed and hooted him as he passed in all his oriental state through the villages.'[3]

After keeping his head down for some time because his reputation as a 'nabob' had been equally bad, Barwell became MP for Winchelsea in 1790. He later, presumably with the agreement of Lord Darlington, 'gained undisputed control of both seats at Winchelsea'.[4] In his parliamentary activity he fulfilled his poor reputation elsewhere by refusing to attend and give evidence to a committee of the House which was inquiring into matters in India. Eventually he had to be 'brought before them under threat of force'.[5] This happened even before he had been elected; only his Winchelsea property and influence could bring about that election and he was reviled by his fellow members from the start. After an undistinguished parliamentary career, he died in 1804 unlamented by those outside his large family at Stansted and leaving two illegitimate children in his local parish.[6]

Lord Darlington then took control. He is an elusive character in the records for, apart from that title, his name also appears as William Harry Vane, Viscount Barnard and, eventually, Duke of Cleveland. He was of liberal mind and fully supported the Reform Act of 1832 in which all his six MPs, including Winchelsea's, voted to abolish their own seats. That is a story belonging to the nineteenth century[7] but mention of it here at least draws to a conclusion the many strange ramifications of Winchelsea's centuries of parliamentary representation which we have encountered in these pages.

It was in 1792, two years after Richard Barwell's first election to the Commons, that William Boys' *Collections for a History of Sandwich* noted that a new common seal for Winchelsea had been engraved and brought into use.[8] The reverse side of the fourteenth century seal had been removed from the town, allegedly to prevent documents being signed in yet another disputed parliamentary election. The missing piece was eventually returned and both seals are currently safely in the corporation's possession.

This brief mention of the seal allows me to correct an omission from my earlier book, *Winchelsea – A Port of Stranded Pride*, where I managed completely to omit a description of the reverse side.[9] Such are the perils of authorship and they are invariably discovered too late! The engraving is principally of Winchelsea's main buildings, the churches of St. Thomas on the right,

St. Giles on the left and a central tower, presumably the town hall. St. Giles is said to be 'caressing that faithful hind by whose milk his life is reputed to have been sustained'. The three niches below St. Thomas's are much easier for us to interpret; they show the martyrdom. The central tower may also have been a watch-tower for the lantern held by the figure depicted there represents Winchelsea's lighthouse. Several sources, including Cooper, say that the bird standing on one of the pinnacles of St. Giles's is there to fill up a blank space in the design.[10] I do not think that medieval craftsmen worked that way. Everything is likely to be of significance and the bird is probably 'an emblem of mercy and peace'.[11] Many people of medieval Winchelsea would have craved such qualities. The lettering round the edge of the reverse has been a great puzzle to scholars. After quoting earlier attempts at translation Cooper arrives at one which has some sense and relates perfectly to the town and the times when the seal was first crafted:

> Pour forth your songs, ye people all,
> To Giles and Thomas praise;
> Lest evil should their flock befall,
> By land or ocean's ways.[12]

Henry Waterman, already mentioned, would have been the first town clerk to use the c.1792 seal on documents. His immediate successor was John Woollett, appointed in 1798. Woollett was a Rye solicitor, as were many of his predecessors and successors. He was a partner in Rye's first bank which may well have been established on the High Street frontage of his own home for he lived where HSBC now has its premises. When he became town clerk of Winchelsea, Woollett set about recording and clarifying the oaths which had to be taken at the Easter Monday Hundred. He put them all in a little book entitled, *WINCHELSEA – Book of Oaths of the Mayor and of other Officers of the Corporation, 1799.* At the end of the eighteenth century those included, quite apart from the ones which are taken by corporation officers to this day, the oaths of the constables, the water-bailiff's sergeant, the attornies, the drivers of the common, the clerks of the market, the searcher and sealer of leather, the common measurer, the common porter and the common carrier. The names of these offices alone give us a flavour of life in Winchelsea in those days. The book also demonstrates the pressures of the job for it starts in a careful copper-plate and finishes in a hurried scrawl! When John Woollett died in office in 1819 his book of oaths was passed to his successor and it has been handed from town clerk to town clerk ever since. Sad to record, the oaths still in use are now held on a computer and reproduced in print. With concern for its care after more than two hundred years I have therefore arranged for the original book to be transferred to East Sussex Record Office as part of Winchelsea's archives which are held there.[13]

John Woollett served Winchelsea's courts as their legal officer during the time that the town was brought almost to its knees by the poverty with which parliament required it to deal. Responsibility, as we have seen, lay with the St. Thomas's Vestry Meeting and the overseers of the poor, but Woollett would have been much involved in hearing appeals. During the year between Easter 1799 and Easter 1800 the overseers paid out just over £523 to sustain paupers and meet bills

(91) The seal of Winchelsea, reverse side.

incurred in maintaining the workhouse and other facilities. That was an enormous sum which had to be raised by levying the poor rate on Winchelsea's residents and landowners. The records show that each time a rate was levied the best amount which could be hoped for was just under £195. This rate was collected twice during the year under consideration and, with various other minor payments, totalled £455, £67 less than the payments made. It is not clear to me how the deficit was covered.

Among the principal ratepayers who will be recognised by readers of this story were Richard Barwell who paid by far the largest amount, Thomas Marten, several times mayor, the Rev. Mr Hollingberry, part of whose assessment was on St. Giles's Churchyard from which he had removed the remains of the church, James Jones, purchaser of Harbour Field, and Richard Maplesden who will feature soon literally making money! The same Thomas Marten received almost more in rent for his premises than he paid in rates.[14] Among others who received considerable

(92) Richard Barwell

sums for services provided for the poor were Richard Maplesden, grocer and draper, James Jones, cordwainer, Walter Fuller, carpenter and joiner, and James Holt, bricklayer and mason.[15] It is noticeable that Thomas Easton, maltster, does not appear in the list! Weekly payments were made through the whole year or part of it to thirty-nine paupers not living in the workhouse. Others received casual payments when needed. Examples of additional payments include: 'for cabbage plants and seeds', 'for work in the [workhouse] garden and mending a wall', 'for hog killing', 'for journey to Rye to get the boys' clothes', to Mrs Howell 'for laying Haisell forth and Dame Waters' and for doing washing' and to the same lady for a journey to Rye 'to see Mr Woollett'.[16] I wish we knew why she had to consult him! Sadly, the ledgers of Woollett's firm, Dawes, Son and Prentice, do not reveal the reason for Mrs. Howell's journey.[17] This multiplicity of assorted responsibilities, selected almost at random from many more, took an enormous amount of time and energy and placed great strain not only on those responsible for administration and supervision but also on those who had to pay.

And all this was happening while Winchelsea was once more on England's most vulnerable coast in time of war.

France had declared war on Great Britain and Holland in 1793, 'firm in the belief that an internal revolution in England was imminent'.[18] It was not. However, trade with the continent was endangered and the English Channel was no longer safe. For Winchelsea that has a distressingly familiar ring. French intelligence made further ill-informed mistakes by making invasion plans on the understanding that 'the people of England were waiting eagerly to welcome their liberators'.[19]

Although there had been discontent, the threat was enough to unite the population in preparations to repel any invasion.

Those preparations made Winchelsea a garrison town. Examinations of men serving in the army, undertaken by the mayor and jurats, indicate the presence of soldiers of two companies of the Wiltshire Regiment of Militia, of the Worcestershire Militia, of the Royal Staff Corps and of the 'Eleventh Royal Veteran Battalion'.[20] These men would have been billeted in the Barrack Houses, adapted from their original use for the manufactory and their presence created a major upheaval in the life of the town. Many soldiers married local girls and many other local girls had illegitimate children who were likely to place additional strains on the parish.

If men from other counties were liable for such service so were men from Sussex, Winchelsea included. A particular need lay in finding recruits to serve in the sadly depleted navy, now so badly needed. An act of parliament required magistrates in boroughs such as Winchelsea to find men who could be pressed into service. The mayor and jurats convened the court to sit on 26 May 1795. Henry Waterman was appointed to oversee the arrangements and he summoned the town constables to receive instructions. They must seek out any men who were 'able bodied and idle', including those who were not conscientiously following a trade or employment, those who could not financially support themselves, any 'rogues, vagabonds or disorderly persons' and anyone who had recently offended against the law of the land, particularly smugglers.[21] This last inclusion may give us a clue as to why the town constables were signally unsuccessful in their search. Three times they came back to court to report that they had found nobody. 'When Captain Ballard from the Board of Admiralty arrived to collect Winchelsea's conscripts, there were none to collect.'[22]

When it came to voluntary service, however, the picture was quite different. Men flocked to the colours. The Infantry Volunteer Corps unit from Winchelsea was raised by Richard Denne, then the owner of Mariteau House. In overall command of the Volunteers was the Lord Warden who acted in place of the Lord Lieutenant because the Sussex men recruited from Seaford, Pevensey, Hastings, Winchelsea and Rye came within the separate jurisdiction of the Cinque Ports. Perhaps it is fortunate that, as during the Second World War, the Lord Warden and the Prime Minister were one and the same person, in this case William Pitt.[23]

It is the activities of the Winchelsea Volunteers which provide us with the first known occasion on which cricket was played in the town. The *Southern Weekly Advertiser* of 5 October 1795 noted that 'a few days hence' the officers and men of this unit 'amused themselves with cricket' and that, in the evening, at an excellent dinner, the officers 'returned to the bottle and, after drinking legal and constitutional toasts till near 12 o'clock, retired to their respective homes in a manner which did great credit to themselves and their entertainers'.[24]

This mention of cricket allows me to introduce for a final time in this story the Earls of Winchilsea whose family name of Finch had been associated with the town since at least 1355; earlier ancestors listed in the 1292 Rent Roll were Herberds or Herberts.[25] The eighth earl was appointed First Lord of the Admiralty in 1742 as a young man. The appointment was not a success and so incensed the Admiral of the Fleet that he 'refused to serve under a civilian novice half a century his junior'.[26] The cricketing connection comes through his heir, his nephew George Finch, the ninth earl. He was an enthusiastic player and a generous benefactor as patron of the famous Hambledon Club and backer of Thomas Lord in the establishment of Lord's. On 14 July 1789, the day of the storming of the Bastille, the ninth earl is said to have been playing cricket at Hambledon in a match between Hampshire and Kent.[27] Surviving records of Sussex cricket in the

(93) William Harry Vane, first Duke of Cleveland

eighteenth century reveal his lordship enjoying occasional success with the bat and taking a commendable number of catches.[28]

Perhaps the most extraordinary way in which Winchelsea contributed to the war effort was through the activities of Richard Maplesden, grocer and draper, of German Street. Banks such as those started by John Woollett and his colleagues in Rye in 1790 began issuing notes which were of denominations too large for everyday use. Ridiculous situations occurred in which several men working together were paid with the same note and had to sort out how they could spend it between them. Men like Maplesden solved this problem by printing their own 'tokens' and exchanging them for notes. The tokens could then be divided between the note-owners and redeemed, originally just in Maplesden's shop. This project proved so useful that in 1794 he 'struck two hundredweights of a Winchelsea halfpenny'. No doubt the Winchelsea garrison made use of them to Maplesden's benefit. With great enterprise, in the same year, he assisted the military outside the town by issuing a halfpenny token for use at the Brighton camp where up to ten thousand men were being held in readiness because of the invasion scare. Maplesden's tokens were used to pay the troops and, although initially inscribed as redeemable in Winchelsea, they were later 'Payable in London or Brighton'.[29] There is no doubting the self-interest and potential profit which motivated Maplesden in setting up his 'network of credit similar to that of the banks' but it is pleasant to record that such a positive contribution to the smooth-running of the war effort originated in Winchelsea.

And so we reach the end of the eighteenth century and the period covered by this book. The major part of the Napoleonic Wars was still to come, bringing further impact on life in the town and, through the Royal Military Canal and the Martello Towers, its view towards the sea. It is sad to leave Winchelsea impoverished by the demands of its poor and disrupted by the presence of the garrison. However, as we have seen, such turmoil is far from untypical of the life of the town in earlier centuries. It would be many years before Winchelsea settled down to develop into the beautiful place so justly proud of its albeit chequered history and so enthusiastic in maintaining its traditions that the resident and the visitor can observe and enjoy today.

EPILOGUE

Winchelsea's mayor, in the early twenty-first century, is no longer entitled to preside at the trial of the town's citizens; neither may he order the execution of the guilty. Indeed, he no longer has any judicial or local government responsibility. In extreme summary, he must now supervise and ensure the proper maintenance of the Corporation's property and fulfil the town's ceremonial function as a head port of the Confederation of the Cinque Ports.

Nevertheless, when the Mayor of Winchelsea seeks the co-operation of the residents in some project for the benefit of the town he invariably receives enthusiastic support. So it was at the millennium. I remarked in *WINCHELSEA – A Port of Stranded Pride* that the town was good at celebrating. That reputation was maintained and enhanced by its millennium celebrations and I feel unable to complete my story of Winchelsea over at least the whole of that millennium without jumping forward two centuries to record another great success.

The mayor at the time, Jurat Robert Beecroft, called a public meeting on 21 November 1998 to consider how the town could mark this very special occasion. Over a hundred residents attended and sixteen nominations to serve on a millennium committee were received and accepted. That initial enthusiasm was to be carried forward throughout what followed, led until Easter 2000 by Robert Beecroft and subsequently by his successors as mayor, Jurats Donald Cameron-Clarke and Roger Neaves. The committee was ably supported by Katharine Manning and Roy Coxon as Hon. Secretary and Hon. Treasurer respectively.

Working through the mass of minutes, newsletters, financial reports and associated documents generated by the committee's hard work[1] has proved quite as intriguing as investigating aspects of Winchelsea's medieval history! However, I cannot let that interest run away with me and must, almost exclusively, confine myself here to brief details about those projects which eventually reached a successful conclusion.

Very early in the committee's proceedings the erection of a beacon to be lit at midnight on 31 December 1999 was proposed. A temporary site at the cricket field for that occasion eventually became a permanent one close to where St. Leonard's Mill stood until 1987. Winchelsea's beacon is now recognised as part of the official national chain of beacons to be lit on special occasions. Sadly, inquiries into the possibility of rebuilding the mill as a millennium project had to be abandoned on grounds of administrative difficulty and cost.

An early suggestion that a 'Domesday Survey' of Winchelsea should be undertaken eventually matured as Melvyn Pett and Dominic Leahy's *Winchelsea at the Millennium*. The town is small enough to allow room in the book for everyone who wanted to be included with brief notes about residents and photographs of them outside their houses. A remarkable record for the future and a sell-out!

The books were joined in the sell-out category by Winchelsea's millennium mugs. These, produced by Rye Pottery for a scheme managed by Denis Hyson, were not only sold but, thanks to the generosity of sponsoring residents, also presented to more than 160 children; all those attending St. Thomas's School and others living in the town.

The people of Winchelsea gathered in force on millennium eve. A children's party and a magnificent fireworks display in the earlier part of the evening were followed later by an ecumenical non-denominational religious service arranged by the Very Rev. Canon Basil O'Ferrall. The lighting of the beacon at midnight preceded a social gathering in the New Hall.

Other associated events during the weeks before and after this included a performance of

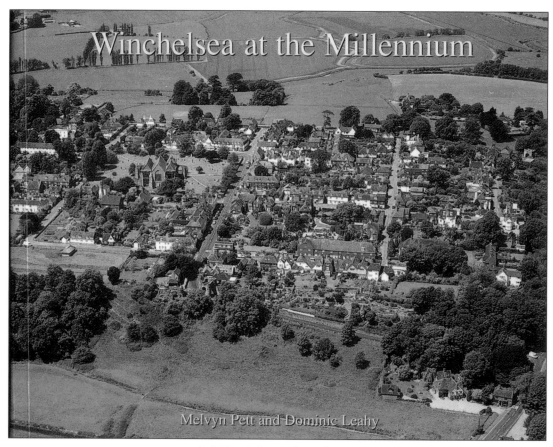

(94) Winchelsea at the Millennium

Messiah by the Winchelsea Singers, the collection of material for a time capsule for burial in the town (here Denis Hyson also took the lead), a boot fair, a flea market, a sale of paintings and other fund-raising activities too numerous for them all to have a mention.

One which is likely to have stuck in the memories of those present is the first lighting of the beacon on its permanent site. This was on 4 August 2000 in celebration of the hundredth birthday of Her Majesty Queen Elizabeth the Queen Mother, Lord Warden of the Cinque Ports. A town picnic on the Cricket Field was attended by many Winchelsea families who, later in the evening, joined a torchlight procession, accompanied by a piper, to the beacon site. As the beacon flared, to the sound of *Amazing Grace,* above mist rising from the valley it was an impressive and moving occasion.

Yet another millennium project was what is known as the Millennium Tapestry. Technically probably better described as a stitched collage, this is now on permanent exhibition in St. Thomas's Church. Many Winchelsea ladies, under the co-ordinating leadership of Margot Leahy, Bren Dunk and Jackie Stevens, undertook to sew a panel and the result was a remarkable representation of Winchelsea, its landmarks and its history. Whenever I examine it I am pleased to find the town clerk, depicted in wig and gown in a corporation procession, taking centre stage!

Nearby stands St. Thomas's Church's own millennium artefact, a magnificent piece of craftsmanship, an altar table bearing the simple legend MM. The late Rev. Peter Ansdell-Evans, an architect and non-stipendiary priest, designed this table and supervised its construction. It has been dedicated in his memory.

The original millennium committee[2] was 'stood down' on 30 September 2000 by which date a total of £9,946 had been raised to fund and support millennium projects. The minutes of that meeting, with pride and full justification, record this as 'an extraordinary feat for a community such as Winchelsea.'

However, considerable further funding was still needed for what is now the most immediately and strikingly noticeable millennium artefact, the town sign. The responsibility for raising the considerable sum needed fell to Jurat Donald Cameron-Clarke as mayor. His success, after much hard work, is clear for all to see for the town sign now stands proudly in German Street and an acknowledgement with the names of donors is prominently displayed in the museum. A sub-committee undertook responsibility for the manufacture and construction. Understandably in view of its size and prominent position, this project, originally suggested at one of the main committee's early meetings, had taken a long time. Principal sub-committee co-ordination was by Jurat Roger Neaves, an architect, who had earlier also taken a leading part in the beacon project. The sign's design, by John Haddock, a Winchelsea resident, was realised with such outstanding craftsmanship that it won first prize in the Traditional Skills section of the 2002 Sussex Heritage Awards. The sign had earlier been officially 'opened' by Mrs. Mary Chetwood whose major contribution to the life of the town over many years was recognised by the invitation to carry out this duty and later by her installation as Winchelsea's first woman freeman since medieval times.

I can only conclude here, having personally been in no way involved, by remarking that the outstanding community spirit epitomised by these extremely successful schemes and events does Winchelsea the greatest credit. Long may that spirit continue.

APPENDIX I

MAYORS OF WINCHELSEA

The following list uses as its base the names displayed in the Upper Court Hall and adheres to the spelling shown there. All additions and corrections discovered since that list was drawn up have been italicised.

Edward I

1295	Gervase Alard Jun
1306	Henry Paulyn

Edward II

1308	Gervase Alard Jun
1313	Robert Paulyn

Edward III

1328	Robert Bataille
1330	Thomas de Meydestan
1333	Henry Vynghe
1346	John Seman
1351	Robert Arnald
1353	Robert Arnald
1354	Robert Arnald
1355	Valentine de Dover
1358	Robert Arnald
1359	Robert Arnald
1362	*John Patevyn*
1363	Robert Badding
1364	Robert Londeneys
1365	John Pettevine
1366	Thomas Sibbe
1369	*Robert Harry*
1374	*Simon Salerne*
1376	Robert Badding

Richard II

1378	William Skene
1379	*Robert Harry*
1382	*William Skene*
1383	*John Pulham*
1384	*Robert Londeneys*
1385	*John Pulham*
1386	*Robert Harry*
1387	Robert Harri
1388	Robert Harri
1389	William Skene
1390	*William Skene*
1391	*Robert Arnold*
1392	*Robert Arnold*
1393	Robert Arnold

1394	*Robert Arnold*
1395	*William Skene*
1398	*Vincent Fynch*
1399	*John Helde*

Henry IV

1400	Vincent Finch
1401	*John Helde*
1404	*John Helde*
1405	*Vincent Fynch*
1406	*John Thunder jnr*
1407	*John Salerne*
1408	*John Salerne*
1409	Roger atte Gate
1410	Roger atte Gate
1411	*John Tunstall*
1412	John Tonstall
1413	*John Tunstall*
1414	*John Tunstall*

Henry V

1415	Roger atte Gate
1416	*John French*
1417	*John French*
1418	*Roger atte Gate*
1419	*Thomas Thunder*
1420	Thomas Thundyr Jun
1421	*John Tamworth*

Henry VI

1422	*Thomas Thunder*
1423	Thomas Thundyr
1424	*Thomas Thunder*
1425	Thomas Fysh
1426	William Worth
1427	
1428	William Worth
1430	Roger atte Gate
1431	John Godfrey
1432	John Godfrey
1433	John Godfrey
	William Fynch
1434	William Fynch

1435	Thomas Thundyr
1436	Thomas Thundyr
1437	William Alard
1438	John Godfrey
1439	Godard Pelham
1440	Godard Pelham
1441	Godard Pelham
1442	Thomas Sylton
1443	Thomas Sylton
1444	Thomas Thundyr
1445	Thomas Thundyr
1446	Godard Pelham
1447	Thomas Thundyr
1448	Thomas Thundyr
1449	Thomas Thundyr
1450	Thomas Wodeward
1451	Thomas Thunder
1452	Thomas Thunder
1453	Thomas Thunder
1454	Thomas Thunder
1455	Thomas Thunder
1456	Thomas Sylton
1457	Symon Farnecombe
1458	Symon Farncombe
1459	Robert Basele
1460	Robert Basele

Edward IV

1461	Robert Basele
1462	John Sylton
1463	John Sylton
1464	Henry Fyshe
1465	Thomas Thunder
1466	Robert Basele
1467	Richard Davy
1468	John Sylton
1469	Thomas Martham
1470	John Phypps
1471	Henry Fyshe
1472	Robert Basele
1473	Richard Davy
1474	Richard Davy
1475	John Sylton

1476	Henry Fyshe		Wyllym Ham	1562	John Pecke
1477	Robert Basele		Wyllym Ham	1563	John Love
1478	John Copyldyke	1520	Wyllym Ham	1564	John Pecke
1479	John Convers		Thos Assheburnham	1565	Goddard Whyte
1480	John Sylton	1521	Thos Assheburnham	1566	Goddard Whyte
1481	John Sylton	1522	Thos Assheburnham	1567	John Love
1482	Walter Moore		Thomas Ensyng	1568	Edward Midelton
		1523	Thomas Ensyng	1569	John Love
	Richard III	1524	Robert Sparowe	1570	John Pecke
1483	Henry Fyshe		George Lowes	1571	Edward Midelton
1484	Richard Davy	1525	George Lowes	1572	*Thomas* Wilford
	John Sylton	1526	George Lowes	1573	Thomas May
		1527	Thomas Foster	1574	Thomas May
	Henry VII	1528	Thomas Foster	1575	John Millward
1485	John Sylton	1529	Thomas Ensyng	1576	Thomas May
1486	Arkenold Silton	1530	Thomas Ensyng	1577	Thomas Fane
1487	Thomas Fyshe	1531	George Lowes	1578	Thomas Fane
1488	Richard Ferett	1532	George Lowes	1579	Goddard White
1489	John Godard	1533	George Lowes	1580	Edward Middleton
1490	John Godard	1534	John Coveley	1581	Robert Pierse
1491	Richard Martham	1535	John Bell	1582	Edward Middleton
1492	Richard Martham	1536		1583	William Morley
1493	George Bartyn	1537	George Lowes	1584	Anthony Stapley
1494	John Godard	1538	Thomas Ensyng	1585	James Fletcher
1495	Henry Stede	1539	Richard Ferett	1586	Adam Moyle
1496	Robert Oxenbregge	1540	Richard Ferett	1587	Adam Moyle
1497	Richard Barkeley	1541	John Bett	1588	Adam Moyle
1498	Richard Barkeley	1542	Richard Ferett	1589	Thomas Egleston
1499	Robert Oxenbregge	1543	Richard Ferett	1590	Thomas Egleston
1500	Robert Oxenbregge	1544	John Watts	1591	John Standen
1501	Robert Sparow	1545	Richard Ferett	1592	John Avery
1502	Robert Oxenbregge	1546	Godard Heman	1593	Thomas Egleston
1503	Thomas Godarde			1594	Thomas Egleston
1504	Harry Fisshe		**Edward VI**	1595	Oliver St. John
1505	William Stonacre	1547	John Smyth	1596	Thomas Egleston
1506	William Parnell	1548	John Watts	1597	George Samson
1507	Thomas Godarde	1549	William Oxenbredge	1598	George Samson
1508	Thomas Godarde	1550	John Hall	1599	Paul Wimond
		1551	George Lowes	1600	Paul Wimond
	Henry VIII	1552	William Eglisden	1601	George Sampson
1509	Thos Assheburnham			1602	George Sampson
1510	Thos Assheburnham		**Philip & Mary**		
1511	Robert Sparowe	1553	Richard Sergeant		**James I**
1512	William Stonacre	1554	William Eglestone		
1513	John Kyrkeby	1555	John Nethersole	1603	Paul Wymond
1514	James Marchall	1556	Thomas Egelstone	1604	George Sampson
1515	James Marchal	1557	Hugh Middelton	1605	Paul Wymond
1516	Moyser Pette			1606	John Avery
1517	Robert Sparowe		**Elizabeth**	1607	Thomas Pelham
	James Marshall	1558	Goddard Whyte	1608	Adam White
1518	James Marshall	1559	William Egelstone	1609	Wilham Bishop
1519	Thomas Ensyng	1560	William Egelstone	1610	Robert Boteler
		1561	John Pecke		

1611	John Eglestone	1657	John Richardson		**Anne**
1612	William Cooper	1658	Thomas Hamon	1702	Thomas Bottle
1613	William Wymond	1659	John Stephensen	1703	John Hopper
1614	John Tyndell			1704	John Hopper
1615	Paul Wymond		**Charles II**	1705	Richard Ashdown
1616	John Eglestone	1660	William Pelham	1706	John Cliff
1617	John Tyndell	1661	John Sampson	1707	Richard Ashdown
1618	William Wymond	1662	George Sampson	1708	Richard Ashdown
1619	Robert Plomer	1663	John Richardson	1709	Thomas Jenkin
1620	John Collins	1664	Thomas Farnham	1710	John Parnell
1621	Edward Avery	1665	William Jordan	1711	John Parnell
1622	Paul Wymond	1666	Thomas Gostrey	1712	Thomas Jenkin (Senior)
1623	John Collins	1667	John Sampson	1713	John Parnell
	Paul Wymond	1668	*John Richardson*		*Thomas Jenkin (Senior)*
1624	Giles Waters	1669	Thomas Waterer		
		1670	Samuel Newman		**George I**
	Charles I	1671		1714	Thomas Jenkin *(Senior)*
1625	George Wymond	1672	Peter Harmer	1715	Walter Pavis
1626	Richard Martin	1673	Richard Sheather	1716	Thomas Jenkin
1627	Robert Boteler	1674	Simon Sharvall	1717	Walter Pavis
1628	Paul Wymond	1675	John Sampson	1718	John Parnell
1629	John Pettit	1676	Walter Roberts	1719	Thomas Jenkin
1630	John Pettit	1677	William Smith	1720	John Parnell
1631	William Thorpe	1678	William Smith	1721	Thomas Marten
1632	George Sampson	1679	William Alderton		
1633	Paul Wymond	1680	Edward Marten		**George II**
1634	Richard Waters	1681	Edward Marten	1722	John Parnell
1635	William Thorpe	1682	Richard Padiham	1723	William Gyles
1636	George Sampson	1683	William Smith	1724	John Parnell
1637	Thomas Harnett	1684	Robert Wares	1725	Thomas Jenkin
	George Sampson			1726	William Gyles
1638	Daniel White		**James II**	1727	John Parnell
1639	William Thorpe	1685	Thomas Hovenden	1728	Thomas Marten
1640	George Sampson	1686	William Alderton	1729	John Parnell
1641	Daniel White	1687	John Richardson	1730	Thomas Marten
1642	William Chanon			1731	John Parnell
1643	John Freebody		**William and Mary**	1732	Thomas Marten
1644	Hugh Beresford	1688	John Richardson		John Parnell
1645	James Batcheller	1689	Edward Marten	1733	William Gyles
1646	William Thorpe	1690	Edward Marten	1734	John Parnell
1647	George Sampson	1691	Edward Marten	1735	William Gyles
1648	William Pelham	1692	Thomas Fuller	1736	John Parnell
		1693	Edward Marten	1737	William Gyles
	The Interregnum	1694	John Richardson	1738	John Pavis
1649	John Sampson	1695	John Richardson	1739	John Jenkin
1650	Simon Mois	1696	John Richardson	1740	Henry Jenkin
1651	William Thorpe		Philip Drinker		William Marten
1652	William Pelham	1697	Philip Drinker	1741	John Parnell
1653	John Sampson	1698	Edward Marten	1742	William Marten
1654	Simon Mois	1699	Edward Marten	1743	John Parnell
1655	Anthony Wells	1700	Edward Marten	1744	John Pavis
1656	George Sampson	1701	John Hopper		

1745	William Marten
1746	John Parnell
1747	Edwin Wardroper
1748	John Parnell
1749	Edwin Wardroper
1750	John Parnell
1751	Edwin Wardroper
1752	John Parnell
1753	John Knight Sen
	William Marten
1754	Edwin Wardroper
1755	William Marten
1756	Edwin Wardroper
1757	William Marten
1758	Edwin Wardroper
1759	William Marten

George III

1760	Edwin Wardroper
1761	Richard Wardroper
1762	Nathaniel Dawes
1763	Richard Wardroper
1764	Walter Gybbon
1765	Richard Wardroper
1766	Walter Gybbon
1767	Richard Wardroper
1768	
1769	William Marten
1770	Joash Adcroft
1771	Nathaniel Dawes
1772	Thomas Marten
1773	William Marten
1774	Thomas Marten
1775	William Marten
1776	Thomas Marten
1777	William Marten
1778	Thomas Marten
1779	William Marten
1780	Thomas Marten
1781	William Marten
	Thomas Marten
1782	John Peters
1783	Thomas Marten
1784	Joash Adcroft
1785	Thomas Marten
1786	Joash Adcroft
1787	Thomas Marten
1788	Joash Adcroft
1789	Thomas Marten
1790	Richard Lamb
1791	Thomas Marten

1792	Richard Lamb
1793	Thomas Marten
1794	George Stace
1795	Thomas Marten
1796	Barwell Browne
1797	Godfrey Scholey
1798	Barwell Browne
1799	John Shakespear
1800	Barwell Browne
1801	Rev Thomas Raddish
1802	Barwell Browne
1803	Rev Thomas Raddish
1804	Thomas Lloyd
1805	Barwell Browne
1806	Thomas Lloyd
1807	Barwell Browne
1808	Rev Thomas Raddish
1809	Barwell Browne
1810	Rev Thomas Raddish
1811	Barwell Browne
1812	Rev Thomas Raddish
1813	Barwell Browne
1814	Rev Thomas Raddish
1815	Barwell Browne
1816	Rev Thomas Raddish
1817	Barwell Browne
1818	Alexander Tullock
1819	Barwell Browne

George IV

1820	Alexander Tullock
1821	Barwell Browne
1822	Alexander Tullock
1823	Barwell Browne
1824	Alexander Tullock
1825	Barwell Browne
1826	Alexander Tullock
1827	Rev Samuel Philip Sheppard
1828	Alexander Tullock
1829	Rev S. P. Sheppard

William IV

1830	Alexander Tullock
1831	Rev S. P. Sheppard
	William Lipscomb
1832	*George Morant*
1833	George Morant
1834	Thomas Dawes
1835	John Tilden
1836	Joseph Hennah
1837	John Beaumont

Victoria

1838	Richard Stileman
1839	Richard Stileman
1840	Thomas Dawes
1841	Richard Stileman
1842	Thomas Dawes
1843	Richard Stileman
1844	*Richard Stileman*
	Joseph Hennah
1845	Joseph Hennah
1846	Joseph Hennah
1847	Joseph Hennah
1848	Joseph Hennah
1849	Joseph Hennah
1850	William Sergeant
1851	William Sergeant
1852	Dr Robert Coker Nash Davies
1853	William Longley
1854	William Longley
1855	William Longley
1856	Charles Robins
1857	Charles Robins
1858	Robert Curteis Stileman
1859	R. C. Stileman
1860	Dr Robert Vaile Skinner
1861	Charles Robins
1862	R. C. Stileman
1863	R. C. Stileman
1864	R. C. Stileman
1865	Charles Robins
1866	Samuel Griffiths
1867	Samuel Griffiths
1868	Dr R. V. Skinner
1869	Dr R. V. Skinner
1870	R. C. Stileman
1871	Rowland Thomas George Legg
1872	Dr R. V. Skinner
1873	R. C. Stileman
1874	R. C. Stileman
1875	Dr R. V. Skinner
1876	R. C. Stileman
1877	R. C. Stileman
1878	Dr R. V. Skinner
1879	R. C. Stileman
1880	R. C. Stileman
1881	Dr R. V. Skinner
1882	Frederic Andrew Inderwick QC MP
1883	R. C. Stileman

1884	R. C. Stileman	1926	Major J. A. Burke	1959	Captain H. Lovegrove CBE RN
1885	F. A. Inderwick QC MP	1927	Major J. A. Burke		
1886	Dr R. V. Skinner	1928	G. M. Freeman KC	1960	Thomas Bruce
1887	R. C. Stileman	1929	Anthony Mallows	1961	Thomas Bruce
1888	Dr R. V. Skinner		Freeman	1962	Anthony Mallows
1889	James Dearle Padgett	1930	Anthony Mallows		Freeman
1890	Dr Ernest William		Freeman	1963	Captain H. Lovegrove
	Skinner	1931	The Lord Ritchie of		CBE RN
1891	F. A. Inderwick QC		Dundee	1964	Ralph Eddowes Garrod
1892	F. A. Inderwick QC	1932	A. Vernon Owen		David Homan
1893	William Martindale	1933	Major J. A. Burke	1965	David Homan
1894	R. C. Stileman	1934	The Hon. J. K. Ritchie	1966	David Homan
1895	George Mallows Freeman	1935	James McGowan OBE	1967	C. C. Croggon
	QC			1968	C. C. Croggon
1896	F. A. Inderwick QC		**Edward VIII**	1969	H. J. Wenban
1897	G. M. Freeman QC	1936	Major J. A. Burke	1970	Captain H. Lovegrove
1898	Dr E. W. Skinner				CBE RN
1899	R. C. Stileman		**George VI**	1971	Lt. Col. P. V. Gray MBE
1900	Dr John Rutherford	1937	Major J. A. Burke	1972	Thomas Bruce
	Skinner	1938	Major J. A. Burke	1973	John B. L. Clark CBE
1901	R. C. Stileman	1939	B. M. McGowan	1974	John B. L. Clark CBE
		1940	Maj. J. P. Wildeblood	1975	D. D. W. Cole CBE
	Edward VII	1941	Lt. Col. Goldschmidt	1976	D. D. W. Cole CBE
1902	F. A. Inderwick KC	1942	Lt. Col. Goldschmidt	1977	Lt. Col. P. V. Gray MBE
1903	R. C. Stileman	1943	Major J. A. Burke	1978	H. Stanley Hargreaves
1904	G. M. Freeman KC	1944	Anthony Mallows	1979	H. Stanley Hargreaves
1905	G. M. Freeman KC		Freeman	1980	W. K. Whitehead TD
1906	Walter Inderwick	1945	Anthony Mallows	1981	Noel A. Eccles
1907	G. M. Freeman KC		Freeman	1982	Douglas H. Turner
1908	Dr J. R. Skinner	1946	Anthony Mallows	1983	Douglas H. Turner
1909	Charles Walter Campion		Freeman	1984	C. C. Croggon
1910	John Cousmaker	1947	Joseph Corbin Rogers	1985	C. C. Croggon
	Anderson	1948	Joseph Corbin Rogers	1986	Noel A. Eccles
		1949	John Knox	1987	G. A. Hughes
	George V	1950	John Knox	1988	G. A. Hughes
1911	G. M. Freeman KC	1951	Commander J.	1989	A. G. Sandeman
1912	Dr J. R. Skinner		Wyndham Cookson	1990	A. F. Tremeer
1913	Col. Wm. Barrington	1952	Anthony Mallows	1991	A. G. Sandeman
	Browne		Freeman	1992	K. W. Chetwood
1914	G. M. Freeman KC			1993	K. W. Chetwood
1915	G. M. Freeman KC		**Elizabeth II**	1994	Maj. P. L. Hoskins
1916	G. M. Freeman KC	1953	Anthony Mallows	1995	Lt. Col. H. G. Dormer
1917	G. M. Freeman KC		Freeman	1996	Lt. Col. H. G. Dormer
1918	G. M. Freeman KC	1954	Commander J.	1997	R. G. Beecroft Ll.B.
1919	G. M. Freeman KC		Wyndham Cookson	1998	R. G. Beecroft Ll.B.
1920	Alfred Osman CC	1955	John Knox	1999	R. G. Beecroft Ll.B.
1921	James McGowan	1956	Joseph Corbin Rogers	2000	D. Cameron-Clarke
1922	James McGowan	1957	Anthony Mallows	2001	D. Cameron-Clarke
1923	W. H. Martindale		Freeman	2002	R. D. Neaves
1924	The Lord Ritchie of	1958	Captain H. Lovegrove	2003	R. D. Neaves
	Dundee		CBE RN	2004	John Dunk
1925	Basil Holmes			2005	John Dunk

APPENDIX II

TOWN (OR COMMON)[1] CLERKS OF WINCHELSEA

The following names survive within the records of the Corporation

1427	Thomas Grevt	1621	Thomas Roberts	1734	Humphrey Butler
1445	Thomas Westynden	1623	Thomas Walwyn	1735	Edwin Wardroper
1461	John Rodys	1627	Thomas Reynolds	1740	Henry Dodson
1492	John Fermor	1630	Washington Reynolds[4]		Edwin Wardroper
1502	William Gregory	1637-38	No appointment	1747	Nathaniel Dawes
1505	John Hales	1639	John Bryant	1753	Charles Stephens
1506	Gervase Cobbes	1641	William Joy		Nathaniel Dawes
1513	William Chapell[2]		Thomas Curteis	1756	Richard Butler (Junior)
1515	Simon Fysshe		William Joy[5]	1763	Edwin Wardroper
	William Chapell	1644	John Puckle	1764	Richard Wardroper
1520	Richard Alcok	1651	Samuel Sampson	1767	Nathaniel Dawes
1521	Richard Sharpe	1652	Thomas Hyder	1769	Jeremiah Curtis
1523	William Chapell	1655	Henry Bromfield[6]	1770	Nathaniel Dawes
1529	John Mores	1660	Stephen Morley	1771	Richard Butler (Junior)
1535	Nicholas Whyte		Samuel Sampson		Thomas Marten
1538	Alexander Welles[3]	1663	Henry Bromfield	1772	Nathaniel Dawes
1544	John Sharp	1667	Joseph Wethered[7]	1773	Henry Waterman
1547	Hugh Lorymayr	1673	Henry Bromfield	1798	John Woollett
1549	Nicholas Harrold		Thomas Tournay	1819	Weedon Dawes
1553	Thomas Hooker	1676	Edward Watson	1822	Henry Butler
1561	John Davison	1678	Walter Roberts	1826	John Lardner
1564	Andrew Peke	1679	Thomas Tournay[8]	1848	Edwin Nathaniel Dawes
1565	John Davison	1680	Samuel Stretton	1876	Walter Dawes
1567	William Johnson	1681	Joseph Bigg	1930	Edwin Plomley Dawes
1570	William Appleton	1682	Samuel Stretton	1961	Charles Croggon
1572	Francis Bolton	1690	Robert Symons	1967	Thomas Bruce
1585	Thomas Fane	1702	Stephen Odiarne	1969	Charles Croggon
1609	Thomas Isted	1709	Henry Brockman	1984	Malcolm Pratt
1618	Samuel Playford	1710	Richard Butler (Senior)		

1. The titles of Town Clerk and Common Clerk are synonymous and interchangeable. The latter may well be the older. Its origin lies in the fact that Winchelsea had four courts, the Hundred which still meets at least annually on Easter Monday, the Assembly which still meets occasionally for the appointment of freemen, the Quarter Sessions and the Court of Record, both of which are now defunct. The town clerk served all four as legal officer. He was therefore common to them all, hence Common Clerk.

2. It seems likely that William Chapell served as town clerk from 1513 until 1528 and that the others named above as serving during that time acted for him at meetings of which details have survived. Simon Fysshe is recorded on 25 April 1525 serving as Solicitor to the Confederation of the Cinque Ports, an ancient office still in existence. He was at that time a jurat of Winchelsea. On 25 July 1525 one of the members of the Winchelsea delegation to Courts of Brotherhood and Guestling was Nicholas Tufton, 'general attorney for the ports with Richard Sharp his clerk'. Sharpe could therefore easily have been a legal officer who had earlier represented the town clerk.

3. On 23 July 1538 Alexander Welles held the office of deputy town clerk and he was later promoted. By 24 July 1543 he was serving as Town Clerk of Hastings and on 15 September 1550 as Town Clerk of Rye, a town of which he was a freeman. John Mores was another who was appointed to a different port. In July 1543 he is recorded in office as Town Clerk of New Romney, a post he held for a number of years. The similarity between many of the meeting dates is because, just as in recent years the Joint Standing Committee of the Confederation has met annually on 21 May when the speakership changes from head port to head port, in those days the Courts of Brotherhood and Guestling met annually during the last week in July to elect the bailiffs who would attend the Great Yarmouth herring fair. The speakership changed at that meeting.

4. Winchelsea seems to have had considerable problems appointing town clerks at this time, and a resolution passed at the mayoring ceremony in 1636 gives a revealing picture of the work involved in those days:-

    'Forasmuch as the said now elected Common Clarke (an ancient Clarke in the Portes) is very aged and weak with infirmities which office (for the goodwill he hath long borne to this towne) he proposes with God's assistance to execute to his utmost endeavours, and forasmuch as it is apparently known that the office is become of small value, no fee or exhibition appertaining thereto, and consisteth of great paines in writing manifold copies and returns of writts, precepts, letters and other matters and causes without reward, and so consequently of more paines than profit. He therefore prayeth due consideration thereof and therefore this Assembly is pleased and firmly granteth and consent to free him from all travel, all other offices, ecclesiastical and civil, scotts, watches etc. And to allow him one pasturage of free gift during his continuance in the office.'

    Sadly it seems that Washington Reynolds died shortly after this without enjoying his one pasturage of free gift for long. For the next two years the appointment of the town clerk was, 'respited at the discretion of the Mayor'.

5. The rather odd entry for 1641 is explained by the following references to the official records of the town and the confederation: On 20 April 1641, 'The place of Towne Clerke being vacant it is thought fitt by the major part of the Corporation viz. Mr. Maior and others that William Joy shall be elected Towne Clerke for the whole year and being in Court was sworn according to usual custom.' Nevertheless on 17 June 1641 at a sitting of the Court of Hundred the record reads: 'Also Thomas Curteis is elected and chosen Common Clarke and hath taken his oath according to usual custom.' Curteis was made a Freeman the same day. Whatever may have been the reason for this change of mind, the Confederation of the Cinque Ports did not approve. At a Brotherhood and Guestling on 27 July 1641 an order was made for the reinstatement of William Joy as Town Clerk of Winchelsea, 'on pain of £10'. Winchelsea complied.

6. In 1659 Henry Bromfield was indicted of the theft of £500 and was ordered to be taken to Middlesex Quarter Sessions by the Chamberlain. Bromfield was formally excluded from keeping the records of the corporation. It was not, however, their money he was alleged to have stolen but that of Richard Bradshaw whose house he had 'feloniously entered'. Presumably he was acquitted because it was the same Henry Bromfield who was re-appointed in 1663 and again, briefly, in 1673.

7. Joseph Wethered appears to have been Winchelsea's least conscientious town clerk. During his period of office the town's records consist almost entirely of blank pages!

8. The Hundred Book record of the mayoring for 1679 states, 'Mr. Thomas Tournay was elected Towne Clerke for the year ensuing upon condition that if Mr. Roberts doe come home again to be resident here on or before the 19th Day of May next then the said Mr. Roberts to officiate the said office of Towne Clerke from that time, otherwise the said Mr. Tournay to be sworn according to custom.' It seems that Mr. Roberts did not return to Winchelsea and that he had lodged the corporation's books with Mr. John Weekes Junior of Westfield. An Assembly held on 30 December 1679 instituted proceedings for their return.

NOTES ON SOURCES

The books and documents (details in bibliography) referred to in these notes are those which I consulted in preparing my text. No attempt has been made to indicate either the original sources or alternatives from which the same information is available. The only exception to this is that where I have obtained information from the published catalogue of Winchelsea Corporation Records, I have added the reference of the listed document referred to. References commencing with D are to my personal collection of Winchelsea documents, cuttings and notes.

Prologue

1. McKisack p.69

1. Through the Mists of Time

1. Eddison p.142
2. Kemp p.48
3. Jessup [HK] p.21
4. *East Sussex News* 16 July 1981 (D21/6)
5. Martins [WT] p.95
6. ESRO WIN 2362/9/41
7. Martins ibid
8. Kemp p.35
9. *Rye and Battle Observer* 2 February 2001 (D55 17)
10. SAC 79 p.203
11. SCM 13 p.674
12. VCH IX p.62
13. Turner p.19
14. Saul p.53
15. VCH II p.126
16. Murray p.24
17. Churchill I p.108
18. Schama I p.72
19. Baines p.3

2. In Foreign Hands

1. SCM 14 pp.37-39
2. SCM 13 pp.674-679; Homan [CSW] pp.1-3
3. SCM 13 pp.676-677; Vidler [HR] p.2
4. Bradbury p.41
5. ibid

3. Seeds of Confederation

1. VCH ii 127
2. ibid
3. Baines p.9
4. EHR 91 p.650
5. Murray p.25

6. EHR 91 p.649
7. Kirkham pp.14-15; Green I. p.73; Baines p.34 inter alia
8. Baines p.8
9. Sylvester p.113
10. for this privilege in the nineteenth and twentieth centuries see Pratt pp.116, 119-121
11. Vidler [RR]
12. Green I. p.17

4. Conquest

1. Burrows p.29
2. Vidler [HR] p.3
3. SCM 13 p.680
4. D29/3
5. DNB II p.484
6. Dawson II Appendix Sheet 6A
7. Bradbury p.215
8. ibid p.224
9. Green I. p.18
10. Murray p.26

5. Domesday and Beyond

1. Morris 5.1
2. SNQ 1 p.162
3. Homan [CW] p.3
4. Saul pp.45, 53
5. SAC 92 p.128; Leslie & Short p.43
6. Vidler [HR] p.4
7. VCH II p.233
8. ibid p.232
9. Eddison [ECHO] p.82
10. SNQ 16 pp.253-255
11. SAC 79 p.200
12. SNQ 16 p.255
13. see Green I. p.12
14. Bavington Jones p.6

15. Green I. p.18
16. Vidler [HR] p.4
17. Murray pp.18-19
18. VCH IX pp.62, 67
19. Eddison p.73
20. Leslie & Short pp.42-43
21. Baines p.9

6. Charters and Honours

1. EHR 91 p.641
2. Murray p.13
3. Vidler [HR] p.6
4. Schama I p.129
5. SAC 71 p.101
6. Eddison [ECHO] p.82
7. Churchill I p.181
8. Burrows p.63
9. ibid
10. Murray pp.30, 31; Sylvester pp.84-87
11. For the story of Winchelsea's attendance at twentieth century coronations see Pratt pp. 116, 119-121, 124.
12. Burrows pp.70-71
13. VCH II p.129
14. Longmate [DTI] p.203
15. Green I. p.19 inter alia
16. Longmate ibid

7. The Alards, the Cogs and the Loss of Normandy

1. Eddison pp.73-4; Sylvester pp.50-51; Poole p.96
2. Cooper pp.5-6
3. Eddison [EOR] p.105
4. Murray p.46
5. Eddison [TDG] p.135
6. SAC 97 p.72
7. VCH IX p.70

8. SAC 61 p.126
9. ibid p.128
10. ibid p.130
11. ibid p.131
12. Kemp p.63
13. Williamson J. p.151
14. Howarth p.44
15. Williamson D. p.81
16. Longmate [DTI] p.202
17. EHR 91 p.638
18. Longmate [DTI] p.207
19. Green I. p.20

8. Louis and Eustace

1. Baines p.8
2. VCH II p.129
3. Cooper p.6
4. Green I. p.20
5. Murray p.35
6. Poole p.484n
7. VCH I pp.492-493
8. Chapman p.28
9. VCH IX p.69
10. Williamson D. p.79
11. Vidler [HR] p.7
12. SAC 23 p.29
13. ibid p.23
14. Rodger I p.54 inter alia
15. SAC 3 p.12
16. VCH II p.130
17. ibid IX p.37
18. Longmate DTI p.232
19. Powicke p.10
20. Longmate DTI p.233
21. ibid pp.233-234; TRHS
    (1904) p.262n
22. Green I. p.21
23. Rodger I p.55
24. D33 18 (p.46)
25. Longmate ibid p.244
26. ibid

**9. Early Friars and
Early Storms**

1. Jessup [HK] p.63
2. Martin p.2
3. Gillingham & Griffiths p.62
4. ibid p.63
5. Jessup [HK] p.63 inter alia
6. Poland p.78
7. Green I. p.21

8. ibid
9. Clark p.11
10. Murray p.33
11. ibid p.84; SAC 23 p.23
12. Williamson D. pp.81-82
13. Churchill I p.208
14. Bavington Jones pp.8-9
15. Baines p.11
16. Legg p.62
17. VCH II p.130
18. Eddison [ECHO] p.69
19. Rodger I p.69
20. SAC 23 p.20
21. ibid p.22
22. Inderwick p.18
23. ibid
24. Eddison p.78
25. D23 4
26. Eddison [ECHO] p.82
27. Eddison p.78
28. Homan [FW] p.2 inter alia
29. Bavington Jones p.57
30. Homan [FW] pp.2-3
31. ibid p.2
32. Eddison [ECHO] p.70
33. Homan [FW] p.3
34. Inderwick p.19
35. Homan [FW] p.4

10. Resumption and Rebellion

1. Vidler [RR]
2. Cooper pp.11-12, Vidler
    [HR] p.9
3. Cooper p.11
4. Williams p.59
5. VCH II p.132
6. ibid
7. Vidler [HR] p.12
8. SAC 23 pp.30-31
9. Murray pp.37-38
10. Churchill I p.218
11. VCH I p.496
12. Chapman pp.31-32
13. EHR 91 p.650
14. VCH I p.501
15. Parry p.274
16. Green I. p.22
17. SAC 23 p.30
18. SAC 4 pp.111-112
19. Williamson D. p.83
20. Ford F. M. pp.30-31

21. SAC 4 p.111
22. Prestwich p.55
23. Burrows p.113
24. Prestwich p.28
25. EHR 54 p.201
26. ibid
27. ibid p.208
28. Powicke p.207

**11. The Road to Final
Destruction**

1. VCH IX p.63
2. Eddison [ECHO] p.70
3. VCH II p.265
4. VCH IX p.70
5. Homan [FW] p.4; Eddison
    [ECHO] p.70
6. see Sylvester p.64
7. Beresford p.15
8. EHD 1189-1327 p.799
9. Eddison p.79
10. Sylvester p.31
11. Eddison [EOR] p.113
12. VCH IX p.69; SAC 79
    p.219
13. D61 20
14. Eddison [EOR] p.113
15. VCH IX p.70
16. VCH II p.47
17. VCH I p.506; CCR 1272-
    1279 p.50
18. Powicke p.411; Murray p.29
19. EHD 1189-1327 p.859
20. Green I. pp.13-14
21. Homan [FW] pp.4-5
22. Eddison [ECHO] p.70
23. Eddison p.79
24. ibid p.144
25. ibid pp.79-80
26. Cooper p.21
27. Inderwick p.19
28. Eddison p.89
29. Calder p.229
30. Floyd p.42; Collard p.9
31. Farrant p.91

12. The Hill of Iham

1. Cooper p.29
2. Powicke p.511n
3. Homan [HW] p.1
4. EHD 1189-1327 p.799

5. Cooper p.29
6. Martins [EUS] p.4; Cooper p.31
7. Prestwich p.310
8. Chambers p.180
9. Powicke p.310
10. *Monségur, an English Bastide* pub. Tourisme en Monségurais (D61 11)
11. Homan [FW] p.20
12. See Pratt pp.199-200
13. Sylvester p.30
14. DNB Vol XV p.731
15. Powicke p.632
16. Prestwich p.264
17. Fiennes p.129
18. Homan [FW] pp.8-12
19. Bois pp.17-18
20. Cooper p.53

13. New Winchelsea

1. Williamson J. p.132
2. VCH VII p.245
3. D28 7
4. Sylvester p.58
5. Martins [EUS]
6. Homan [FW] p.23
7. Martins [QQ] p.10 inter alia.
8. Martins [EUS] pp. 5 & 32 inter alia
9. Homan [HW] p.100
10. Homan [FW] p.26
11. Cooper pp.44-53
12. Inderwick p.92
13. ibid pp.70-74
14. D43 10
15. Martins [EUS] p.29; Swinden p.18
16. Knowles and Hadcock p.311
17. Chizlett [DG] p.8
18. Martin [EUS] p.29
19. ibid pp.30-31
20. Sylvester p.61
21. Pratt p.7
22. Churchill I p.239
23. Powicke p.636

14. The Cellars

1. Williamson D. p.11

2. VCH II p.177
3. Sylvester p.198
4. ibid
5. ibid p.200
6. James pp.76-77, 138
7. Martins [EUS] p.6
8. ibid p.37
9. ibid pp.37-41
10. *Medieval Undercrofts and Town Houses* by P. A. Faulkner (Studies in Medieval Domestic Architecture, 1975 pp.118-133) referred to in Martins [EUS] pp.41-42
11. ibid p.42
12. Homan [FW] following p.38; D29 7
13. D63 7
14. Pers. Comm. Dominic Leahy who refers particularly to Fitchen; D59 4
15. Pers. Comm. Bernard Doherty; Martins [QQ] p.19
16. Pers. Comm. John Gooders; D52 18

15. The Other Survivors

1. Martin p.145
2. Nairn & Pevsner p.635
3. Martins [QQ] p.102
4. See Pratt p.55
5. ibid p.18
6. Poland p.78
7. Martins [QQ] p.99
8. Pers. Comm. David Martin
9. Blair et. al.
10. ibid p.19
11. Saville, Malcolm p.15
12. Cooper p.123
13. Blair et al p.21
14. *Daily Telegraph - Books Supplement* 8 March 2003 p.3 (D61 21)
15. Inderwick p.108
16. Martins [CH] p.5
17. Martins [QQ] p.24
18. Homan [FW] p.35
19. Martins [QQ] p.23
20. ibid p.41

21. ibid
22. See Pratt pp.147, 149
23. Martins [QQ] p.19
24. ibid p.34
25. see ESRO WIN 2362/9/27
26. Pers. Comm. Clive Chizlett (D54 14)
27. SAC 88 p.37

16. Escape, Enmity and Expedition

1. Bagley p.14
2. Saul p.45
3. Baines p.27
4. ESRO WIN 442
5. Schama I p.196
6. Homan [HW] p.5
7. Powicke p.498n
8. VCH II p.43
9. VCH IX p.75
10. Poland p.79
11. Homan [CSW] p.4
12. Poland pp.80-82
13. Martins [QQ] p.101
14. Cooper pp.144-145
15. Homan [HW] p.16
16. Burrows p.120
17. D33 18 (p.46)
18. Burrows ibid
19. D33 18 (p.46)
20. Murray p.33
21. VCH II p.132
22. ibid
23. Platt pp.61-62
24. Chapman p.37 (although she gives the date incorrectly as 1294)
25. Hardy pp.45-46
26. CPR 1292-1301 p.149
27. Sumption I pp.81-82
28. Homan [HW] p.18
29. Martins [QQ] pp.17, 19, 25, 36, 42, 50, 52, 54, 60.

17. The Crisis

1. DNB Vol. 21 p.626
2. Denton p.7
3. ibid
4. Homan [CW] p.8
5. Denton p.11
6. DNB ibid p.627-8

7. Prestwich p.403
8. ibid
9. ibid p.404
10. Denton p.87
11. Inderwick pp.101-102
12. Saul p.113
13. EHR Vol. 91 p.643
14. Homan [HW] pp.28-31
15. Sylvester p.178
16. SAC 5 p.276
17. Prestwich p.111
18. Denton p.109
19. Cooper p.57
20. Powicke p.682
21. Inderwick p.103
22. Homan [HW] pp.49-50
23. CPR 1292-1301 p.306
24. Powicke p.683
25. Denton p.174
26. Prestwich p.521
27. Denton p.179
28. ibid p.206
29. ibid p.15
30. McKisack p.69
31. Denton p.16
32. Powicke p.717
33. Denton ibid

18. The Admirals

1. Longmate [DTI] p.255
2. Powicke p.655
3. Sylvester p.220
4. ibid pp.138, 140
5. Green I. p.23
6. Sylvester p.221
7. ibid
8. Williamson J. p.116
9. Sylvester p.221
10. Huxford p.307
11. Jessups [CP] p.110
12. Sylvester p.96
13. Homan [HW] p.43
14. Taylor p.7
15. Burrows p.130
16. Prestwich p.499
17. Homan [HW] pp.46-47
18. Powicke p.715
19. Cooper p.60
20. Prestwich p.514
21. Homan [HW] p.44
22. Burrows p.131

23. Rodger I p.131

19. Misdemeanours Multiply

1. Sylvester p.210
2. Cooper p.118
3. Murray p.153
4. ibid p.32
5. ibid
6. Sylvester p.217
7. Green I. p.25
8. SAC 61 p.134
9. Homan [HW] p.57
10. Cooper p.63
11. Ford F. M. p.7
12. ibid
13. VCH II p.136
14. Murray p.122
15. VCH II p.136
16. Jessups [CP] p.26
17. Vidler [HR] p.18; D33 16 p.16
18. Homan [HW] p.63
19. ibid p.64
20. Platt p.107
21. ibid
22. McKisack p.65
23. VCH II p.136
24. Homan [HW] p.70
25. Sylvester p.157
26. Ford F. M. p.7
27. Murray p.33
28. Homan [HW] p.79
29. ibid p.80
30. VCH II p.137

20. From Wine to War

1. Homan [HW] pp.47-48
2. ibid p.48
3. Martins [WT] p.97
4. Homan [FW] p.40
5. Homan [HW] p.48
6. Sylvester p.205
7. SAC 70 p.104
8. ibid p.106
9. James p.11
10. Homan [HW] p.47
11. ibid pp.58-60
12. Homan [CW] pp.70-72
13. Martins [QQ] p.105
14. ibid
15. ibid p.94

16. Cooper p.67
17. Homan [CW] p.57
18. Poland p.44
19. Homan [HW] p.77
20. Sylvester pp.204-205
21. James pp.5-6
22. ibid p.16
23. ibid p.128
24. Sylvester pp.139, 142
25. Homan [HW] p.92
26. Martins [QQ] pp.87-88
27. Rodger I p.63
28. VCH II p.234
29. Green I. p.25
30. Cooper p.69
31. ibid
32. James p.18
33. McKisack p.361
34. James p.16
35. Homan [HW] p.111

21. Bailiffs Malicious ...

1. Homan [HW] pp.65-66
2. ibid pp.66-67
3. ibid p.67
4. ibid
5. ibid p.68
6. Sylvester p.100
7. Vidler [HR] p.18
8. Cooper p.65
9. Homan [FW] p.61
10. ibid pp.61-66
11. Cooper p.65
12. Turner p.177
13. Homan [HW] p.71
14. VCH I p.508
15. see Pratt p.46
16. HPC 1386-1421 I p.751
17. Homan [CSW] p.17
18. Homan [HW] p.82
19. ibid p.84
20. Homan [CSW] p.18
21. Homan [HW] p.84
22. SNQ 8 p.5
23. Martins [QQ] p.93

22. ...and a Bailiff Maligned

1. Murray p.132
2. Homan [HW] p.104
3. Murray p.123
4. McKisack p.121

5. ibid p.153
6. Churchill I p.264
7. Homan [HW] p.105
8. this account based on
   Homan [HW] pp.105-108;
   Homan [CW] pp.42-44
9. Neillands p.111
10. Sumption II pp.7-8
11. Schama I p.225
12. ibid
13. Neillands p.111
14. Schama I p.232
15. McKisack p.306
16. Jessup [HK] p.64
17. Saul p.161
18. Homan [HW] p.135
19. Eddison p.144
20. Jessup [HK] p.70
21. Cooper pp.73-74
22. Homan [HW] pp.118-119

23. The War Develops

1. Cooper p.69
2. Sumption I p.264
3. Martins [EUS] p.8
4. Rodger I p.97
5. Longmate [DTI] p.267
6. Sumption I pp.320-321
7. Rodger I p.99
8. Longmate [DTI] p.268
9. Neillands p.84
10. Howarth p.51
11. Cooper p.70
12. Sumption I p.450
13. SAC 78 p.211
14. Sumption ibid
15. VCH II p.138
16. Sumption I p.391
17. Murray p.211
18. CCR 1343-1346 p.581
19. Murray p.212
20. Sumption I p.499
21. Churchill I p.269
22. Howarth p.371
23. Sumption I pp.506-507
24. ibid p.510
25. Homan [HW] p.117
26. Murray p.213
27. EHR 91 p.645
28. Baines p.14
29. Cooper p.71

30. Sylvester p.154
31. ibid p.218
32. Neillands p.110

24. The Battle of Winchelsea

1. Homan [HW] p.119
2. Longmate [DTI] p.273
3. Sylvester p.201
4. James p.129
5. Rodger I p.104
6. SCM 9 p.477
7. ibid p.478
8. ibid p.555
9. ibid p.479
10. Carter p.167
11. SCM 9 p.552
12. ibid
13. Cooper pp.74-79
14. Longmate [DTI] p.273
15. Kemp p.64
16. SCM 9 p.553
17. ibid p.554
18. Sylvester p.179
19. Williamson D. p.119
20. Sumption II p.67
21. ibid
22. Rodger I p.104
23. Sumption II p.67
24. ibid p.68

25. A Decade at Home …

1. Homan [HW] pp.117-118
2. ibid p.118
3. Sylvester pp.74, 76
4. Williamson J. p.92
5. Cooper pp.140-141
6. Homan [HW] p.121
7. Cooper p.85
8. Hufton & Baird p.3
9. Homan [CW] p.24
10. Cooper p.136
11. CP Vol. VI p.651
12. Murray p.8
13. Cooper p.120; VCH II
    p.237
14. Homan [HW] p.122
15. CCR 1354-1360 p.315
16. Homan [HW] p.137
17. VCH II p.266
18. HPC 1386-1421 I p.751
19. CCP p.279

20. HPC ibid
21. VCH IX p.37
22. Martins [EUS] p.29
23. Homan [HW] p.127
24. Martins ibid p.28
25. Pers. Comm. David Martin
26. Pers. Comm. Christopher
    Whittick; Martins ibid p.20
27. Turner p.54

**26. …and Devastation from
Abroad**

1. Neillands pp.130-131
2. ibid p.155
3. Sumption II p.309
4. Cooper pp.80-81
5. Homan [HW] p.134
6. ibid p.131
7. Sumption II p.436
8. ibid
9. Longmate [DTI] p.276
10. Sumption II p.437
11. ibid
12. CCR 1360-1364 p.101
13. Homan [HW] p.135
14. ibid p.136
15. Martins [EUS] p.26
16. ibid p.7
17. Seward p.217
18. Hewitt p.20
19. Sumption II p.437
20. ibid p.445
21. Neillands pp.159, 201

27. Determined Defence

1. Homan [HW] p.137
2. ibid p.137
3. ibid p.138
4. SCM 1 p.451
5. D26 7 24 April 1993
6. *Bournemouth Echo* 23 April
   1993
7. ibid
8. Churchill I pp.282-283
9. Sylvester pp.182-183
10. CCR 1369-1374 pp.114-
    115
11. ibid pp.188, 200
12. Sumption II p.584
13. Turner p.40
14. Homan [HW] pp.140-141

15. Cooper pp.83-84
16. McKisack pp.244-245
17. Homan [HW] pp.142-144
18. Cooper p.88
19. Homan [HW] p.150
20. Vidler [HR] pp.26-27
21. Homan [HW] p.150;
    Burrows pp.150-151
22. Russell Chapter 11; Cooper
    p.89
23. Baines pp.4-5
24. Vidler pp.27-28; VCH II
    p.140

28. Attacked Again

1. Martins [EUS] pp.8-9
2. Homan [HW] p.155;
   Cooper p.93
3. Homan ibid pp.155-156
4. VCH IX p.118; SAC 53
   p.80
5. Rodger I p.112
6. Russell Chapter 11
7. Homan [HW] p.156
8. Homan [FW] p.49
9. VCH II p.140
10. Homan [CW] p.12
11. ibid p.13
12. D22 23; D34 18; D49 16
13. Schama I p.247
14. Longmate [DTI] p.284
15. ibid
16. SNQ 3 p.190
17. VCH II p.140; Cooper p.92
18. HPC 1386-1421 I p.42
19. ibid p.766
20. Eddison p.98
21. HPC ibid; CPR 1381-1385
    pp.425-426
22. Eddison ibid
23. Turner p.50
24. Homan [HW] p.159
25. ibid

29. Troubled Times Continue

1. Homan [HW] p.160
2. Longmate [DTI] p.284
3. ibid
4. ibid pp.286-287
5. VCH IX p.67
6. McKisack pp.446-447

7. Homan [HW] p.163
8. Murray p.56
9. EHR 91 p.646
10. Homan [HW] p.165
11. SAC 79 p.204
12. Cooper p.94
13. Baines p.190
14. VCH II p.261
15. HPC 1386-1421 III p.342
16. SAC 9 p.296
17. SAC 69 pp.181-182
18. HPC 1386-1421 I p.752
19. HPC ibid II p.57
20. Homan [CSW] p.23
21. HPC 1386-1421 III
    pp.150-151
22. Cooper p.159
23. Martins [EUS] p.27
24. Homan [HW] pp.166-167
25. HPC 1386-1421 III p.151
26. HPC ibid p.342
27. Homan [HW] p.169-170
28. HPC 1386-1421 II p.219

30. Towards New Walls

1. Homan [HW] pp.168-169
2. SAC 82 pp.136-137
3. Cooper p.140
4. Jacob p.289
5. SAC 28 p.94
6. Jacob pp.27-28
7. Martins [EUS] p.26
8. VCH IX p.75
9. Hannah p.366
10. Homan [FW] pp.80-81
11. CIM 1399-1422 pp.278-
    283
12. Martins [EUS] p.9
13. ibid p.15
14. ibid p.26
15. ibid p.28
16. ibid
17. Turner p.64
18. Homan [FW] ibid.
19. Martins [EUS] pp.10, 22
20. Neillands p.202
21. Williams p.60
22. Howarth p.59
23. Kemp p.71
24. Cooper p.96
25. Allmand p.113

26. VCH IX p.70
27. HPC 1386-1421 II p.504
28. SAC 4 p.123
29. Neillands p.210
30. Jacob p.158

31. Extraordinary Ordinances

1. Homan [HW] pp.163, 177
2. ibid p.176
3. Longmate [DTI] pp.315-
   316
4. Homan ibid p.178
5. ibid p.179
6. Eddison p.105
7. HPC 1386-1421 IV
   pp.610-611
8. SAC 8 pp.202-206; ESRO
   WIN 616/2

32. Piracy Persists

1. Green I. p.27
2. SAC 4 p.122
3. Jessups [CP] p.118
4. Williamson D. p.85
5. Kemp pp.136-137
6. Sylvester p.160
7. D33 18 (p.53)
8. James p.120
9. Homan [HW] p.171
10. Jacob p.134
11. Homan [HW] p.183
12. ibid
13. Cooper p.101
14. D60 2
15. ESRO WIN 435 ff.4-5
16. SAC 8 p.207
17. VCH II p.142
18. WCR p.17 [ESRO WIN 53
    fo.30r]
19. Cooper p.104
20. SAC 120 p.144
21. VCH II p.144
22. ibid p.147
23. ESRO RYE 47/2/19
24. ibid 47/20/2
25. D19 13
26. Mayhew p.98
27. Sylvester p.163
28. ESRO RYE 47/93/6; WCR
    p.25 [ESRO WIN 55
    fos.245v-247v]

29. Cordingley pp.251-252

33. Principally of Pilgrimage

1. D29 6
2. See Cooper pp.45 & 152
3. D29 6 gives the full inscription
4. Homan [HW] p.137
5. Vidler p.24
6. Neillands pp.164-5, 177
7. Windeatt
8. ibid p.12
9. ibid p.147
10. D29 5
11. Carter pp.175-177; EHD IV 1327-1485 pp.1216-1218
12. Homan [HW] p.198
13. Cooper pp.98-99
14. Ford F. M. p.72n
15. Saul p.191
16. Taylor p.13
17. Homan [CSW] p.26
18. Ford F. M. p.72n
19. D61 19
20. Cooper p.98
21. Homan [HW] p.181
22. Martins [WT] p.99
23. Bavington Jones p.58
24. CCP pp.1-2
25. ibid pp.2-3
26. ESRO WIN 435 f.3

34. A Long War's End

1. Topp p.89
2. Murray p.207
3. ibid
4. HPC 1386-1421 I p.752
5. CCP p.18
6. Homan [HW] p.192
7. ibid
8. Burrows p.158
9. ibid
10. VCH II p.143
11. Cooper p.102; CPR 1446-1452 p.270
12. Homan [HW] p.195
13. ibid pp.195-196
14. Gairdner I p. 109
15. ibid
16. Churchill I p.333

17. Homan [HW] p.197
18. Neillands p.287
19. James pp.44-45
20. Cooper p.102
21. ibid pp.102-103
22. Homan [HW] p.202
23. Cooper p.102
24. Homan [HW] p.197
25. EHR 91 p.651
26. Rodger I p.154; EHR 91 ibid
27. Dyer p.264
28. Cooper p.104

35. Beer and Buildings

1. D19 20
2. CCP p.70
3. CCP p.108
4. Williamson J. pp.103-104
5. Cooper p.105
6. ESRO WIN 435 fo.3
7. Cooper p.245
8. Homan [CSW] pp.24-26
9. Homan [CW – Chantries Supplement] p.18
10. Homan [HW] pp.182-183
11. VCH II p.261
12. Homan [CW – Chantries Supplement] pp.10-11
13. ibid p.10
14. ibid p.15
15. Martins [QQ] p.99
16. Homan ibid pp.19-21
17. Blair et. al. p.19
18. ESRO WIN 435 fo.6
19. ibid fo.8
20. ibid
21. Cooper p.191
22. Sylvester p.155n
23. Homan (HW) pp.208-209
24. Salzman p.271
25. D22 9; VCH II p.143
26. Martins [EUS] p.10
27. ibid
28. ibid p.47
29. ibid
30. Martins [QQ] p.35
31. Martins [EUS] p.48
32. Pers. Comm. Roger Davey (D52 15)
33. Martins ibid

34. VCH IX p.64
35. Martins ibid

36. Hostilities Renewed

1. Homan [CW] pp.5-6
2. SCM 10 p.818
3. CCP p.144
4. HPC 1509-1558 III pp.358-359
5. Green I. p.28
6. Burrows p.222
7. Schama I p.289
8. Longmate [DTI] p.369
9. Green I. p.28
10. ibid
11. Schama I p.292
12. VCH IX p.69
13. D57 7 p.26; Schama ibid
14. D19 7
15. VCH II p.144
16. ibid
17. Homan [CSW] p.41
18. CCP p.201
19. ibid
20. ibid p.169
21. ibid p.170
22. Murray pp.196-197
23. CCP p.xxxvi
24. Murray p.193
25. VCH II p.18
26. Mayhew p.61
27. SAC 120 p.143
28. ESRO WIN 51 [CW] fo.39r
29. ibid
30. Martins [EUS] p.19
31. see Appendix 2
32. SAC 120 ibid

37. Dissolution

1. Jessup [HK] p.64
2. Lee p.167
3. Schama I p.310
4. Briggs p.129
5. Leslie and Short p.47
6. Martin p.144
7. ibid
8. SAC 92 p.36
9. Martin ibid
10. CCP p.221
11. Poland pp.82-83

12. HPC 1509-1558 I p.648
13. SAC 28 p.94
14. Poland p.83
15. Martin p.145
16. Homan [CW] p.85
17. ibid pp.85-86
18. Homan [CSW] p.13
19. SAC 28 p.94
20. SAC 122 p.113
21. Chizlett [KE] p.5
22. Saul p.206
23. Schama I p.318
24. Martins [EUS] pp.30-31
25. ibid p.31
26. ibid p.29
27. Pilbeam & Nelson p.4
28. Report from His Majesty's Commissioners for inquiring into the Administration and Practical Operation of the Poor Laws (1834) p.7
29. ibid
30. ibid
31. D6 p.10
32. Martins [QQ] p.89
33. Homan [CSW] p.31
34. SAC 114 p.48

38. Winchelsea's Castle

1. Martins [QQ] p.96
2. Homan [HW] p.209
3. Biddle et. al. p.21
4. ibid
5. Longmate [DTI] p.377
6. Biddle et. al. p.25
7. Steane p.51
8. Biddle et. al. p.89
9. Cruickshank p. 41
10. Steane ibid
11. Homan [CW] p.90
12. Cooper p.176
13. HPC 1558-1603 III p.618
14. Biddle et. al. p.123
15. ibid pp.40-41
16. CSPD 1625-1626 p.220
17. Biddle et. al. p.41
18. Martins [EUS] p.23
19. Biddle et. al. p.32
20. Longmate [DTI] p.382
21. Biddle et. al. p.30

22. Ford F. M. p.121
23. Biddle et. al. p.1
24. Rutherfurd p.201
25. VCH II p.144
26. SAC 8 p.208

39. Winchelsea's Custumal

1. VCH IX p.35
2. D62 28
3. CCP p.243
4. The Homan/Wise translation is at SNQ 6 pp.65-70, 97-100, 129-132, 161-163
5. see WCR pp.86-88
6. For W. M. Homan's own summary of the custumal clauses, rather more detailed than what follows, see Homan [FW] pp.82-92
7. SNQ 6 p.68
8. Mayhew p.208
9. SNQ 6 p.162
10. WCR p.14 [ESRO WIN 52 fo.163r]
11. Martins [EUS] pp.30-31
12. HPC 1509-1558 II p.87 gives five years of his mayoralty; the Court Hall list which I have followed only four.
13. Eggleston p.2
14. ibid
15. HPC 1509-1558 II p.87
16. ibid p.88
17. WCR p.16 [ESRO WIN 52 fo.188v]
18. ibid [fo.189r]
19. ibid [fo.190r]
20. Martins [EUS] p.11
21. Eddison [TDG] p.138
22. Biddle et. al. p.7
23. Mayhew p.235

40. A Plea to the Queen

1. Mayhew p.294
2. Baines p.45
3. HPC 1509-1558 I p.263
4. ibid p.448
5. HPC 1558-1603 I p.307
6. ibid

7. ibid III p.619
8. CCP p.291
9. ibid p.265
10. ibid p.267
11. ibid p.272
12. WCR p.13 [ESRO WIN 52 fo.146r]
13. VCH II p.151
14. Mayhew p.238
15. VCH II ibid
16. Murray p.178
17. CCP p.315
18. ibid
19. This order was put into effect – see WCR p.19 [ESRO WIN 53 fo.147v]
20. CCP p.315
21. Martins (EUS) p.11
22. ibid
23. SCM 23 p.351
24. SCM 24 p.34
25. ibid
26. Inderwick pp.21-22
27. WCR p.13 [ESRO WIN 52 fo.142r]
28. Cooper p.106
29. ibid pp.106-107
30. ibid p.107 quoting Jeake
31. ibid
32. WCR p.19 [ESRO WIN 53 fo.124v]
33. Chapman p.60

41. Residents and Revenues

1. ESRO Rye 47/6/48
2. ibid
3. ibid
4. D47 p.24
5. WCR p.18 [ESRO WIN 53 fo.70v]
6. SAC 117 p.171
7. Cleere and Crossley p.159
8. Goodsall p.40
9. Straker pp.114-121
10. Goodsall ibid
11. VCH II p.229
12. Mayhew p.256
13. ibid p.308
14. ESRO WIN 53 [CW] fo.210
15. ESRO WIN 2222

16. ESRO WIN 53 & 54
17. ESRO WIN 54 [CW] fo.50
18. ESRO WIN 53 [CW] fo.176
19. ESRO WIN 54 [CW] fo.54
20. Murray p.183
21. APC 1586-1587 p.51 [D42 p.94]
22. CCP p.347
23. HPC 1558-1603 III p.610
24. WCR p.24 [ESRO WIN 54 fo.51v]
25. Seward p.153
26. WCR p.22 [ESRO WIN 53 fo.231v]
27. ESRO WIN 2359/1/1 [Introduction to listing]
28. Cooper pp.108-110
29. ESRO WIN 2359/1/1
30. Cooper pp.108-109
31. For a list of the properties liable see Pratt p.265
32. WCR p.19 [ESRO WIN 53 fo.142r]
33. ESRO WIN 2359/1/1

42. Armada Alert

1. Longmate [DTI] p.442
2. Williamson J. p.209
3. Martins [QQ] p.105
4. SAC 8 p.209
5. ibid p.210
6. Jessups [CP] p.28
7. D62 10 p.4
8. WCR p.24 [ESRO WIN 54 fo.22v]
9. Green I. p.29
10. Bavington Jones p.10
11. SAC 11 p.152; VCH II p.152
12. Jessup [HK] p.105
13. Longmate [DTI] p.443
14. Jessup ibid
15. Longmate [DTI] p.471
16. Sylvester p.163
17. EHR Vol. 91 p.646
18. ESRO WIN 2361/1
19. HPC 1558-1603 III p.108
20. ibid
21. ibid I p.307
22. Martins [EUS] p.26

23. SAC 122 p.113
24. Martins [QQ] p.94
25. Sussex History No. 24 pp.16-17
26. ibid p.17
27. *Imago Mundi* – The International Journal for the History of Cartography No 47 (1995) p.41
28. Copy at ESRO ACC 8194
29. *Imago Mundi* ibid p.40
30. CCP p.358
31. ibid
32. SAC 122 p.120
33. Cooper p.111
34. WCR p.24 [ESRO WIN 54 fo.145v]
35. CCP p.356

43. Grief for the Godfreys

1. HPC 1558-1603 II p.119
2. ibid
3. Horsfield I p.486
4. HPC ibid p.118
5. Baines p.11
6. ibid
7. CSPD 1603-1610 p.19
8. ibid p.24
9. ESRO RYE 47/64/16
10. CSPD 1603-1610 p.18
11. Strutt II p.109
12. CSPD 1603-1610 p.258
13. ibid p.473
14. ibid p.487
15. VCH II p.154
16. CSPD ibid p.509
17. Homan [CW] p.30
18. Martins [EUS] p.11
19. Pilbeam & Nelson p.5
20. ibid
21. Cooper p.211
22. ibid p.212
23. ibid pp.212-213
24. ibid p.164
25. Biddle et. al. p.151
26. see Cooper p.246
27. ibid p.164
28. ibid p.165
29. ibid pp.165-166
30. ibid p.166
31. ESRO WIN 55 [CW]

fo.113
32. ibid fo.176; ESRO WIN [CW]56 fo.133

44. The Corporation in Confusion

1. Eddison p.127
2. Jessups [CP] p.30
3. SAC 27 pp.172-173
4. Horsfield II Appendix 2 p.72
5. ibid
6. CSPD 1623-1625 p.185
7. CCP p.431
8. ibid pp.442-443
9. ibid p.445
10. ibid p.446
11. ibid p.460
12. ESRO WIN 64 fos.2-3
13. Hibbert p.91
14. ibid.
15. CSPD 1625-1626 p.232
16. Murray p.164
17. CSPD 1625-1626 p.11
18. ibid p.21
19. Longmate [IF] p.13
20. ibid
21. CCP p.xxvi
22. CSPD 1625-1626 pp.423-424
23. ibid p.432
24. Cooper p.214
25. ibid
26. CCP p.425
27. ibid pp.425-426
28. See Appendix 2 p.250
29. CCP p.xxxiii
30. ibid
31. ESRO AMS 2381
32. See Blair et. al. pp.12-13
33. ESRO AMS 2381

45. Civil War and Commonwealth

1. Schama II p.74
2. ESRO RYE 47/118/11
3. ESRO RYE 47/118/8
4. Jessups [CP] p.29
5. Longmate [IF] p.18
6. ibid pp.17-18
7. VCH II pp.156-157

8. Longmate ibid p.18
9. VCH II p.157
10. ibid p.155
11. Cooper p.179
12. Watson p.86
13. Fletcher p.92
14. Martins [QQ] p.100
15. Homan [CW] p.27
16. Jessup [HK] p.112
17. Longmate [IF] p.21
18. Thomas-Sandford pp.203-204
19. CCP p.481
20. ibid pp.476, 479-481, 487, 488-489; ESRO WIN 64 fo.89
21. CCP pp.479, 481
22. D40 1 p.12
23. SAC 8 p.211; Goodsall pp.138-139
24. Longmate [IF] p.33
25. Taylor p.77
26. Longmate ibid p.34
27. Huxford pp.129, 162
28. ESRO WIN 64 fo.83
29. Thornton p.342
30. DNB VII p.17

46. Restoration and Responsibilities

1. DNB VII p.11
2. ibid
3. Green I. p.93
4. Murray p.208
5. Baines p.12
6. SCM 10 p.819
7. ESRO WIN 64 fo.100
8. Martins [EUS] p.19
9. ESRO WIN 64 ibid
10. HPC 1660-1690 III p.35
11. Bright p.349
12. Horsfield II Appendix 2 pp.72-73
13. Briggs p.161
14. Green I. p.29
15. Longmate [IF] p.73
16. Cruickshank p.68
17. D53 5
18. ESRO PAR 511/34/3/8
19. Tomalin p.294; D53 5
20. Hunter & Gregory p.127

21. Martins [QQ] p.91
22. Martins [EUS] p.11
23. Baines p.129
24. Briggs ibid
25. Martins [QQ] p.100
26. HPC 1660-1690 II pp.316
27. HPC 1660-1690 I p.504
28. ibid p.503
29. HPC 1690-1715 II p.777
30. HPC 1660-1690 I p.504
31. Cooper p.170
32. Clifton p.3
33. ibid p.4

47. Sequestration and Ships

1. Taylor p.98
2. ibid p.99
3. ibid p.98
4. Homan [CW] p.7
5. Ford W. K. p.42
6. Cooper p.242
7. Clifton p.4
8. ESRO WIN 58 [CW] fo.315
9. Martins [QQ] p.100
10. ESRO WIN 60 fo.9
11. CCP p.545
12. ibid p.546
13. Kirkham p.15
14. Jessups [CP] p.39
15. Cooper p.186
16. D31 9
17. Longmate [IF] p.121
18. Letter: 7 Nov 1942: Hugh Whistler of Battle to W. M. Homan included within ESRO AMS 2407.
19. ibid
20. ESRO WIN 2362/9/56
21. ibid
22. D36 4; D63 10
23. HPC 1690-1715 II p.777
24. ESRO WIN 60 fo.68
25. HPC ibid p.778
26. ibid
27. HCJ 27 February 1701
28. ibid 3 & 5 May 1701
29. ibid 3 May 1701
30. Ford F.M. p.73
31. Fiennes p.129
32. ibid

33. Cooper pp.184-185
34. ibid p.185

48. Visitors and the Control of Votes

1. D20 6
2. Homan [HW] p.266
3. D20 6
4. Inderwick p.57
5. Homan [FW] p.38
6. D63 6
7. ESRO SAY 662
8. see also Pratt p.151
9. Briggs p.161
10. Sussex Almanac 1995 (D38 2 p.3)
11. Chizlett [TE] p.4
12. Ogley et. al. p.8
13. Ford F.M. p.148
14. ibid
15. Homan [CW] p.69
16. Hufton & Baird p.53
17. D45 22
18. HPC 1690-1715 II p.777
19. ESRO WIN 60 fo.78
20. Pers. Comm. Major J. LeB. Freeman (D56 16)
21. HPC 1715-1754 I p.370
22. ESRO WIN 62 fos.82 & 87
23. HPC 1690-1715 II p.779
24. ESRO WIN 64 fo.161
25. ESRO WIN 482-497
26. ESRO WIN 64 fo.166
27. ESRO WIN 622
28. see Pratt pp.51-52
29. Farrant p.20
30. ibid
31. ibid

49. The New Harbour Starts and Stalls

1. Cooper p.181
2. ibid p.183
3. Vidler [HR] p.67; ESRO RYE 47/45/12
4. Vidler ibid
5. Saville, Michael pp.7-8
6. Jessups [CP] p.29
7. Saville, Michael p.9
8. ibid p.10
9. Farrant p.92

10. Collard p.38
11. Monod pp.193-194
12. Saville, Michael pp.11-12
13. SAC 109 p.23
14. Cooper p.111
15. SAC 11 p.181
16. ESRO WIN 60 fo.237
17. ibid
18. Hufton & Baird p.41
19. ESRO SAY 3871: 12 October 1734
20. ESRO WIN 64 fo.202
21. ibid
22. CCP p.xvi
23. ibid p.xvii
24. ibid pp.596-597
25. Ford W.K. p.101
26. Homan [CW] p.27
27. ibid p.15
28. ibid p.16
29. ESRO PAR 511/37/3/11
30. D27 p.38

50. Jeremiah's Journey

1. Farrant p.88
2. ibid p.92
3. HPC 1715-1754 I p.370
4. ibid
5. ESRO AMS 3215
6. HPC 1715-1754 I ibid
7. HPC 1754-1790 II p.80
8. Stevenson p.191
9. ibid p.186
10. ibid
11. HPC 1754-1790 III p.194
12. Martins [EUS] p.12; Stevenson p.187 (the latter includes a full list of Nebitt's property in the area.)
13. ESRO WIN 2138
14. see also Appendix 2
15. Stevenson p.188
16. D53 5
17. SAC 127 pp.259-260
18. CCP p.559
19. Hufton & Baird p.25
20. Longmate [IF] p.149
21. ibid
22. Farrant pp.91-92
23. ibid p.92
24. ibid

25. ESRO PAR 511/40/2/1

51. Cambric and Causes

1. ESRO PAR 511/35/1/1
2. ibid
3. VCH II p.258
4. ibid
5. Cooper p.121
6. Stevenson p.187
7. Martins [EUS] p.12
8. Pett & Leahy p.48
9. Baines p.139
10. VCH II p.258
11. Ford F.M. p.74
12. Cooper p.121
13. ESRO PAR 401/33/19
14. ESRO PAR 401/33/20
15. ESRO WIN 2206
16. ESRO WIN 216
17. ESRO WIN 61 fo.80
18. Holyoake p.98
19. Jessup [HK] p.135
20. ESRO PAR 511/40/2/1 (sheet for 1767)
21. Jessup [HK] pp.136-137
22. Pers. Comm. Janet Stevenson, D63 3
23. ESRO PAR 511 ibid
24. Martins [EUS] p.12
25. D54 4 p.1
26. Homan [CW] p.69
27. D54 4 ibid
28. Cooper p.216
29. Stevenson p.190
30. ibid; D63 3
31. Stevenson p.191

52. Two Reverend Gentlemen

1. Rengert p.30
2. VCH II p.41
3. SCM 15 p.284
4. Homan [CSW] p.34
5. Park p.3
6. Rengert ibid
7. Park p.2
8. ibid p.3
9. Hattersley p.394
10. Park ibid
11. Homan [CW] p.91
12. Huxford p.382
13. ibid

14. ESRO AMS 2396 p.110
15. Huxford p.383
16. ESRO AMS 2396 p.112
17. ESRO WIN 2156
18. ESRO WIN 2172 et. seq.
19. ESRO WIN 2185, 2186
20. ESRO WIN 2189 et. seq.
21. Davey p.xx
22. ibid
23. ibid p.259
24. ibid pp.257-259
25. Homan [CW] p.26
26. ibid p.27
27. Homan ibid p.16
28. ESRO PAR 511/1/1/2 fo.100; Homan ibid p.6; D43 7
29. Homan [CSW] pp.32-33
30. Homan [FW] p.36
31. ESRO AMS 2490 Bk.4 p.18
32. Martins [QQ] p.99
33. ibid p.100
34. Haining p.164
35. ibid
36. SCM 29 pp.226-228
37. SAC 8 p.223
38. ESRO PAR 511/12/1
39. ibid

53. The New Harbour Finishes and Fails

1. Saville, Michael p.14; D63 4
2. Saville, Michael p.15
3. ibid p.17
4. Collard p.39
5. Saville, Michael p.17
6. Collard p.41
7. Homan [CSW] p.38
8. Fraser p.142
9. ESRO WIN 520
10. ESRO WIN 521
11. ESRO WIN 513
12. ESRO WIN 519
13. ESRO WIN 263
14. ESRO WIN 262
15. ESRO WIN 264
16. DNB IV p.1158
17. ibid
18. HPC 1754-1790 II p.256
19. Churchill III p.166
20. Longmate [IF] p.202

21. HPC 1754-1790 I p.458
22. ibid

54. War Again

1. Oldfield III Cinque Ports
   p.90
2. Holmes p.38
3. Bessborough p.62
4. HPC 1790-1820 III p.149
5. Bessborough p.64
6. Ellacott pp.40-41
7. See Pratt pp.46-47
8. Williams p.59
9. See Pratt pp.186-187
10. Cooper p.200
11. D43 8
12. Cooper p.201
13. D62 9; ESRO WIN
    2359/3/5

14. ESRO AMS 2329 1799-
    1800
15. D49 14
16. ESRO AMS 2329 ibid
17. ESRO DAP 235/6 & 235/8
18. Churchill III p.232
19. Longmate [IF] p.212
20. ESRO WIN 1987-1999
21. Pratt pp.21-22
22. ibid
23. SAC 122 pp.168-169; VCH
    I p.535
24. see Pratt p.232
25. Cooper pp.88, 159
26. Rodger II p.242
27. Green S. p.17
28. McCann pp.145, 148, 149,
    151-152, 156-160
29. Jenkins pp.22-23; Dalton &
    Hamer p.258

Epilogue

1. The minutes of the
   Winchelsea Millennium
   Committee are in my care
   awaiting transfer to
   Winchelsea's archives at East
   Sussex Record Office.
2. Members of this hard-
   working committee not
   already mentioned in the
   text were:
   Knightley Chetwood, Terry
   Cuthbert, Alfred
   McKenney, Michael Melvin,
   Tony Moore, John Morgan
   OBE, David Peters and
   Allan Pope.

BIBLIOGRAPHY

This list includes only the volumes which are referred to directly in the text. Unpublished work marked ESRO is available on the shelves of the Search Room at East Sussex Record Office.

Allmand	*Henry V* by Christopher Allmand (1992)
APC	*Acts of the Privy Council*
Bagley	*The Book of Rye* by Geoffrey S. Bagley (1982)
Baines	*Historic Hastings* by J. Manwaring Baines. Amended and revised edition (1986)
Bavington Jones	*The Cinque Ports, their History and Present Condition* by J. Bavington Jones (1903)
Beresford	*New Towns of the Middle Ages* by Maurice Beresford (1967)
Bessborough	*Enchanted Forest, The Story of Stansted in Sussex* by The Earl of Bessborough with Clive Aslet (1984)
Biddle et. al.	*Henry VIII's Coastal Artillery Fort at Camber Castle, Rye, East Sussex* by Martin Biddle, Jonathan Hillier, Ian Scott and Anthony Streeten. Oxford Archaeological Unit (2001)
Blair et. al.	*The Winchelsea Tombs Reconsidered,* by Claude Blair, John A. Goodall and Philip J. Lankester published in 'Church Monuments' No. 15 (2000)
Bois	*A Constitutional History of Jersey* by F. de L. Bois (1972)
Bradbury	*The Battle of Hastings* by Jim Bradbury (1998)
Briggs	*A Social History of England* by Asa Briggs. New Edition (1994)
Bright	*The Diary of Samuel Pepys, Volume II* Edited from Mynors Bright (1906) Revised and re-set (1953)
Burrows	*Historic Towns – Cinque Ports* by Montagu Burrows (1892)
Calder	*The English Channel* by Nigel Calder (1986)
Carter	*The Forgotten Ports of England* by George Goldsmith Carter (1951)
CCP	*A Calendar of the White and Black Books of the Cinque Ports 1432-1955* Ed. Felix Hull (1966)
CCR	*Calendar of Close Rolls*
Chambers	*The French Bastides and the Town Plan of Winchelsea* by G. E. Chambers. Archaeological Journal No. 94 (1937)
Chapman	*Royal Visitors to Sussex* by Brigid Chapman (1991)
Chizlett [DG]	*On Dangerous Ground* by Clive Chizlett (2003)
Chizlett [KE]	*The King's Evil* by Clive Chizlett. (2000)
Chizlett [TE]	*Taken to Extremes* by Clive Chizlett (2004)
Churchill	*A History of the English Speaking Peoples* - Volumes I-IV by Winston S. Churchill (1956-1958)
CIM	*Calendar of Inquisitions Miscellaneous (Chancery)* Preserved in the National Archives. Volume VII (1968)
Clark	*A Short History of Rye* by Kenneth Clark (1991)
Cleere & Crossley	*The Iron Industry of the Weald* by Henry Cleere and David Crossley (1985)
Clifton	*A Short History of the Church of Our Lady of Consolation and St. Francis, West Grinstead* by Margaret Clifton
Collard	*A Maritime History of Rye* by John Collard. Second Edition (1985)
Cooper	*The History of Winchelsea – One of the Ancient Towns added to the Cinque Ports* by William Durrant Cooper (1850)
Cordingley	*Life Among the Pirates – The Romance and the Reality* by David Cordingley (1995)
CP	*The Complete Peerage* (1926)
CPR	*Calendar of Patent Rolls*
CSPD	*Calendar of State Papers (Domestic)*

Cruickshank	*Invasion – Defending Britain from Attack* by Dan Cruickshank (2001)
Dalton & Hamer	*The Provincial Token-Coinage of the Eighteenth Century* by R. Dalton and S. H. Hamer (1910)
Davey	*East Sussex Land Tax 1785* by Roger Davey. Sussex Record Society Vol. 77 (1991)
Dawson	*History of Hastings Castle* by Charles Dawson (1909)
Denton	*Robert Winchelsey and the Crown 1294-1313* by J. H. Denton (1980)
DNB	*The Dictionary of National Biography – The Earliest Times to 1900* Ed. Sir Leslie Stephen & Sir Sidney Lee (Reprinted 1917 et. seq.)
Dyer	*Everyday Life in Medieval England* by Christopher Dyer (1994)
Eddison	*Romney Marsh – Survival on a Frontier* by Jill Eddison (2000)
Eddison [ECHO]	*Romney Marsh – Environmental Change and Human Occupation in a Coastal Lowland* Ed. Eddison J., Gardiner M. and Long A. Oxford University Committee for Archaeology Monograph 46 (1998)
Eddison [EOR]	*Romney Marsh – Evolution, Occupation, Reclamation* Ed. Eddison J and Green C. OUCA Monograph 24 (1988)
Eddison [TDG]	*Romney Marsh – The Debatable Ground.* Ed. Jill Eddison. OUCA Monograph 41 (1995)
Eggleston	*William Eglestone of Winchelsea and some of his Descendants* by Ben Eggleston (1995) Unpublished (D40/1)
EHD	*English Historical Documents* 1189-1327 (1975), 1327-1485 (1969)
EHR	*English Historical Review* Vol. 91(1996), Vol. 54 (1939)
Ellacott	*The Bastards of Westbourne* by Peter Ellacott. Westbourne Local History Group (1996)
ESRO WIN [CW]	Christopher Whittick's expansion of the original published edition of Winchelsea Corporation Records (see WCR). Available at ESRO.
Farrant	*Sussex Depicted – Views and Descriptions 1600-1800* by John H. Farrant. Sussex Record Society Volume 85 (2001)
Fiennes	*The Journeys of Celia Fiennes 1685- c.1712* (Illustrated Edition) (1982)
Fletcher	*A County Community in Peace and War* by Anthony Fletcher (1975)
Floyd	*Wynchelse: A Geographical and Historical Study of an Ancient Town* by Professor B. N. Floyd (1962) Unpublished (D2)
Ford F. M.	*The Cinque Ports – A Historical and Descriptive Record* by Ford Madox Ford (1900)
Ford W. K.	*Chichester Diocesan Surveys 1686 and 1724* by Wyn K. Ford. Sussex Record Society Volume 78 (1994)
Fraser	*A People's History of Britain* by Rebecca Fraser (2003)
Gairdner	*The Paston Letters* Edited with an introduction by James Gairdner (1986)
Gillingham & Griffiths	*Medieval Britain – A Very Short Introduction* by John Gillingham and Ralph A. Griffiths (1984)
Goodsall	*The Eastern Rother* by Robert H. Goodsall (1961)
Green I.	*The Book of the Cinque Ports* by Ivan Green (1984)
Green S.	*Lord's – The Cathedral of Cricket* by Stephen Green (2003)
Haining	*The English Highwayman – A Legend Unmasked* by Peter Haining (1991)
Hannah	*County Coast Series - The Sussex Coast* by Ian C. Hannah (1912)
Hardy	*Longbow – A Social and Military History* by Robert Hardy 3rd Edition (1992)
Hattersley	*A Brand from the Burning – The Life of John Wesley* by Roy Hattersley (2002)
HCJ	*House of Commons Journal*
Hewitt	*Organisation of War Under Edward III* by H. J. Hewitt (1966)
Hibbert	*Charles I* by Christopher Hibbert (1968)
Holyoake	*Wellington at Walmer* by Gregory Holyoake (1996)

Holmes	*Wellington the Iron Duke* by Richard Holmes (2003)
Homan [CSW]	*Chronique Scandaleuse of Winchelsea* by W. M. Homan (1944) Unpublished (ESRO AMS 2497)
Homan [CW]	*The Churches of Winchelsea* by W. M. Homan (1939) Unpublished (ESRO)
Homan [FW]	*The Founding of Winchelsea* by W. M. Homan (1940) Unpublished (ESRO)
Homan [HW]	*History of Winchelsea 1292-1800* by W. M. Homan (1942) Unpublished (ESRO)
Horsfield	*The County of Sussex* (2 volumes) by T. W. Horsfield (1835)
Howarth	*Sovereign of the Seas* by David Howarth (1974)
HPC	*History of Parliament – The Commons*
Hufton & Baird	*Scarecrows Legion – Smuggling in Kent and Sussex* by Geoffrey Hufton and Elaine Baird (1983)
Hunter & Gregory	*An Astrological Diary of the Seventeenth Century by Samuel Jeake of Rye 1652-1699* Ed. Michael Hunter and Annabel Gregory (1988)
Huxford	*The Arms of Sussex Families* by J. F. Huxford 1982
Inderwick	*The Story of King Edward and New Winchelsea* by F. A. Inderwick (1892)
Jacob	*The Oxford History of England – The Fifteenth Century 1399-1485* by E. F. Jacob (1961)
James	*Studies in the Medieval Wine Trade* by M. K. James (1971)
Jeake	*Charters of the Cinque Ports* by Samuel Jeake (1728)
Jenkins	*Sussex Money* by Peter R. Jenkins (1987)
Jessup [HK]	*A History of Kent* by Frank W. Jessup. Revised Edition (1995)
Jessups [CP]	*The Cinque Ports* by R. F. and F. W. Jessup (1952)
Kemp	*The History of Ships* by Peter Kemp (2000)
Kirkham	*Ryennium – Ancient Rye at the Millennium* by Josephine C. Kirkham (2000)
Knowles & Hadcock	*Medieval Religious Houses in England and Wales* by David Knowles and R. Neville Hadcock (1971)
Lee	*This Sceptred Isle 55BC – 1901* by Christopher Lee (1997)
Legg	*English Coronation Records* Ed. Leopold G. Wickham Legg (1901)
Leslie & Short	*An Historical Atlas of Sussex* Ed. Kim Leslie and Brian Short (1999)
Longmate [DTI]	*Defending the Island – From Caesar to the Armada* by Norman Longmate (1989)
Longmate [IF]	*Island Fortress – The Defence of Great Britain 1603-1945* by Norman Longmate (1991)
Martin	*Franciscan Architecture in England* by A. R. Martin (1937)
Martins [CH]	*The Court Hall, High Street, Winchelsea, East Sussex* by David and Barbara Martin (1999) Unpublished (ESRO)
Martins [EUS]	*An Extensive Urban Survey Assessment of Winchelsea, East Sussex* by David and Barbara Martin (2002) Unpublished (ESRO)
Martins [QQ]	*A Quarter by Quarter Analysis of Winchelsea, East Sussex* by David and Barbara Martin (2002) Unpublished (ESRO)
Martins [WT]	*Archaeological & Historic Landscape Survey – Land at Winchelsea – Part 3: Winchelsea Town* by David and Barbara Martin (1994) Unpublished (ESRO)
Mayhew	*Tudor Rye* by Graham Mayhew (1987)
McCann	*Sussex Cricket in the Eighteenth Century* by Timothy J. McCann. Sussex Record Society Volume 88 (2004)
McKisack	*The Oxford History of England – The Fourteenth Century 1307-1399* by May McKisack (1959)
Monod	*The Murder of Mr. Grebell – Madness and Civility in an English Town* by Paul Kléber Monod (2003)
Morris	*Domesday Book – Sussex* Ed. John Morris (1976)
Murray	*The Constitutional History of the Cinque Ports* by K. M. E. Murray (1935)

Nairn & Pevsner	*The Buildings of England – Sussex* by Ian Nairn & Nikolaus Pevsner (1965)
Neillands	*The Hundred Years War* by Robin Neillands. Revised Edition (2001)
Ogley et. al.	*The Sussex Weather Book* by Bob Ogley, Ian Currie and Mark Davidson (1991)
Oldfield	*An Entire and Complete History Political and Personal of the Boroughs of Great Britain* by T. B. H. Oldfield (1792)
Park	*Wesley Methodist Chapel – A Brief History* by Rev. Cynthia Park (1995)
Parry	*An Historical and Descriptive Account of the Coast of Sussex* by J. D. Parry (1833)
Pett & Leahy	*Winchelsea at the Millennium* by Melvyn Pett and Dominic Leahy (2000)
Pilbeam & Nelson	*Mid-Sussex Poor Law Records 1601-1835* by Norma Pilbeam and Ian Nelson. Sussex Record Society Volume 83 (2000)
Platt	*Medieval Southampton – The Port and Trading Community AD 1000-1600* by Colin Platt (1973)
Poland	*The Friars of Sussex* by E. B. Poland (1928)
Poole	*The Oxford History of England – Domesday Book to Magna Carta 1087-1216* by A. L. Poole. Second Edition (1955)
Powicke	*The Oxford History of England – The Thirteenth Century 1216-1307* by Sir Maurice Powicke. Second Edition (1962)
Pratt	*Winchelsea – A Port of Stranded Pride* by Malcolm Pratt (1998)
Prestwich	*Edward I* by Michael Prestwich. New Edition (1997)
Rengert	*John Wesley at Winchelsea* by H. J. Rengert Sussex Life April 1970
Rodger I	*The Safeguard of the Sea – A Naval History of Britain, 1660-1649* by N. A. M. Rodger (1997)
Rodger II	*The Command of the Ocean – A Naval History of Britain, 1649-1814* by N. A. M. Rodger (2004)
Russell	*The English Intervention in Spain and Portugal in the Time of Edward III and Richard II* by P. E. Russell (1955)
Rutherfurd	*The Forest* by Edward Rutherfurd (2000)
SAC	*Sussex Archaeological Collections* (1848-Present)
Salzman	*English Trade in the Middle Ages* by L. F. Salzman (1931)
Saul	*The Oxford Illustrated History of Medieval England* Edited by Nigel Saul (1997)
Saville, Malcolm	*The Story of Winchelsea Church* Nineteenth Edition. Revised and retold by Malcolm Saville
Saville, Michael	*Smeaton's Harbour 18th Century Tragedy or Farce* by Michael Saville (D56 17)
Schama	*A History of Britain* Vol. I 3000 BC-1603 (2000) Vol. II 1603-1776 (2001) Vol. III 1776-2000 (2002)
SCM	*Sussex County Magazine* (1926-1956)
Seward	*Sussex* by Desmond Seward (1995)
SNQ	*Sussex Notes and Queries* (1926-1971)
Steane	*The Archaeology of Medieval England and Wales* by John M. Steane (1984)
Stevenson	*Arnold Nesbitt and the Borough of Winchelsea* by Janet Stevenson (SAC 129 pp.183-193, 1991)
Straker	*Wealden Iron* by Ernest Straker (1931 Re-published 1969)
Strutt	*A Complete View of the Dress and Habits of the People of England* by Joseph Strutt. (1842)
Sumption I	*Trial by Battle – The Hundred Years War I* by Jonathan Sumption (1990)
Sumption II	*Trial by Fire – The Hundred Years War II* by Jonathan Sumption (1999)
Swinden	*The History of Great Yarmouth* by Henry Swinden (1772)
Sylvester	*Maritime Communities in Pre-Plague England: Winchelsea and the Cinque Ports* by David Sylvester. Ph.D. Thesis. Fordham University, New York. (1999) Unpublished (ESRO)

Taylor	*The Sea Chaplains – A History of the Chaplains of the Royal Navy* by Gordon Taylor (1978)
Thomas-Sandford	*Sussex in the Great Civil War and the Interregnum 1642-1660* by Charles Thomas-Sandford (1910)
Thornton	*Hastings – A Living History* by David Thornton (1987)
Tomalin	*Samuel Pepys – The Unequalled Self* by Claire Tomalin (2002)
Topp	*Sussex Prisons* by John Topp. (1991) Unpublished (ESRO)
TRHS	*Transactions of the Royal Historical Society*
Turner	*Town Defences in England and Wales* by Hilary L. Turner (1971)
VCH	*The Victoria County History of Sussex* Vol I (1905) Vol II (1907) Vol VII (1940) Vol IX (1937)
Vidler [HR]	*A New History of Rye* by L. A. Vidler (1934)
Vidler [RR]	*Riddles of Rye* by L. A. Vidler (1925) (D29 9)
Watson	*Charles I* by D. R. Watson (1972)
WCR	*Winchelsea Corporation Records – A Catalogue* Ed. Richard F. Dell (1963)
Williams	*The Heraldry of the Cinque Ports* by Geoffrey Williams (1971)
Williamson D.	*The Mariners of Ancient Wessex* by David Williamson (1998)
Williamson J.	*The English Channel* by James A. Williamson (1959)
Windeatt	*The Book of Margery Kempe* translated with an introduction by Barry Windeatt (1985)

Note: *New Winchelsea, Sussex – A Medieval Port Town* by David and Barbara Martin with contributions by Jill Eddison, David Rudling and David Sylvester and *Excavations in Winchelsea, Sussex, 1974-2000* Edited by David Martin and David Rudling, both published by Heritage Marketing and Publications Ltd. (2004) were not available in time for completion of my text but most of the information contained within them is also included in sources cited above. I have, however, been able to make use of the former in writing captions.

INDEX

excluding preliminary pages, appendices and mentions of source authors in the text